Molding
the
Hearts and Minds

Molding the Hearts and Minds

Education, Communications, and Social Change in Latin America

John A. Britton
Editor

Jaguar Books on Latin America
Number 4

A Scholarly Resources Inc. Imprint
Wilmington, Delaware

©1994 by Scholarly Resources Inc.
All rights reserved
First published 1994
Printed and bound in the United States of America

Scholarly Resources Inc.
104 Greenhill Avenue
Wilmington, DE 19805-1897

Library of Congress Cataloging-in-Publication Data

Molding the hearts and minds : education, communications, and social
    change in Latin America / John A. Britton, editor.
        p,   cm. — (Jaguar books on Latin America ; no. 4)
    Includes bibliographical references.
    ISBN 0-8420-2489-1. — ISBN 0-8420-2490-5 (pbk.)
    1. Education—Latin America—History. 2. Education—Social
aspects—Latin America. 3. Latin America—Social conditions.
I. Series.
LA541.M577   1994
370'.98—dc20   93-41937
                                                                      CIP

The paper used in this publication meets the minimum requirements
of the American National Standard for permanence of paper for printed
library materials, Z39.48, 1984.

Acknowledgments

Several people have made important contributions to the completion of this volume. Colin MacLachlan and Bill Beezley offered encouragement at several stages in its development. Elsie Rockwell, Elaine Lacy, and Mary Kay Vaughan provided stimulating ideas at the 1993 CLAH-AHA session on Mexican education. Many of the contributors to this volume were generous in allowing the reprinting of their work and also gave useful suggestions for the volume as a whole.

The Francis Marion University Release Time Committee made the job more manageable by allowing me to reduce my teaching load in the spring of 1993. The head of the FMU history department, Richard Chapman, held the institution's bureaucratic burdens to a minimum and also had the professional integrity to insist that scholarly work in general and this volume in particular should have a legitimate place in the academic life at the institution.

A special recognition goes to Kevin Healy and Maria Barry of the Inter-American Foundation for the use of the rotafolio illustrations. Professor Donna Goodman of the FMU Department of Fine Arts gave essential assistance in their preparation for publication and Joe James of the modern languages department worked with me on the translation of the captions. Jerry Chamness, manager of the FMU print shop, also lent a helping hand.

Richard Hopper and his highly professional staff at Scholarly Resources—especially Laura Cunningham and Amy Rashap—tolerated my sporadic work habits and helped to bring this project to completion.

And, finally, I express my gratitude to Josefina Vázquez of El Colegio de México, whose patience and wisdom helped me as a lowly graduate student make a start in the field over two decades ago. This volume is dedicated to her.

Contents

Introduction

The traditional concept of education—pupils learning under the guidance of a teacher in a classroom—has been the focus of many important and useful studies. In recent years, however, social critics have emphasized that much important learning takes place outside the classroom. While the one-room, rock-walled school perched on a mountainside in the Peruvian Andes and the bustling, crowded, urban school in a barrio of Mexico City are central to education, they share the spotlight in this volume with adults in night school learning basic literacy, factory laborers reading the pages of a working-class newspaper, and potential consumers watching the parade of enticing products march across a television screen.

Two commentators have gained international recognition for both their criticisms of long-established educational methods and their emphasis on the importance of schooling outside the traditional classroom: Ivan Illich, a Catholic theologian by training and a social critic by choice, did most of his writing on educational issues in Mexico in the 1960s and 1970s; and Paulo Freire, a Brazilian academic, developed his acute awareness of the perspective of the urban poor by drawing from his own childhood experiences. Although controversial, their criticisms have continued to hold the attention of a wide audience that shares their interest in the impact of bureaucracy on education and the potential for informal learning outside the classroom.

Moving beyond the work of Illich and Freire, an even broader perspective places education within the expanding systems of communication. Individuals learn not only in school but also through the newspapers, magazines, pamphlets, political speeches, commercial advertising, and popular entertainment that have become increasingly available to large numbers of people. At the same time, these media have become dominated by large publishing houses, motion picture and television companies, advertising agencies, political parties, and governments that employ new methods of gaining public attention. Sometimes called marketing (if a product or personality is introduced to a mass audience) or propaganda (if a government or political movement attempts to build a mass following), these methods of dispersing messages are considered in this volume alongside customary themes in education.

Social change—defined here as a basic alteration in the ideas, structures, and practices of a society—is the second crucial theme in this volume. Fledgling students often perceive Latin American history before the rise of Fidel Castro as a vast, calm sea where only a few violent storms, such as the Spanish Conquest of the early 1500s and the independence movements of the early 1800s, break the placid surface into rolling waves of social turmoil and political unrest. As the student delves more deeply, however, the winds of social change appear again and again, sometimes in the form of gradual transformations, as in the expansion of public schooling among the lower strata of society in the nineteenth and twentieth centuries, and sometimes in more dramatic phenomena, as in the hurricane force of revolutionary movements that rely on propaganda and schooling to broaden and deepen their influence. This volume will explore both types of social change—the gradual and the dramatic.

An example of the more gradual type of change is the University Reform movement of the early twentieth century. Until then most Latin American universities had been strongholds of tradition and elitism where the dominant minority held firm control. But as new ideas began to penetrate these select circles, the university curriculum expanded to include courses on contemporary social, political, and economic problems. Universities also opened their doors to offspring of disadvantaged classes— the workers and peasants, for example. Within a few decades many universities had undergone fundamental changes; males and females of lower-class origins were studying sociology, political science, and economics on the campuses previously reserved for sons of the privileged few.

The widening participation of the lower strata of society in formal education posed problems for the elites who held political and economic power. On one hand, some members of the elite saw in the masses potential sources of strength for their nation as educated, productive citizens and as consumers of mass-produced goods. On the other hand, those more interested in power were concerned that the lower strata, once educated and generally aware of its disadvantaged position, would turn against the existing government and economic systems in an effort to gain access to political institutions and to improve its material living conditions. Under these circumstances, schooling and the flow of information throughout society often became an exercise in social control whereby the elite attempted to curb the thrust of mass participation or at least divert its energy into channels that would do little to alter basic power structures.

The Colonial Legacy and the Nineteenth Century

The Spanish and Portuguese erected educational systems that catered to their American empires and the elites who dominated the political, economic, and religious structures. Most of the population received little or no formal schooling, partly because the empires were built on labor-intensive enterprises that depended on heavy, repetitive work in mines, fields, and factories. Formal classroom instruction did not readily fit into these practices. Latin America was also a multi-ethnic society in which government offices and private property were generally in the hands of Spaniards or Portuguese and their descendants in America. The unschooled labor force was made up of slaves from Africa, native Americans who were often trapped in burdensome manual jobs, and an ever-growing number of people of mixed ethnic backgrounds who were struggling to rise above their humble origins. Under these conditions literacy rates in the newly independent states of the early 1800s were low. In general, less than a fourth of the population could read and write. After extensive efforts in Argentina, the literacy rate there rose to perhaps 50 percent by the end of the century, but in most Latin American countries the illiterate continued to outnumber the literate.

Elites in these countries were increasingly uncomfortable in spite of their advantaged position. With the spread of democracy and the doctrines of the Enlightenment (the European intellectual movement that emphasized rational thought and based much learning on experience rather than theory), a few members of the elite came to accept the notion that economic prosperity, political unity, and cultural maturity required a broadly educated population. Most of the elite, however, saw mass education as a challenge to the existing political and social hierarchies. An educated but impoverished and powerless lower class would eventually resent and perhaps rebel against the existing social order. In the view of many of the elite (or *gente decente*, as historian Mark Szuchman terms them in Selection 1), along with the fundamentals of reading and writing, the schools had to convey a sense of the proper order within a structured society. In both Guanajuato, a provincial city in Mexico (Selection 2 by Angela Thompson), and Buenos Aires, the commercial and political center of Argentina, elites carefully designed the curriculum and operations of the schools to reinforce the existing hierarchy.

In the nineteenth century many governments used the Lancaster system, which is discussed by Szuchman (Selection 1) and Thompson (Selection 2). An innovation of British educator Joseph Lancaster, the plan called for older, more advanced students to instruct pupils in the lower grades and was inexpensive because it allowed one teacher to supervise several grade levels in the same school. The Lancaster system sparked interest in the middle 1800s, but the actual application of the program had mixed results. Falling into disfavor in the last decades of the century, it was replaced by methods that enjoyed varying degrees of success.

Argentina's Domingo Faustino Sarmiento, a professional educator and member of the "Generation of 1837," was influenced by the public school system of the United States. As an educator and, later, as president of Argentina (1868–1874), Sarmiento devoted his energies to the creation of a public school system that was to play a crucial role in the expansion of literacy in that country. Various levels of government in Uruguay, Chile, Argentina, and Mexico began to apply more financial resources to education, but with uneven results. Because of reliance on state and local rather than national funding, relatively wealthier areas, such as commercial centers like Buenos Aires and the tier of states in northern Mexico, had more effective school programs than less affluent areas.

Undergraduate students in the United States often have difficulty grasping the historical importance of the Catholic church in Latin America. While the United States separated the institutions of church and state early in its history, most Latin American countries endured a bitter and sometimes violent rivalry between the Catholic church (which was predominant throughout the region) and opponents of its continued control of important institutions. During the long colonial period that stretched over three centuries, the church operated most institutions of learning, from the primary level to the university, and its doctrines were usually a part of the curriculum. With the arrival of the secular emphasis in the Enlightenment of the 1700s and the accomplishment of independence in the early 1800s, many leading political and cultural figures began to argue that education should be secularized, which meant that the civil government was to take over primary responsibility for education and that its religious content was to be reduced. In some cases anticlericals—opponents of the political, economic, cultural, and educational influence of the church—called for an end to all church involvement in education, including the closure of all church-run schools. Angela Thompson's article (Selection 2) discusses a gradual form of secularization.

Universities in Ferment

The unrest often associated with Latin American universities is a relatively recent development. Generally following the examples of the universities founded in Mexico City and Lima in the 1550s, higher education in the region reinforced the twin pillars of the empire: the Catholic church and the colonial administration. The curriculum was largely abstract, emphasizing scholasticism and theology. One function of the universities was to help provide the colonies with an educated priesthood, and they also offered training in law and medicine for the sons of prosperous creoles (people of European descent born in America). These tradition-bound institutions, however, were destined for change. During the independence period and for the remainder of the nineteenth century, new ideas continued to penetrate the universities. The Enlightenment, with its stress on science over religion, experimentation over rote memorization, and reform over tradition, gradually made its way into most curricula. By the early 1900s many scholars were leading their students in explorations of new fields of study such as sociology, economics, and political science, which held much relevance to the immediate concerns of their respective countries.

Chile's experience during this period offers an example of how a political and cultural elite attempted to adjust to these new influences. Through the nineteenth century Chile's educational leaders reformed the curricula of the Instituto Nacional (National Institute), the country's preeminent secondary school, and its senior partner, the University of Chile. In spite of the sometimes controversial reforms and other substantial changes, these institutions remained the training grounds for Chile's governing elite. Only a few talented and lucky sons of middle-class families made their way through the narrow academic channel of upward mobility into the nation's governing class. Chile's period of political stability (1830s to 1890s) and the decorum of its political elite seemed to be a reflection of the university and the Instituto Nacional. As historian Gertrude Yeager has observed, the Instituto was an important part of elite consolidation:

> Although it represented itself as the official custodian and interpreter of national culture, the Instituto also labored to set its clientele apart from other Chileans. Instituto professors and administrators apparently found no conflict between these functions. By promoting social distinctions or class consciousness, the Instituto contributed to the formation of a more durable elite, which reinforced national identity and implemented authentically Chilean policies.[1]

The Chilean formula for elite control of the higher levels of education was more successful than most efforts, but it and similar arrangements in other countries began to unravel in the late 1800s. In many Latin American countries intensified thrusts of economic and social change challenged universities and related institutions. The expansion of international trade and investment, the growth of modern transportation and communications, the early stages of industrialization, and the arrival of large numbers of immigrants meant far-reaching alterations in many areas. University faculty and students turned to the disciplines of sociology, economics, and political science to try to explain the challenges that confronted their countries. The lingering outmoded traditions of colonial schooling, the lack of funding for new university programs, and the continued prevalence of open elitism often spurred student activists to call for reform. When officials were slow to act or ignored such demands, the universities became centers for the protests and demonstrations that sometimes spawned significant political movements.

The University Reform movement that arose at Argentina's University of Córdoba in 1918 is an example of this phenomenon. Students demanded and eventually achieved the ouster of a proclerical rector and the establishment of a new form of university governance that included democratic procedures and increased student involvement. The push for change also reached beyond the walls of the university. Under the new arrangement, the University of Córdoba accepted larger numbers of students from lower-income backgrounds, and its teaching and research were to include more emphasis on contemporary issues.[2]

The reform of the University of Córdoba was but one of many cases in which student and, at times, faculty activism became indicators of broader and deeper social trends. Higher education, with its traditional role of elite formation, soon became more an object of conquest than an impenetrable barrier for the sons and daughters of the middle and lower classes. University reform quickly spread to other countries, thereby taking on the characteristics of an international movement. Its origins and general purposes had several parallels in other countries, such as Peru. In 1919 students at the venerable University of San Marcos successfully challenged its antiquated administrative structure and joined with a national student-worker movement that helped to launch the fifty-year political career of Víctor Raúl Haya de la Torre (Selection 3). These movements in Argentina, Peru, and elsewhere in Latin America shared a somewhat eclectic tendency toward the left of the political spectrum, with much talk and writing about socialism and Marxism.

Student activism and university reform carried over into national politics not only in Argentina and Peru but also in Mexico, Cuba, and other countries, thereby leaving a lasting imprint on modern Latin American history. Not all of those who emerged from the university reform were leftists. José Vasconcelos, a university administrator and Catholic traditionalist, gained international acclaim as Mexico's minister of education from 1920 to 1923 and ran a vigorous but ill-fated campaign for the presidency in 1929. Vasconcelos seemed to be the exception, however, as leftist ideas—Marxism, anarchism, populism, and their many variations—gained adherents among faculty and students. While a law student at the University of Havana in the late 1940s, Fidel Castro was active in campus politics for more than a decade before he seized power in Cuba in 1959 (see Selection 10 for an account of Castro's education policies in the early 1960s). And in 1968 a series of protests by university and high-school students in Mexico City led to a bloody confrontation with police and armed forces in one of Latin America's most dramatic and violent acts of recent government repression (Selection 4).

Revolution

The timeworn elitist institutions of the colonial period and the nineteenth century could not withstand the demands for the substantial and at times radical innovations that arose within the universities in the early decades of the twentieth century. Student and faculty advocates of reform came from a larger society in which similar tendencies were also under way. This section provides some examples of the relationship between education and the most pronounced type of social change: revolutionary movements that propose to alter the fundamental political, social, and material structures of a country. Because of the magnitude of disorder, disruption, and violence commonly associated with these movements, they leave a legacy of confusion and controversy. Nevertheless, they allow the student of the history of social change to examine the sometimes impractical and bungled—and sometimes astute and effective—attempts to bring about change on a massive scale.

Twentieth-century Latin America has witnessed an expansion and intensification of social unrest. The region has felt the impact of at least half a dozen uprisings in which peasants, workers, intellectuals, and other disadvantaged or disaffected groups have attempted to alter the basic power structure of their countries. The case studies in this section involve five such movements: 1) the Mexican revolution that erupted into a decade of disorder and strife after 1910 and continued with sporadic surges of government-directed social and economic change until 1940; 2) the revolution in Guatemala that centered on the attempts of the national government to improve the lot of peasants and workers from 1944 to 1954; 3) the populist movement that enabled Juan Perón to hold power in Argentina from 1945 to 1955; 4) the Cuban revolution of 1959 that brought Fidel Castro to power with the opportunity to remake Cuban society; and 5) the Nicaraguan revolution of 1979, which drew support from an aroused general populace to overthrow the dictatorship of the Somoza family in the hopes of fundamental socioeconomic change. Similar movements took place elsewhere in Latin America, such as the short-lived Cuban revolution of 1933, the Bolivian revolution of 1952, and the electoral victory of socialism in Chile in 1970. But the selected cases considered here, while admittedly a subjective grouping, provide grounds on which to study the main themes under consideration in this volume.

For the purposes of understanding these selections, the reader is encouraged to look at revolution from two perspectives. The first concerns the roots of the revolution, or, to put it another way, how the revolutionary movement recruited its supporters. This type of activity is far removed from the typical classroom and is generally closer to the University Reform movement in that ideology and persuasion become more important than pedagogy, lectures, and other forms of academic activity. In this interaction, propaganda—the attempt to convince a person or group to join the movement—becomes crucial.

The second perspective concerns what happens after the revolutionaries have gained control of the government. The basic question now turns to the results of the revolutionary government's efforts to stimulate change. Here education is often touted as a means of solving social inequities and opening new economic opportunities for disadvantaged groups.

The Roots of Revolution

The origins or "causes" of revolution are often recognized by academic analysts years after the events took place so that in some of their analyses history is read backward; that is, it contains an element of hindsight. One would think that the decade before 1910, for example, must have harbored some of the causes of the Mexican Revolution of 1910. But, unfortunately for the sake of simplified narrative, this revolution did not have a single dominant personality or organization that provided a focal point for events during the critical decade. Observant historians have identified several revolutionaries who fought for power but nevertheless failed to gain control of the movement. Among them were, in the words of James Cockcroft, "the Precursors," who were led by the Flores Magón brothers. They formed the PLM (Partido Liberal Mexicano or Mexican Liberal party), but it won few converts and had ceased to be a major factor in Mexican politics by 1912. Other radical groups, such as the anarchist-inspired labor unions, had considerable success in some areas, but, as John Hart has documented, they fell victim to the military and political power struggles of the period. In Cockcroft's words, "Mexican intellectuals, except for the Precursor Movement prior to Madero's triumph (1910–1911) and the PLM radicals after it, generally were radicalized by revolutionary events, rather than serving to radicalize events."[3]

The essay by María Elena Díaz (Selection 5) explores the content and role of the satiric penny press for workers, which consisted of several inexpensive journals directed at working-class readers in the decade before the outbreak of the revolution. Although these publications catered to an audience that was to play a crucial role in the revolution, Professor Díaz finds little evidence of radical, anticapitalist, prorevolutionary ideas in their pages. Perhaps the revolutionary potential in this situation was simply the appearance of publications with a specialized appeal to the working class in a country where these people generally had been left out of serious discussion of national politics and economic policy.

The Sandinista victory over the Somoza dictatorship in 1979 developed in an entirely different way. Rather than a series of unconnected and unfocused revolutionary movements, the Sandinistas' strategy combined popular Nicaraguan folklore—especially the heroic image of Augusto César Sandino, who was that nation's ardent anti-imperialist warrior of the 1920s—with a flexible formulation of Marxist theory. This unique combination, as discussed in Selection 6 by Donald Hodges, became the means by which a handful of revolutionaries persuaded large numbers of their compatriots to follow them. Hodges's thoughtful analysis reveals that "historical hindsight" has some validity. The Sandinistas built a system of education and propaganda that helped to shape the decisive events of 1979, a decided contrast to the Mexican experience, in which revolutionary persuasion and propaganda seemed to have relatively little impact in the early stages of the movement.

Revolutionary Governments and Social Change

Selections in this section explore the role of education as an instrument of change in the hands of revolutionary governments. What changes did the new national leaders attempt to enact? How effective were these governments in producing the desired changes? The reader is cautioned to expect ambiguities and even contradictions in the revolutionary programs.

The Mexican revolution had its share of contradictions; the radical rhetoric of the 1920s and 1930s that promised a new way of life for the masses often ran up against the realities of deeply entrenched poverty and limited government resources. The large burst of government-directed social and economic change during the presidency of Lázaro Cárdenas (1934–1940) is a good example. This shrewd former general, who impressed contemporary observers with his ability to outwit his conservative foes, also managed to break through revolutionary ambivalence and deliver a blow to U.S. and British oil companies with his decision to expropriate their Mexican properties in the climax to a lengthy labor dispute. In addition, Cárdenas attempted a vigorous land reform program that included the conversion of large, privately owned estates into *ejidos*, or Mexican-style, village-owned collective farms.

His education program took on huge challenges as well. Mexico's ambitious Six Year Plan of 1934 decreed that socialism was to be the official doctrine in the country's schools. Many overly anxious people in the United States believed that some type of socialist state was in the making along their southern border. But historian Mary Kay Vaughan has discovered a more complex story (Selection 7). The national government directed rural teachers to establish a quickly assembled socialist curriculum in the classroom, but, as Vaughan's findings make clear, the peasants and their sons and daughters were not receptive to this imposition from outside their communities. The revolution in this case was at work on two distinct levels: the national government and its ambitious plans, and an aroused peasantry and its hopes and expectations. As might be expected in an open, revolutionary environment, these two forces clashed.

Rough parallels existed between the revolutions in Guatemala and Mexico. In both cases loosely structured, somewhat disorganized revolutionary coalitions overthrew dictators (Jorge Ubico in Guatemala and Porfirio Díaz in Mexico) who had held on to power in spite of growing unrest. In the subsequent period of experimentation and change, Guatemala, like Mexico, experienced fluctuations in the intensity and direction of reform. Guatemala, however, had only ten years (1944–1954) to develop its programs, while Mexico took the larger part of three decades (1910–1940).

During Guatemala's crucial decade, Protestant missionaries, who served both as teachers in basic literacy skills and as proselytizers for their churches in rural areas, felt the effects of policy vacillations. Virginia Garrard Burnett (Selection 8) discusses the shift from government encouragement of and cooperation with the missionaries under President Juan José Arévalo (1946–1950) to a distant and at times hostile relationship under his successor, Jacobo Arbenz Guzmán (1950–1954).

Argentina provides an ominous example of the risks associated with popular movements. Many Argentines had enjoyed the benefits of a broadly based school structure from the elementary level to high school, and a growing number attended the country's universities. The rise of a military-dominated government during World War II, however, presented the possibility that this system would become the tool of an authoritarian regime. Ruth and Leonard Greenup were in Argentina when the military government came under the influence of the aggressive, colorful Colonel Juan Perón who, with his dynamic wife, Eva Duarte de Perón, inspired widespread excitement and support among the working class. In Selection 9 the Greenups describe the government's heavy-handed methods, which jeopardized Argentina's educational institutions through political manipulation, bureaucratic intimidation, and police-state tactics.

Fidel Castro's overthrow of Fulgencio Batista in 1959 stimulated more international attention than the Guatemalan revolution and even more controversy than the policies and politics of Perón largely because the bearded revolutionary projected a charismatic presence at the same time that he moved into a close relationship with the Soviet Union. Joseph Roucek's contemporary assessment of Castro's educational program (Selection 10) explores an issue that was paramount in the 1960s: to what extent had communism taken hold in Cuba and, in this case, in Cuban schools?

Problems of Institutionalization

Although this section emphasizes the problems associated with the emergence of large educational and media institutions, the student of modern Latin America should be familiar with its positive accomplishments. The previous sections on university reform and revolution may leave the impression that schools and universities in Latin America were usually caught up in social turmoil and political agitation, but this impression is incorrect. Most of Latin America did not undergo major social revolutions. And most school teachers and university professors dealt with their students as usual on a day-to-day basis in which learning and its associated problems were their main concerns.

These routine operations included a variety of classroom situations. Students who attended the large and often crowded urban schools in rapidly growing cities from Santiago, Chile, to Monterrey, Mexico, found education a vital tool for survival in the competitive world of commerce, business cycles, and inflation typical of the shift toward private enterprise economics in recent years. Students who attended isolated rural schools in the rugged mountains of Mexico and Central America or in the Andes chain of South America regarded education as a mediator between their traditional culture and the the onrushing tide of modern civilization.

In spite of the formidable challenges outlined above, the educational systems of many Latin American countries have responded with considerable success. The growth of literacy in the region during the twentieth century, for example, is an impressive achievement by almost any standard. Most governments have enlarged their school systems from their nineteenth-century concentration in a few prosperous urban and commercial centers to reach previously isolated rural areas. This expansion has had a marked impact on literacy rates. While statistics are not always reliable and are subject to varying interpretations, the overall improvement is undeniable.

TABLE 1. Literacy Rates in Selected Countries

Argentina		*Brazil*		*Mexico*	
1869	24%	1872	16%	1900	22%
1895	46%	1920	30%	1920	40%
1949	89%	1939	57%	1940	52%
1990	94%	1990	74%	1990	88%
Chile		*Bolivia*		*Guatemala*	
1875	26%	1900	17%	1893	11%
1945	76%	1945	15% to 35%	1945	20%
1990	90%	1990	75%	1990	48%

Sources: Carlos Newland, "La educación elemental en Hispanoamérica: desde la independencia hasta la centralización de los sistemas educativos nacionales," *Hispanic American Historical Review* 71, no. 2 (May 1990): 358; Herbert S. Klein, *Bolivia: The Evolution of a Multi-Ethnic Society* (New York, 1992), 227; *Pan American Yearbook* (New York, 1945); and Paul Goodwin, ed., *Global Studies: Latin America* (Guilford, CT, 1990).

One of the most difficult tasks in education has been the provision of schools in isolated communities where, only a generation or two earlier, no such institutions existed. Nineteenth-century education, whether in the hands of the Catholic church, Protestant missionaries, individual tutors, or local officials, usually reached only a small part of the population. A few countries, however, benefited from the determination of advocates of mass education, such as Argentina's Domingo Sarmiento and Uruguay's José Pedro Varela, who, in the last decades of the 1800s, led the expansion of their national school systems. Under the guidance of Minister of Education José Vasconcelos in the early 1920s, Mexico also broadened its schools to include the children of many illiterate parents. In all three cases, the main impetus for change came from the national government, which seemed to be the only institution in those countries that possessed the material resources and political will to carry out such massive undertakings. This pattern, accompanied by much political rhetoric and many pedagogical promises, became the established practice in most countries of the region in the first decades of the twentieth century.

The Challenges of Bureaucratization and Centralization

Carefully worded plans endorsed by a corps of teachers, administrators, and politicians do not tell the whole story. In 1926, for instance, the Mexican government created the Casa del Estudiante Indígena (House of the Native American Student) in Mexico City to break through the cultural barriers that separated the modern centers of social and economic development from small rural communities. The purpose of this new school was to educate a selected group of young native males from provincial villages so that they could return to help bring modern education to their home communities. The results of this experiment were impressive in terms of the young Indians' response to the opportunity to learn, but the larger consequences were unexpected and, in terms of the purpose of the program, counterproductive. Most of its graduates chose to seek jobs in Mexico City or some other urbanized area rather than return to their villages. The story of the Casa depicts one of the problems of rural education: the better students often left home for what they perceived to be the greater opportunities and excitement of the city. This outcome also indicates another difficulty: a well-meaning program sometimes produces results that are harmful to its intended beneficiaries. The rural villages lost some of their more capable young people and remained on the fringes of national life. Finally, in 1932, the Mexican Ministry of Education closed the Casa in order to divert its funding to other purposes.[4]

The Q'eros Indians' relationship with Peru's national government likewise contained unexpected consequences, frustration, and even farce. A small, cohesive community of native Americans located near the ancient Indian city of Cuzco, the Q'eros had retained their traditions since the days of the Inca Empire. The Peruvian government, intent on expansive modernization in the 1970s, allocated materials for the construction of a national network of rural schools. Although the building material shipped to the Q'eros was adobe, which becomes moisture-laden and crumbles in the humid, high-mountain atmosphere, the village council accepted the misdirected benevolence and stored the adobe blocks in its old stone-walled schoolhouse. John Cohen's documentary captures this and other elements in the tenuous relationship between the Q'eros and the "educated" world outside their community.[5]

Mexico's experience with the Casa and the Q'eros' response to the good intentions of the Lima government underscore the uncertainties involved in social change led by central bureaucracies. Administrative misdirections and mistakes combine with the expansion of these large institutions to produce situations that contain some potential for benevolent results (such as higher literacy rates and the expansion of technical skills) as well as ambiguous or even unintended outcomes. Students, such as the graduates of the Casa, used their learning to maximize their personal potential in ways not anticipated by their teachers.[6]

The process of institutionalization can also combine the noblest of aims—schooling for every citizen—with the tendency in modern governments to accumulate layers of bureaucracy. Much of this layering is open to political appointments and the cancerlike expansion of functions and officials. The Hispanic proclivity for labyrinthine government reinforces this tendency. Many administrative hierarchies protected themselves with their claims to be the best hope for the elevation of the younger generation, but critics have noted that these governments often use literacy campaigns and public education in general to build support for their administrations. Such self-serving efforts undermine the stated goals of providing students with the knowledge and confidence to assume the initiative in politics and at work.

Probably the more typical difficulties posed by bureaucratization revolved around a new form of elitism (or perhaps a resilient but revised form of the older elitism). Educational bureaucracy spawns a world of its own, carefully structured to harmonize with the larger economic and political trends of the day, but also top-heavy and unresponsive to the backgrounds and needs of the very students these educational institutions identified ostensibly as their primary beneficiaries—the children of the working class, the peasantry, and the struggling middle class.

One of the leading critics of this system was Ivan Illich, an Austrian-born Catholic theologian and social critic who in the 1960s and 1970s made Cuernavaca, Mexico, his base of operations. Illich challenged the basic assumptions used by the founders of mass education in Latin America. He charged that "the school systems of Latin America are fossilized records of a dream begun a century ago. The school pyramid is abuilding from top to bottom throughout Latin America."[7]

The "top" was made up of politicians and administrators who exercised their political and management skills to impose a system that brought few benefits to the ordinary citizen. Illich blamed the lockstep graded curriculum, the pompous claims of meritocracy (promotions and other rewards to students who master the curriculum), and the insensitivity of this mechanistic approach for what he saw as the general failure of education. He argued for "deschooling," or the breakup of this expansive and expensive system because of its failure to supply the skills and expertise needed by the sons and daughters of ordinary citizens.[8]

A second critic of the heavily bureaucratized schools was Brazilian Paulo Freire. While Illich directed most of his judgment against the upper levels of the education establishment, Freire started at the bottom of the structure—the classroom—to devise alternatives to the prevalent pedagogy. Based largely on practical classroom experience, his discussions and writings attracted a wide following not only in Latin America but also in the United States and Europe. Selection 11 by John W. Donohue describes Freire's explication of his ideas on a visit to Fordham University in New York in 1972. In Selection 12, Kevin Healy discusses the application of Freire's ideas in a rural education program for Bolivian women in the late 1980s, a program that went beyond the rudiments of literacy to address issues of power and social/ethnic discrimination in Bolivian society.

The Impact of International Institutions: Images and Ideas from Abroad

Both Freire and Illich point out the weaknesses of formal schooling and the need to look beyond customary classroom approaches. They and other observers of the broader social and cultural trends of the twentieth century have concluded that the school is only one of many institutions that provide children and adults with a steady barrage of information and images. The school in the age of the modern media must compete with the influence of mass-circulated newspapers, magazines, and comic books; films; television; and popular music. U.S. domination of film production and television programming has created special problems in many Latin American countries, where a sense of national identity has developed unevenly. This problem became particularly evident in the popular films and television series exported from the United States in the 1950s and 1960s. Through the display of houses, furniture, automobiles, and clothing, the media's version of the living standard of the "average" family in the United States became a prominent feature in the entertainment of millions of Latin Americans.

The heavy use of U.S.-style advertising in Spanish and Portuguese for products ranging from soft drinks to cigarettes to automobiles created a fascination with the way of life portrayed in these persuasive pieces of marketing. In the view of Alan Wells, the author of a pioneering study of the impact of U.S. television in Latin America, the purveyors of Madison Avenue methods of advertising quickly gained the upper hand in large cities throughout the region (Selection 13).

The stream of images from the United States into Latin America was not limited to the work of the entertainment and advertising industries. As historian Gerald K. Haines makes clear in Selection 14, in order to reinforce its foreign-policy goals, Washington played a major role in the creation of a media image of the United States in Brazil during World War II and afterward in the early phases of the Cold War. Emerging as a countermeasure to Axis propaganda during World War II, this media image continued to expand and evolve in response to the perceived threat of a Communist menace in the 1950s and 1960s.

Two Bolivian educators developed a series of illustrated *rotafolio* textbooks to explain to their adult students the importance of outside forces in their lives. This illustration depicts the impact of the mass media (*"comunicación dominante,"* or "dominant communication") as compared with the influence of the classroom (*"comunicación popular,"* or "popular communication"). The mass media "speak of the interests of a small [and powerful] group and impose an alien culture and reality." The classroom "speaks of the necessities, reality, and native culture of the local community." (See Selection 12 by Kevin Healy.)

The impact of this propaganda, along with the extensive influence of U.S. television programs, films, and advertising, directly affected the teachers' tasks. Most educators attempted to provide their students with skills in reading, writing, and mathematics, the fundamentals in their respective national culture and history, and some discussion of current events. The U.S. media campaign against communism and related movements helped shape the ideological debates in much of Latin America. The powerful lure of the fast, hypnotic commercials and the longer programs and feature films seriously competed with schools for the attention and sometimes even the attendance of students. Unfortunately, the classroom teacher had to face these challenges with limited budgets that provided little support for equipment, books, and media aids to counteract popular mass culture.

Not all international influences, however, have produced troublesome results, as the activities of the United Nations Education, Science, and Cultural Organization (UNESCO) prove. The transition from the life of the rural village to the complex and competitive environment of the city affects every developing country and many industrialized countries. Since the late 1940s UNESCO has been working toward an approach to this problem through rural schooling. While highly sensitive to its revolutionary heritage and national uniqueness, the Mexican government cooperated with UNESCO and, as Selection 15 by Elaine Lacy reveals, has been doing so since the 1950s.

Conclusion

The role of education exists within the larger context of the flow of information and images through expanding systems of mass communication. In both education and communication, Latin America has experienced an intrusion of foreign cultures. The powerful impact of U.S. entertainment and advertising over the last century has competed with the lingering importance of Spanish, Portuguese, British, and French influences and the rise of new players in this game of cultural hegemony—the Germans and the Japanese.

In spite of the multiplicity and momentum of these influences, the concepts of national identity and culture remain alive, and the educational system is often the main vehicle for their cultivation. Governments, intellectual leaders, and the general public are often sensitive to the arrival of foreign films, television programs, advertisements, and news coverage that contain stereotypical views of their countries, their cultures, and Latin America in general. Education and the national mass media offer the means by which to mount campaigns against foreign influences. The kind of patriotic nationalism employed by Juan Perón in Argentina in the 1940s and early 1950s and, on the far left, by Fidel Castro in Cuba in the 1960s are two obvious examples. In a sense, Castro not only adopted Communist ideology but also used it to assert Cuba's national identity against the United States.

While the internationalization and privatization associated with the "New World Order" of the 1980s seemed inevitable to many commentators, each country maintained deep reservoirs of national, regional, and local autonomy. On one level, many Latin American television stations and networks began to turn away from direct foreign influences through their own popular dramas, or "telenovelas." More significant, the application of Freire's pedagogy in the mountains of Bolivia indicated that local communities and the concerns of their people could thrive within a carefully designed national education program. Although their values and ways of life were threatened by the onrush of modern, commercial culture from the affluent sections of cities and large towns, these common folk—descendants of the proverbial peasant—have found ways to deal with the tidal wave of modernization through the flexible use of information supplied by the schools and mass media.

The implication of these struggles supports the notion that education has been and continues to be an important factor in Latin American social change. The old elitist ideas and practices of the nineteenth century that limited primary education to a privileged few and university schooling to an even smaller minority felt the rumblings of the University Reform movement and the earthquakes of the Mexican, Guatemalan, Argentine, Cuban, and Nicaraguan revolutions. The old elitist structures did not withstand these seismic shocks intact, but elitism itself did not disappear. Social change has had its limits. Although the public schools and universities opened their doors to the offspring of the disadvantaged, providing more avenues for upward mobility, exclusive private schools and expensive private universities maintained barriers between those in the upper echelons and those below.

The rise in literacy rates and the migration of those in search of better jobs revealed that the poor were not ignorant and passive; but, ironically, the very process that provided reading and writing skills and technical training for society in general also contained another type of elitism—that of an administrative corps atop the bureaucratic and political power structures. Organizations whose admirable purposes included literacy campaigns and rural outreach programs also tended to rely on impersonality and political manipulation and were largely insensitive to individual and regional differences. Freire and Illich warned of the dire consequences of these tendencies. For though many tensions arise from the interaction of people and bureaucracies, the outcomes of these struggles are difficult to predict.

Notes

1. Gertrude M. Yeager, "Elite Education in Nineteenth Century Chile," *Hispanic American Historical Review* 71, no. 1 (February 1991): 98.

2. Richard J. Walter, *Student Politics in Argentina: The University Reform and Its Effects, 1918–1964* (New York, 1968). For another perceptive study of a university reform movement, see Mark Van Aken, "The Radicalization of the Uruguayan Student Movement," *The Americas* 23, no. 1 (July 1976): 109–29.

3. James D. Cockcroft, *Intellectual Precursors of the Mexican Revolution* (Austin, 1971), 232. See also John M. Hart, *Anarchism and the Mexican Working Class, 1860–1931* (Austin, 1978).

4. Ramon Eduardo Ruiz, *Mexico: The Challenge of Poverty and Illiteracy* (San Marino, CA, 1963), 142–57.

5. Originally broadcast as "Patterns from the Past" on the Nova series for the Public Broadcasting System and now available through "The Works of John Cohen: Anthropology, Music, Film" from the University of California Extension Center for Media, Berkeley, California.

6. Historians have begun to study the interaction between Mexico's system of rural schools and local communities. Two innovative studies that stress the assertiveness of villagers in the shaping of their education and the education of their children are: Elsie Rockwell, "Schools of the Revolution: Enacting and Contesting State Forms (Tlaxcala, 1910–1930)," in *Everyday Forms of State Formation: Revolution and the Negotiation of Rule in Modern Mexico*, ed. Gil Joseph and D. Nugent (Durham, NC, in press); and Mary Kay Vaughan, "Rural Women's Literacy and Education in the Mexican Revolution: Subverting a Patriarchal Event?" in *Creating Spaces, Shaping Transition: Women of the Mexican Countryside, 1850–1990*, ed. Mary Kay Vaughan and Heather Fowler Salamini (in preparation).

7. Ivan Illich, "The False Ideology of Schooling," *Saturday Review of Literature* 53, no. 42 (October 17, 1970): 56–57, 68.

8. Ivan Illich, *Deschooling Society* (New York, 1970).

I The Colonial Legacy and the Nineteenth Century

1 Mark D. Szuchman ◆ In Search of Deference: Education and Civic Formation in Nineteenth-Century Buenos Aires

The school often served as a focal point in the relationship between a nation's elite and the undereducated masses. A specialist in nineteenth-century social and cultural history, Mark Szuchman explores this relationship in Argentina's crucial decades of the 1820s and the 1830s.

In the excitement of independence, many Argentines saw education as an opportunity for self-improvement for the lower classes. But two of the most prominent Argentines of the era disagreed with this assumption. The reader should give special attention to the contributions of the administration of Juan Manuel de Rosas, Argentina's dominant political figure of the period, and Domingo Faustino Sarmiento, the intellectual leader of the "Generation of 1837," to this discussion of the roles that schools should play in the formation of the nation's social and political systems.

Education and the Civic Consciousness

Government authorities and civic leaders in Buenos Aires were moved to train the city's youth by their sense of a longstanding Western tradition: that education was the fundamental instrument for reconstituting political leadership. Beyond this, the purpose of education rested on the creation and reinforcement of moral and political ideals suitable to the general welfare, but always within the practical context of the continued leadership of the *gente decente* [social and political elite]. The Enlightenment had paved the way for the execution of this more generalized purpose by substituting the traditional and authoritarian ideal of the loyal

From Mark D. Szuchman, "In Search of Deference: Education and Civic Formation in Nineteenth-Century Buenos Aires," *SECOLAS Annals* 18 (March 1987): 5–21. Reprinted by permission of the author.

1

subject with the progressive ideal of the participatory citizen.[1] By the start of the nineteenth century, the school was meant to serve as the medium by which "to inspire in children the habit of order, the sentiments of honor, love of truth, the search for justice, [and] respect for their peers."[2] In the course of the postrevolutionary period in Buenos Aires, notions related to the education of youth were also formulated within a generalized apprehension over the failure to maintain social and political stability. Thus, the need for strengthening the moral basis of the educational curriculum was perceived with greater urgency by the authorities and the *gente decente*, as expressed by the *porteño* [resident of the port city Buenos Aires] critic who asserted that "moral education is the first item of importance which should be considered." His logic carried its own imperative: the youth must be taught to love work, because "it is well known that every hard-working man is an excellent member of society; the man who works all day has very little time left to perpetrate crimes."[3] As the idea took hold that the establishment of order needed to begin with the children, the roles played by the public and private schools took on greater dimensions than those normally associated with formal education.[4] The subject of childhood education will be discussed within the context of the social and political values of the dominant elites. The "model" of citizenship that these custodians of order tried to implant forms the backdrop of the analysis.[5]

The number of urban educational establishments tended to increase in the first half of the century. In 1815, the city was served by thirteen elementary schools, five of which were administered directly by the religious orders, but in all of which the curriculum was based on church doctrine. These primary schools were attended by over 1,200 students, estimated to represent barely 5 percent of the school-age children.[6] Increases in the school population were registered very slowly; for example, 130 students attended the elementary school in the parish of La Piedad in 1815, while only 126 were enrolled three years later.[7] Similarly, school enrollments throughout the city increased barely 5 percent between 1815 and 1817. Moreover, parishes fluctuated significantly from one year to another in the total number of registered students. This was indeed a checkered record for a group of revolutionary leaders whose educational ideology had committed them to casting off the Spanish system which, in the words of alcalde Prudencio Sagari, had been aimed at "keeping us ignorant in order to perpetuate our slavery and [the Spaniards'] despotism."[8] But by 1872, approximately 107 public schools and 120 private institutions operated within the city.[9] Over 7,700 students, or nearly 22 percent of the school-age population—defined by the government as children between the ages of six and fifteen, who then numbered nearly 36,000 boys and girls—were attending classes.[10]

The basic nature of the interplay between education and social advancement was redefined after independence. The advancement derived from formal training during the colonial period had been inherently individualistic; education had been considered a surplus commodity of a sort, which could be marketed insofar as it had situated the educated individual in competition for place. The returns on the investment of education had been largely self-centered: the individual, along with his family, would reap the benefits of salaries and other emoluments, in addition to the contacts that would further one's position in this clientelistic society.

Independence furthered the importance given by the state to the system of education by politicizing it. Learning became a construction which included both the infusion of ideological content into the curriculum, and the belief—derived from the republican ethos among the original revolutionaries—that formal training was a basic element of the new and liberal communitarianism. Thus, General Manuel Belgrano's motive force in founding public schools in Jujuy in 1813 was patently political: he held the ultimate goal of education to be"the formation of the citizen's conscience."[11]

In other attempts at fostering a republican consciousness, the revolutionary leadership of Buenos Aires early on ordered the dissemination of the *Social Contract* among the school children in elementary grades.[12] More than a decade later, the educational authorities required students on vacation to read the daily record of the sessions of the short-lived national congress in 1826, so that they "would learn the rationale on which our nation's constitution is founded."[13] The results of the new curricula were expected to contrast sharply with the particularistic privileges associated with the hierarchical society of castes which had existed under the defunct monarchical regime. The content of the curriculum that pertained to civics and history would, of course, extol the visionaries who held progressive values, but the fundamental responsibility given to the curriculum was to provide the community with young men and women upon whom the nation could rely for spiritual and material progress. Formal training would continue to furnish the means that would advance individuals, and their families would continue to be the recipients of their children's success. Yet, the new republican ideology held that benefits from such advancement must be shared beyond the narrow confines of the private, individual, and familial worlds. Liberal reformers of the revolutionary era were thus adding a novel and divisive ingredient into the realm of education by challenging the traditional dominance of the family and the household over the child, particularly during his formative years.[14]

In the view of social conservatives in Buenos Aires, however, the revolutionary principles which affected children served to form the "Jacobin family," wherein "paternal authority was forced to relax by the intervention of the State in all conflicts."[15] Insofar as schooling had the potential to disestablish traditional community norms, conservatives in Buenos Aires and other areas where early nineteenth-century reformers held political influence were justified in their fear of a consequent alienation of their children: in the revolutionary ideology, republican virtues were public virtues established by extra-familial interests, and the achievements of the nation's youth became the foundations of the nation's, not simply the family's, progress. Moreover, if the inspiration for reform was republican, its instruments came from cultural environments which were historically antagonistic to the Iberian traditions: "Instruction should not be limited only to instructing," preached one of the city's liberal weeklies in 1817, "it is necessary to form the heart, to awaken and stimulate its useful, lofty, and patriotic sentiments; in sum, we are obliged to inculcate virtuous habits in our children. . . . Happy are those nations which know how to form the inheritors of their rights . . . , and the zealous guardians of *order* [original emphasis]."[16]

If "nation" was still more an aspiration than a reality in a disunited revolutionary Argentina, the ideal was no less powerful a decade later. Indeed, the ideal, which combined order with deference to authority, became increasingly urgent after the completed revolution and the schismatic country of the 1820s.[17] As occurred with other theoretical formulations of the era, however, educational and cultural ideals, too, conflicted with political, financial, and ideological cycles.[18] For example, in serving Juan Manuel de Rosas, Minister [Tomás de] Anchorena went on to instruct the Inspector of Schools in a written directive of March 11, 1831, that not only must school employees wear the red emblems in support of the Federalist party led by Rosas, but it also became the duty of the students to wear them "while making clear to them the origins for such a determination in a manner calculated to instill in them love and respect for the [Federalist] System and for the Laws of their Fatherland."[19]

Thus, from the first republican moments, matters related to education would not stand apart from matters political and military. One of the clearest examples of this inseparable relationship comes from a simple but telling event in 1821. A brigantine sent from Buenos Aires to the southern coastal town of Patagones contained cargo which included fresh supplies of "weapons, ammunition, uniforms, tools, and some money to repair the forts, and twelve artillery pieces of high caliber and gun carriages." The supervision of this shipment was predictably in the hands of a military officer, Colonel Don Gabriel de la Oyuela, who had also been given command of the military detachment of twenty men on board, but who additionally had been provided by the Buenos Aires cabildo with "the most complete training necessary to begin teaching the youth of that important population."[20]

Because of the close relationship between education and the formation of political values, the officials of learning establishments had to deal with the effects of their fragile and conflictual society. Not surprisingly, Rosas required that the membership of each school board be selected by the *juez de paz* [justice of the peace] of every provincial district and urban barrio.[21] Moreover, the financial picture of the decade of the 1830s was much more conducive to military and police expenditures than to educational or other non-military needs.[22] Teachers went without salaries for months; their schools, reported the authorities in July 1829 following Lavalle's uprising, were "looted horribly by hordes of criminals." A teacher in the outlying town of San José de Flores was forced to flee from his post and take up a new one in Buenos Aires's Monserrat parish. These were just a few of the consequences that schools suffered at the hands of a troubled political environment.

Warnings of all these consequences and laments by observers notwithstanding, the pervasiveness of war—or at least of a military stance— was difficult to eradicate. This was a contradiction—the desire for peace and the militarization of society—which became evident in the nature of prizes that were sometimes awarded to primary school children who had received good grades. It became customary during much of the nineteenth century for political and school authorities to hold public exams and contests. The ritual of examining children's learning in public in the manner of a competition, followed by award ceremonies and festivities, was a tradition which contained important functions and derivatives. For example, the works of school children, which would sometimes be put on public display in the barrios' churches and in government buildings, served as moral exemplars for other children and as stamps of approval for the teachers who could thereby be served further in their own search for additional employment as private tutors.[23] More important still, the public ritual of judgment and observation of children's school performance served as an overt expression of the state's nominal concern for education, and it clearly established the solid nexus that joined the style and content of learning to the political values held by the governing authorities in power at any given time. The rituals of 1816, for example, included the public reading of a congratulatory note that had been sent by the governor to Don Rufino Sánchez, director of one of the city's public elementary schools. In it, the political authorities lauded his pedagogical efforts and the high levels of achievement demonstrated by his students. This time, the coveted prizes consisted of weapons.

> It was an honorable exam on general subjects which the 8 students under your direction rendered on the afternoon of the 28th of last month at the Church of San Ignacio. . . . As reward for their brilliant performance, I offer 8 carbines with bayonets which you should present to them in my name to each one of them, along with a copy of this note; let each of these weapons from this day on accompany them as a prize for their studies, and let them use it only for defending their sacred religion and the rights of their fatherland, without ever bringing shame to these honors.
>   Please also accept a carbine and a pair of pistols for your own individual use as a well-deserved reward for your virtuous earnestness.[24]

The most fundamental differences that divided Argentine thinkers on the subject of education, however, were related to functional aspects, such as what role education might play in molding the human resources that would be responsible for the country's political and economic development. On such issues, the child—as a developmental and dynamic concept—was largely missing from their considerations. To be sure, attitudes about the nature of the child were instrumental in determining the nature of his training in school. The case of Buenos Aires suggests that official educational policies could become sources of conflict between the domestic and the public spheres. Prior to 1830, the growing demand for educational facilities resulted in the increased role of the state in the socialization of the child outside the family's protective circle. For conservative Catholics during the anticlerical Rivadavian era, progressive and lay education posed a serious danger to traditional values: when, for example, Bernardino Rivadavia decreed the end of autonomous teaching responsibilities by Franciscans in their monastery in February 1824, he gave as his reason the crisis of confidence in the education preparedness of the religious orders and their inability "to provide the state with the guarantees it expects to receive in such matters."[25] For their part, liberal parents in the conservative restoration headed by Rosas underwent the difficulties inherent in the same conflict, albeit obtained from ideological opposites.[26] Thus, the composition of the Juntas Inspectoras was changed in the alternation between the liberal and conservative regimes. Under Rivadavia, each school board was composed of the local justice of the peace and two residents; but beginning in 1830, shortly after Rosas's coup, each board was brought under the government's closer scrutiny by replacing one of the residents with the Ministro del Culto, a sort of minister of religion who invariably was a priest. These changes formed part of a generalized turn away from the secularizing trends of the liberal past, and instead, toward a reinsertion of the clergy into various institutions of learning and high culture.[27]

The children's attendance and the quality of training they received in public schools were positively correlated, and, in turn, both depended equally on the socioeconomic positions of their families. "As soon as parents believe that their children have managed the barest understanding of the first lessons in reading and writing," reported several teachers in 1819, "they resolutely try to remove them from school, and they thus deprive them of the greater enlightenment which could make them more developed and which could raise their general standing in the community."[28] In the end, the financial dependence of lower-class parents on their children and the state's insistence on childhood education created tensions which were never fully eliminated. It remained for a more efficient system of monitoring school attendance at the start of the twentieth century to make compulsory education a reality.[29] In the meantime, even children from humble positions who were determined to complete their education ran into disappointing realities.[30]

School Regimen and Parental Resistance

The lack of cooperation by parents in educational matters was not simply the result of rural backwardness nor of their own illiteracy. Among the city's *gente decente*, too, school authorities and teachers found many recalcitrant fathers and mothers who objected to specific educational reforms, such as the monitorial system, which had been ardently welcomed by progressive liberals in the late 1810s. The monitorial system was predicated on enlisting proficient students as aides in the instructional regimen—thereby maximizing the number of students while minimizing expenditures—and on completely subordinating every child in the classroom to the teacher's demands. In this context, the drill became one of the monitorial system's all-important features, and—by way of the insistence on instantaneous responses to questions and to unspoken signals—the students' attention was supposed to be assured.

This so-called monitorial system of simultaneous instruction had been originated in England by Andrew Bell and Joseph Lancaster in the late 1790s. Their contribution to the field of education rested on a "scientific" approach to the curriculum, which was intended to be systematic, consistent, and economical. These procedures represented the pedagogical version of the rationalism which pervaded the Industrial Revolution. The educational regimen also reflected the industrial entrepreneurs' deep concern for workers' efficiency and absenteeism by including detailed plans for the classroom in order for the teacher to monitor the students' behavior and attendance. It resulted in an odd combination of progressive didactics, authoritarian rule, and impersonal attention.[31]

The system's economy was based on the use of children who, upon mastering the material, would then teach other children. These monitors were responsible not only for the execution of the concept of peer education but also for monitoring behavior and enlisting fellow students in guarding the orderliness of the classroom. Social control was thus applied to the children by other children, albeit under the adult supervision of the school's inspector, all within an authoritarian structure which contained many elements of public embarrassment for students who broke the rules. Indeed, Lancaster outlined in great detail the various "Instruments and Modes of Punishments," which included the use of shackles and yokes, suspending incorrigibles from the roof, the proclamation of students' faults before the whole school, and other forms of humiliation.[32] This authoritarian style of treatment, coupled with its publicly punitive rituals, was especially suitable to the *porteño* political elites of virtually all ideological preferences, as eager to establish orderliness among the youth as it was to restore order in the nation.

Not surprisingly, the Lancasterian model of instruction, which was first imported to Buenos Aires in 1818 and fully applied in the 1820s, was hailed by influential spokesmen as the greatest and most efficient innovation in the field of pedagogy.[33] To the enlightened, it carried the legitimacy borne out of its English origins; to the rational, it offered scientific design; to the liberal and the anticlerical, it became positively associated with secularism; and to the authorities, always short of capital, it promised economy.[34] Still, families reportedly resisted the implementation of the Lancaster method of teaching and continued to ignore additional pleas by the officials to give the new system a chance.[35]

Evidently, educational reform had become an additional element of community division, as policies and programs that threatened to undermine patriarchal authority were opposed by the older traditionalists. Their educational formations had served them well, and they saw the subordination of the child—and his mind—to the household as essential for the maintenance of the societal order. For their part, educational reformers insisted on the close interplay among their stated goals of intellectual development, political independence, and the general progress of a people. In some ways, the two constructions represented a generational split.

The *porteño* child in the early nineteenth-century school received his training in sociability within a framework designed to instill in him an acceptably inferior position in domestic society and an unquestioningly deferential attitude toward authority. Reading and writing exercises, reinforced by constant drill, formed the typical mechanisms used for instilling these patterns of sociability, or *urbanidad*, as the school subject was formally known. This drive to inculcate a deep sense of subordination among children was shared equally by liberals and conservatives. "We have just happily seen in practice the Lancaster system, by which not only do the children learn to read and write, but they also become accustomed to order," reported the utopian liberals of 1821.[36] During Rosas's regime students and faculty alike were required to wear the red pins that signified loyalty to the federalist party. The wording of the decree of May 1835 contained a logic easily found in the earlier liberal and republican rhetoric: "The government is convinced that when children are made to observe the laws of the country from the time of their infancy, and thereby they are taught the respect owed to the authorities, such impressions become permanently engraved."[37] For their part, hardened and more realistic liberal voices expressed themselves even more fully: "From subordination emanates good order," wrote Sarmiento in 1836, "and it is therefore of the utmost importance that the students respect and obey their superiors without any contradiction or opposition to their orders; failure to do so should be considered one of the greatest personal flaws, and by the same token, the most severe penalties available to the school should be applied in such cases."[38] Indeed, Sarmiento's ideological liberalism in political matters generally, although it did not extend much to children, displayed the contradictory mixture of respect for the need of children to be educated with the application of measures which severely restricted their behaviors. These were, in fact, the contradictions registered among members of the Generation of '37, hardened liberals whose pragmatism arose out of the ashes of the military and political conflicts of the postrevolutionary era.[39]

The hardening of attitudes by the Generation of '37, so succinctly expressed by Sarmiento, its most famous pedagogue, contrasts sharply with the tenets of the previous generation of liberals of the period shortly following the May Revolution. In time, however, the Rousseauist requirement that education contribute to the flowering nature of childhood and to the evolution of a society was forcefully complemented by the Kantian call for constraint and for the inculcation of habit in the youngsters' preparation that he or she may follow faithfully the rules of conduct imposed from above. Thus, the tumultuousness of the independence era resulted in a curious consensus: Argentine reformists and traditionalists came to agree that the supreme guide to life was the law of duty, which was always more or less in opposition to the promptings of inclination.

Not surprisingly, Sarmiento devoted a significant number of regulations to monitoring the behavior of students, and to the punishment appropriate to every type of infraction.[40] Thus, Sarmiento's charter allowed for six degrees of severity in punishments, ranging from "sweet and loving warnings," to denials of various privileges, to religious penance, and finally, to expulsion "in cases of absolute impertinence," but no mention is made of paddling. By design, an uncritical solidarity with the community in which the youngster lived was fostered early. Here, as in the political realm, the common weal and the peaceful order were held to depend upon blind deference to established authority.

Until mid-century, educational thinkers and essayists writing on the subject of childhood generally did not consider young children to be naturally endowed with critical thinking abilities. Indeed, the attitude suggested by a number of school teachers resembled the theories of [John] Locke on the youthful acquisition of knowledge. Along with some of his seventeenth-century contemporaries, Locke believed that, upon birth, children's brains were devoid of any content; knowledge and aptitude were nothing more than the child's capacity to fill his head with the facts provided to him by others and by experience. Neither the innate ability of children to learn nor the cognitive prowess of the human mind were recognized. Thus, it was not until after the 1850s that any attention was paid to devising teaching techniques that would capitalize on the child's own abilities to learn. Until then, most educators felt the need to shape children's minds in a clearly hierarchical, unilateral, and adult-centered manner, allowing virtually no latitude for youngsters to develop and employ their own analytical skills.[41]

The daily activities of children in school did not allow for much free interplay between teacher and student. There was no such thing as discussion of the educational subjects to any meaningful degree: teaching was unidirectional and hierarchical, always stemming from the teacher and not subject to debate among students; indeed, successful education was deemed to rest more on the teacher's total domination of the class than on his own mastery of the material. Thus, the two basic instruments of instruction for each subject matter included the monologue and the attendant practice-and-drill session. A typical schedule for the elementary public schools of Buenos Aires included either a six- or a seven-hour day depending on the school, always divided into two sessions.[42] It was a pedagogical system that required a great deal of passivity on the part of the youngster, thereby conspiring against students with short attention spans.[43]

The characteristics of the educational system of Buenos Aires would remain basically unaltered until the 1850s. Then the school regimen, the formative experiences of teachers, and the definitions of childhood with their attendant epistemological concerns would compromise the line of considerations that distinguished the old from the new approaches to the education of youth. As precedent to action, however, the very purpose of childhood learning had to undergo a fundamental redefinition, while the role of the state in the field of education would need to be expanded considerably. The fall of Rosas signified that the extremely hierarchical structure of learning within the classroom and the ad hoc nature of the personnel and the curriculum were subjected to review and amendment.

The Political Dimensions of Educational Reform

The arrival of liberal reformers to political power in the 1850s carried significant consequences for the educational system. Not since the Revolution of 1810 had men come to political leadership with a renewed sense of the value of education; they demonstrated a heightened awareness of the pedagogue's power to shape the political consciousness of the citizenry. In addition, they brought into play a greater sensitivity to the innate learning processes of children. If the reforms did not attain significant increases in the percentage of literate *porteños*, at least the needed infrastructure was put in place for the quantitative increases in school attendance which would be registered at the turn of the century.[44]

At the base of the changes lay a functional definition of the masses, which clearly distinguished the conservatism of the Rosas era from the liberalism of the Generation of '37. Rosas's political elites considered the illiteracy of the *gente de pueblo* [common people] to be the natural condition of a prepolitical folk. In other words, ignorance of matters of the mind—as distinguished from matters associated with the practical end of artisanry and rural functions—was inherent to a people who not only lacked political influence, but also were destined never to have it. As such, the *gente de pueblo* represented the large majority of Argentines, who posed a threat only insofar as they could be led into battle by a politically calculating individual. Without such an opponent, however, the *gente de pueblo* merely served the ends of the governing elite. Malleable and unable to apprehend neither the subtleties of the art of politics nor the machinations of their patrons, plebeians were in no need—indeed, they were not capable—of being redeemed. Instead, they merely served as clients and servants of their custodial elites.

Allowing for the considerable philosophical differences found among the liberals of the Generation of '37, they presented a significantly different definition of the purpose of the masses. Post-Rosas liberals certainly held the illiterate and rustic peoples in disdain, much as did their conservative counterparts, but they distinguished themselves from both their liberal predecessors and from the conservatives on the basis of two facts.

The first was simply generational: they had breathed the stimulating and rarefied atmosphere of the romantic socialists who believed in the perfectability of all segments of mankind. They thus stood in sharp contrast to the traditional elites who accepted the immutability of the ignorant state commonly found among the lower classes. The second distinction derived from the experiential level, to the extent that the Generation of '37 viewed the nature of Argentine and Spanish-American politics as historically conflictual, and it was from the acceptance of this reality that they defined the value of a literate public.

These two realities synthesize the explanation for the actions of the Generation of '37 in matters of education: the redeemability of the ignorant masses was possible not only as a universal proposition of unavoidable progress, but it also figured as a local and urgently needed prescription for the elimination of armed struggle as the all-too-predictable means to the resolution of conflict. These calculations were clearly aimed at the realignment of the mental states related to identifications, for the average individual in Argentina identified his political self with one individual leader or another and his respective retinue. The Generation of '37, by contrast, aimed at the popular identification with the abstract, specifically, with the state, thereby eliminating two historical tendencies: the dispersal of political authority among the surfeit of actors in the constellation of power, or, conversely the centrifugal tendency of hegemonic caudillismo.

The second half of the nineteenth century was the ripe time for these ideas to be tested, for they circulated in the realm of values attendant a capitalism which, already quite mature in parts of Western Europe, was now advancing with greater strength than ever across the Atlantic. The growing presence of market forces was altering radically the nature of contractual obligations, including the rights and obligations among citizens, and between citizen and state. Within the material realm, the oral promise and the broken vow proved inadequate to the exigencies of financial transactions. Along with more stringent requirements of accountability for human will, the market was inculcating the needed lesson of attending to the remote consequences of human action.[45] What was true of the world of industry, commerce, and finance had become obvious also to the political inheritors of the more than forty years of tensions encompassed by the revolutionary and Rosas eras: that private promises of friendship and political loyalties among caudillos served poorly as mechanisms for the maintenance of stability, and that alternative means had to be found to attain a more stable basis for action and for accountability.[46] At the legal end of things, codified and constitutional principles would be established which would, in due course, at least provide relatively clear standards of appropriate political behavior. But at the much more complex level of establishing normative action, education was considered to be the principal mechanism that over the long run would alter popular character and the *gente de pueblo*'s disposition toward authority. They would no longer be easily at the disposal of political adventurers and caudillos; they would instead make their own political calculations on the basis of reasoned will. The age of caudillos would come to an end, not so much because such men would cease to arise from within the ranks of the politicized gentry, but because of the uncertainty that they would command a mass following. Public action, which before depended on the ability to muster men of arms, would come to depend on garnering affinities to political ideas. Freedom could not be guaranteed except by an educational system "made to fit a generation's new necessities, breaking its old habits," wrote Esteban Echeverría while living in exile in Montevideo.[47] Echeverría's goal was to establish a society that, in the course of history, would be able to exercise sovereignty through the use of reasoned thought rather than through the traditional visceral motivations. The link he traced between education and political action was more discrete than the first generation of revolutionary liberals: "only the prudent and rational part of the social community is called to exercise that sovereignty."[48]

Thus, these liberals considered prudence, rationality, and conscientious political action to depend on the ability of the majority of the Argentine public to internalize the values generally associated with contemporary Western Europeans: delay of gratification, attention to remote consequences, conceptualization of the self as a functioning member of the social and political community. The basis for success in these projected constructions would rest on the ability—not the willingness—of the public to learn and act out these new behaviors. Willingness, or rather, the will to have these values and behaviors adopted by *porteños* rested with the state, which enlarged its responsibilities to include education and the regularization of the educational system. Education was thus a metaphor for civic apprenticeship unto a new generation of leaders who endowed themselves with the mantle of political power on the basis of their self-asserted intellectual superiority. In a way, this represented an updated liberal variant of the political schema of the traditional Thomist perspective on authority; the purpose of the supreme political organization known as the state was to rise above the fallibility of the popular constituency in order to consummate public action in accordance to a higher morality and for the benefit of the common good in opposition to private consideration.[49]

Conclusions

The hegemony of the generation of men who followed upon Rosas's fall was justified by their insistence on turning the problematical masses into passive elements of society.[50] The *hommes de lettres* then simply had to fulfill their charge of molding the masses in accordance with the contemporary sense of a civic society. Men of ideas ruled, therefore, by virtue of their tutorial talents, the political novelty of which was based upon the added element of education to the realm of public action. Furthermore, the new liberals' concepts related to the masses, and their education represented a significant departure from the revolutionary liberal ideology of the 1810 generation. To the revolutionaries, education formed the means to the liberation of each and every individual of the community in the common pursuit of republicanism; it was an ideal with direct lines of argumentation to the Enlightenment's optimism related to mankind's political future. The course of the revolution, and the subsequent erosion of the constitutional ideal, had dramatically demonstrated to the young liberals who grew up under the caudillo political order the need to eliminate the individual from active participation in exchange for his passivity, in effect his depoliticization. If for Belgrano the classroom had been the cauldron in which the ingredient of fervent republicanism would stir up Americans seeking liberty, for Sarmiento it represented the containment of passion and the instrument for inculcating subservience to the abstraction of the state.

The ultimate goal of the education process did not and could not stand apart from matters more overtly political, though not more importantly so. It represented the planned elimination of the atomization of popular loyalties and the depersonalization of authority. The cessation of an Argentina defined as a political construction of hostile regions would come through efforts exerted by two forces pushing from opposite ends of the societal structure toward a common center. From the top, that is, from the structures of government and its executive officials would come the pressures to conform via the organized political parties—associations, really—and from the accumulation of military prowess capable of eliminating regional dissidence by the hegemonic employment of updated warmaking technology. From the bottom came the pressures for a peaceful and longitudinal program of education, by which generation after generation of youngsters would come to understand political authority as defined by the moral superiority of the abstraction of nationhood, unified in its common goal of peace, and deferring to men of letters—not war lords—in the interest of stability.

Notes

1. Gregorio Weinberg, "A Historical Perspective of Latin American Education," *CEPAL Review* 21 (December 1983), p. 45.

2. *El Censor*, April 24, 1817.

3. *El Lucero*, October 21, 1829.

4. Yet, while education as a mechanism for improving society in general figured prominently within the value-system of the city's literate group, it was still widely accepted that the effects of education on individuals depended primarily on the socioeconomic positions into which they had been born. This was the internalized value-system of a widow left alone with six children who, in 1825, requested and received a government scholarship for her fourteen-year-old son to "be accorded the education to which he is entitled by his distinguished social origin, even if he [now] figures among the poor." AGN X-6-1-6. Inspección de Escuelas, 1826–1836. Similarly, the people who applied to one of twelve government-sponsored scholarships in support of their sons in 1826 registered high social positions and respectability, even if they were undergoing financial difficulties. They included men such as Mariano Vico, the army's Surgeon General who had served in Paraguay, Uruguay, and Peru, and Antonio Pirán, former *regidor*, conciliar, and prior of the Buenos Aires *consulado*. The functional purposes in the relationship between knowledge and class position were instilled in Argentines early in their lives. This was the lesson taught to youngsters, for example, by the principal of the elementary school in the town of San Fernando when in 1830 he told them that the best prevention of misfortune "came by way of study and application in your infancy . . . , guiding yourselves by the irrefutable principle that knowledge enlightens the rich and facilitates the livelihood of the poor." AGN 6-1-2. Instrucción Pública, 1821–1836.

5. The concept of "model" or "style" of education as an expression of the elites' dominant values is argued in Gregorio Weinberg, "A Historical Perspective of Latin American Education," *CEPAL Review*, 21 (December 1983), pp. 39–41.

6. *El Censor*, April 24, 1817.

7. AGN X-6-1-1. Instrucción Pública, 1812–1835.

8. Ibid.

9. AGN. Censos 1405–1406. *Censo Nacional de Escuelas del 20 de diciembre de 1872*. Provincia de Buenos Aires. Cuadros de Capital, B. III–B. IV.

10. República Argentina, *Primer Censo de la República Argentina* (Buenos Aires, 1872), p. 26.

11. The school regulations drafted by Belgrano himself called for a teacher who should be concerned with instilling in his students "a love for order, respect for religion, moderation and sweetness in dealings with fellow men, a deep sense of honor, a sense of love toward virtue and science, a sense of abhorrence toward vices, a favorable disposition toward work [and] selflessness, contempt for anything materially extravagant or luxurious in matters of food, dress and other necessities of life, a spirit of nationalism that would guide them to work for the public well-being rather than for private benefit, and a higher valuation given to everything that is American over and above anything foreign." Quoted in Manuel H. Solari, *Historia de la educación argentina* (Buenos Aires, 1976), p. 41. See also AGN X-6-1-1. Instrucción Pública, 1812–1835.

12. Torcuato S. Di Tella, "Las raices de la controversia educacional argentina," *Los fragmentos del poder. De la oligarquía a la poliarquía argentina.* Ed. Torcuato S. Di Tella and Tulio Halperin Donghi (Buenos Aires, 1969), p. 291.

13. AGN X-6-1-6. Inspección de Escuelas, 1826–1836.

14. Indeed, educational and social reformers throughout the West shared the hope that progressive schools would drive a salutary wedge into the habits and loyalties which traditionally had been shaped and maintained by home and church. Mary Jo Maynes, *Schooling in Western Europe: A Social History* (Albany, 1985), pp. 80–81.

15. Juan Agustin García, *La ciudad indiana. Buenos Aires desde 1600 hasta mediados del siglo XVII* (Buenos Aires, 1955), p. 96.

16. *El Censor*, May 15, 1817.

17. The search for stability was also expressed in the relationship between political order and education, as illustrated by the following comment, written by a *porteño* in 1827 who urged the masses to read a treatise published by London's Society for the Promotion of Useful Knowledge: "A paternal and just government receives the natural support of the people when they become enlightened. The spread of knowledge brings with it this decorous submission, which is supportive equally of both power and public order. Learned men obey better than do ignorant men." *Crónico Política y Literaria*, June 16, 1827.

18. In an oblique reference to the military conflicts which ensued from the antagonisms between federalists and unitarians and from the generally acrimonious style of relations, Ramón González Gorostizu, secretary of the Society for the Promotion of Enlightenment of the town of Chascomús, equated education with social and political stability: he hoped that the town's elementary school "would eliminate the animosities engendered by the state of ignorance." AGN X-6-1-1, Instrucción Pública, 1812–1835.

19. AGN X-6-1-2. Instrucción Pública, 1821–1836.

20. *El Argos de Buenos Aires*, June 23, 1821.

21. Thus, in 1830, Minister Tomás Guido instructed every *juez de paz* in the province to prepare reports which would include lists of suitable candidates, the condition of every school, and the list of all students and faculty. See *Circular* of January 22, 1830, in *El Lucero*, January 23, 1830. A more dangerous feature of the era, whether during the May Revolution or during the sporadic rebellions that dotted the first decades of the century, were the military storms which would sometimes blow down the structures of learning in both subtle and direct ways. For example, during the military and political disturbances of the years 1827–1829, which were marked by Lavalle's revolt, the execution of Governor Dorrego, uprisings in the provinces, and the eventual coming to power of Rosas, schools were forced to shut down for lack of funds or were occupied and ransacked by armed bands. See the *Considerando* of the edict of September 28, 1830, which closed down the Colegio de la Provincia de Buenos Aires.

22. Tulio Halperin Donghi, *Guerra y finanzas en los orígenes del Estado Argentino (1791–1850)* (Buenos Aires, 1982), pp. 169–183.

23. See, for example, *El Lucero*, December 18, 1829.

24. AGN X-6-1-1. Instrucción Pública, 1812–1835.

25. Ibid.

26. Differences of opinion on matters of education among members of any given community could also be encountered on such subjects as the contents of the curricula, the extent to which religious dogma should occupy the children's

daily classroom experience, or the extent of influence parents would have in determining the appointment of teachers. Such disagreements divided the citizenry furiously: formerly sociable neighbors would stop talking to each other, and it was not unusual for tempers to flare and for insults to be shouted across rooms where school board meetings were held. Ibid.

27. For example, when José Ignacio Grela, the Director of the Buenos Aires Public Library, resigned for reasons of health in November 1833, the government appointed a priest, Father José María Terrero, as replacement. AGN X-6-1-2. Instrucción Pública, 1821–1836.

28. In a similar vein, Juan Alexo Guaux, the teacher of the primary school of the humble barrio of San Telmo, informed his superiors that because of "the poverty of so many parents, they cannot provide their children with the required educational materials." Guaux was asking approval from the Director of Schools, Don Manuel Bustamante, for a plan to provide the paper, ink, and quills to the needy students out of his own pocket, to be repaid by the parents sometime later. But such parents often failed to see any economic value in educating their children; "I cannot bring [the children] by force," wrote José María Conde, a teacher in the county of Concepción, "and their parents either do not want to send them, or if they do send them they remain uninterested in their advancement." AGN X-6-1-1. Instrucción Pública, 1812–1835. Similarly, José Rodríguez, the teacher in the town of Morón, was convinced in 1825 that the cause for the "very small" number of students attending school was the placement of the children by their parents at the service of the town's bakers to sell sweet cakes on the streets. AGN X-6-1-6. Inspección de Escuelas, 1826–1836.

29. For the mixed results of the compulsory education law, see Hobart A. Spalding, Jr., "Education in Argentina, 1890–1914: The Limits of Oligarchical Reform," *Journal of Interdisciplinary History*, III (Summer 1972), pp. 31–61.

30. See memorandum of Felipe Senillosa to Minister of War, May 22, 1816. AGN X-6-1-1. Instrucción Pública, 1812–1835.

31. Joseph Lancaster, *The British System of Education: Being a Complete Epitome of the Improvements and Inventions Practiced at the Royal Free Schools, Borough-Road, Southwark* (London, 1810), p. 25.

32. Ibid., pp. 34–38.

33. Juan Carlos Vedoya, *Historia de la instrucción primaria en la República Argentina* (Tandil, 1984), pp. 11–14.

34. In fact, Joseph Lancaster confidently asserted that "a class may consist of many number of scholars, without limitation to any particular number." Lancaster, *The British System*, p. 3.

35. AGN X-6-1-1. Instrucción Pública, 1812–1835.

36. *El Argos de Buenos Aires*, August 25, 1821.

37. Manuel H. Solari, *Historia de la educación argentina* (Buenos Aires, 1976), p. 89.

38. Domingo F. Sarmiento, *Constitución del código de señoritas se Santa Rosa de América . . . ,* con advertencia de Ismael Bucich Escobar (Buenos Aires, 1939).

39. For an overview of the tenets held by the Generation of '37, see José Luis Romero, *A History of Argentine Political Thought*, trans. Thomas F. McGann (Stanford, 1963), pp. 126–154.

40. He did this, for example, in the charter he prepared in 1836 for a girls' school in the Province of San Juan: "If the non-application, disobedience, and transgression of constitutions should go unpunished," he wrote in that charter,

"such misbehaviors would become so frequent that the hard work and vigilance of the headmistress and others in charge of education would be in vain." Sarmiento, *Constitución*, pp. 17–18.

41. Indeed, this attitude toward children, far from being unique to *porteños*, was widespread enough to have become a leitmotiv in modern Spanish American fiction; thus, José Arcadio Buendía, the patriarch in Gabriel García Márquez's *One Hundred Years of Solitude*, shared in the belief that children's minds were essentially empty vessels: "He was always alien to the existence of his sons, partly because he considered childhood as a period of mental insufficiency." Gabriel García Márquez, *One Hundred Years of Solitude* (New York, 1970), pp. 23–24. This line of thought, which threads some of the sentiments regarding youth reaching back into the Buenos Aires of the late eighteenth and early nineteenth centuries, was noted in the chronicler Azara's comment that a child who may have asked a question would not be given much attention; instead, he would be treated in all likelihood with disdain and be dispensed with by a deceitful answer. Juan Agustín García, *La ciudad indiana*, p. 97.

42. AGN X-6-1-1. Instrucción Pública, 1812–1835.

43. The authority of teachers depended not only on their moral superiority by virtue of their pedagogical status but also on their assertedly indisputable knowledge of the subject matter; teachers would thus broach no question or doubt from any student on the execution of the curriculum. Students who questioned the established procedures ran the risk of public humiliation heaped on university students who dared to question the educational system; for attitudes toward such students at the School of Medicine of the University of Buenos Aires, see the exchanges published in *El Lucero*, July 23, December 1, December 2, and December 4, 1830.

44. For a study of the achievements and shortcomings of the educational system under the generation of 80, see Spalding, "Education in Argentina."

45. Thomas L. Haskell, "Capitalism and the Origins of the Humanitarian Sensibility," (Part 2), *American Historical Review*, 90 (June 1985), pp. 551–555.

46. Halperín Donghi, *Revolución y guerra*, p. 417.

47. Esteban Echeverría, *Manuel de enseñanza moral* in *Obras completas*, Vol. IV, p. 327, quoted in José Ingenieros, *La evolución de las ideas argentinas* (Buenos Aires, 1946), pp. 316–317.

48. Esteban Echeverría, *Dogma socialista* (La Plata, 1940), in Romero, *A History of Argentine Political Thought*, p. 145.

49. Glen Dealy, "Prolegomena on Spanish American Political Tradition," *Hispanic American Historical Review*, 48 (February 1968), p. 57; Ronald C. Newton, "On 'Functional Groups,' 'Fragmentation,' and 'Pluralism' in Spanish American Political Society," *Hispanic American Historical Review*, 50 (February 1970), pp. 1–29.

50. Tulio Halperín Donghi, *Una nación para el desierto argentino* (Buenos Aires, 1982), p. 12.

2 Angela T. Thompson ◆ Children and Schooling in Guanajuato, Mexico, 1790–1840

Much like the citizens of distant Buenos Aires, the residents of Guanajuato, Mexico, expressed a sense of idealism and optimism in their education policies from the late 1700s to the early 1800s. Historian Angela Thompson documents the expansion of educational opportunities for the lower classes and for women of diverse social backgrounds, but she also stresses the limited effects of these well-meaning reforms. Thompson's research interest is in the field of eighteenth- and nineteenth-century social history, with special emphases on children and family life. She is currently working on a study of families and children in the mining communities of Guanajuato. In the selection below, she carefully analyzes the goals and accomplishments of elite-directed education. Of special note is her conclusion concerning "the ambiguous intentions of local elites and their failure to fund adequately the expansion they advocated."

Concern about the education of children and the role of children in a changing society engaged the attention of officials, intellectuals, and concerned citizens alike in Spain and in parts of its vast empire in the late eighteenth and early nineteenth centuries.[1] As part of their program of transforming the empire into a modern, economically progressive entity, the liberal reformers of Spain's Bourbon monarchy envisioned the establishment of free public instruction, particularly at the primary level, that was to go beyond the traditional religious instruction offered in most schools during the colonial period. In response to directives issued by the Spanish crown, towns throughout the empire, including those in New Spain, began to reform both the content and structure of public instruction. Even after the people of New Spain declared their independence from Spain in 1821 and named their new nation Mexico, this reforming impetus continued at the local level, particularly after the formation of the Mexican republic in 1824. The consequences of the renewed interest in education and children, however, varied from locality to locality. This essay is a case study that examines how the city of Guanajuato, Mexico, developed a public education system beginning in the 1790s and how the new state of Guanajuato used the public school system of its capital city as the basis for expanding public education throughout the state to both

From Angela T. Thompson, "Children and Schooling in Guanajuato, Mexico, 1790–1840," *SECOLAS Annals* 22 (March 1992): 36–52. Reprinted by permission of the author.

urban and rural areas. The study ends in 1840, when Guanajuato adopted a different approach to public education.[2]

This study follows several lines of inquiry into the development of public schooling in Guanajuato. The first is to see if Guanajuato's educational system developed as did that of Mexico City, where the foundation of post-Independence local schools can be traced to late eighteenth-century Enlightenment reforms in education and society. These made the period from the 1780s to the late 1830s a transitional period in the development of schooling in the national capital.[3] Another is to assess the tendency toward variation following Independence in 1821, when some localities such as Puebla and Jalisco approached issues of education differently and continued to do so even after the national government tried to institute uniform educational reforms in 1883.[4] A third is to see if Guanajuato's experience bears out the argument that local orientation in the development of education undermined the development of a national identity and led to constant civil strife and political instability during the early republican period.[5] Additionally, this study will evaluate how schooling affected the socialization, or the way values are transmitted from generation to generation, and the life course of Mexican children, a topic that has been only partially developed in previous studies of Mexican education during this period.[6]

Several factors make Guanajuato an appropriate local case study. With its economy based upon silver mining and agriculture, Guanajuato contained an ethnically and socially diverse population in both rural and urban settings totaling approximately 55,000 people in the city of Guanajuato and almost 400,000 in the entire province in 1792.[7] Guanajuato was also distant from the area around Mexico City, where national policy heavily influenced local policy. Finally, the city, and later state of Guanajuato, were innovative and aggressive in expanding public instruction at the primary level in both rural and urban areas after Independence, despite the fact that the region's economic and financial resources were severely reduced by destruction of mines and ranches during the Independence period.

Schooling in the Late Colonial Period

Until the late eighteenth century, Mexican children had few options for basic education at the primary and preprimary level. These were dames schools, pious schools, convent schools, private schools, and tutors, all of which served mostly the wealthy or the very poor and the Indians. In 1779, however, a royal decree ordered towns to establish free primary schools. While the measure was particularly designed for the poor, it also included all children, both girls and boys, of any social or ethnic background without access to schools. In conformity with the decree, municipalities in Mexico established more public secular schools and religious primary schools.[8] Likewise, Guanajuato's municipal council began to open schools and appointed a public school commissioner.

In Guanajuato, children who attended school during the last decades of the colonial period may have started schooling as young as age three. At this age their first school experience was usually at a dame's school, called an *amiga*. Informal, private institutions that resembled nursery schools, *amigas* were to be found in Mexican towns at least until the late 1830s. The school, in which a small fee was charged, was usually held in the home of the woman teacher, the *amiga*, and featured little more than memorization of the catechism. In fact, the women who conducted these establishments needed only to know prayers and Christian doctrine. They did not have to be literate.[9] Guanajuato had a few of these establishments. For example, the historian and diplomat Lucas Alamán attended the *amiga* of Josefa Camacho in Guanajuato during the 1790s.[10]

From about the ages of five to twelve, a child may have attended one of three types of primary schools: a private primary school, a secular public primary school, or a pious school (*escuela pía*). Private schools were directed by teachers who were members of a teachers' guild. By the last decades of the eighteenth century, Guanajuato and surrounding villages had several private schools serving about a hundred boys. In addition, Guanajuato began to establish secular public primary schools in the 1790s, perhaps earlier, for there was at least one functioning in 1791, a school for boys.[11]

Even so, until the 1810s most school children in Guanajuato, attended an *escuela pía*. *Escuelas pías* were free primary day schools that towns and parishes funded. Usually held in parish churches or convents where priests or nuns conducted classes, *escuelas pías* were established to provide education to poor children and to children who lived in areas without schools. Like *amigas*, the primary purpose of *escuelas pías* was religious instruction, but they also offered reading, writing, and *buena educación*—how to act and behave. By the early 1780s Guanajuato had at least two *escuelas pías* for boys, the Escuela de Cristo in the parochial church and one run by the Bethelemite order in their convent near their hospital.[12] In 1792 the town council planned an *escuela pía* for 300 non-Spanish girls to be run by the parish priest.[13] The establishment of these and other schools was in direct response to the imperial order of 1779. By 1813 there were six publicly funded primary schools that served over five hundred children in the city: two secular schools for boys, two for girls, and two *escuelas pías*, both for boys.[14]

The curriculum stressed religious instruction and manners in all primary schools, whether they were private, pious, or public secular schools. Padre Ripalda's catechism and *Máximas de buena educación* were part of the primary curriculum well into the nineteenth century.[15] Additionally, most schools offered basic reading, writing, and spelling, and following 1810, "política civil y moral," or civics. In 1820, for example, Spain decreed that students in all of the empire's public and private schools and in the universities read and study the Constitution of Cádiz, which had been recently restored.[16] Part of the curriculum was gender specific. Girls learned various kinds of needlework and sometimes drawing; private and convent schools sometimes offered music and domestic economy, subjects rare in free schools. Boys learned a wider variety of subjects including calligraphy, grammar, arithmetic, history, and art.[17]

Children usually attended school for six hours a day, from eight to eleven in the morning and from two to five in the afternoon, Monday through Friday. They also attended on Saturday mornings. School ran all year round, closing only for holy days, for a week in September, and during Christmas and Easter, making approximately twenty days of vacation a year.[18]

In addition to requiring towns to provide primary instruction for all their children, eighteenth-century Spanish Bourbon reformers revived interest in vocational training, which they saw as a way to invigorate the economy. Thus a few institutions were established primarily to teach vocational skills, and some existing schools added such training to their curriculum. Even girls received vocational training in various textile crafts such as weaving and needlework. Vocational training was gradually incorporated into Guanajuato's schools, replacing the rapidly disappearing formal apprenticeships that ceased in Guanajuato after 1805.[19] Schooling, however, probably did not interfere with informal apprenticeships, if such persisted, for most apprenticeships began during the early teenage years, after primary schooling would have been completed.

Few children continued formal education beyond the primary level, for most went to work by age thirteen. In the entire city of Guanajuato in 1792, only twenty boys aged thirteen to fifteen were students, and all but two of those were Spaniards; therefore, their families were probably able to pay for their education (Table 1). Of students over sixteen, only seven Spanish males were listed (Table 2). No students in Guanajuato were over age twenty-one, though some students at this level from Guanajuato attended school elsewhere, again those from well-off families. In fact, public schooling as it developed in this period was intended to enhance, not interfere with, the traditional family work regimen by developing children's work skills so that they could enter the workforce at the traditional ages of twelve to fifteen.

TABLE 1. Occupations of Mestizo and Spanish Males Ages Thirteen to Fifteen, Guanajuato, 1792, Excluding Most Mineworkers*

	Mestizos		Spaniards	
	N	%	N	%
Artists	2	2.7	1	0.9
Artisans, other	2	2.7	1	0.9
Peddlers	7	9.5	1	0.9
Muleteers/Drivers	3	4.1	4	3.6
Barbers	-	-	2	1.8
Construction Workers	6	8.1	8	7.2
Students	2	2.7	18	16.2
Clerk/Scribes	-	-	8	7.2
Ironworkers	5	6.8	6	5.4
Food Service Workers	5	6.8	3	2.7
Silversmith/Refiners†	2	2.7	15	13.5
Apparelmakers	15	20.3	25	22.5
Servants	20	27.0	9	8.1
Traders	2	2.7	5	4.5
Watchmen/Porters	1	1.4	3	2.7
Laborers	2	2.7	2	1.8
Totals	74	100.2**	111	99.9**

*Includes all males eligible for future military service; excludes all mineworkers and most refinery workers except those who intended to be soldiers; excludes Indians and most mulattoes because they were not subject to conscription and were therefore not listed by occupation.
**Does not total 100 percent because of rounding.
†Includes one youth who was a mineowner; he volunteered for military service.

Source: AGN, Padrones, Vol. 32.

Traditionally, girls did not attend school beyond ages ten to twelve except for the few in special colleges or convent schools, most of whom were orphans. Rarely did girls receive more than rudimentary instruction. On the other hand, boys who attended school beyond the primary level had several options: Latin grammar school, college (*colegio*),

TABLE 2. Occupations of Mestizo & Spanish Males Ages Sixteen to Twenty-five, Guanajuato, 1792, Excluding Most Mineworkers*

	Mestizos		Spaniards	
	N	*%*	*N*	*%*
Artists	12	6.4	29	9.2
Artisans, other	5	2.7	11	3.5
Peddlers	13	7.0	5	1.6
Muleteers/Drivers	6	3.2	15	4.7
Barbers	1	0.5	8	2.5
Construction Workers	12	6.4	21	6.6
Students	-	-	7	2.2
Clerk/Scribes	1	0.5	21	6.6
Ironworkers	9	4.8	15	4.7
Food Service Workers	19	10.2	27	8.5
Silversmith/Refiners†	1	0.5	28	8.9
Apparelmakers	41	21.9	43	13.6
Servants	38	20.3	43	13.6
Traders	10	5.3	26	8.2
Watchmen/Porters	13	7.0	9	2.8
Laborers	6	3.2	8	2.5
Totals	187	99.9**	316	99.7**

*Includes all males eligible for military service; excludes most mineworkers and refinery workers except those who were also soldiers; excludes Indians and most mulattoes.
**Does not total 100 percent because of rounding.
†Includes several mineowners.

Source: AGN, Padrones, Vol. 32.

seminary, convent school, or military academy. Some had tutors. A very few went to a *colegio mayor*, a college that offered instruction beyond the secondary level, or to the country's only university in Mexico City, which offered advanced degrees in law, medicine, or theology. Guanajuato had one college for its male youths at the end of the eighteenth century, the Real Colegio de la Purísima Concepción. As a result of Bourbon efforts to make mining more efficient and profitable, a mining college, the Real Seminario de Minería, was established in Mexico City to bring science and technology to the aid of the mining industry. Established to train engineers, this school was especially beneficial to the economy of Guanajuato (where a mining school is now located), and many of its graduates worked in Guanajuato's mining industry. Sons of mining families also trained there, as did Lucas Alamán, whose family was involved in the mining business.[20]

The perennial problems that all local schools experienced from the 1780s to 1821 were twofold: lack of funds and lack of qualified teachers. Guanajuato's college closed intermittently during the decades of the 1780s and 1790s for lack of instructors.[21] Even when there were teachers, they were not assured of salaries. At times teachers virtually had to beg for their pay. In June 1791, the viceroy demanded that the town council pay the salary of primary teacher Gregorio Rodríguez, which the council finally did two months later.[22] During the decade following the 1810 uprising that began Mexico's Independence movement, teachers had to make numerous requests to city school officials before they received their salaries. To raise funds for teacher salaries, the city imposed a small matriculation fee upon students, but teachers complained that many of their students could not afford the fee and thus had stopped coming to school. The directors of two of the city's primary schools refused to collect the fee and begged the city to pay their salaries instead. Teachers also complained that they lacked school supplies and that their school buildings were in poor condition.[23] Doroteo Romero, the director of one of the boys' primary schools went without pay for three years, from 1815 to 1818.[24] These problems suggest that quality and availability of instruction varied. Nevertheless, some teachers were dedicated enough to remain at their posts for years at a time despite problems with salaries and facilities. José Francisco Camargo, director of one of the boys' primary schools, taught in that school for at least twenty-three years, from 1802 to 1825, and María Josefa Rocha y Mazo taught for at least twenty-four years, from 1808 to 1832.[25] They all contributed to the expansion of public instruction.

Despite problems with funds, teachers, and facilities, the three decades before Independence formed a transitional period for development of public education in Guanajuato, for it was during that time that the foundation for a comprehensive system of public schools was laid. In 1796 the town council appointed a commissioner of schools who also was a member of the town council. The first commissioner was Agustín Marañón. A *mayordomo*, or administrator, served under the commissioner and handled the dispersal of funds and other administrative tasks. Establishing an administration that was primarily responsible for public instruction facilitated the development of municipal, and later state, public school systems. During most of the colonial period private individuals, town councils, parishes, or convents administered primary schools as part of their myriad responsibilities. By 1810 public school officials, instead of the traditional teachers' guild, certified teachers.[26] Further extending the late eighteenth-century initiatives in education, the Spanish Constitution of 1812 and decrees issued by the Cortes of Cádiz mandated the establishment of educational administrations throughout the empire to assume the responsibilities of the teachers' guild that the Cortes abolished. The new republican state governments established in 1824 adopted and modified the administrative structure established earlier.[27]

Public Instruction in the Post-Independence Period

By 1821, when Mexico declared its independence from Spain, the structure and administration of formal education had been significantly reorganized from the rather haphazard system of the colonial period into an institution increasingly controlled by local governments. In Guanajuato local government had taken control to an even greater degree than in other localities, such as in Mexico City, where private and church influence remained strong. In 1826 the new state of Guanajuato, following the spirit of the Spanish Constitution of 1812 and of the 1824 Mexican Constitution, placed public school administration under joint state and municipal funding and administration, with state-mandated curriculum and secularized instructors. In fact, by 1815 none of the public primary schools in the city of Guanajuato used clergy as instructors. A commissioner appointed by the municipal council continued to administer the city schools. Following Independence, local school administrations experimented with new teaching methods and attempted to revise curriculum to meet the needs of the new nation. Private schools and convent schools continued to provide instruction to children in the state, but their influence was eclipsed by the proliferation of the new public schools.

Although public schools were secularized by removing priests and nuns from the classroom, the curriculum retained a strong religious component well into the nineteenth century. Indeed, the primary purpose of one new method employed soon after Independence in some areas, the Lancasterian method, was to teach the Bible simultaneously to large numbers of students. Furthermore, modernization of administrations, implementation of new teaching methods, and modifications to curriculum, many of the texts and teaching manuals used in the 1820s and 1830s were the same as those used before Independence. Padre Ripalda's catechism and *Máximas de buena educación* remained the basic texts at the primary level.[28] A teaching manual on penmanship and manners first published in 1798 was still being used in 1840.[29]

Despite a lack of significant change in the curriculum and the continuing predominance of religious content, the state of Guanajuato in the

1820s and 1830s made instruction available to many more children, both male and female, perhaps its greatest accomplishment in the area of education. The state constitution of 1826 and, later, legislation by the state congress mandated all towns and villages to establish public primary schools for the purpose of teaching children to be religious, patriotic, and useful citizens. To this end, the state's first governor, Carlos Montesdeoca, urged municipalities to employ the Lancasterian method.[30]

The Lancasterian method was pioneered by an Englishman named Joseph Lancaster in the late eighteenth century. His system of instruction, called the mutual method, was widely adopted because it was theoretically effective and economical in that it used older students to convey instructions from a master teacher to younger students. In that way large numbers of young children could learn the Bible, reading, writing, and arithmetic. One master teacher could handle as many as two hundred students.[31] The method also instilled discipline by the use of surveillance, monitors, and rules, initiating what one scholar has called a "disciplinary revolution" linked with the development of market economies.[32] Thus Lancaster's method intended to fulfill two economic purposes: to deliver instruction economically and to produce obedient, productive citizens. The method also imposed a measure of social control through its emphasis on discipline and on being obedient Christians. Furthermore, the method provided the basis for training primary teachers.

The city of Guanajuato had already explored the feasibility of implementing this method even before Governor Montesdeoca urged its use. The city wanted to stretch its limited financial sources to provide schooling to all of its school-age children and to educate its children to be obedient and productive Christians, goals that some council members felt the Lancasterian method promised to fulfill. On January 3, 1824, the Guanajuato city council first discussed the possibility of implementing the Lancasterian method in the city's existing public primary schools.[33] In this respect Guanajuato differed from Mexico City, where the method was used primarily in special Lancasterian schools, which were private schools founded by Lancasterian societies formed specifically to promote the mutual method.[34] For a time the city adopted the Lancasterian method for use in only one of its boys' schools. Then in June 1827 the city council voted to use it in all of its primary schools, but only after a great deal of debate, for some members questioned the method's compatibility with teaching Catholicism. They believed that most Catholics needed only to know the catechism, not how to read the Bible.[35]

To implement the method in all of its schools, the city needed teachers who were trained to use it. After several unsuccessful attempts to find a Lancasterian teacher, in 1827 Guanajuato sent its own teachers, Doroteo

Romero and Ignacio Luna, both of whom had been with the city's schools for many years, to Mexico City to the Lancasterian normal school there, a private institution, to be trained in the mutual method. By December 6, 1827, Romero and Luna had passed their examinations and returned to Guanajuato to help implement the mutual method in all city schools.[36] Romero became director of the city's first normal or teacher training school, La Escuela Normal Lancasteriana, established on December 10, 1827, as part of the boys' primary school that he directed.[37] Luna was appointed director of the city's second public school for boys. Soon thereafter, the city hired two other teachers, Ignacio Vargas, to teach military exercises to boys, and Antonio Acevedo, to teach reading and mathematics using the mutual method.[38] In 1828 the director of one of the public primary schools for girls, María Josefa Madrid de la Rocha, and her assistant also received certification to teach the mutual method. Rocha's school was then established as a normal school for females. This was an extraordinary event in the history of Mexican education, for Guanajuato's female normal school predated female teaching academies even in the United States.[39]

Both of these normal schools were structured as training laboratories, for they were established in already existing primary schools where student teachers learned by serving as assistants to a master teacher. The Lancasterian method lent itself very well to such a purpose, since it used older students to teach younger ones. In the case of Guanajuato, females as well as males had equal opportunity to train as teachers. Normal schools provided both the justification and the opportunity for women to enter higher education in Mexico and Latin America. The method also spurred the implementation of adult education in night schools. Thus, the Lancasterian method in Guanajuato was responsible in part for providing educational opportunity to more children and to people of all ages and both sexes and for increasing employment opportunities for both women and men.[40] The normal schools also provided the teachers that the state needed to fulfill its mandate to establish schools in all towns and villages. By 1832, twenty-one towns and villages in the state had at least two public primary schools, one for each sex.[41] An 1839 report on school enrollments in the city of Guanajuato and its suburbs indicated that 1,371 children were enrolled in both public and private primary schools in the district. School enrollments had more than doubled since 1813, increasing from 5 to 15 percent of the school-age populations.[42] Still, many school-age children in Guanajuato obviously did not attend school.

The school experience for children attending schools in Guanajuato in the 1820s and 1830s did not change substantially from the twenty years previously, nor did the school environment. The daily schedule was the same: eight to eleven in the mornings and two to five in the afternoons. Schools had the same weekly schedule: Monday to Friday and Saturday mornings. Complaints were often made about the number of vacation days taken, even though the traditional twenty days continued to be the norm. Attendance and individual student progress seemed a minor concern of teachers and school authorities, for attendance and regular student evaluations were rarely mentioned until after 1840. Although teachers and authorities occasionally complained that parents did not send their children to school regularly, only school regulations published in 1840 mention the necessity of taking attendance, charting each student's progress, and fining parents who were remiss in sending their children to school, one step toward compulsory attendance.[43] School children still spent much of the school day memorizing the catechism and learning religious doctrine, etiquette, and correct behavior, although more emphasis was placed on learning these activities through reading and writing exercises. Yet, despite the increasing emphasis on reading and writing, it is not clear if levels of literacy increased as the opportunities for primary education increased. Nor is it clear if the new *catecismo civil* that was supposed to be introduced at the primary level was usually taught. In addition, curriculum remained gender specific. Girls still concentrated on rudimentary skills and learned various methods of needlework, while boys studied mathematics and grammar, although now the emphasis was on Castilian grammar rather than Latin. Girls learned only basic arithmetic, as part of their writing lessons. Unlike the late colonial period, however, girls, like the boys, took public examinations.[44]

School officials in this period demonstrated a measure of sensitivity to the needs of school children by trying to improve facilities to make them safer and more comfortable for the children, but lack of funds often waylaid their good intentions. Authorities expressed concern that one of the girls' schools was uncomfortable and the building too narrow, but they did little to alleviate the situation.[45] Regulations issued in 1840 stipulated that all tables and benches have rounded corners so that children would not hurt themselves.[46] Attitudes toward punishments and treatment of students expressed by school officials following Independence also indicated some compassion for children, for they urged teachers to be amiable and to inspire confidence in their students. Officially, teachers were prohibited from beating children as punishment. The punishment for laziness, for example, was demotion and reprimand rather than blows.[47] Whether or not teachers followed these suggestions is another question. Perhaps the Lancasterian method mitigated disciplinary problems. This method also promoted strict but benevolent discipline, as Guanajuato's school officials advocated.

In addition to expanding primary instruction, the state of Guanajuato reestablished its college for male youths in 1828 as a state-sponsored institution that offered professional training.[48] Initially, the name of the school was similar to that of the colonial college it replaced, and the rector was the same secular priest, Marcelino Mangas, who had held the position before Independence, but he held the position only for a short time.[49] Soon after being reestablished as a state institution, the college began to modernize its curriculum to train lawyers, notaries, engineers, merchants, and teachers, professionals that the state needed. Science gradually replaced the traditional emphasis on religion and philosophy. After 1831, the state government awarded scholarships to promising but poor students from around the state so the entire state could benefit from the college. Manuel Doblado, for example, from a rural village west of the city, received a scholarship to attend the college in Guanajuato. He later became governor of the state. The college later added a program to prepare students to attend the university in Mexico City.[50] In 1831 the first public library in the city opened within the college, and a few years later the college offered its first courses in medicine.[51]

Conclusion

The development of public schooling in Guanajuato from the late eighteenth century until 1840 conformed to and contradicted patterns noted elsewhere in Mexico. Guanajuato organized and gradually secularized education, as happened elsewhere, in response to Enlightenment reforms of the late eighteenth century, but it did so primarily by establishing in the 1790s a government-controlled school system that laid a firm foundation for expansion during the first few decades after Independence. That foundation was evident in the continuity of administrative structure and personnel. After Independence, Guanajuato developed its own approach to educating the region's children by establishing a state administration of public schools, determining curriculum, setting school regulations, and adopting the Lancasterian method, which was being used in Mexico City in special private schools, with the intention of developing a comprehensive public school system that would serve all children in the state. Furthermore, Guanajuato was innovative. For example, its education commissioner assumed the responsibilities of the teachers' guild even before the Spanish Cortes abolished the guild, and the city opened a public normal school for females.

Guanajuato's efforts, however, yielded mixed results. While many more children in the state by the 1830s had the opportunity to attend school, the principal purpose of extending schooling to all children was not yet fulfilled; thus the economically and socially progressive society that public schooling was to help create did not emerge. Much of the fault lies with the ambiguous intentions of local elites and their failure to fund adequately the expansion they advocated and to enforce the regulations they issued, although both the city and state had persistent problems in funding the increasing responsibilities they assumed during the nineteenth century. While they adopted the liberalism of Enlightenment ideology, they subscribed to it only in part. Their liberal intentions were evident in that they established a secularized, government-funded public school system that offered instruction free, theoretically, to children of all social groups and in that they established a specialized school administration to expand schools, certify teachers, and make the curriculum and the quality of instruction consistent in all public schools. Furthermore, their intent to use public schools to make economically productive and educated citizens of all children in order to improve society was a liberal ideal.

Nevertheless, while Guanajuato's leaders adopted liberal ideas, they retained a large measure of traditionalism in the education of children. The substance of the primary curriculum, for example, emphasized religious instruction and behavior. Although liberalism in education did not intend to undermine the teachings of Christianity, Spanish liberalism was determined to suppress the influence of the Catholic clergy in education and in society. While Guanajuato successfully suppressed the influence of church personnel in public instruction, local leaders hesitated in going beyond the traditional religious instruction based on the catechism, for they wanted to teach local children to be good Catholics, not just good Christians. Learning to read the Bible, for example, was not a priority in curriculum reform. Furthermore, local leaders intended public schools to be institutions of social control; teaching correct behavior, including a child's place in the social and family hierarchy, remained an important part of the primary curriculum. Also, the primary curriculum continued to emphasize learning skills through imitation, memorization, and practice rather than acquiring knowledge through observation and study. Practicing reading, writing, spelling, arithmetic, manners, religious ritual, drawing, and needlework (for girls) and military exercises (for boys) took up most of the schoolday, leaving little time for studying history, geography, science, or literature, subjects that might have fostered a stronger sense of nationalism, of national purpose, and a continuing desire to learn and explore. Because only a minority of children who attended primary school received additional instruction in academics at a higher level, it is very likely that the lack of focus on these subjects at the primary level failed to educate children sufficiently to be citizens of a republic that had aspirations of being democratic and economically progressive. Lack of adequate funding also prevented teaching more than rudimentary skills, for schools often lacked money to buy books and supplies. Lack of funding also prevented many children from attending school, for there simply were not enough schools, although negligent parents may have prevented a minority of children from attending.

Despite the failure to reform the content of curriculum significantly and to provide all children with an opportunity to attend primary school, the city and state of Guanajuato did begin the process of expanding schooling and made considerable progress in that direction by 1840. This study has only just begun to examine the consequences of that expansion, but two in particular deserve emphasis here. One was the establishment of the two Lancasterian public normal schools in the city of Guanajuato that provided a reliable local source of teachers, allowing the state to open more schools, and that extended educational and employment opportunities for both males and females. This was particularly important for females, who had few educational opportunities beyond the primary level and fewer viable job opportunities.

Another consequence was significant changes in the life course of children who attended school. First, school children left home and the supervision of parents, siblings, relatives, or guardians at younger ages to be supervised and taught by others, thus changing the method of socialization and broadening its content.[52] Also, schools tended to segregate children by age and sex, producing a restricted social environment in which children spent more time with peers than with people of all ages, as they would have done at home. This was especially the case in schools that employed the Lancasterian method. Third, for some small children, attending school constituted a positive change in that at school they were more closely supervised, whereas at home they may have been neglected by busy parents, guardians, or remiss siblings. At least, both government and church officials in Guanajuato complained of parental neglect of small children, which sometimes resulted in serious injury or death. Finally, primary schooling, which was usually segregated by sex with same-sex teachers, may have had a more significant impact on the life course of boys, because by attending school they would have left the supervision of females at an earlier age—around ages five or six instead of ten to twelve—to be supervised and socialized by adult males. Furthermore, after Independence, learning military exercises became a regular part of the primary curriculum in public schools for boys. These changes in the lives of boys who attended public schools may have been a factor in the increasing militarization of Mexican society in the nineteenth century, for the period from ages five to twelve is the most impressionable period in the life of a child.

Important questions remain to be answered. What effect did expansion have on levels of literacy? How did it affect the social structure? To what degree was compulsory schooling enforced? And did compulsory schooling help to prevent the exploitation of the labor of small children which, if the work was long and arduous, could prejudice their health? Even so, it is clear that the educational program in Guanajuato achieved significant results. Taking the cords of Enlightened Spanish policy, the educational reformers of Guanajuato interwove them with local threads to make a material that was uniquely appropriate for its place and time. Furthermore, the maintenance—indeed the development—of Guanajuato's program of educational reform through the turbulent years after 1810 demonstrates yet another line of continuity across the historiographical cleft of the Independence period.

Notes

1. Mexican writer José Joaquín Fernández de Lizardi and journalist José Barquera wrote on this topic during this period. For a discussion of official and general interest see Dorothy Tanck de Estrada, *La educación ilustrada (1780–1836)* (Mexico City: Colegio de Mexico, 1977).
2. In 1839 and 1840, the state of Guanajuato issued new regulations to govern its school system, including measures to force parents to send their children to school and means for better record-keeping. This phase is not treated here.
3. Tanck de Estrada, pp. 5–14, 203.
4. Various studies have shown that local areas set their own local educational goals, organized school administration, selected their own teaching methodologies, and determined curriculum. See Mary Kay Vaughan, "Primary Education and Literacy in Nineteenth-Century Mexico: Research Trends, 1968–1988," *Latin American Research Review* 25: 1 (1990): 31–66.
5. This argument is developed in the classic study by Josefina Zoriada Vázquez, *Nacionalismo y educación en México* (Mexico City: Colegio de Mexico, 1970), pp. 1–4.
6. See, for example, Vázquez, cited above. In fact, *educación* in the Mexican context meant the total formation, or in contemporary terms, socialization, of the child. Generations of Mexican children that grew up before the end of the eighteenth century were socialized primarily within the family with contributions made by community religious institutions. Ariès and others have argued that modernization and changes in schooling in the eighteenth and nineteenth centuries were factors that greatly changed children's lives, for the worse in some respects, by limiting their freedom. Philippe Ariès, *Centuries of Childhood: A Social History of Family Life* (trans. Robert Baldick, New York: Vintage Books, 1962). For studies that evaluate causes and consequences of life course changes see Tamara K. Hareven, ed., *Transitions: The Family and Life Course in Historical Perspective* (New York: Academic Press, 1978).
7. Archivo General de la Nación, Padrones, Vols. 30–33.

8. The order is quoted in Archivo Histórico de Guanajuato (hereafter AHG), Educación Pública (hereafter EP), 1791–1845, November 2, 1813, Fray Antonio de San Francisco to José Francisco Robles.

9. Tanck de Estrada, pp. 160–65.

10. J. Jesús Rodríguez Frausto, "Lucas Alamán," *Biografías*, tomo I (Guanajuato: Universidad de Guanajuato, Archivo Histórico, 1960), número 2.

11. In 1792 Marfil had a small private school for boys that was probably a boarding school. There was also one in Guanajuato run by a Spaniard. Archivo General de la Nación, Padrones, Vol. 31.

12. AHG, Eclesiástico, February 7, 1783.

13. AHG, EP, 1791–1845, February 20, 1792, Manuel de Quesada to Ayuntamiento.

14. AHG, EP, February 6, 1811, Virrey to Ayuntamiento; November 2, 1813, Convento de Belén, Fray Antonio de San Francisco to José Francisco Robles; November 2, 1813, José Francisco Camargo to José Francisco Robles; November 3, 1813, María Lucía Gadea and Basilio Beñares to José Francisco Robles, November 4, 1813, María Guadalupe Moscosos to José Francisco Robles.

15. AHG, EP, 1791–1845, November 2, 1813, Fray Antonio de San Francisco to José Francisco Robles; and November 1, 1834.

16. AHG, EP, 1791–1845, April 20, 1820.

17. AHG, EP, 1791–1845, November 2 and 4, 1813. The city of Guanajuato had no convents for females during this period, and there were only a few in the region.

18. Ibid.

19. AHG, Protocolos de Cabildo, various years, 1780 to 1805.

20. Rodríguez Frausto, "Lucas Alamán," número 2.

21. AHG, Actas de Cabildo (hereafter AC), 1783–1787, January 29, 1784, f. 195.

22. AHG, EP, 1791–1845, June 15, 1791, Revillagigedo to Ayuntamiento. Perhaps because he was not paid regularly, Rodríguez decided later to leave the city's school and open his own private school in 1802. AHG, EP, 1791–1845, April 28, 1802, Manuel Sairumon to Ayuntamiento.

23. AHG, EP, 1791–1845, May 2 and August 4, 1817, Doroteo Romero to Ruperto Rocha; August 18, 1817, María Josefa Rocha y Mazo to Ruperto Rocha.

24. AHG, EP, 1791–1845, August 27, 1818, Doroteo Romero to Ayuntamiento.

25. AHG, EP, 1791–1845, April 28, 1802, and October 2, 1825; November 4, 1813, and June 16, 1832.

26. AHG, EP, 1791–1845, various years, see especially August 6, 1801, and November 4, 1813.

27. Nettie Lee Benson, *La diputación provincial y el federalismo mexicano* (Mexico: El Colegio de Mexico, 1955), p. 19. Tanck de Estrada, pp. 23–24.

28. The editions of some texts show their longevity. For example, *Máximas de buena educación* was first published in 1774 in Mexico City. The last edition was published in Querétaro in 1876. Pedro Antonio de Septien published an edition of *Máximas* in 1841 under the title *Breves lecciones de moral y urbanidad*.

29. Archivo Histórico de la Alhóndiga de Granaditas (Guanajuato) (hereafter AHAG), Educación, 180, *Reglamento General para las escuelas de primera enseñanza del departamento de Guanajuato*, 1840, pp. 17–25.

30. AHAG, Constitución política del Estado Libre de Guanajuato, April 14, 1826, Título VI, Instrucción Pública.

31. For a discussion of the Lancasterian method in Mexico, see Tanck de Estrada, pp. 230–39.

32. David Hogan, "The Market Revolution and Disciplinary Power: Joseph Lancaster and the Psychology of the Early Classroom System," *History of Education Quarterly* 29:3 (Fall 1989): 381–417.

33. AHG, AC, January 3, 1824.

34. Tanck de Estrada, p. 237. She points out that the state of Jalisco also mandated use of the mutual method in its public schools.

35. AHG, AC, 1827–1828, June 16 and 17, 1826.

36. AHG, AC, 1827–1828, December 6, 1827.

37. AHG, AC, 1827–1828, December 6 and 15, 1827.

38. AHG, AC, December 22, 1827.

39. AHG, EP, 1791–1845, October 17, 1828, Carlos Montes de Oca to the vice governor. The teacher training schools in Guanajuato were specifically named "normal" schools from their date of establishment. For purposes of comparison, in the case of teacher training for women, Mexico was ahead of other places. Catharine Beecher founded her Hartford Female Seminary in 1823. But she did not advocate training women regularly for teaching until 1830. Furthermore, her school was a private school. Kathryn Kish Sklar, *Catharine Beecher: A Study in American Domesticity* (New Haven: Yale University Press, 1973), pp. 59, 95.

40. AHG, EP, 1791–1845, August 30, 1843, Demetrio Montes de Oca to Ayuntamiento.

41. AHG, EP, 1791–1845, January 27, 1832, Report from José Pérez Marañon.

42. AHG, EP, 1791–1845, November 2 to 4, 1813; August 22, 1839, Report on schools in Guanajuato and suburbs.

43. AHG, EP, 1791–1845, March 29, 1838, José María Soltis to Prefectura de Guanajuato. AHAG, Educación, Folletos, 180, *Reglamento General para las escuelas de primera enseñanza del departamento de Guanajuato* (Guanajuato: Impreso por Juan E. de Oñate, 1840), pp. 3–7.

44. AHAG, Educación, Folletos, 180, *Reglamento General*, 1840, pp. 31–35. AHG, EP, 1791–1845, March 29, 1838, José María Solís to Prefectura de Guanajuato. AHG, EP, 1791–1845, January 20, 1828, Benigno Bustamante to Ayuntamiento.

45. AHG, EP, 1791–1845, January 18, 1833, Carlos Montes de Oca to Ignacio Rocha.

46. AHAG, Educación, Folletos, 180, *Reglamento General*, pp. 3–7.

47. AHG, EP, 1791–1845, March 29, 1838, José María Solís to Prefectura de Guanajuato. AHAG, Educación, Folletos, 180, *Reglamento General* 1840, pp. 29–31.

48. AHAG, República Restaurada, Educación y Escuelas, 614, J. Jesús Rodríguez Frausto, "Datos sobre el Colegio del Estado," s.f., p. 6.

49. Rodríguez Frausto, "Datos," p. 7.

50. AHAG, De Victoria a Santa Anna, Educación y Escuelas, 414, June 29, 1831.

51. Rodríguez Frausto, "Datos," p. 7. This college would be the focus of educational innovation in the state at the end of the nineteenth century and would evolve into a state university in the twentieth century.

52. Some argue that expansion of schooling also extended the length of childhood, for example, Ariès, cited above. That phenomena is not apparent in the first half of the nineteenth century in Mexico, where the expansion of schooling

occurred mostly at the primary level at the ages that children were considered children anyway, and afterward most youths were supposed to assume their traditional place in the workforce, mostly as helpers and trainees and usually at the side of a parent or family member. Even as youths, Mexican children theoretically were not expected to perform work in an adult capacity, but to learn job skills by training under a father or relative.

II Universities in Ferment

3 Jeffrey L. Klaiber, S.J. ◆ The Popular Universities and the Origins of Aprismo, 1921–1924

Peru was one of several Latin American nations to experience a rising tide of student activism in the 1920s. Historian Jeffrey Klaiber, formerly a missionary in Peru who has taught at the Universidad Católica in Lima, has a long-standing interest in the broader impact of education in Latin America. In this selection, he describes the founding of popular universities in Peru. These institutions were not formal, degree-granting universities but consisted, rather, of a few professors and students who presented lectures and seminars for working-class people. Although somewhat innocuous sounding, the popular universities served a larger purpose in that they formed a link between the University Reform movement and the working class. The reader should be alert to the work of Víctor Raúl Haya de la Torre in the popular universities and their part in the emergence of his political party, Apra (Alianza Popular Revolucionaria Americana, or Popular Revolutionary Alliance of America). Also important is the rivalry between Haya de la Torre and another Peruvian radical, José Carlos Mariátegui.

A multitude of events and currents of thought influenced the formation and rise of the Peruvian Aprista movement: the Mexican and Russian revolutions, the University Reform movement, the emergence of organized workers' groups, the rise of foreign economic expansionism, and the impact of the ideologies of Marxism, socialism, and nationalism. Most of the studies of the Aprista movement, however, have tended to emphasize its intellectual indebtedness to the University Reform movement, with little attention paid to the immediate and proximate way in which the Peruvian university students reacted to the reform movement.

From Jeffrey L. Klaiber, S.J., "The Popular Universities and the Origins of Aprismo, 1921–1924," *Hispanic American Historical Review* 55, no. 4 (November 1975): 693–715. Reprinted by permission of *Hispanic American Historical Review*.

Between the beginning of the University Reform movement in Peru in 1919 and the appearance of the Aprista movement in 1924 several important events occurred that decisively shifted the University Reform movement into politics and stamped the Peruvian movement with several original characteristics distinguishing it from other university-based reform movements in the rest of Latin America. The most significant of these events was the founding of the González Prada Popular Universities for workers by Haya de la Torre and his companion students at San Marcos University in 1921. The purpose of the centers originally was to further the aims of the University Reform movement by bringing the benefits of culture and learning to the poor and uneducated. When President Augusto B. Leguía suppressed these centers in 1924 and exiled most of the leaders, Haya and his companions turned their cultural movement into the Aprista movement and later into the Peruvian Aprista party.[1]

The Aprista movement did not, therefore, flow directly out of the general University Reform movement. On the contrary, for the three short but intense years in which they operated legally and publicly, the Popular Universities served as the vital testing ground for most of the ideology of the Aprista party. Furthermore, the Popular University experiment provided the Peruvian reformers with a key asset lacking in other university-based reform movements of the period, namely, an intensive and relatively lengthy experience of mutual collaboration before being subjected to political repression.[2] Perhaps even more significantly, the longevity and continued mass support of the party in the face of electoral defeat and persecution throughout the 1930s and early 1940s may not have been due solely to its reformist program, but also to the ability of the Aprista leaders to deal effectively with their lower class constituency, a skill acquired in large part in the Popular University experience.

Since the turn of the century the concept of the Popular University had been germinating as part of the general thrust of the University Reform movement throughout Latin America. The All-American Student Congress of Montevideo of 1908, the first of its kind in Latin America, had proposed the creation of university extensions to spread the cultural wealth of the old and very elitist universities to the new working classes emerging in many parts of Latin America. As envisioned in its simplest form, the university extension involved nothing more than the sending out of a few professors and students to dictate lectures on diverse subjects for the benefit of the workers. The Peruvian delegates, under the leadership of Víctor Andrés Belaúnde, implemented the Montevideo proposal by creating the University Center in Lima in 1908 and by collaborating in the first university extension in Peru, created that same year.[3] This pilot project, however, failed, like many others, because of lack of organization.[4]

The need to break down the social barriers that isolated the university from the lower classes and to convert it into an instrument of national integration was a constant theme of subsequent student congresses held in Buenos Aires in 1910 and Lima in 1912. In 1913, the Universidad Popular Mexicana was founded under the inspiration of the leaders of the Ateneo, Pedro Henríquez Ureña, Antonio Caso, Alfonso Reyes, and José Vasconcelos. This center of learning for workers in Mexico City operated as a subsidiary of the Ateneo and depended on the voluntary good will of professors and students for its existence. It closed down in 1922 due to lack of funds.[5] Another Popular University was organized in Córdoba a year before the outbreak of the student movement of 1918, but it does not seem to have made a major impact on subsequent events. Although the first National Congress of Argentinian Students proclaimed the creation of university extensions or "social universities" to be an essential goal of their reform, no notable popular center resulted from the Córdoba movement in Argentina. In creating their own popular universities, the Peruvian students implemented and advanced in a much more concrete way the social aims of their Argentinian counterparts.[6]

In 1917 the Peruvian students created their own Federation of Peruvian Students (Federación de Estudiantes Peruanos, or the FEP). Although the Peruvian students were stimulated by the action of the Argentinian students, the immediate impetus leading to the creation of the Popular Universities was the alliance formed between the students and the textile workers of Lima during the first successful strike for the eight-hour day in 1918–19. The strike broke out in a textile plant in Lima run by the William R. Grace Company in December 1918, and by the end of December all of the textile plant workers of Lima and many other workers had joined in a citywide sympathy strike. When a meeting of the Workers' Committee established to formulate the demands of the strikers was broken up by President José Pardo's troops, the workers issued an appeal to the FEP for aid. The newly created FEP acted swiftly in response to the workers' appeal by appointing a committee of three students to act as a liaison between the workers and students. One of the three designated was Haya de la Torre, who soon became the dominant figure in sealing the alliance between the workers and students. On January 15, 1919, President Pardo granted the eight-hour day to all Peruvian workers. One of the immediate results of the strike, at the urging of Haya de la Torre, was the establishment of the Textile Federation, to include the approximately 1,200 textile workers in Lima.[7]

When President Pardo continued to harass both students and work-ers, the Workers' Committee called for a joint student-worker general strike in May. By this time, however, the students had set into motion their own university reform movement. Dissatisfaction with the cautious moves of the FEP led to the creation of a University Reform Committee, to force more energetic action in favor of student demands. The commit-tee, headed by Jorge Guillermo Leguía, and composed of Haya de la Torre, Luis Alberto Sánchez, Jorge Basadre, Manuel Seoane, and other promi-nent student leaders, demanded the removal of eighteen professors at San Marcos, the suppression of certain courses in ecclesiastical discipline, complete renovation of the university government, student participation in policy decisions, and academic freedom for professors.[8]

The tense situation in Lima was heightened by the visit of Alfredo Palacios, the Argentinian socialist, who regaled the students with his re-ports of the reform advances of the Argentinian students. The general strike, which broke out on May 27, the day after Palacios's departure from Lima, paralyzed the city and eventually led to the fall of Pardo, who was prematurely ousted by the newly elected president, Augusto B. Leguía. Leguía seized the opportunity to strengthen his position by acceding to the demands of both the students and the workers. In September 1919, he issued a decree that effected the first major university reform in Peru since 1855.[9] In October, Haya was elected president of the FEP, and one of his first actions was to call for a general congress of Peruvian univer-sity students to implement the objectives of the university reform in Peru. Leguía strengthened his liberal image by offering to subsidize the con-gress, set to meet in 1920. The year 1919 closed with reform victories gained on two distinct fronts: the factory and the university. But the aims of both had been achieved through mutual collaboration, a fact that was to influence deeply the ideology hammered out at the student congress of 1920, as well as the whole subsequent history of Peruvian unionism and politics.[10]

The first National Congress of Peruvian Students convened on March 11 in Cuzco and closed on March 20. The preparatory committee and the direction of the congress were in the hands of Haya de la Torre as president of the FEP. Delegates attending were from the four Peruvian universities, San Marcos (Lima), San Agustín (Arequipa), La Libertad (Trujillo), and the University of Cuzco. The congress developed through two phases, the first of which was dominated by enthusiasts who champi-oned the causes of patriotism and nationalism. In the second phase, the more serious and organized students under Haya de la Torre's leadership took command of the congress. They fought to channel the general ideal-ism of the students into a concrete project, the creation of the Popular

Universities.[11] Haya had proposed the creation of a Popular University to the FEP on two previous occasions, but the idea was rejected both times.[12] Now, however, with the prestige of the office of the presidency of the FEP behind him, and buoyed by the success of the alliance between the students and the workers a few months earlier, Haya pressed again for action on the creation of a Popular University.

The actual proposal for the creation of the Popular University was made halfway through the congress. Under the direction of Haya de la Torre, the students drew up a fourteen-point resolution, defining the nature of the Popular University. The first point of the draft resolution stated that the Popular University was to be under the supervision of the Student Federation, and not attached directly to San Marcos, as in the case of the old university extension concept. Other points envisioned a double cycle of courses to be offered to the workers: in the first cycle emphasis would be placed on inculcating a greater appreciation of national culture, and in the second the emphasis would be on specialized and technical instruction. The methodology to be employed called for a maximum of student involvement and the use of a pedagogy adapted to the popular level. The tenth point called for the Popular Universities to generate other projects, such as community co-ops, libraries, recreation facilities, and medical centers for workers.

Although the resolutions declared that the aim of the Popular University was cultural, they also urged the Popular University to involve itself in "all workers' conflicts."[13] This somewhat ambiguous stance between a purely cultural and a more political orientation created a tension that would characterize the short life of the Popular University. Ultimately, the political orientation would win out, thereby causing the downfall of the Popular University.

The purpose of the Popular University was to carry the culture and learning of the traditional and largely middle- and upper-class national universities to the lower classes. On the occasion of the twenty-fifth anniversary of the founding of the Popular University, Haya de la Torre summarized the students' objectives in creating it: to educate the people, to redeem Peru from social injustice, and to erect a monument to the memory of González Prada.[14] This equating of education with social justice was inspired in large part by an older liberal populism, which looked to education as essential to any revolutionary transformation of Peru. As early as 1858 Francisco de Paula González Vigil had called for the creation of night schools for adults, to teach them to read and write and to inculcate in them a sense of national pride.[15] But the man closest to the students in time and spirit was, of course, Manuel González Prada. More than anyone else, González Prada had foreshadowed the popular university movement by calling for an alliance between workers and students, in order to overthrow the currently existing oppressive class structure in Peru.

Many of González Prada's antiestablishment, populist ideas were set down in his speech delivered to the Bakers' Union in Lima in 1905. He looked with contempt upon the time-honored notion of the superiority of the intellectual over the manual laborer. He compared the interdependence of the brain and the muscles of the human body with the work of the intellectual and the manual laborer in society. Both functioned together, but in different ways. No one could say that the work of one is more valuable than the other. He warned the intellectual not to assume that he alone knows the road to justice in society. On the contrary, the intellectual must become a revolutionary who both stimulates the masses to action and follows the masses when they act. Furthermore, the working classes, once awakened from their slumber by the revolutionary intellectuals, will naturally tend to fight for what is their proper due in society. To those timid souls who would cringe before what they see as a rising tide of barbarians, González Prada proclaimed the populist's creed: "We are not the inundation of barbarism, but the deluge of Justice!"[16]

Like many liberals of the nineteenth century, González Prada believed in the basic goodness of the common man and in man's natural propensity to choose what is best for himself, when given a chance. At the same time, however, he never defined the exact nature of the coming era of justice, nor did he map out a clear program of how this universal justice was to be achieved. He died in 1918 without ever seeing his ideas fructify into any large scale or organized movement, although he had greatly influenced the different groups of workers and students. Haya himself fell sway to this radical populism in frequent conversations with González Prada shortly before the latter's death. The Popular University was not baptized with González Prada's name until 1922, however, in order that the new project not provoke opposition from the many conservative critics of Prada before it had even begun.[17]

The student congress appointed Haya in charge of preparing the ground for setting up the Popular University. The first Popular University was officially inaugurated in Lima on January 21, 1921, in the Palacio de Exposición, which was then the center for the FEP, and was in the 1950s converted into an art museum. All four dailies of Lima carried full news accounts of the inauguration, and a round of applause in the senate was accorded the new cultural project.[18] A second Popular University center was created in the small textile town of Vitarte outside Lima. These "universities" were not, of course, accredited institutions of higher learning in the usual sense of the word. Rather, they were centers of cultural improvement for uneducated lower-class workers and their families. They offered no degrees, required no tuition, and depended entirely upon the good will of their teachers and students to function. The different centers of the Popular University operated at night and were open to all workers, many of whom were women. Financially, the Popular University received a token sum of 50 soles a month from the FEP.

The teachers at the Popular University were nearly all students or professors at San Marcos University in Lima recruited by Haya de la Torre, who had been elected the first rector. Many of these first teachers, who gave their time voluntarily and gratuitously to the Popular University, represented some of the leading lights of the post-World War I student generation of Peru. Raúl Porras Barrenechea, later to win fame as a historian, conducted courses on American literature, and Jorge Basadre taught Peruvian history in the Popular University. Oscar Herrera, a science student at San Marcos and decades later the rector of Federico Villareal University in Lima, gave classes on geography and astronomy. Others among the teachers were Luis Heysen, the future Aprista leader; Eudocio Ravines, the one-time Communist and later director of *La Prensa*; and in 1923, José Carlos Mariátegui. Years later, some of the teachers—such as Nicolás Terreros, Jacobo Hurwitz, Luis Bustamante, and others—would become founders of the Communist Party in Peru, while Mariátegui would form his own socialist party.[19] Luciano Castillo, who also taught at the Popular University, later formed a distinct socialist party.

The main organizer behind the Popular University, however, was Haya de la Torre, who, besides functioning as rector, also taught geography and social history. He appointed the teachers, organized most of the cultural and social activities, and, with his speaking abilities, drew the largest crowds. The editors of *El Obrero Textil*, the principal organ of the Peruvian textile workers and a staunch supporter of the Popular University, even felt it necessary to refute in an editorial a claim made by one of their readers that without Haya de la Torre there would be no Popular University.[20]

The students of the Popular University were mainly workers or field laborers from the coastal haciendas. At times as many as a thousand workers would gather in the hall of the Palacio de Exposición to listen to the more popular lecturers, such as Haya de la Torre or Mariátegui. In Vitarte, where the Popular University became the main attraction and diversion in the town, anywhere from 70 to 400 men, women, and children crowded into the local cinema where the classes were held twice weekly.[21] In Lima the vast majority of the students were Spanish-speaking mestizos. At Vitarte, some 10 miles inland, most of the students were mestizos who belonged to the local textile union, but many Quechua-speaking laborers from the neighboring haciendas also rode in by horseback to attend the lectures. Like many coastal towns, Vitarte was a focal point of transition from the more Indian rural culture to the more mestizo town culture. At the public outings of the Popular University in Vitarte, for example, the men wore ordinary worker's dress, but the majority of the women still wore the typical Indian garb of the highlands.[22] In general, however, as most of the Popular Universities functioned in coastal towns and cities, the majority of the students tended to be acculturated Spanish-speaking workers, usually associated with the new and growing labor movement.

Many of the worker-students had been participants or leaders in the strike for the eight-hour day. Among them was Arturo Sabroso, a young anarchist and coeditor of *El Obrero Textil*. Years later Sabroso would be the founder and first president of the powerful Confederation of Peruvian Workers, and close ally of Haya de la Torre in politics. For Sabroso and many other workers, the Popular University was the medium for their conversion from petty anarchism to organized labor and national politics.[23] Furthermore, their enthusiasm for cultural self-improvement at the Popular University was a natural expression and continuation of their new political awakening. The Popular University thus served to bring together into an institutionalized setting, which demanded regular face-to-face contact and exchange of ideas, the student activists and workers who collaborated in the strike of 1918–19.

Although the student-teachers aimed to expose their students to the full range of subjects and courses taught at the regular university, in practice they tended to emphasize the newest and most attractive subjects or ideas. In his lectures on geography, Haya attempted to synthesize his readings in Hegel, Marx, and Spencer, to demonstrate the impact of land on man and the formation of human culture. Humberto del Aguila, a law student at San Marcos and cofounder of *La Razón* with Mariátegui, gave a course in the history of the Inca civilization and also expounded on the latest developments in the theory of evolution to his audience.[24] Although academic subjects such as history, geography, and science were taught, the emphasis was placed more on practical subjects that would directly benefit the lives of the workers: personal hygiene, first aid for home and factory, and, most important, reading and writing, for the vast majority of the students were illiterate. Care was also taken to include artistic appreciation in the program, and from time to time the Popular University offered courses in music, painting, ceramic-making, and cloth-weaving, the last two being ancient arts among the Incas.[25]

The student-teachers also presented lectures highlighting the values of studying Incan culture and history in order to foster the cult of *indigenismo*. They encouraged their students to cultivate an interest in Indian arts and customs and to learn Quechua. In accordance with this objective, the Popular University held evening social gatherings (*veladas*) from time to time; at these native artists would perform traditional dances of the highlands and play the *quena*, the typical Indian flute. These meetings usually ended with a speech by one of the teachers on the need to "vindicate" the rights of Peru's long-oppressed Indians.[26] At the same time, each Popular University had a section for "Indian Affairs," to teach Spanish to the Indian students and to attend to their particular needs.[27] In general, however, there were few Indians, and the lectures on *indigenismo* were intended primarily to awaken a new pride in Peru's past and to create a sense of solidarity among the workers with the Indians.

From the outset, the student reformers at Cuzco had resolved to overcome the great social and psychological barriers that divided themselves from the lower-class workers whom they intended to teach. They employed a didactic style calculated to catch the attention of their students, most of whom suffered from a social inferiority complex in the presence of members of a higher social class. Furthermore, most of the workers were exhausted after a full day's work. Haya and his companion students discovered that they had to be "part teacher and part showman" to keep the workers' attention. One of the important techniques that Haya and the others developed was a question-and-answer dialogue with the students. Other didactic techniques included the use of colorful posters of slogans that condemned alcoholism or coca chewing.[28] Public student recitals were held to instill in the students a sense of self-confidence. Morality plays were presented on the stage of the cinema in Vitarte. Once a month on a Sunday afternoon the workers put on a short morality play to demonstrate the evils of alcoholism or to extol the virtues of hard work.[29]

From the very beginning the Popular University waged a war on alcoholism among the workers. The young student-teachers gave lectures and admonitions to the workers on the ill effects of drinking, and they disseminated literature against it at every opportunity. They organized picnics on the weekends among the workers, which were intended in part to convince the workers that healthy recreation was possible without recourse to alcohol. At other times these outings were organized to foster a greater appreciation of nature, in particular the natural beauty of Peru's countryside. Implicit, also, in the purpose of these outings was the desire to heighten the sense of unity between the workers and their teachers. This effort to inspire the workers to appreciate the values of the resources of their own country led to the institutionalization of one of these outings, which came to be known as the "Feast of the Plant" (*Fiesta de la*

Planta). Each year this holiday was celebrated in Vitarte, with a mixture of solemnity and festivity, by thousands of workers from Lima and the surrounding towns.[30]

Along with the temperance campaigns, the Popular University also conducted sanitation drives. In January 1922, the Popular University initiated a campaign to prevent the spread of typhoid by urging all restaurants to keep their facilities clean.[31] Moreover, the students of medicine who taught at the Popular University gave special instructions to the workers on the dangers of venereal diseases. These efforts to improve the cultural and physical lot of the workers won widespread approval in the beginning. Most of the leading dailies of Lima, *El Comercio*, *El Tiempo*, *La Crónica*, and *La Prensa* carried regular feature articles on the activities of the Popular University during the first two years of its existence. *La Prensa* even carried twice-weekly summaries of the lectures given at the Popular University throughout most of 1921, until President Leguía closed it down for its antigovernment stand. *El Tiempo* reported with approval in one article that the workers of Lima had ceased to flock to the local bar on payday as a result of the labors of the Popular University.[32] *La Prensa* acclaimed the Popular University for its educational achievement among the workers.[33]

The first anniversary of the Popular University was marked by the announcement of the decision to establish new Popular University centers in other parts of Peru. Within a short period of time six new centers were established in Lima alone. The first Popular University center to be established outside the Lima area was that of Arequipa in January 1922, under the direction of the students of San Agustín.[34] Within the next few months Popular University extensions were established in Huaraz, Puno, Ica, and even in the faraway jungle department of Madre de Dios.[35]

After the first year of the Popular University, Haya accepted an invitation of the YMCA, of which he was an active member, to attend a youth congress in Uruguay. He made use of the opportunity to tour many cities in southern Latin America, including Buenos Aires, where President Hipólito Yrigoyen commended the young student leader for the work of the Popular University.[36] Indeed, the fame of the Popular University in Peru had traveled far and wide. When Haya visited Havana after his exile from Peru, he found the Cuban university students eager to set up their own Popular University in imitation of that of Peru. At Haya's behest they founded the José Martí Popular University on November 9, 1923. In Chile the José Lastarria was founded, the Justo Arosemena in Panama, the Emiliano Zapata in Mexico, which lasted until 1937, and several others throughout Latin America.[37]

The success of the Popular University in Peru increasingly began to overshadow other aspects of the University Reform movement. Carrying the culture directly to the people had now assumed an importance outweighing the demand to remold traditional structures within the older universities. Revitalization of the nation through the establishment of voluntary centers of popular education and culture now seemed a far more efficient plan of action than waiting for the older universities to train the needed number of scholars and technicians to raise the educational level of the people. That would take generations to do what the Popular University could conceivably accomplish in a decade. Shortly after his exile, Haya wrote enthusiastically to the Argentinian students that the González Prada Popular University would one day become the "great social university of Peru," which would "sing the repose of the other" (San Marcos).[38]

Given the openly proclaimed social orientation of the Popular University, it was inevitable that it would become involved in politics sooner or later. For the first two years of its existence, the Popular University operated mainly as a cultural center and refrained from engaging in overt political activities. Nevertheless, among the San Marcos student-teachers were to be found many young activists with strong Marxist and anarchist leanings who used the Popular University as a platform for their ideas. The Popular University tolerated this free expression of thought, for it fit in well with the proclaimed liberty of speech of the student reform movement in general. The social aims of the Popular University had been loudly proclaimed but never clearly defined. The motto of the Popular University succinctly summed up this noncommittal stance: "The Popular University has no dogma but that of Social Justice."[39] All factions were invited to enter the classrooms of the Popular University, although, of course, this liberality extended only to those who showed an interest in improving the lot of the Indians and the working class. In the minds of some of the young reformers, this meant freedom to teach the workers the benefits of the new social system of the Soviet Union.[40]

On a few occasions, the Popular University sponsored projects that served to channel the social impulses of the workers into concrete action. When the 5,000 workers of the American Copper Company in La Oroya went on strike in May 1921, the students and teachers of the Popular University took up a collection to send food and supplies to the strikers and their families.[41] Such protest moves, however, were sporadic and spontaneous. They represented the lingering anarchical strain left over from the strikes of 1918–19 before the union movement had gotten under way. Such anarchism also carried with it, in a modified way, overtones of the anticlericalism of González Prada, whose words were framed on the walls of the Popular University: "In Peru there are four million illiterates, thanks to the clergy and the politicians."[42]

The full politicization of the Popular University occurred as the climax of a series of protracted clashes between Leguía and his critics after he seized power in 1919. Among the earliest critics of Leguía were three journalists of *El Tiempo*, César Falcón, Humberto del Aguila and José Carlos Mariátegui, who founded an anti-Leguía magazine, *La Razón*, in 1919. Shortly thereafter, Leguía pressured the most brilliant of the three, Mariátegui, to depart to Europe on a four-year journalistic scholarship. The other two aligned themselves with the Popular University, as did Mariátegui on his return from Europe in 1923. On the university scene, Haya de la Torre headed a list of thirty-two students who denounced the Student Federation for according Leguía the title, "Mentor of the Youth."[43] In reaction to a speech by Víctor Andrés Belaúnde protesting his antiuniversity policies, Leguía closed down San Marcos in May 1921.[44]

The Popular University, too, had increasingly fallen into government disfavor. More and more it was viewed as a hotbed of radicalism by conservative elements. *El Comercio* had long since dropped the Popular University from its columns, and *La Prensa*, which Leguía had closed down and turned into a government newspaper in 1921, took a more critical stance toward the activities of the Popular University. In May 1923, Mariátegui returned from Europe, and Haya invited him to lecture at the Popular University and to collaborate in directing the new organ of the Workers' Federation and the Popular University, *Claridad*, which Haya had founded in March of that year. By coincidence, the announcement of Mariátegui's first lecture, on the impact of revolutionary Russia on the modern world, appeared on May 23, the date on which the Popular University launched its most serious venture into politics: the protest movement against the consecration of Peru to the Sacred Heart.[45]

The Popular University spearheaded the protest against Archbishop Emilio Lissón's planned ceremony. Weeks before the announced date for the ceremony, Haya de la Torre organized a number of dissident groups, Protestants, Catholics, anarchists, students, and workers of the Popular University into a single protest block, "The Popular Front of Manual and Intellectual Workers."[46] On the day of the consecration, Haya and several thousand workers and students, most of them affiliated with the Popular University, marched through the streets of Lima denouncing the plans of the archbishop and the president. In the face of such opposition, Archbishop Lissón was forced to suspend the ceremony.[47] After two workers were killed by government troops during the march, the Popular University issued a manifesto summoning all workers and students of Peru to join in a nationwide strike.[48] The various workers' unions and groups of Lima promptly cooperated. From that moment on, Leguía looked for his opportunity to destroy the Popular University, which had overtly become a center of political dissent against his regime.

After May 23 the government launched a steadily intensifying campaign against the Popular University. *La Prensa* voiced the dictator's sentiments by frequently denouncing the Popular University as a center of Bolshevism because it fostered a dangerous fraternization between workers and students.[49] On July 16 the police disrupted with gunfire the inaugural ceremonies for the new Popular University center of Callao in the Palacio de Exposición. In October, in the midst of the student elections for the presidency of the FEP, in which Haya ran for a second term against Manuel Seoane, the police seized and deported Haya from Peru. The government then closed down the Popular University centers and *Claridad*.

In the belief that the main source of trouble had been removed, the government permitted the Popular University to reopen in January of the following year. Oscar Herrera assumed the title of rector, and Mariátegui took over the direction of *Claridad*. With Haya gone, however, Mariátegui emerged as the undisputed center of attention and natural leader of the Popular University. He was the only lecturer at the Popular University who had won fame in his own right before coming to teach there.[50] The workers respected him because they knew that he had begun as a worker himself, and the intellectuals admired his brilliance and force of conviction. Mariátegui's first reaction to the Popular University after he returned from Europe was one of skepticism. His studies in Marxism in Italy convinced him of the need to ground the class struggle in a clear-cut strategy and to gird it with discipline. He was disconcerted both by the lack of a well-defined class consciousness at the Popular University and by the somewhat formless orientation that guided it. Years later, after he had definitively broken with Haya, he referred to the Popular University as an "instrument of intellectual domination by the petty bourgeoisie."[51]

Nevertheless, Mariátegui had returned from Europe with the intention of working for the creation of a class party, and he found the Popular University a useful platform from which he could develop his ideas and attract a following. When he learned of the protest march planned for May 23, he at first objected because he believed that that kind of activity resembled old-fashioned anarchism, which was ineffective because it was sporadic and emphasized short-term over long-term goals.[52] Later, however, he reconciled himself to the protest movement because May 23 symbolized the end of the Popular University as a cultural project and its blood baptism as a center of social protest. After that day, Mariátegui believed that the university students of Peru had left behind them their naïve notions of reforming Peru merely by exerting themselves to raise the cultural and educational level of the lower classes.[53]

Mariátegui steered the Popular University toward the left and used it as a platform to preach the ideals of revolutionary Marxism. The new *Claridad*, which appeared in January 1924, revealed the extent of this radical departure from the more or less undefined political orientation of the pre-May 23 days. In it Mariátegui declared that the "Popular Universities are not agnostic or colorless institutions like the university extension." Rather, they are schools that exist for the "creation of a proletarian culture."[54] At the sixth anniversary of the founding of the Popular University, Mariátegui addressed the workers on the significance of the Popular University. The Popular University had gone through two stages in its development, Mariátegui observed. In the first stage, which ended on May 23, 1923, the Popular University consolidated the workers and broke the class bonds that tied them to the *civilista* regime of Leguía. But in the second stage, dominated by Mariátegui, the Popular University took a more critical view of the struggle and defined its objectives more sharply. Whereupon, Mariátegui proposed the formation of a sociological seminar to study and apply the Marxist historical analysis to the problems of Peru. This seminar was to be the core nucleus of the Popular University.[55]

The early part of 1924 was marked by premature hopes of overcoming the difficult times as tensions eased up. In September of that year, however, the Leguía regime set about with greater earnestness completing the business left unfinished after deporting Haya de la Torre by closing down the Popular Universities in Trujillo, Arequipa, Cuzco, Vitarte, Barranco, and Lima.[56] Even more damaging, between September 1924 and the early part of 1925 the leading teachers of the Popular University were all deported: Oscar Herrera, Luis Bustamante, Eudocio Ravines, Jacobo Hurwitz, Nicolás Terreros, Luis Heysen, Manuel Seoane, Enrique Köster, and many others.[57] Along with the teachers many leading labor leaders and workers from the Popular University were also deported. The Popular University of Lima—which alone of all the others in Peru managed to weather the storm and reopen—maintained a shadowy, underground existence until 1927. After 1924, however, the tone of the meetings was overtly political, and little pretense was made of fulfilling the original cultural finality of the Popular University.

In the meantime, Haya and his student companions brought Apra into existence in Mexico in May 1924. From then until the time they returned to Peru in 1930–31, most of the essential points of the Aprista ideology were further clarified and refined. The Aprista's decision to convert Apra into a political party designed to win power in Peru was the pretext that

Mariátegui used to break with Haya and form his Socialist Party in 1929, along with Eudocio Ravines and Ricardo Martínez de la Torre. Mariátegui strongly objected to the populist, multiclass character of the Aprista movement, as well as to its more moderate stance on imperialism.[58] Other former teachers of the Popular University also began to part company with Apra for the same ideological reason. Nicolás Terreros and Jacobo Hurwitz broke away from the Aprista cell in Mexico and joined the Communist International.[59]

Although the history and ideological development of the Aprista movement itself lie outside the scope of this study, a few observations may serve to underline some of the ways in which the original González Prada Popular Universities influenced the origins and orientation of that movement. Significantly, one of the first acts of the new party in Peru was to recreate the Popular Universities, this time no longer as independent autonomous cultural centers, but rather as integral organs of the Aprista party. The stated aims of the newly restored Popular University were to "educate the Peruvian people, raise their moral standards, inculcate in them a love for their country, wage war on alcoholism, and prepare the people to lead honest lives as citizens of the country."[60]

However noble and disinterested the ends of the new Popular University were, its life was as secure or insecure as the party with which it was associated. One of the first acts of Sánchez Cerro after assuming power was to harass and eventually close down the Popular University centers. When the Aprista members of parliament protested this action, the dictator seized the occasion to expel twenty-three of them from Parliament in February 1932.[61] Shortly afterward, Apra was forced to enter its first period of underground existence, from 1932 to 1945, interrupted by a brief breathing spell after the assassination of Sánchez Cerro in 1933.

During the period of clandestine existence, the Popular University lived an active but precarious life, functioning in the homes of Apristas at night. Under Sánchez Cerro there were some five Popular University centers operating in different parts of Lima. The important role that the Popular University played in the lives of party members is illustrated by the example of Aprista political prisoners on the prison island of San Lorenzo off the coast of Callao, who established an improvised "Popular University" among themselves. They held surreptitious "classes" from 1942 until May 1945, when the party was officially legalized throughout Peru under President Manuel Prado.[62]

After President José Luis Bustamante y Rivero was overthrown by General Manuel Odría in October 1948, the Aprista party was outlawed once again, and the Popular Universities reverted to the techniques of underground life, still fresh in the memories of all Apristas. When the party was legalized in 1956 in exchange for its support of Manuel Prado's second term, the Popular University also surfaced publicly. The Popular University of Lima continues to function as an adjunct of the Aprista party, within the confines of the general party headquarters. It offers free nocturnal classes to workers in the technical arts, English, accounting, and the handicrafts. Each year, also, Haya de la Torre delivers a series of lectures at the Popular University on such diverse topics as Toynbee's concept of history or Aprista political strategy.[63]

The impact of the original González Prada Popular University, however, went far beyond the initiative to recreate the popular universities within the party. In many ways, the party itself was an extension and a fulfillment of the aims and objectives of the first Popular University, a reality frequently stressed by Aprista leaders. In his presidential acceptance speech in August 1931, Haya declared that the Aprista movement had arisen indirectly from the university reform movement, but directly from the Popular University.[64] On another occasion he called the Popular University the "vanguard" of the Aprista movement.[65] One of the lessons that the future Aprista leaders learned during the Popular University experiment was that they could not solve many particular problems without a total political transformation of the entire country. For example, Haya cited the discovery by the young student reformers that the lack of good hygiene among the workers was not due merely to lack of proper instruction, but to their low economic status as well.[66]

Ideologically, the Apristas described their movement as a "Popular Front of Manual and Intellectual Workers." This concept had, of course, originated much earlier with González Prada. Haya himself proposed the formation of a "Popular Front of Manual and Intellectual Workers" in a speech that he gave to workers and students at the University of Trujillo in 1922.[67] The term did not acquire its later great significance for the Apristas, however, until 1923, when the leaders of the protest movement of May 23 first designated themselves with that title. This same multiclass populism appeared in the Aprista program drawn up by Haya in Mexico after his exile in 1924.

Recent studies have questioned Apra's claim to be a broadly based national party, particularly as regards the Indians. In the 1931 election, for example, Apra drew 44 percent of its vote from the northern coastal departments, 30 percent from Lima, and only 26 percent from the rest of Peru. The key to Apra's strong appeal in the north seems to be its strong anti-imperialist rhetoric, which served to consolidate the highly organized sugar hacienda workers and certain middle-class groups, both of which felt themselves displaced and exploited by the great foreign-owned sugar monopolies. By way of contrast, in the more backward and less-industrialized south and central sierra region, the Indians perceived little threat from foreign imperialism. According to this interpretation, the rapid growth of Apra was due more to special social conditions affecting coastal workers than to its reformist, pro-Indian propaganda.[68]

Nevertheless, even in light of this more correct appraisal of Apra as primarily a regional and urban labor party, it still came the closest to being the only really national party in the 1930s and 1940s in Peru. The much smaller and more ideologically rigid Socialist and Communist parties, for example, failed to offer a program as comprehensive and as elastic as that of Apra, which brought together such diverse and newly politicized groups as urban factory workers, hacienda laborers, university students, and the lower middle class. While there were undoubtedly unique social conditions that brought these groups together in 1931, it is also important to stress that the successful collaboration of students and workers in the Popular University had predisposed future Aprista and pro-Aprista leaders to think in terms of populist strategies long before Apra became a reality in Peru.

The Apristas have also been criticized for failing to translate their *indigenista* rhetoric into effective pro-Indian legislation.[69] Nevertheless, both the Popular University and Apra played an important role in making the issue of Indians' rights a subject of national controversy. The cult of *indigenismo* had, of course, been in vogue long before the Popular University. González Prada, Clorinda Matto de Turner, Joaquín Capelo, and others had strongly influenced the university generation of the early twentieth century, as well as certain workers' groups in Lima. But the Popular University, with its glorification of Peru's Indian past and fostering of Quechua, Indian dances, and artwork, turned *indigenismo* into a popular cultural form among the working classes. For these largely mestizo workers, the new *indigenismo* served as a cultural expression of their new political awareness. For the middle-class university students who taught them, it served as a vehicle of expression for their new reformist nationalism. Similarly, the Popular University's advocacy of woman's rights carried over into Aprista ideology in the 1930s.[70]

Undoubtedly, one of the most important influences of the Popular University on the Aprista party was its sense of a cultural and educational mission to the rest of the nation. After the electoral defeat in October 1931, Haya assured his followers that the mission of Apra was not to "arrive at the Palace," but to teach and uplift the people. Apra would still govern Peru, Haya declared, because to govern meant to educate, inspire, and redeem the people. Haya compared Apra to a "school," the principal function of which was to raise the cultural level of the Peruvian people.[71]

Furthermore, the Aprista program of 1931 reflected the Popular University's general objective of improving not just the mind, but the total person as well. The Popular University's emphasis on personal hygiene, physical fitness, and honesty in dealing with others foreshadowed the Aprista stress on moral and physical fitness as a key to national regeneration. Likewise, the Aprista proposal for the establishment of centers of public sanitation stemmed from the public health campaigns of the Popular University. Finally, in their educational program the Apristas called for the establishment of agricultural schools, specialized workers' schools, and "popular universities" throughout the country.[72]

The popularity of Apra as well as its capacity to survive sustained political repression in the 1930s in Peru must be attributed in great part to its all-encompassing program, which offered an integral solution to both the personal and social problems of the lower classes. The key to understanding this totalizing thrust of Apra is found in its origins in the Popular University, which functioned as a combination civic club, labor union, self-help cooperative, and social and educational center for the lower classes. Perhaps the greatest lesson that the young student reformers learned during their three-year experience in the Popular University was that fundamental social reform in Peru could not be accomplished solely through the spontaneous efforts of private individuals to improve certain aspects of the lives of the lower classes. Rather, they came to realize that the social regeneration of Peru could be effected only through a total transformation of all of society itself. It was this realization—that culture, education, and politics are ultimately inseparable—which led to the transformation of the Popular University into the Aprista movement in 1924 and which decisively shaped Aprista ideology in 1931 and thereafter.

Notes

1. Some of the more important works in English on the Aprista movement are Harry Kantor, *The Ideology and Prgram of the Peruvian Aprista Movement* (Berkeley, 1953); Fredrick B. Pike, *The Modern History of Peru* (New York, 1967); Grant Hilliker, *The Politics of Reform in Peru* (Baltimore, 1971); and Peter F. Klarén, *Modernization, Dislocation, and Aprismo* (Austin, 1973). Although all of these works offer good general coverage of the Aprista movement, none deal at length with the Popular Universities. For a critique of both the literature and conflicting viewpoints on Apra, see the article by Richard Lee Clinton, *"Apra: An Appraisal," Journal of Inter-American Studies and World Affairs*, 12 (Apr. 1970), 280–297.

2. For a viewpoint that stresses the positive contributions of Latin American university students to social change, with reference to the Peruvian Aprista movement, see Kevin Lyonette, "Student Organizations in Latin America," *Interna-*

tional Affairs, 42:4 (Oct. 1966), 655–661. An opinion which de-emphasizes the role of the students in affecting national change is expressed by Alistair Hennessy, "University Students and National Politics," in Claudio Veliz, ed., *The Politics of Conformity in Latin America* (New York, 1967), pp. 119–157. A survey of the literature in this area is found in John Petersen, "Recent Research on Latin American University Students," *Latin American Research Review*, 5:1 (Spring 1970), 37–58.

3. Victor Andrés Belaúnde, *Mi generación en la universidad (1900–1914)* (Lima, 1961), pp. 123–128.

4. Luis Alberto Sánchez, *La universidad no es una isla* (Lima, 1963), p. 138.

5. John S. Innes, "The Universidad Popular Mexicana," *The Americas*, 30:I (July, 1973), 110–122.

6. The most comprehensive study of the reform movement in Latin America is by Gabriel del Mazo, one of the principal leaders of the movement in Argentina: *La reforma universitaria*, 6 vols (Buenos Aires, 1941). Although del Mazo has been criticized for overemphasizing the importance of Córdoba as the beginning of the reform movement, he offers a more balanced overall view of the proper role of other pre-Córdoba movements in the rest of Latin America in his later works. See also Gabriel del Mazo, *El movimiento de la reforma universitaria en América Latina* (Lima, 1967). Two studies that emphasize the roots of the Peruvian reform movement in Peru itself are Jesús Chavarría, "A Communication on University Reform," *Latin American Research Review*, 3:3 (Summer 1968), 192–195; and Mark J. Aken, "University Reform before Córdoba," *HAHR*, 51:3 (Aug. 1971), 447–462.

7. A detailed chronicle of the strike is found in Ricardo Martínez de la Torre, *Apuntes para una interpretación Marxista de historia social del Perú*, I (Lima, 1947), 395–461. Another account of the strike, which emphasizes Haya's role, is found in Luis Alberto Sánchez, *Haya de la Torre y el Apra* (Santiago, 1954), pp. 49–69.

8. Victor Raúl Haya de la Torre, *¿A dónde va Indoámerica?* (Santiago, 1935), p. 192.

9. Julio C. Tello, *Reforma universitaria* (Lima, 1928), pp. 137–38.

10. For a study of the close relationship between Apra and labor, which dates back to the period of the strike for the eight-hour day, see James L. Payne, *Labor and Politics in Peru* (New Haven, 1965), pp. 116–125. See also Robert J. Alexander, *Organized Labor in Latin America* (New York, 1965), pp. 112–122.

11. Del Mazo, *La reforma universitaria*, II, 36; vol. II also contains a chronicle of the student congress and of the Popular University, written by Enrique Köster, pp. 15–60.

12. *Boletín de las Universidades Populares González Prada* (Apr. 1946), p. 15.

13. Del Mazo, *La reforma universitaria*, II, 45–46.

14. *Boletín de las Universidades Populares González Prada* (Apr. 1946), pp. 12–13. Haya de la Torre's reflections on the university reform movement appear in many of his different works: *Construyendo el Aprismo* (Buenos Aires, 1933), pp. 155–166; *Ideología Aprista* (Lima, 1961), pp. 72–108; and his article "Latin America's Student Revolution," *Living Age*, 331:4291 (Oct. 15, 1926), pp. 103–106.

15. Francisco de Paula González Vigil, *Importancia de la Educación Popular* (Lima, 1948), pp. 113–116.

16. Manuel González Prada, *Horas de lucha* (Lima, 1964), pp. 47–55. For an overall study of González Prada's thought and influence, see Eugenio Chang Rodríguez, *La literatura política de González Prada, Mariátegui y Haya de la Torre* (México, 1957).

17. Felipe Cossío del Pomar, *El indoamericano* (Lima, 1946), p. 55.

18. *El Comercio*, Jan. 24, 1921, p. 1; *La Prensa*, Jan. 24, p. 4. See also *Mundial*, Jan. 28, 1921, p. 20.

19. Sánchez, *Haya de la Torre*, pp. 80–81.

20. *El Obrero Textil*, Mar. 1923, p. 2.

21. Josefina Yarlequé de Marquina, *El maestro o democracia en miniatura* (Lima, 1963), p. 39. The author, a schoolteacher and eyewitness of the Popular University in Vitarte, discusses the impact of the Popular University on the town. Also, personal interview with Sra. Yarlequé de Marquina, Vitarte, July 27, 1967.

22. Ibid. Photographs of the students at these festive gatherings are found on pp. 52, 91. For a contrast in the degree of westernization, see the photographs of the students in Lima, *Mundial*, Jan. 28, 1921, p. 20.

23. Personal interview with Arturo Sabroso, Lima, Aug. 8, 1967. For a hostile view of Sabroso's pro-Aprista involvement, see Martínez de la Torre, *Apuntes*, II, 237–274.

24. Haya de la Torre, unpublished photostatic summaries of the lectures given at the Popular University, 1921–1923. In the private collection of Haya de la Torre, Vitarte.

25. Ibid.

26. *La Prensa*, Mar. 8, 1921, p. 6.

27. *Claridad*, July, 1923, p. 9. The same article also refers to the "great number" of Indians who had begun to come to the Popular University as a result of its literacy program. There were, however, other indications that few Indians, in fact, attended the Popular University. In a lecture to the workers in Vitarte, Haya de la Torre urged them to do whatever they could to attract Indians to the Popular University. Yarlequé de Marquina, *El maestro*, pp. 59–60.

28. Personal interviews with Haya de la Torre, Lima, August 8, 9, 11, and 12, 1967. Haya believes that much of his skill in dealing with large crowds, especially semiliterate workers, was acquired during his teaching experience in the Popular University.

29. Yarlequé de Marquina, *El maestro*, pp. 47; 80–83.

30. Del Mazo, *La reforma*, II, 23. During the period of persecution in the 1930s, the Apristas continued to celebrate the "Feast of the Plant" in Vitarte as a symbol of resistance. *Apra*, Lima, Feb. 1, 1934, p. 3.

31. *La Prensa*, Mar. 18, 1922, p. 2.

32. *El Tiempo*, Jan. 25, 1922, p. 7.

33. *La Prensa*, Mar. 5, 1921, p. 1.

34. *El Tiempo*, Jan. 29, 1922, p. 9.

35. *El Obrero Textil*, May 1924, p. 3.

36. Cossío del Pomar, *El indoamericano*, pp. 82–83.

37. Luis Alberto Sánchez, *La universidad latinoamericana* (Guatemala, 1949), pp. 205–206.

38. Cossío del Pomar, *El indoamericano*, p. 71.

39. Del Mazo, *La reforma*, II, 110.

40. *La Prensa*, Mar. 5, 1921, p. 4.

41. *La Prensa*, June 14, 1921, p. 2.

42. *Claridad*, July 1923, p. 20.

43. Sánchez, *Haya de la Torre*, p. 57. See also the editorial by Haya de la Torre protesting Leguía's substitution of the FEP by a government-controlled university center. *La Prensa*, Mar. 3, 1921, p. 1.

44. Carlos Enrique Paz Soldán, *De la revolución a la anarquía universitaria* (Lima, 1922), pp. 35–36.

45. *La Crónica*, May 23, 1923, p. 10.

46. Some examples of the many propaganda appeals issued by the Popular University against the consecration may be found in *El Tiempo*, May 21, 1923, p. 2; *El Comercio*, May 22, 1923, p. 4.

47. *El Comercio*, May 26, 1923, p. 3.

48. *La Crónica*, May 24, 1923, p. 3. A later Aprista version of the events of May 23, 1923, may be found in Manuel Seoane's work, *La revolución que el Perú necesita* (Arequipa, Peru, 1965), pp. 99–103.

49. *La Prensa*, Oct. 5, 1923, p. 3.

50. Later, however, Mariátegui found it necessary to reject the notion that he owed his fame or political ideas to the Popular University. Martínez de la Torre, *Apuntes*, II, 336.

51. Ibid., p. 258.

52. Ibid., p. 467.

53. José Carlos Mariátegui, *Siete ensayos de interpretación de la realidad Peruana* (Santiago, 1955), p. 104.

54. *Claridad*, Jan. 1924, p. 5. Many supporters of the Popular University did not admit that it had changed its orientation after the departure of Haya de la Torre. See, for example, the editorial in *El Obrero Textil*, Apr. 1924, p. 1.

55. Martínez de la Torre, *Apuntes*, II, 271.

56. *Claridad*, Sept. 1924, p. 6.

57. Del Mazo, *La reforma*, II, 272.

58. The somewhat bitter exchange of correspondence between Mariátegui and Haya in which they broke off their relationship is found in Martínez de la Torre, *Apuntes*, II, 296–299. A pro-Aprista history of events and the ideological development of Apra in exile from 1924 until 1930 is found in Cossío del Pomar, *El indoamericano*, pp. 111–208.

59. Martínez de la Torre, *Apuntes*, II, 281.

60. *Apra*, Lima, November 30, 1933. Some evidence that the memory of the old Popular University was kept alive is provided by another Aprista periodical of the 1930s, *Libertad*, Lima, Feb. 9, 1931, p. 2.

61. *Apra*, Nov. 12, 1933, p. 5.

62. *Boletín de las Universidades Populares* (Apr. 1946), pp. 3–4.

63. Ignacio Campos, *Coloquios de Haya de la Torre*, 3 vols. (Lima, 1965). Much information on the role of the Popular University within the party was obtained through frequent conversations at the Aprista Party Headquarters in Lima in the summer of 1967 with the current director of the Popular University, Orestes Rodríguez.

64. Haya de la Torre, *Política Aprista*, 2nd ed. (Lima, 1967), p. 43.

65. Haya de la Torre and José Ingenieros, *Teoría y táctica de la acción renovadora y antiimperialista de la juventud en América Latina* (Buenos Aires, 1928), p. 26.

66. Haya de la Torre, *Construyendo el Aprismo* (Buenos Aires, 1933), p. 169.

67. Sánchez, *Haya de la Torre*, p. 115.

68. This view of Apra as primarily a regional labor party has been especially developed by Klarén, *Modernization, Dislocation, and Aprismo*, and Hilliker, *The Politics of Reform in Peru*.

69. See, for example, the article by Thomas M. Davies, Jr., "The *Indigenismo* of the Peruvian Aprista Party: A Reinterpretation," *HAHR*, 51:4 (Nov. 1971), 626–645.

70. A sample of the pro-feminist propaganda of the Popular University may be found in *Claridad*, July, 1923, p. 11. Similar views on the role of women in society appear in the Aprista party platform, Haya de la Torre, *Política Aprista*, pp. 11, 22.

71. Haya de la Torre, *Ideología Aprista*, pp. 108, 192.

72. Haya de la Torre, *Política Aprista*, pp. 22–23.

---

4 Donald J. Mabry ◆ The Great Conflict

The explosion of violence that took place in Mexico City's Tlatelolco housing project on October 2, 1968, was one of the most dramatic confrontations between a student movement and a government in Latin American history. Although the full magnitude of this event continues to elude even the most astute analysts, the deaths of these students (the exact number remains uncertain) was, for many young Mexicans, the defining event of their generation. President Gustavo Díaz Ordaz's administration (1964–1970) had based part of its popular support and historical legitimacy on its claim to be the successor to the revolutionary governments of the period from 1910 to 1940. But in the view of many students and their supporters, the unleashing of the military and police forces against the Tlatelolco demonstration destroyed the regime's popularity and undercut its legitimacy.

The Díaz Ordaz government, it must be stated, was caught in a difficult situation. Mexico was the host for the 1968 Summer Olympics, and his government had expended much effort and a large portion of its budget to prepare the physical facilities for these games. Mexico was on display as live television covered the Olympics for a huge international audience. As the date for the opening of the Olympic games drew nearer, student unrest continued. The government acted with sudden repression to eliminate the possibility of worldwide embarrassment.

The government's commitment to the staging of the Olympic games underscored one of the students' main complaints: Mexico's limited resources were needed to deal with other, more pressing needs, such as primary, secondary, and higher education; road building; food subsidies;

From Donald J. Mabry, *The Mexican University and the State: Student Conflicts, 1910–1971* (College Station, TX, 1982), 261–67. Reprinted by permission of Texas A&M University Press.

and medical care for the poor. To the protestors the presence of the Olympics was an artificially imposed event on a nation that needed other forms of government activism.

The author of this selection, Donald Mabry, is a versatile and prolific historian whose research interests and publications include the political right in twentieth-century Mexico, Mexico's relations with the United States, and the Latin American drug trade. As Mabry's narrative of events opens, the CNH (Consejo Nacional de Huelga, or National Strike Committee) has just staged a peaceful demonstration at the Zócalo, the large, open square in front of the government's executive offices in Mexico City. The scene then switches to UNAM (Universidad Nacional Autónoma de México, or the National Autonomous University of Mexico).

To revitalize the movement, the students reached back into the history of Mexican student movements and staged another giant march to the Zócalo, but this time in silence. Perhaps as many as 250,000 persons walked without talking, the only sounds coming from footsteps and the rustle of signs and clothing. By going in silence, the demonstrators avoided any possible confrontation with government forces. More important, they demonstrated that the movement was still alive and that the Consejo Nacional de Huelga (CNH) was still in control. Even critics of the movement had to be impressed at the discipline involved in the undertaking.[1]

The government rekindled the violence by sending the army to take over the Universidad Nacional Autónoma de México (UNAM) on September 18. Why the soldiers who were stationed on the edges of the campus were suddenly called into action remains something of a mystery; the official government explanation was that UNAM had become a center of subversion (which was true), controlled by non-UNAM forces (which was not true), and the government had had to act to clear out this subversion so that normal academic activities could be resumed. The rationale was lame, for numerous schools were centers of subversion (in the sense that the students and their allies were trying to alter the existing political order), and the army occupation meant the end of all academic activities. When the army moved onto the campus, soldiers arrested everyone on sight, some fifteen hundred including parents attending examinations. One goal was to arrest the CNH, but most of its members who were there escaped. Unable to meet in a single place, the CNH had to yield authority to its central coordinating committee. The government, for its part, announced the next day that the army would give up UNAM when university authorities asked for its return; public outrage had had its effect.[2]

The choice of UNAM, rather than the Instituto Politécnico Nacional (IPN) or some other school, for the invasion revealed the importance of UNAM in the movement. Since the army had invaded the IPN in 1956, a similar invasion in 1968 would have been less controversial than that of UNAM. The IPN and some of its vocational schools, where the movement started, were also centers of radicalism and thus likely targets of government ire. UNAM, however, was *the* elite institution and a long-term foe of whatever government was in power. [Gustavo] Díaz Ordaz apparently had a special dislike for the university. At least his government believed that UNAM was the center of the movement and that crushing the university would crush the movement.

The army invasion of UNAM sparked a wave of violence and then the military takeover of the IPN. Street battles between students and their allies, on the one hand, and the army and police, on the other, erupted on September 19, continuing intermittently for days. Voca [Vocational School] #7 near Tlatelolco again became a major battle scene. Porras attacked Prepa [University Preparatory] #4 and El Colegio de México, a prestigious private university, early on September 20, and then hit Voca #5, Prepa #5, and Prepa #9 on the twenty-third. Tensions rose. An army lieutenant killed a *granadero* [member of the government's paramilitary antiriot unit] in the Tlatelolco housing project because the policeman [had] assaulted his mother. [Javier] Barros Sierra resigned on September 23, under pressure from Congress and the executive branch. He believed his task hopeless. More serious, however, the army and police fought students on the IPN campus the same day. That evening and during the following day, it took control of the IPN. The CNH, which had planned to meet there, moved to the Tlatelolco housing project, which became the unofficial headquarters of the movement.[3]

This massive use of force disoriented the movement, as the government intended, but did not stop it. The UNAM junta rejected Barros Sierra's resignation, but he lost some of the moral authority he had had in the movement. Soldiers in jeeps, armored cars, and tanks guarded the main streets of the city, giving the Olympics' host city a strange appearance, for the welcoming signs and banners proclaiming peace and brotherhood floated above these armed contingents. The CNH held a mass meeting on the twenty-seventh in the Plaza de Tres Culturas in Tlatelolco, but it was clear that much of the spirit of the movement was gone; the leaders present called for another to be held there on October 2, followed by a march to the IPN, one [that] they hoped would give new life to the movement. These were tense days for the students, however, for the army and police patrols were effectively breaking the momentum of the movement, and the leaders had to move constantly and secretly to avoid arrest. The willingness to use the army against UNAM and the IPN stifled much of the vocal support of the students and encouraged critics to speak more loudly.

The government sent signals that it believed it had won. On September 28, Díaz Ordaz named two representatives, Jorge de la Vega Domínguez and Andrés Caso (son of Alfonso), to begin the dialogue with the students. The latter were making even greater efforts to convince the government and the public that they would not interfere with the Olympic Games, as some charged, and were willing to have an Olympics truce. They publicly refused to meet with the presidential representatives, however, until the troops were pulled out of UNAM. On September 30, the troops withdrew from the national university, leaving behind them broken equipment, vandalized buildings, and a record of thefts. Quietly, CNH members and the presidential representatives began meeting. On October 1, no one bothered the CNH when it held two meetings on the UNAM campus. Agustín Yáñez, public education minister, began talking of educational reform during the week before October 2. Arrests of persons accused of criminal acts and subversion continued but posed little threat to the movement. CNH representatives met with Vega Domínguez and Caso on October 2 to discuss the demands.

In the late afternoon of October 2, the crowd began to gather in the Plaza of Three Cultures to hold still another rally, to be followed by a march to the IPN campus to protest the presence of troops there; a historic event was in the making, but not the one the organizers had intended. The atmosphere was tense, for army tanks, jeeps, trucks, and soldiers were stationed near the plaza, but they had become a common sight and no efforts were made to prevent persons from assembling. By 6 P.M., a crowd of several thousand, some say five, some say ten, had gathered in the historic plaza with its mixture of Aztec, Spanish Colonial, and modern Mexican architecture. Some were residents of the adjoining Nonoalco-Tlatelolco housing project; men, women, and children had joined the students in what had become a commonplace diversion from the humdrum of everyday life. The plaza had several assets as a meeting place. The army had not taken control of it as it had the IPN or UNAM, and its open area allowed large numbers to congregate. Many residents of the housing project had demonstrated sympathy for the student cause, so the organizers knew they were in friendly territory. The plaza was easily reached from all parts of the city. More important, the Chihuahua building (the apartment buildings were named after states) had a large fourth-floor balcony from which orators could address the crowd below.

The rally was, in fact, a signal of the waning power of the student movement. Its numbers could not approach those reached earlier. The presence nearby of the army unnerved many, and rumors wormed through the crowd that government agents were present. After a few almost perfunctory speeches, leaders announced that the march to the IPN was called off, that it was too dangerous and might provoke a violent reaction from the army.

Shortly after six o'clock the rally became a nightmare as soldiers invaded the plaza, shooting into the crowd. The government contended that the troops advanced in response to sniper fire from the buildings. The reality was different. Shortly before the advance, a helicopter, circling the area, dropped two flares. Soldiers and policemen in the crowd, dressed in civilian clothes, donned white gloves on their left hands, or wrapped them in white handkerchiefs, to identify themselves from the mass. As the soldiers advanced, killing and maiming as they assaulted the fleeing, panic-stricken crowd, some of these white-gloved personnel entered the Chihuahua balcony and arrested those present, taking the opportunity to strike at will or to force them to lie where there was the greatest danger of being hit by flying bullets. Television crews from ABC and CBS, in town for the Olympics, filmed some of the action until they too had to flee to safety. The government forces were attacking everyone, and foreign newsmen were important targets. The films leave little doubt that the army initiated the violence and that innocent women and children were attacked.[4]

The massacre lasted for hours. Crowds fled in waves from one part of the plaza to another, only to turn and run again. Soldiers fired toward the center at the crowds and at each other; the crossfire was indiscriminate. Some soldiers, including those on the balcony, cried "Olympic Battalion!" to identify themselves to their fellows as members of the elite squad organized to provide protection during the games to celebrate peace and brotherhood. Tanks and other armored vehicles blocked passage, but at least their cannonns were not fired into the crowds or the buildings. Students died; children died; women died; and soldiers died. No one knows how many. Certainly more than the fifty-seven the government claimed, perhaps as many as the three hundred the students claimed. Some of the dead and injured were carted away in Red Cross and Green Cross ambulances, when the army finally let them do their work, but others were taken away in military vehicles. Students and their allies claimed that bodies were burned by the government to hide the death toll. There were fires that night in Military Camp One in Chapultepec Park, from which these army units had come and to which the thousands of arrested were taken. Blood flowed that night; the Aztecs had returned to human sacrifice. The elders were devouring their young.[5]

The Tlatelolco massacre made no sense except that it stopped the movement a few days before the Olympic Games opened. Even if one accepts the government argument that snipers had begun to fire from the buildings, one is hard-pressed to explain why soldiers fired again and again into a crowd. Standard procedure would have been to clear the plaza of the crowd and then use sharpshooters against snipers. The goal of the maneuver must have been different. Nor could it have been the arrest of the CNH leaders, most of whom were gathered on the balcony, for agents could have arrested them without any army assault. Certainly, some of the deaths and injuries were the result of poor leadership and panic among the soldiers, who did not know what to do in the face of gunfire, but the white-gloved agents' act of grabbing leaders in the crowd so that they could be shot bespoke another purpose. The government had failed to stop the movement by taking UNAM and had failed again when soldiers occupied the IPN. The Olympics were only days away. Frustrated, angry, irrational men decided to end the movement quickly, not fully realizing that unleashing the army would result in such a catastrophe. Undoubtedly, they intended that some would die and others would be hurt, but that must have seemed a small price if the result was the death of the movement and the arrest of the CNH.

Faced with the infamy of its actions, the government immediately tried to justify those actions. The rationales offered were not surprising. Student snipers fired first; machine gun fire from the Chihuahua building brought in the army to protect the crowd and the residents. Confessions of "leaders" proved that the entire student movement was a conspiracy to install a Communist regime in Mexico and to thwart the Olympics, Sócrates Campos Lemus, of the CNH and IPN, "confessed" that the goal was the abolition of existing institutions and the creation of a workers'-farmers' state, that six snipers were stationed in Tlatelolco to fire on soldiers and *granaderos* if they tried to break up the meeting, and that a number of distinguished intellectuals and politicians had financed the movement. The army, for its part, produced a list and photographs of arms it found in buildings around the plaza; these "proved" that there was a revolutionary conspiracy.

Confessions and arrests of known leftists are easily arranged, although the validity of such confessions is dubious, but the arms list reveals the weak case of the government. Found were three submachine guns, fourteen .22-caliber rifles with telescopic sights, five shotguns, four carbines, twenty-one revolvers, ten angle irons, 425 shotgun shells of 12 and 16 gauge, nine hundred .38-caliber cartridges, 1,850 cartridges for the twenty-twos, twenty of .38 caliber, five of 7 millimeter, equipment for recharging cartridges, a radio transceiver, some dynamite, and a few other minor pieces. Since over 70,000 persons lived in the 144 buildings, the list is surprising only because so few weapons were found. More weapons would probably have been found in the same number of apartments along Lake Shore Drive in Chicago. As evidence that a revolution was planned or that an army was needed in Tlatelolco, the list did not vindicate the stupidity and cruelty of government officials responsible for its release.

The student movement of 1968 died in Tlatelolco on the night of October 2; the burial took place on December 1, when the strike was officially ended. Those student leaders who were not killed or arrested on October 2 went into hiding in the city or disappeared into the states or exiled themselves in countries around the world. Other students absented themselves as well; it was not a good time to stay in Mexico City. The horror of Tlatelolco lent credence to the widespread belief among students and their supporters that the government was killing or imprisoning students months after October 2; perhaps it was. Some prisoners were not sentenced for over a year after their arrest. The Olympics came and went, for the Olympic Committee, by a close vote, decided not to withdraw from Mexico. A rump CNH (now in the hands of diehards) made announcements to the media and held various meetings with the two presidential representatives. The six demands were never met. More political prisoners filled the Mexican jails. . . . Students became more apathetic and suspicious; some retreated into drugs and drink, sex and cynicism. . . .

Student strikes have not ended permanently at UNAM. Local strikes in *facultades* and *escuelas* continue. After the memory of 1968 is dim enough and a cause célèbre is discovered, UNAM students will once again shut down the university in protest. Students will continue to be concerned about grades, examination policy, and unpopular teachers and administrators, as well as social and political issues. But these strikes or movements will forever be different from what they once were. The horror of Tlatelolco will hang over UNAM for decades to come.

Notes

1. IPN (Instituto Politécnico Nacional) students had used the tactic in the 1950s, and physicians had used it in 1965. On the physicians, see Evelyn P. Stevens, *Protest and Response in Mexico* (Cambridge, MA, 1974), 213. See also Luis González de Alba, *Los días y los años* (Mexico City, 1971), 116–124, for a participant account of the march and the strategy behind it.

2. González de Alba, *Los días*, 128–129. Daniel Cosío Villegas in "Como en Gracia: Los siete años de una tragedía," *Excelsior*, Sept. 28, 1968, took the view that the army occupation was unjustified because the army was winning.

3. Bert Quint of CBS News reported student sniper fire in his televised report, Sept. 24, 1968, CBS News, Vanderbilt University Television Archives. See also *El Sol de México*, Sept. 24, 1968, Roll 2, #128, Instituto Nacional de Antropología e Historia, microfilm collection on students.

4. See videotapes from ABC News and CBS News for Oct. 3, 1968, Vanderbilt Television Archives.

5. Octavio Paz, *The Other Mexico: Critique of the Pyramid* (New York, 1972) makes this argument.

III Revolution

The Roots of Revolution

---

5 María Elena Díaz ◆ The Satiric Penny Press for Workers in Mexico, 1900–1910: A Case Study in the Politicization of Popular Culture

In the decade before the outbreak of the revolution, Mexico saw the appearance of newspapers intended for a working-class readership. María Elena Díaz explores the content of these newspapers during this crucial period in Mexican history. Born in Havana, Cuba, Díaz earned a master's degree in anthropology at the University of Chicago and a doctorate in history at the University of Texas. Her subject in this essay—the "penny press"—consisted of inexpensive (therefore "penny") publications intended for working-class readers. Mexico had experienced some industrialization in the late 1800s so that by the first decade of the twentieth century there was an audience for this type of publication. Students should focus their attention on the subjects covered in the pages of the penny press and, in particular, on the presence (or absence) of evidence of working-class discontent in the years preceeding the revolution of 1910.

In 1908 an editorial in *El Diablito Rojo*, itself a penny journal, made some disparaging, yet revealing, remarks regarding the impact of the penny press of the time on Mexican workers:

> There is hardly a worker in Mexico [today] who every morning does not bring to his workshop or leave at home the paper of the day in addition to the small papers dedicated to workers which he acquires with

From María Elena Díaz, "The Satiric Penny Press for Workers in Mexico, 1900–1910: A Case Study in the Politicization of Popular Culture," *Journal of Latin American Studies* 22 (October 1990): 497–525. Reprinted by permission of the author and the *Journal of Latin American Studies*.

real pleasure. In the big paper [the worker] looks for the daily news . . .
in the small weekly he looks for a joke, a caricature, an anecdote; something that can distract or instruct him. . . .

But is that small press useful to its readers? . . . No: the journals
constituting the small press all call themselves defenders of the worker
and preach a dangerous gospel: hate of the bourgeois . . . [so that to-
day] The worker already sees the bourgeois as an ogre. . . .

The small press does not . . . demonstrate to the worker the evils
brought about by rebellion or violence, instead it tries to flatter the proletariat, indeed defending it in its own way when it is victimized, but
only by fomenting in him a bad attitude toward his work.[1]

Several important characteristics of these journals that will be discussed at some length in this article are referred to in the above passage:
the widespread diffusion of the penny press among Mexican workers in
the years before the revolution; the entertaining, educational and political functions of these popular weeklies; and the depiction of issues on
working-class consciousness and class conflict in their pages. These observations immediately suggest the significance of a popular press tradition in the making of the Mexican working class.

Most histories of the working class have consisted of institutional
studies on the formation and development of the Mexican labor movement.[2] The prominent place that the Mexican Revolution holds in the ideology and historiography of that country, however, has also inevitably
brought much attention to bear on questions dealing with the role of labor
in the revolution. Traditionally, as if to highlight the revolutionary thrust
of Mexican labor, most works dealing with the prerevolution period have
understood labor's militancy as reflected in the major strikes of those
years, the (recurring) influence of revolutionary ideologies such as anarchism, and the role of the Mexican Liberal party and of anarchist leaders
such as the Flores Magón brothers.[3] More recently, however, Rodney
Anderson has questioned the preeminence of anarchist ideas in the years
preceding the revolution and has drawn a picture of a Mexican working
class steeped instead in the ideology of liberalism, a political tradition
hegemonic over wider urban sectors of Mexican society.[4] Similarly, Alan
Knight, in his revisionist study of the Mexican Revolution, has done much
to deflate the alleged revolutionary role of the Mexican working class
during those years.[5]

In this article, I wil show through careful textual analysis that the
ideological currents that found expression in the pages of the widely read
satiric press for workers represented either a democratic liberal embrace
of the "people" or, more specifically, the "worker's" causes, or the latter's
adherence to the cause of democratic liberalism. Given the sociological
significance that, I will argue, this penny press had in its time, the (less

revolutionary) political tradition it reflected and disseminated must have also played a major role in the making of the Mexican working class. In this sense, the evidence represented by these penny weeklies overwhelmingly supports Anderson's and Knight's revisionist contentions. But, while Anderson tends to play down the class consciousness of the nascent Mexican working class, the discourse emanating from these satiric publications, I will claim, evinces a rather vigorous sense of working-class consciousness (albeit not a revolutionary one).[6] In fact while, properly speaking, nothing much was new in terms of content in the liberal opposition discourse of these satiric journals, what was somehow new, at least in the press tradition, was precisely the specifically working-class perspective that was wedged into the democratic liberal discourse in most of these papers.

A great deal of emphasis will be placed in this article on the actual language and discourse found in the pages of these penny journals. The purpose is not only to convey as vividly as possible the voices of the papers of the period but, more importantly, to draw out the meaning that lies in both content and form, and point out its implications. Indeed, what can be described as *popular* in these publications lies in their tone and journalistic style. Furthermore, a good part of the defense of the worker carried out by this press related to the cultural sphere: in the way it highlighted class-related ways of speaking and being in the world. In fact, the very existence of this press constituted a cultural affirmation of the popular tradition, vis-à-vis more elite-oriented journalistic traditions.

Finally, this article also attempts to call the attention of the social and cultural historian to the merits of this penny press as a source. For these satiric weeklies effectively document popular attitudes and reactions to the myriad (major and minor) events of the day: a typhus epidemic, a strike, the advent of trams, inflation, scandals, temperance campaigns, entertainment, etc. It is clear that these cultural texts have a much wider relevance to researchers than has previously been acknowledged.

Although Mexican society was not to witness the formation of a strong labor movement until after (and as a result of) the Mexican Revolution, the decades of the 1860s and 1870s had already witnessed an effervescent movement of labor into mutualist societies and a wide diffusion of ideas related to the merits of such associations. At the forefront of this movement were alleged "anarchists" who had emigrated from Europe, particularly Spain, bringing to Mexico ideas and experience in labor organization. Later, with the consolidation of the Porfirian regime in the 1880s, most of this activity was curtailed together with most of the opposition to the federal government. The most radical tendencies of the nascent labor movement were subdued by co-optation, and/or force, before they had a chance to crystalize. It was not until the turn of the century, and coinciding with the emergence of Mexico's first industrial proletariat, that much of the previous labor activity started reconstituting itself. The opening of the twentieth century witnessed a resurgence of labor protest as well as political opposition to the regime.[7] An important aspect of this resurgence was the re-emergence of a bolder, more independent and combative press and, along with it, these often overlooked penny weeklies.

The antecedents to this popular penny press are found in two other journalistic traditions of the nineteenth century. Parallel to the nascent tradition of a working-class press in the 1860s and 1870s, another kind of publication had already made its acerbic presence felt. A significant proliferation of illustrated satiric publications after the 1840s, and particularly during the 1870s, dealt with national politics and addressed the main issues of the day: monarchism versus republicanism, anticlericalism, and various liberal positions depending on partisan loyalties. Directed to the well-educated public and to polite society, they were sophisticated in their discourse, full of classical and learned allusions, and they relied on an intellectual and political framework far removed from the cultural universe inhabited by the popular sectors of Mexican society. In short, this nineteenth-century satiric press constituted a vehicle for expression and an arena of political debate for the Mexican elites.

By the first decade of the twentieth century, however, these two traditions of journalism—a worker's press and an elite satiric press—without disappearing themselves, gave way to a new phenomenon: a satiric penny press directed at the working class. Unfortunately, these popular publications for workers have been neglected not only by labor and social historians, but also by most surveys and histories of Mexican journalism.[8] Apparently scholars have not considered them respectable or significant enough to merit their attention—a fact which may betray an attitude similar to that of many contemporaries, namely a dash of scorn for a popular discourse considered "vulgar" by groups with somewhat different cultural habits and tastes. Not until recently have these penny weeklies for workers received some attention, but this has been mainly in relation to their graphic aspect. This interest has been due to the reappraisal of their main illustrator, José Guadalupe Posada—an artisan printmaker of popular Mexican themes who has been called "the Father of Mexican Art" by no less than Diego Rivera, one of the great exponents of the Mexican muralist art tradition.[9] The journalistic value of these periodicals as vehicles of the social, labor, and political currents of the time, however, and their semiotic value as artifacts of popular culture—due to their accessibility for their readers and the possibility of communicating with a wide new audience for their writers—have not been properly examined.[10]

On the other hand, satiric papers such as *El Hijo de Abuizote* and *El Colmillo Público* enjoy a high reputation in Mexican historiography for their staunch opposition to the Porfirian regime and for their popularity. The anarchist connection of the former via the Flores Magón clique and the Liberal Clubs, and that of *El Colmillo* with the Mexican Liberal party are well known and have been frequently underscored in the literature.[11] And yet, in spite of their purported revolutionary aura, both of these satiric weeklies had a more definite "middle-class" character—both in tone and content—than any of the penny weeklies for workers. The references made in these papers and the way in which their satiric attacks were encoded presupposed more sophisticated interlocutors than those sought out by the penny press for workers. Moreover, the objects of satire in these two weeklies more often than not had to do with the intrigues of high politics; and when allusions were sometimes made to the experience of "the people," the latter were portrayed in a generic way—more as Mexican citizens, perhaps even poor Mexican citizens, than as Mexican workers.

In contrast, the lively and biting penny weeklies for workers introduced and identified themselves with headings such as: (*El Papagayo*) "Independent weekly, jester, fond of a bit of fun, scourge of the bourgeoisie and of bad comedians, defender and unconditional comrade of the working class" or, more soberly, as in the case of *La Araña*, "Independent weekly for workers." This new genre appropriated and literally popularized the more elitist satiric press of the nineteenth (and twentieth) century. Similarly, it imbued the all too frequently dull and sober tradition of the worker's press with a new tone and style which made it immediately accessible and far more appealing to the politically uninitiated common man and to those not intellectually inclined among the working class. For this was, after all, an illustrated press designed to entertain—compact, varied, easy, and fun to read. Whatever their political and didactic functions, these satiric journals never lost sight of their ludic function, a feature that no doubt accounted for a good deal of their success.

The boom in this new genre at the turn of the century is apparent in the fact that, out of thirty-six satiric periodicals listed for that decade in one of the most complete bibliographic compilations, at least fifteen—or 40 percent—explicitly identified themselves as weeklies for workers.[12] In marked contrast, none of the satiric papers listed for the previous century identified itself in its program or heading as directed at "workers." Furthermore, for a small press, the circulation of these periodicals does indeed seem impressive. Although there are no reliable and exact figures for their circulation, *La Guacamaya*, one of the most successful to judge by its longevity, claimed a peak figure of 29,000 copies in several issues.[13] In comparison, the circulation of the important and popular official daily *El Imparcial* ran from 40,000 to 100,000.[14] These figures suggest a relatively wide diffusion of the satiric penny weeklies for workers and point to the sociological significance of this press for its capacity to disseminate ideas and to shape public opinion. In this sense, these popular journals merit at least as much attention as any of the other more "respectable" opposition papers of the period.

While it has been almost impossible to determine who was behind these penny papers, some evidence seems to point to minor writers of comedies and poetry, lawyers, and perhaps individuals related to the small printing business, that is, James Cockcroft's "low-status intellectuals," as well as some educated artisans.[15] The writers, however, sometimes stressed their "humble" origins, working-class extraction and their solidarity with the people.[16] At any rate, the social origins of the owners, editors, or contributors does not necessarily determine the class character of these satiric papers except in the most reductionist of senses.[17] Rather, what may better define the character of these cultural texts is their intended audience and the groups who identified with, appropriated, and consumed them. The analysis of the discourse found in the pages of these penny weeklies will attempt to demonstrate their popular working-class character. In addition, the contexts in which this press circulated constitute an index of the occupational character of the audience for these weeklies.

These satiric penny papers seem to have circulated widely and to have reached "workshops, factories and rural work centres," as attested by one of these journals.[18] Letters and complaints by workers from factories and workshops appearing in these publications further support this contention.[19] Furthermore, these weeklies reached other states beyond the capital, mainly through distribution mechanisms such as subscriptions and agents who received special rates by the hundreds.[20] Textile factories, given the huge potential audience they represented in a concentrated area, seemed particularly suitable places for their sale and distribution. But given the subversive quality of most of these weeklies, their distribution in workplaces was not always easy. One paper protested that it did not circulate in the factory of Santa Rosa, Nogales, because workers there were afraid of a Mr. Flores, "the scarecrow of the papers that defend the working class." The latter did not allow any salesman around the town nor in the factory, and he even tried to intercept the weeklies arriving by mail. Any worker who dared to promote any of these papers would immediately be fired.[21] The incident gives a glimpse of the distribution mechanisms of this particular press and of the kind of obstructions its circulation could find.

In short, as the contemporary remarks of *El Diablito Rojo*, quoted at the beginning of this article, suggested: the satiric penny press was indeed a popular press directed to and consumed by workers. Its popular character lies both in the working-class audience to which it catered and among which it circulated, and beyond that, in the true "rank-and-file" quality of this press, manifested in its more entertaining and commercial aspects.

The next characteristic of these satiric weeklies that I wish to examine is the emergent sense of working-class consciousness found in the discourse that informs their pages.[22] As already mentioned, the character of these satiric journals was explicitly predicated upon the self-designated function of "defending the working class." As such, their main purpose was adamantly, and often fiercely, to denounce the attitudes and practices of groups considered antagonistic to the working class and to do so with one of the most powerful rhetorical tools of subversive discourse: satire. The logos of these papers literally illustrated this purpose: that of *La Araña* (The Spider) typically pictured a spider trying to catch several upper-class individuals dressed in frock coats, while other elements of society such as the police, clergy, and tram conductors—all favorite targets of satire and symbols of the alliance characterizing the Porfirian regime—were already caught up in its deadly web.

A rough and brief analysis of the social categories used in the discourse of these journals reveals that the category of "working class" seemed to refer to both independent artisans and industrial workers. The workshop and the factory are the recurrent contexts of the workers depicted in these journals, while the office or commercial settings hardly ever cropped up.[23] Similarly, the term did not seem to encompass rural workers or peasants, who tended to be ignored by this press, nor did it include the Indian population itself. Furthermore, the sectors to which the term applied can be specified further if we scrutinize the groups to which this category was opposed—the "we" versus the "other." The main category to which *el obrero* (the worker) was usually opposed was *el burgués* (the bourgeois), and less often to *el capitalista* (the capitalist). This main opposition recurred constantly and was apparent in most of the logos and programs of these papers. Other categories, however, joined in with that of "the bourgeois" (or instead of him) in opposition to that of "the worker." An issue of *La Guacamaya* pointed to these elements succinctly in a caricature entitled "Modern Calvary."[24] In it, a man termed "working class" is crucified while his heart is pierced by a man with a lance entitled "overseers and masters." At the foot of the cross, men dressed in frock coats and labeled "bourgeois" gather in their hats blood-coins coming out of the worker's wound. The relationships are clear: the overseers directly oppress, extort, and victimize the worker, and the bourgeoisie obtains the benefits and profits. Thus, even though there were variations in the specific form that class consciousness acquired in the different papers, the boundaries of solidarity between groups seem to be quite uniform. The main polarization posed was therefore between the bourgeois and the worker, and other variations such as administrators, masters or owners of workshops, contractors, and foremen became apparent in the cases of abuses recurrently reported in the pages of some of these satiric papers. Also apparent is the fact that not all wage workers were included in the category of "workers," as can be seen from the exclusion of foremen and overseers.

Another category appeared recurrently in the discourse of these weeklies—*el pueblo* (the people)—pointing to a social identity less distinct than that discussed above. Though more diffuse, however, the term did not embrace all sectors of society indiscriminately, as in the Micheletian tradition of republicanism where it is roughly equivalent to the citizens of a republic: workers, peasants, petty bourgeois, and bourgeois.[25] Rather, and in accordance with the new currents of social reformism also prevalent in Europe, particularly after the 1840s, the term applied to the "lower classes" (the traditional "populace") and embodied a latent sense of class conflict. Widespread in these papers also is a pervasive hostility towards the *rotos*, the slang term employed by the urban poor to refer to the middle classes who sought upward mobility and differentiation from the lower echelons of society.[26] Hence, in these periodicals, the term "the people" acquired a specific reference, as became manifest in its frequent use as a rough equivalent to "the worker," especially in contexts not strictly related to labor. As such, it was often opposed to the very same groups as the latter.[27] Indeed, what seems to be taking place is the conflation of the republican term "the people" with a laborist current—often with utopian socialist resonances—whose main category is that of "the worker."

At the forefront of the battles taken up by the penny press were the battles fought in the cultural domain of language itself (and the attitudes reflected therein).[28] One of the most pervasive protests in these penny journals—and one reflecting a strong awareness of class distinctions and conflict—was that against the prejudices and scorn with which the well-to-do regarded the worker. *La Cagarruta* perceptively drove this point home in noting that "those who wear shirts and have calloused hands" were called "drunkards of *pulquerías* [shops where pulque, a native alcoholic beverage, was sold], while "those who wear suits and frock coats, whose artistic heads are well combed and perfumed," were termed "decent people."[29] And *El Diablito Bromista* complained that the subsidized press usually depicted workers as "drunkards," "lynchers," and "debased."[30] Similarly, *El Papagayo* complained that the worker in Mexico was not considered "a rational being, but a beast of burden."[31] Finally, with an unusual sensitivity to linguistic behavior, *El Diablito Rojo* observed that the scholar called the people "populace/the well-off [called him], scum/. . . the aristocrat, plebeian/ and the rich, rag tag." *El Diablito Rojo*, on the other hand, called him "brother, comrade."[32]

A way of responding to such scorn was, of course, to retaliate with similar terms, applying epithets such as "greedy," "cruel," and even "imbecile" to the bourgeoisie, thus using language as a weapon. At other times, however, the reaction of these periodicals to the prejudices of polite society was to counteract these by advancing a more respectable view of the worker. Such alternative views, for instance, would depict the worker as more noble and respectable and often showed the influence of Proudhonian utopian socialism in its strong re-evaluation of manual labor. In an editorial piece entitled "Who Is the Worker?" in one of the most progressive satiric papers, *Don Cucufate*, the latter view was advanced in the following way:

> The worker is the indefatigable fighter who makes a society great, he is the thermometer of the great machine of progress. . . . He is the Herculean arm of the arts and sciences who builds statues and immortal temples; he is the one who founds cities and makes them powerful with the strong beat of his hammer . . . he is the great artery of humanity.[33]

This quasimythical (and "proto-Brechtian") vision of the worker extolled in lofty discourse the value of physical labor, seeing it as the basis of civilization and progress. It set the common man within the particular context of labor from which his relation and contribution to society derived. But above all, it portrayed him as a positive, active, and creative social being, and as a historical agent.

In many journals, however, this defense took on a patronizing tone as when workers were portrayed as "the helpless and destitute," as the "wretched souls" always victims of ill-treatment, or as the "destitute classes," "the humble," and "the poor."[34] This secular view of God's poor, where the worker is portrayed in a predominantly passive way, as a victim of superordinate groups and social evils, was common to some currents of humanitarianism prominent in the discourse of certain brands of reformist republicanism, although not even the most radical currents of anarchism in the Spanish Peninsula, for instance, ever rid their discourse totally of such Christian resonances either.[35] While the former view tended to correspond to the most progressive currents of laborism and political

thought of the time, it sometimes coexisted with the latter one stressing
the workers' meekness.

Working-class consciousness was most obviously manifested in these
penny journals, however, in their discussions of labor issues and in what
this type of discourse presupposed. Although the labor protests of this
press exhibited a relatively wide range of positions, the views extolled in
their pages did reveal an assimilation of the fundamental notion that man
qua worker was entitled to certain legitimate rights—a principle which
by no means had always been clear and transparent to workers, not to say
to other sectors of society. An editorial entitled "Think, Workers, That a
King in Former Times Could Not Provide Himself with the Satisfactions
That You Enjoy Today" appearing in *Don Cucufate*, drove the above points
home with a tartness possible only through satire. The piece, one of the
most devastating to appear in the penny press of the decade, satirized the
official press's view on workers' rights and aspirations, the logic behind
that view, and the conformity and acquiescence that the press expected
from this class:

> Just like that, in a sententious and doctrinaire tone, "El Imparcial" [the
> official daily] states:
>   A worker complains of a certain abuse; of a particular injustice
> etc. etc.? . . . Bad show. He should remember that the kings of former
> times, in comparison to today's workers, were wretched. . . .
>   And workers who have all these comforts, who are paid so well,
> who are treated as high-class ladies in their workshops. . . . What do
> they want? The millions of Carnegie for a single hour of work?[36]

At stake are conflicting notions of workers' rights: the official and
parodied one shared by certain sectors of Mexican society, and the implied one which legitimized the workers' right to fair labor conditions.
The recognition of such a principle constituted a major landmark in the
formation of working-class consciousness, and its implementation would
presuppose the forging of new political and social realities. In this sense,
the history of the Mexican working class, or rather of the Mexican labor
movement, is the history of how those rights were conceptualized at different points; and only beyond this point, of the practical struggle to bring
about their implementation against the opposing views and interests of
other groups.

While not all the satiric papers for workers manifested the same awareness and commitment to labor issues, there was a certain uniformity among
them as to what were regarded as the main "abuses," "extortions," and
"injustices," that "bourgeois" and other oppressors perpetrated against
the working class at that time. Ill-treatment, reduction of wages (and/or
inadequate ones), unpaid overtime, fines, arbitrary firings, the *tiendas de*

raya (company stores), usury, and the problem of *enganchadores* (labor contractors) were the recurring issues at the forefront of the labor protests found in these papers. More rarely, but also raised, were the issues of child labor, the eight-hour day, and Sunday rest.[37]

Significant as well, in a few of the papers, was the nationalist tone adopted by some of the labor protests. While there were some satiric attacks against gachupines (Spaniards), those against Yankees were more prevalent.[38] Some of these weeklies, particularly the virulent "anti-Yankee" *El Diablito Bromista*, protested at the privileged treatment given to the foreign worker and the discriminatory treatment and work conditions of the Mexican vis-à-vis the "sons of Uncle Sam." Similarly, as early as 1900, an editorial entitled "How Much Our Cousins Love Us!" in *El Diablito Rojo* complained that the Empresas del Ferrocarril del Distrito paid Yankee conductors 120 pesos a month; but that after Mexican workers had been trained for the job they were only paid forty-five pesos a month.[39]

Generally speaking, most of these papers called for or published cases of abuses, at some point or another hoping to correct them by denouncing them publicly in their pages and by calling them to the attention of the pertinent authorities. In this sense, participation by the public was a major feature of some of these weeklies for workers, particularly *La Guacamaya*, and the publication of letters and complaints became a major weapon to combat "injustices."[40] Sometimes it is difficult to determine whether this practice of dealing with concrete and isolated cases of abuse in specific localities was due to self-censorship or to a lack of articulateness—since, after all, continuously reported cases added up to a general experience. The following denunciation relating to one of the textile factories, which seem constantly to have bred conflict, was concrete and to the point, and in many ways a representative one:

> The mere name of the Metepec factory produces in workers an effect not unlike a shower of boiling water. The factory of folly, of abuses, and of tyrannies has invented another genre of exploitation. Now, instead of paying with money, it pays with chips that only have value in company stores. And the authorities, don't they intervene? Can it be because this is not an anti-reelection club?[41]

Although polite appeals to authorities to look into and remedy a situation were common in this press, this particular piece mocked the inefficacy of authorities in the resolution of such problems. The final remark cynically implies that authorities were ready to intervene only in cases of political opposition, but not when owners or administrators infringed the law regarding workers. At any rate, the implication of these protests usually was that the role of authorities ought to be to guarantee the implementation of the law and to mediate and ensure justice in cases of labor conflict.

What seems to be a major distinguishing factor in these weeklies, however, is the kind of action considered legitimate in the face of abuse, and, more specifically, their attitudes toward the strike. Since this was still a delicate issue at the time, support for it was often qualified (although a few straightforward statements of principle can be found in the most radical papers) and lack of support was implicit in the absence of coverage or mention of the issue. The papers themselves made this distinction, as an issue of *El Chile Piquín* attested. The latter dedicated a front page caricature entitled "First Enema for *La Guacamaya*" to a criticism of this paper for not maintaining a pro-labor line by ignoring the railroad workers' strike of 1905. And in an editorial entitled "The Defenders of The People?" in that same issue, it stated that, at the beginning, *La Guacamaya* had carried its program of defense loyally, but proof that it no longer cared for the oppression of the poor lay in the fact that *it had not covered the strike* of the railroad workers (my italics).[42] Thus, according to the radical view, covering a strike was equated with defending workers' rights, and implicitly (and sometimes explicitly) with support of the strike's objectives and its legitimacy as a means of resistance. Other issues, however, such as the role and purpose of association, and the extent of group solidarity and articulated class conflict, separated the stances of these papers as well, although perhaps not in such a clear-cut manner as that of the strikes.

A spectrum of orientations, then, made its way into this—by no means homogeneous—small press for workers. Perhaps the main currents at stake were those represented by the three most important weeklies in this satiric press tradition: *El Diablito Rojo* (1900–1901/1908–1910), *El Diablito Bromista* (1903–1910), and *La Guacamaya* (1902–1911). The fact that these three major penny papers had the fortune to survive for several years is a sign of a stability and popularity rarely achieved at this time by an independent press, and particularly by the small press business, where penny journals appeared and disappeared in just a matter of months. Briefly, *El Diablito Rojo* represented a brand of reformist mutualism, critical of the politically co-opted workers' associations of the period. While, at least initially, the staunchest opponent of the Porfirian regime among its colleagues of the small press, its radical protests remained for the most part political. In labor matters, on the other hand, *El Diablito Rojo* represented the most conservative position in the labor spectrum: it often decried class conflict, opposed trade unionism, and denounced strikes. In fact, this paper peddled an unashamedly middle-class ethos and assumed a patronizing tone that somehow set it apart from the rest of the penny press for workers. Its somewhat excessive helpings of respectability, however, must not have been a total liability for apparently it did enjoy an audience among the working class.[43]

El Diablito Bromista, on the other hand, represented the most consistently radical position in this press. In labor matters it emphasized class conflict, was an exponent of the nascent trade unionism, and advocated the strike. Politically, it was an outspoken critic of the Porfirian regime, particularly after 1904. Finally, *La Guacamaya*, the most commercially oriented of the three, tended to be somewhat eclectic and erratic. It nonetheless manifested a vigorous, although somewhat spontaneous and intuitive, sense of class conflict. Similarly its support of the strike was not always consistent or clear. While, during its first years, it refrained from direct political attack and on occasions opportunistically took a pro-Porfirian politican stance, after 1906 it became an opponent of the regime, and later sponsored Bernardo Reyes as its presidential candidate. The next section will examine at greater length how these different positions were articulated.

Th most moderate labor orientation among these papers translated into the mutualist tendencies which had been gaining ground since the latter half of the nineteenth century. The key to the type of society promoted was the "material" and "spiritual" progress of workers through self-help, an idea that took hold during a period in which the absence of work benefits and pensions for the working class grew into major issues. The idea of spiritual progress was based on the need for the "regeneration of the worker" through education—moral, civil, and intellectual.[44] By the turn of the century, these societies, though progressive in their conception, were beginning to be discredited for their failure to fulfill their purpose. In an editorial entitled "Mutualism Among Mexican Workers, Neither an Element of Progress, Nor a Source of Well-being," *El Diablito Rojo* criticized these societies, declaring that:

> Mutualism has not fulfilled its promises . . . [today] it is nothing but a contract by which a member contributes a weekly amount of money in exchange for certain conditional aid in case of necessity and as long as the latter continues to pay his contributions.[45]

It went on to regret that these associations had been turned into "electoral clubs" and made to march in electoral demonstrations. But, on the other hand, *El Diablito Rojo* also criticized those associations that settled their conflicts through strikes.[46]

Instead, *El Diablito Rojo* promulgated the "regeneration" of the worker via savings, thrift, and education; that is, his material well-being was to be achieved through the workers' ability to accumulate some "capital," rather than through any concerted pressure and collective action to improve his working and living conditions. To improve these, this paper was a firm proponent of cooperative savings banks for workers—a position that was clearly influenced by Louis Blanc's brand of utopian socialism.[47] Likewise, spiritual "regeneration" was to be achieved through education and through the assimilation of a set of values associated with a yearning for respectability—above all, hard work, "hygenic recreation," good manners, intellectual progress, dedication to domesticity, cleanliness—which were designed to edify the members of that class and integrate them into "society," i.e., civilization.[48] What was in fact being promoted was really a synthesis between some laborist currents of utopian socialism and a democratic liberalism which never abandoned the fundamental notion of laissez-faire—now to be accessible to the worker and artisan. The emphasis here was on the need to integrate "the (wretched) people" into the Mexican nation as first-class citizens as a recognition of their contribution to the nation as laboring classes.

While most journals saw the need, promulgated by liberalism, for the intellectual and civic education of workers—and indeed, to a certain degree, this could be said to be one of the functions carried out by these weeklies—the systematic diatribes on morality and respectability that filled the pages of *El Diablito Rojo*, particularly after June 1908, were not found in other papers. Nowhere was the rather bourgeois patronizing ethos of that weekly more clearly revealed than in its own criticism of the discourse found in other penny journals for workers. According to *El Diablito*, the small press had presented the "bourgeois" as "a synonym of tyranny . . . bourgeois, for them, is the boss, the capitalist, the owner. All those whom the worker has to serve." And to this it responded: "No, dear worker friend. The bourgeois is the educated people . . . ; the worker that has attained some comfort . . . for a worker can also be a bourgeois."[49]

Diametrically opposed to the position described above was that of *El Diablito Bromista* and other more short-lived radical papers such as *La Palanca, Don Cucufate,* and *El Chile Piquín.* In the discourse of these weeklies, the resistance function of workers' organizations was closely linked to the idea of the strike. This, precisely, constituted the key element of the emerging notions of trade unionism of the time. In a piece in 1905 denouncing the abuses to which railroad workers were subjected and particularly in relation to the complaint that they were not being paid for overtime, the *Chile Piquín* commented:

> It is about time that the worker was respected by those who exploit him, but to reach that goal it is necessary that all the artisan guilds unite so

that in that way they will be able to resist successfully the terrible pressure of the capitalist. . . . Union gives strength. . . . As long as we remain disunited and on our own, enterprises will try to extort us infinitely.[50]

The idea of organization for the purposes of exerting pressure and fighting the capitalist went far beyond the mutualist ideals of workers' self-help. Clear in this piece as well is the sense of overt class struggle between opposing interests—again a conceptual leap from the isolated cases of the "bad bourgeois" and isolated abuses in workshops. Pieces like this represent the form that the denunciation of abuse often took in the discourse of the more radical papers. And although appeals to authority were usually made in constitutional terms and the discourse did not tend to overstep such constitutional boundaries, this labor orientation nonetheless called for organized action by workers as a protection from abuse, judiciously refusing to rely exclusively on the authorities' disposition to ensure justice. Underlying this, however, this most progressive current of labor still conserved an ideal of government or the liberal state in which it was capable of standing above such labor conflicts and mediating between antagonistic groups.

Labor conflicts and strikes were registered by this press as early as 1900, but particularly after the appearance of *La Guacamaya* in 1902. Although indirectly mentioned, Cananea was not overtly discussed anywhere in this press, perhaps because these weeklies did not circulate there.[51] Railroad strikes, however, made their way into this press, as well as protests and spontaneous strikes in small workshops.[52] The bulk of the complaints in these penny weeklies, however, were related to labor strife in the textile factories in every part of the nation. *El Diablito Bromista* noted early the "infinite abuses" perpetrated in these factories which could be inferred from the "constant correspondence" it claimed to receive from those centers.[53] Río Blanco—the locus of perhaps the major strike in the decade—appeared often in these papers. We know that at least *La Guacamaya* circulated in this factory around the time of the major strike in January 1907 because, a few months earlier, it had protested that 165 papers had been confiscated from its distribution agent in that town after a complaint about the factory had appeared in its pages—one incident, among many, that shows that these papers were not really free from the harassment of authorities and factory administrators. *La Guacamaya* then admonished the authorities of Río Blanco that if they did not want the attention of the journal:

to look again into the matters [abuses] of that factory, (if the reports stop) it will be because [the management] doesn't give us [any further] motives for doing so, for our duty as honest journalists is to bring into the open the defects not only of the political administration but also private ones whenever the helpless worker is extorted.[54]

The reverberation of the Río Blanco strike of 1907 could still be felt a year later in editorial comments and in commemorations of the events. In fact, one of the most devastating cartoons attacking the Díaz regime ever published in this press was in connection with the violent repression of that strike. For the annual homage to Porfirio Díaz on April 2, *La Guacamaya* published a caricature in which workers offered Díaz a wreath of skulls with a banner that read: "Workers of Río Blanco, 7 January, 1907."[55] The tragic labor events were clearly politicized here and directly linked to the caudillo Díaz. After this strike, the penny weeklies took up labor issues with renewed intensity, but their editorials began to grow more theoretical. It is hard to say whether the trend toward generalizations and abstractions was deliberate or a reflection of a temporary reduction in labor discontent.

The working-class consciousness manifested in these penny journals was, however, by no means apolitical. For beyond the properly labor issues found in these satiric weeklies for workers, a discourse is apparent in which more purely political notions and protests were articulated as well. The political discourse of these penny journals—sometimes referred to as "Jacobinism"—approached all the classic issues of nineteenth-century democratic liberalism but gave these a popular twist as it reinforced its own sense of class consciousness. Indeed, the republican notion of sovereignty residing in the people acquired literally a popular meaning: more and more "the people" were defined as the popular and laboring classes (though the term did not yet seem to apply, in these papers at least, to the peasantry and the Indian population). This popular angle made issues intelligible and palatable to this sector of Mexican society, and transformed liberal protests into political causes championed by the working class.

Perhaps the major political notion disseminated by these weeklies was that of a constitution as a national institution representing the law (as against arbitrary rule) and guaranteeing the *rights* of a citizen, however these may be defined. Attacks on the regime's callous behavior in trampling on political rights guaranteed by the Constitution of 1857 were ubiquitous and varied from abstract statements to more concrete ones hitting out at Díaz's caudillismo, lack of effective suffrage and freedom of the press. It is interesting to observe the ways in which the critiques appearing in this press handle the fundamental issues of this type of democratic republicanism for the consumption of their intended audience.

One recurring issue in the penny press—and a favorite target of satire—was the arbitrariness of the police. The figure lay close to the daily experience of the common man and illustrated well some of the basic notions of constitutionalism. The hostility against the gendarme—a symbol of authority par excellence in popular culture (and often a veiled one for the regime)—was gaily and irreverently manifested through ridicule, and no vestiges of legitimacy can be found associated with him in the pages of this press. Portrayed as a brute, corrupt, and a drunkard, he embodied the antithesis of law and order, the negation of justice, and the rule of force. His constant persecution of, and intrusion into, the everyday life of the common man was resented, while his discriminatory application of the law against the people and his subservience to the well-off and powerful did not go unnoticed. A caustic piece written in slang and entitled "The Love for the Police" rhetorically asked:

> Why is it that our comrades have so much respect for the police? Why that love, those caresses, that obsequiousness toward them? . . . There are many individuals in the police who forget the circumspection that the guardians of order should have, and talk to their comrades and have drinks with them . . . ; they are *compadres* of such and such a tavern owner; and when they remember they are the authority, this is to hit with his stick, and make use of their gun and make all kinds of arbitrary acts and run down whoever comes in their way. . . . That is why things between the people and the police are as they are. Indeed grim![56]

One of the central issues at stake in the liberalism of most of these papers was precisely the extension and implementation of the political rights entailed in a democracy to "the people"—where this term acquired the meaning examined before in this paper. The awareness of the stark differences that separated rich and poor, and the "double standard" to which each group was subject before the law constituted key notions in the political discourse of these papers. They surfaced particularly in some comic popular vignettes, which were a permanent feature in these satiric periodicals. In the following excerpt from one vignette, two characters pondered with irony the discriminatory treatment and extortions to which the people, in contrast to the rich, were subject. It dealt with the issue of obligatory bathing decreed by the authorities to fight an epidemic of typhus that had broken out in Mexico City at the time. This measure elicited strong resentment and ridicule from the satiric press mostly because of the logic behind it and the practices of the police, who arbitrarily detained and mistreated people in the streets to take them to public baths. Two men talked in a tavern:

—And since we are talking about baths, tell me, why is it that the popu-
lace are being pulled by the hair to be sent to the baths?
—Ah! You are such a fool, the thread always breaks at its weakest point.
—Does that mean then that only the rich truly enjoy that individuality?
—Obviously, but since when is this not so? Don't you see that there are
always differences in everything?
—I see! That I did not know, but I am noticing now, and if I am right
that means that the real people have to be extorted and s . . . upon, since
after all they are humble and shut up.
—Now you are speaking the sole truth.[57]

These sketches were a standard feature in most of these penny weeklies. They constituted one of the most original aspects of these journals
and merit a study of their own. Written in Mexican popular dialect, some
are practically impossible for an outsider to the subculture to decipher.
The translation into standard English quoted above has lost the ingenuity
of its discourse and the forcefulness of its rhetoric, wherein lay most of
its humor and part of its meaning. The best exponents of the genre constitute true pieces of virtuosity that take pleasure in speech play—punning,
making use of double meanings, or simply experimenting with the possibilities of the dialect. These languages games—known as *albures*—are
still a widespread popular practice among the Mexican lower class and
flourish particularly in the setting of the bars and *pulquerías*. Their appearance in these periodicals constitutes an example not only of the use
of popular customs as a way of appealing to and entertaining a specific
audience, but also of the utilization of folklore as a vehicle for transmitting ideas of social and political protest.

Present as well in the discourse of these weeklies, although not so
prevalent as other motifs, was the anticlerical theme—a central issue in
the liberalism of the nineteenth century. These protests, when in fact they
appeared, were directed, for instance, against the laxity manifested in the
implementation of the Reform Laws against the clergy and the church.
The latter were depicted in these journals as corrupt extorters of the people,
and as the symbols of the dark "antirational" forces of dogmatism.[58]

More important, however, were the patriotic themes diffused by this
press as part of its civic educational campaigns. The major symbols of
this secular mythical discourse were the figures of Cuauhtémoc—symbol
of the indigenous resistance to the Spanish Conquerer; Miguel Hidalgo y
Castilla—the "father of the Mexican Nation" who had fought for the liberation of foreign oppression and independence; and finally, Benito
Juárez.[59] Juárez was perhaps the central historico-mythical figure of democratic liberalism, not only because of his association with the Constitution of 1857 and the Reform Laws, but also because he was proclaimed

"the Son of the People," because of his "humble" and sometimes specified "Indian" origins. In this way, he was made to represent as well the
interests of "the people."[60] A speech made by the "Jacobin" Guillermo
Prieto, and published in a paper, made this point clear by stating that
Juárez was, more than anything, a "symbol" of patriotism, and that was
why "not the knowledgeable nor the privileged classes; not the artisans
of power and wealth, but the wretched and suffering people appropriate
him, bless him and praise him as a benefactor and as a father."[61] Sometimes the patriotism of the people—who were the ones to die for the country and who celebrated the civic holidays—was counterposed to the lack
of national sentiments among the well-off.

The thrust of this patriotic sentiment was the right to sovereignty
without any foreign intervention and domination. While often directed to
the celebration of the historical event of independence from the Spanish,
this patriotic sentiment could sometimes be turned into virulent attacks
against the United States—particularly in the case of *El Diablito Bromista*
which consistently published cartoons and pieces with anti-imperialist
themes.[62] Briefly, the main grievances associated with this issue were the
invasion and occupation of Mexican territory by the United States; the
Díaz's government's over-friendly attitude, servility to, and alliance to
the Northern "cousins," and, perhaps closer to the workers' experience,
the already mentioned complaints about the abuses that "foreign capital-
ists" perpetrated against Mexican workers.

Most of these penny papers not only enunciated liberal constitutional
notions, they also took up in their pages opposition campaigns against
manifestations of "bad government" at provincial levels, and, more significantly, against Porfirio Díaz and his cronies as well. Indeed, ridicule
of the caudillo must have constituted an important psychological and political weapon against the regime; even though the discourse of these
weeklies never reached the point of questioning the liberal republican
system itself.

It is often difficult to identify correctly the political orientation of
these journals due to the censorship of the press during the Porfirian regime—a pervasive complaint in these penny journals. Their silence or
lack of open and direct attacks against the regime cannot always be interpreted as support for it since they often subjected themselves to self-
censorship, particularly in political matters. *El Duende*, for instance, stated
in its program that it would not deal "with issues of high politics for, in
the times in which we unfortunately live, the emission of thought is suppressed by *la psicología* [the slang term used for censorship]."[63] A statement such as this, however, entailed in itself a protest and presumably
indicated some kind of opposition.

But despite the possibility of self-censorship, certain patterns can be discerned. Pro-government positions, for example, can be inferred in journals such as *El Pinche* and *La Tranca*, two short-lived penny journals, for though occasionally suggesting some protest, they seemed to be characterized, contrary to the rest of the papers, precisely by their lack of political content. Instead, miscellanea of a frivolous nature with little or no social content whatsoever filled their pages. The case of *La Guacamaya*, on the other hand, is more interesting and complex, for while its satires and labor protests were among the most cutting ones, it had taken, up to 1906, an apparently pro-government position, as its occasional "homages" to Porfirio Díaz attest.[64] A caricature entitled "A Dance of *Compadres*" that appeared early in this weekly illustrates well how some of these papers could carry out their critiques without implying any political involvement. In this cartoon, various exploiters of "the people" —"bourgeois," "contractors," "clergy," and "tram conductors"—danced together and stepped over him, while a "policeman" toasted the health of his compadres.[65] Nowhere in sight are there symbols of higher political figures.

More often, however, these periodicals betrayed some opposition— however veiled—to the Porfirian regime and always did so from the political stance of a democratic and constitutionalist liberalism. At stake was often a critique of different aspects of the Díaz regime, without touching the top of the pyramid. The implication of this was often ambiguous: either the caudillo was above such abuses and a victim of his surrounding groups, or implicitly he was behind all of them. Hence, most weeklies started out by launching their satiric attacks against the police, then against higher echelons in the political machine such as governors and jefes politicos, the *científico* groups and even the armies of "friends" and adulators of the president.

El Diablito Rojo, however, "broke the ice" as early as April 1901 and began to involve the caudillo directly in its critiques. It protested the adulation of Díaz—whom it termed "the God Man"—even by the so-called independent press; called state governors "sultans"; and also attacked caciques and public employees. Indeed, its indictments were directed against the whole governmental apparatus, including other groups, such as the clergy, as well.[66] In its following issue, however, it went all the way and raised the fundamental issues of the liberal critique, openly proclaiming its opposition to the regime. It ended its editorial in the following bitterly ironic tone:

> But then . . . Down with the Constitution which is only good to be torn into pieces! Down with the Reform Laws which everybody steps over! Long live the dictatorship! Long live the friars! Long live the Yankees

who are the ones who control! Down with patriotism! Down with shame!
Long live Belém [the jail] which awaits us![67]

El Diablito Bromista, while a strong and consistent opponent of the
regime, did not publish an openly anti-Porfirian cartoon until 1904, when
the re-election crisis of that same year was under way.[68] *La Guacamaya*,
as already mentioned, had been either apolitical or declaring support for
the Porfirian "peace" until 1906, when it became strongly anti-Díaz. At
the end of the decade, it supported Bernardo Reyes for the presidency
(although later compromised and called only for his vice-presidential
candidacy).

At any rate, by 1908 the three satiric papers which had managed to
survive were expressing their opposition and political attacks in an
increasingly direct and unambiguous way. In contrast to the above-
mentioned cartoon of 1904 entitled "A Dance of Compadres," for instance,
a somewhat similar caricature in 1908 was made explicitly political. In it,
the bourgeois, the clergy, the military, and the *científicos* danced around
Porfirio Díaz to the well-known tune of a children's game called "Doña
Blanca."[69] In the center, Díaz, "Our Lord," stands in his presidential chair
diligently handing bags of silver and gold to "Doña Blanca." On one side,
and excluded from the "circle," a wretched and sweating figure of "the
people" stands watching. It should be noted that in both caricatures the
element of class consciousness is present and iconographically depicted
by placing the figure of "the people" in the foreground and in opposition
to the other groups—a common strategy in these cartoons to portray the
popular point of view of the weekly. The key distinction between the two
cartoons, however, lies in the latter's explicit portrayal of political figures as allies of other civilian groups; and the whole crowd—the Porfirian
political machine and its cronies—as the oppressors of the people.

By 1909, however, the cartoons and the direct political attacks against
Porfirio Díaz were toned down once more in these papers. The critiques,
as in earlier periods, were again directed against more diffuse social and
political evils—as if the genie of a free press set loose for a few years had
been put back into the bottle by the so-called *psicología*.

To sum up, despite the more or less open political discourse and tactical opposition to the Porfirian regime, there were further distinctions
and latent tensions among these weeklies on the issue of how far resistance and reform should go; and this was particularly manifest on the
labor question which we have examined at some length. In general, however, without sacrificing its entertaining function, this popular press attempted to politicize and educate the emerging Mexican working class
along the principles of democratic liberalism. And, while the grievances
of the laboring class and the people were eventually associated with the

supposedly liberal regime of Porfirio Díaz, the relevance of that system and of a state that should protect and mediate labor's rights was never brought into question.

The emergence and wide diffusion of this (quasi-commercial and political) penny press for workers represents the appearance of a new institution in the popular culture of the time. One, in effect, which narrowed its "popular" constituency to an urban "working class" by delineating this identity against other groups, by focusing particularly on issues related to that group, and by expressing them in the language of that group. The working-class consciousness, however, and class conflict displayed in this press—where indeed currents of utopian socialist thought could indeed be felt—was placed within the dominant discursive context of a reformist democratic liberalism. For at no point was the system of production and the political structures questioned in their totality—in any kind of antiprivate property and antistatist discourse—as properly socialist and anarchist positions would demand (at least in principle, if not always in practice). Radicalization of the working class would require first an apprenticeship in that yet "ideal system" of democratic liberalism and an exhaustion of the possibilities it offered to labor. Hence, without completely discarding the possible influence of anarchism in the emerging labor movement of the pre-revolution decade, perhaps it is fair to say that its role has been exaggerated, particularly if the discourse of this widely disseminated workers' press is examined, and if these penny weeklies are in fact any guide to the ideas that went into the making of the Mexican working class. Indeed, the constitutionalist path taken by the Mexican labor movement in 1915 perhaps should not be surprising, given the notions and views circulating widely among Mexico's urban workers in the decade before the revolution.

Notes

1. *El Diablito Rojo*, 22 June 1908, p. 2.
2. Most labor histories of Mexico tend to start with the Mexican Revolution, while previous periods are dealt with in terms of "background" material. Barry Carr, *El movimiento obrero y la política en México, 1910–1929* (Mexico, 1976); Marjorie Ruth Clark, *Organized Labor in Mexico* (North Carolina, 1934); A. López Aparicio, *El movimiento obrero en México* (Mexico, 1958).
3. Jorge Basurto, *El proletariado industrial en México* (Mexico, 1975); John Hart, *El anarquismo y la clase obrera mexicana, 1860–1931* (Mexico, 1980); James D. Cockcroft, *Intellectual Precursors of the Mexican Revolution, 1900–1913* (Austin, 1968). Moisés Navarro's study of labor during the Porfiriato in Daniel Cosío Villegas (ed.), *Historia moderna de México: el Porfiriato. La vida social* (Mexico, 1957), pp. 344–76, attempts to cover other currents influencing

labor as well, but remains an impressionistic account and one which is too narrow in its choice of sources.

4. Rodney D. Anderson, *Outcasts in Their Own Land: Mexican Industrial Workers, 1906–1911* (Dekalb, Ill., 1976); "Mexican Workers and the Politics of Revolution, 1906–1911," *Hispanic American Historical Review* vol. 54 (1974) pp. 94–113.

5. Alan Knight, *History of the Mexican Revolution* (Cambridge, 1986). "The Working Class and the Mexican Revolution, 1900–1920," *Journal of Latin American Studies*, vol. 16, Part I (1984), pp. 449–59.

6. Anderson seems to assume that because democratic liberalism is a bourgeois ideology, it somehow precludes working-class consciousness. Thus he sees Mexican workers steeped in this ideology speaking as "working Mexicans," rather than as "Mexican workers." See his "Mexican Workers," p. 113.

7. A. López Aparicio, *El movimiento obrero*, pp. 103–15; Hart, *El anarquismo*, pp. 59–80 and 112–39; Cockcroft, *Intellectual Precursors*.

8. Important histories of Mexican journalism such as Stanley Ross's *Fuentes para la historia contemporánea de México: periódicos y revistas* (México, 1965), vol. I; and the article "Periodismo" in José R. Alvarez (ed.), *Enciclopedia de México* (México,1977), vol. X, pp. 222–56, either mention them as a genre in passing or ignore them altogether. Even Manuel González Ramírez in his specialized work on the political cartoon in *Fuentes para la historia* focuses exclusively on well-known satiric periodicals such as *El Hijo de Abuizote* and *El Colmillo Público* but seems totally oblivious to this other tradition; note how his reference to Posada's cartoons deals exclusively with the period after the revolution.

9. There is a prolific literature on Posada and some on the satiric penny press which he illustrated but mostly written from an aesthetic point of view. The most recent, and one of the best, is *Posada's Mexico*, edited by Ron Tyler (Washington, D.C., 1979). For Diego Rivera's homage to Posada, see p. 123.

10. Some important exceptions to this trend have been Anderson, *Outcasts*, who has made some use of this press to document the textile strikes of the period, and, more obliquely, the political ideology permeating Mexican workers at the time. Also William D. Raat, in "The Antipositivist Movement in Prerevolutionary Mexico, 1892–1911," *Journal of Interamerican Studies and World Affairs*, 19 (Feb. 1977), pp. 83–98, briefly examines some political issues raised in this press. Finally, Charles Cumberland refers to them in passing and although, in terming them "truly proletarian papers," he recognized their significance properly, he misidentified them as anarchist and socialist. See *Mexican Revolution* (Austin, 1952), p. 25.

11. See, for example, Victor Alba, "The Mexican Revolution and the Cartoon," *Comparative Studies in Society and History*, vol. 9, no. 2 (Jan. 1967), pp. 121–36; Manuel González Ramírez, *Fuentes: la caricatura política* (México, 1979); Cockcroft, *Intellectual Precursors*.

12. Jefferson R. Spell, "Mexican Literary Periodicals in the Nineteenth Century," *Modern Language Association of America*, vol. 52 (1937), pp. 308–12, and "Mexican Literary Periodicals in the Twentieth Century," *Modern Language Association of America*, vol. 54 (1939), pp. 848–52. One of the thirty-six satiric journals listed by Spell, only six are identified as directed to workers. In my own examination of the publications found in the University of Texas (UT)

collection, I have found that, for the decade of 1900–1910, nine other satiric journals in Spell's list were also dedicated to the "defense of workers." For the nineteenth century, Spell did not list a single satiric journal dedicated to workers. A preliminary examination of at least those satiric publications found in the UT collection for that period confirmed this.

13. *La Guacamaya*, 5 Dec. 1907, p. 3. This weekly published the figures for its press run for a period of five months. They fluctuated between 19,000 and 29,000. *El Diablito Rojo* reported on 22 June 1908 (p. 2) that 25,000 issues of the penny press circulated in Mexico. The less popular and short-lived *Don Cucufate* reported a press run of 12,500 in its issue of 29 July 1906.

14. Ross, *Fuentes*, vol. I, p. xxiv, and "Periodismo" in *Enciclopedia de México*, p. 247. The widespread oppositional weekly of Flores Magón, *Regeneración*, increased from 11,000 to 30,000 by 1906, according to Cockcroft in *Intellectual Precursors*, p. 124. The best-known opposition satiric weekly *El Hijo de Ahuizote* had a circulation of 24,000 according to González Ramírez, *Fuentes*, p. xxvi.

15. Rafael R. Rodríguez, founder of *La Guacamaya*, was said to be sympathetic to the working class "of which he had also formed a part" (*La Guacamaya*, 23 Aug. 1906, p. 2). A rival weekly claimed that Rodríguez was a comedian "who did not know anything about labor issues" (*La Palanca*, 4 Sept. 1904, p. 3). Fernando Torroella, the latter's successor after 1906, and owner of other short-lived penny papers, wrote poems which often appeared in the "literary section" of these journals, and also published poetry books (see *El Duende*, 15 Nov. 1904, p. 4). In an editorial, Torroella also mentioned other contributors to *La Guacamaya*, among whom was a Rafael Solórzano, described as "skilled with the pen and with the hammer" (*La Guacamaya*, 23 Aug. 1906, p. 2). Often the address of the journal's director, to whom all matters regarding the weeklies were to be sent, was an *imprenta*, or printshop, pointing to the possible involvement of typographers in the business of the penny press. Further evidence of this may be the fact that many of these papers advertised popular novels published in their own press. *La Chihuantlahua*, for instance, offered a coupon worth ten cents in its issue of 11 Oct. 1906, for what it termed the "beautiful" novel *The Ripper of Women*. Furthermore, José Guadalupe Posada, the cartoonist for most of these papers, worked in a printshop and at the time had the status of an artisan, not of an "artist," as today may be imagined. Finally, at least one of the directors of the most "educational," and rather middle-class, weekly *El Diablito Rojo*, was Jacobo E. Escalante, a lawyer as indicated by his title of *licenciado*; see issue of 1 July 1901, p. 4.

16. See *La Guacamaya*, 23 Aug. 1906, p. 2. *El Chile Piquín*, 26 Jan. 1905, p. 2. *El Diablito Rojo*, 25 May 1908, p. 2.

17. This issue has been particularly debated with the advent of the commercialization of popular culture. See Iain Chambers, *Popular Culture and the Metropolitan Experience* (London, 1987). E. P. Thompson approaches the problem in yet another way in his brilliant discussion of the "style and tone" of the radical writers Hazlitt and Cobbet. See *The Making*, pp. 746–62.

18. *El Diablito Rojo*, 22 June 1908, p. 2.

19. Rodney D. Anderson has read hundreds of workers' letters appearing in these and other papers and they would appear to echo the concerns expressed in the penny weeklies. "Mexican Workers," p. 96.

20. *La Guacamaya* had agents in several locations: Orizaba, San Luis Potosí, Aguas Calientes, Toluca, Hidalgo del Parral, and Guanajuato. See the list of these

agents with standing debts published in the issues of 18 Jan. 1906, p. 2; and 2 Sept. 1902. It definitely circulated in the factory of Río Blanco (13 July 1906, p. 2). *El Eiablito Bromista* reopened its operations in 1 Oct. 1906 after a suspension of several months with a feature welcoming complaints from "the operators of textile factories and from all workers in general," p. 3. *El Diablito Rojo* circulated, at least in 1900, in Zacatecas, Peubla, and Guanajuato. See its debtors' list in issue of 8 Oct. 1900, p. 2.

21. *El Diablito Rojo*, 11 June 1900, p. 3. This is an interesting incident for, while apparently circulating among workers, at that time *El Diablito* dealt more with political protest than with properly labor issues.

22. The term "working-class consciousness" is used here in a Thompsonian sense—meaning the subjective/cultural expression of the objective experience of class in a particular historical moment and vis-à-vis another class. This sense of class consciousness does not, however, necessarily imply a "revolutionary" consciousness.

23. One of the cultural expressions of class is the precise meaning that the term assumes at different historical moments. The term "working class" today, for instance, tends to refer only to industrial workers. The transformation in meaning already undergone by the term at the turn of the century—as reflected in this penny press—is even more marked if contrasted with its use in the nineteenth-century press, where, according to Arturo Obregón, it tended to aggregate artisans, office workers, and, in general, all wage workers. See "La prensa obrera," p. 37.

24. *La Guacamaya*, 5 Dec. 1902, p. 1; and *El Chango*, 28 May 1904, p. 1.

25. For a discussion of the Micheletian concept of "the people," see David James Fisher, "The Origins of the French Popular Theatre," *Journal of Contemporary History*, vol. 12 (1977), pp. 461–97.

26. The use of the term in these journals corroborates the definition given in Francisco J. Santamaría, *Diccionario de mejicanismos* (Mexico, 1974).

27. For an explicit statement of the sense of the term "*el pueblo*," see *El Moquete*, 16 Feb. 1905, p. 2.

28. The following discussion on the ideological struggle over language, sign, or naming carried out in the pages of this press is based on the ideas of the well-known Marxist language theoretician Mikhail Bakhtin.

29. *La Cagarruta*, 20 Dec. 1906. p. 4.

30. *El Diablito Bromista*, 14 July 1907, p. 3. This exact characterization of "workers" and "the people" is common to other countries as well. See P. Lidsky, *Los escritores contra la comuna* (Mexico, 1971), p. 109.

31. *El Papagayo*, 17 July 1904, p. 2.

32. *El Diablito Rojo*, 2 July 1900, p. 2. The original text reads as follows: "El sabio te llama populo/El roto, peladaje/. . . El aristócrata, plebe/El rico, desarrapado/*El Diablito* te dice mano, guadarnís, valenciano."

33. *Don Cucufate*, 17 Sept. 1906, p. 3.

34. *La Chintatlahua*, 23 Sept. 1906, p. 2; and 21 Oct. 1906, p. 2.

35. For similar humanitarian currents permeating a reformist republicanism in France, see Maurice Agulhon, *The Republican Experiment, 1848–1852* (Cambridge, 1983), pp. 9–11 and 20–21. For socialist and anarchist discourses in Spain, see Iris Zavala, *Románticos y socialistas: Prensa española del XIX* (Madrid, 1972), pp. 131–32.

36. *Don Cucufate*, 20 Aug. 1906, p. 2.

37. On the specific issues of the eight-hour day and child labor, see *La Guacamaya*, 8 Sept. 1902, pp. 1–2, and 7 June 1906; *El Diablito Bromista*, 8 Oct. 1905, p. 2.

38. See for instance references to gachupines in *El Moquete*, 5 May 1904, pp. 1–2; *La Chinhuantlahua*, 30 Sept. 1906, p. 2; *El Diablito Bromista*, 15 Nov. 1903, p. 1. It is hard to say why attacks against this group are not more prevalent in this press given the widespread stereotypes and prejudice against gachupines in Mexico. Perhaps it is due to the fact that such stereotypes were more related to individuals in the commercial sector and did not fit so well the main targets of attack in this press, i.e., the "bourgeois" and the "overseers."

39. *El Diablito Rojo*, 25 June 1900, p. 2. *Primo* (cousin) was a term often employed for North Americans to satirize the kinship relation implied. For other related protests, see *El Diablito Bromista*, "Contempt for the National Worker," 20 Oct. 1907, p. 2; 26 Jan. 1905, p. 2; "Mexican Capital and Yankee Enterprises," 6 March 1904, p. 2; *La Guacamaya*, 3 May 1906, p. 1; *El Chile Piquín*, 19 Jan. 1905, p. 2.

40. Most of the journals put their columns at the disposition of workers to report abuses. See, among others, the program of *El Pinche*, 18 Jan. 1906, p. 2; *La Tranca*, 21 July 1906, p. 2; *El Duende*, 15 Nov. 1904, p. 1. Not all of them actually published many direct protests from workers, however. Only *La Guacamaya* seems to have followed this policy consistently, at least until about November 1907, when a shift toward more abstract pieces from the editor coincided with a change in the administration of the paper. See issue of 22 Oct. 1907, p. 2.

41. *La Palanca*, 12 Oct. 1904, p. 2. The list, however, is endless since many weeklies continuously reported abuses. See, for example, *El Papgayo*, 28 Aug. 1904, p. 2. *La Guacamaya*, 4 and 18 July 1906, p. 2.

42. *El Chile Piquín*, 2 Feb. 1905, p. 2. Indeed, the latter may have been pointing to a change in policy related to a new administrator of the paper. The change took place around December 1905, at the latest. The new administrator, Fernando Toroella, who had directed and/or collaborated for two other satiric weeklies in 1904, eventually became the owner of the popular *La Guacamaya* around August 1906.

43. *El Diablito Rojo* did not explicitly identify itself as a worker's weekly until June 1908, when its head changed into "a worker's combat weekly," and its editorials became systematically dedicated to issues of mutualism and the edification of workers. During its initial period (1900 to 1901), however, it only had a "special section" dedicated to "mutualism" and labor issues. See issue of 7 May 1900, p. 2.

44. *El Diablito Rojo*, 11 Feb. 1901, p. 2; *Don Cucufate*, 5 Aug. 1906, p. 2.

45. *El Diablito Rojo*, 8 June 1908, p. 2. See also *El Diablito Bromista*, 1 Oct. 1905, p. 3.

46. *El Diablito Rojo*, 25 May 1908, p. 2.

47. G. D. H. Cole, *Historia del pensamiento socialista: Los precursores, 1789–1850* (Mexico, 1957), vol. I, pp. 171–79; and M. Agulhon, *The Republican Experiment*, pp. 35–37.

48. For *El Diablito Rojo*'s tenacious crusades for respectability see, among other issues: 26 Oct. 1908, p. 2; 30 March 1908, p. 2; 14 Dec. 1908, p. 2; 19 April 1909, p. 2.

49. *El Diablito Rojo*, 22 June 1908, p. 2.

50. *El Chile Piquín*, 22 June 1905, p. 2. See also issue of 25 Jan. 1905, p. 2. For statements in support of the principles behind the strike see: *La Palanca*, 20 Nov. 1904, p. 2; *El Diablito Bromista*, 31 May 1903; 3 Feb. and particularly 14 Feb. 1904, p. 2; 6 Jan. 1907. For the role of government as mediator see *El Diablito Bromista*, 31 May 1908, p. 2.

51. *Don Cucufate*, 29 July 1906, p. 3, for instance, noted that 300 Mexican workers had been assassinated by "Green's cronies" who had violated the national territory and not by Mexican federal troops, as a paper in Texas, *El Alacrán*, had reported.

52. *Don Cucufate*, for instance, celebrated the happy conclusion of this strike. See issue of 20 Aug. 1906, p. 1. See also *Chile Piquín*, 2 Feb. 1905, p. 2.

53. *El Diablito Bromista*, 7 Aug. 1904, p. 2.

54. *La Guacamaya*, 13 July 1906, p. 2: "*La Guacamaya* in Río Blanco." For other incidents of harassment, see *El Diablito Rojo*'s report quoted on p. 8.

55. *La Guacamaya*, 9 April 1908, p. 1. See also *El Diablito Bromista*, 6 June 1907, p. 2; and 7 July 1907, p. 2, where it analyzed the current strike of "more than 1,500 workers" just months after the "massacre of January that had left so many deaths behind."

56. *El Diablito Rojo*, 26 Feb. 1901, p. 4. For other protests against the police, see *El Diablito Bromista*, 4 July 1907, p. 1; *Don Cucufate*, 3 Sept. 1906, p. 1; *La Guacamaya*, 12 March 1908, p. 1; *La Chihuantlahua*, 23 Sept. 1906, p. 1; *El Diablito Rojo*, 14 Feb. 1901, p. 2.

57. *La Guacamaya*, 26 April 1906, p. 3. The original text reads as follows: — Y ya que hablamos de baños dime, ¿cómo se explica eso de que a todos los peladitos los llevan a puro chaleco a la regadera?/ —A que tu tan a . . . maje, el hilo se revienta por lo más delgado . . ./ —¿Quere decir que solo los rotos gozan de la mera endividualidá?/ —Me parecen rieles, pos si no ahora cuando, ¿no ves que en todo hay sus diferencias?/ —¡Ah! Pos no lo sabino yo, pero ya me voy fijando y asigún me pienso eso quere decir quial verdadero pueblo hay que estorcionarlo y jo . . . robarlo quialcabo es humilde y calla./ —Hasta que adijiste la mera neta.

58. *El Papagaya*, 11 Sept. 1904, p. 1. *El Chile Piquín*, 2 March 1905, p. 1. See also the series of anticlerical cartoons in *La Guacamaya*, 8 Feb. 1906, p. 1; 12 April 1906, p. 1; and 19 April 1906, p. 1. In reality, the most consistently anticlerical worker's penny weekly was *La Guacamaya*; others, for the most part, ignored this theme. There were, however, some satiric penny weeklies like *El Jacobino* (1901) and *El Padre Eterno* (1908) consisting solely of anticlerical campaigns, but these were directed to a general public and were not "worker's" papers.

59. On these national holidays, special "serious" issues were often dedicated to patriotic figures. On Cuauhtémoc see: *El Diablito Bromista*, 18 Aug. 1907, p. 4 and 8 and 16 Sept. 1907, p. 2. On Hidalgo see: *Don Cucufate*, 17 Sept. 1906, p. 1; *La Guacamaya*, 21 July 1902, p. 1; *El Diablito Bromista*, 18 July 1903, p. 3. On Juárez see: *La Guacamaya* 21 July 1902, p. 1; *El Diablito Bromista*, 18 July 1907, p. 3.

60. *Don Cucufate*, 29 July 1906, pp. 1–2; *El Chile Piquín*, 20 July 1905, pp. 1–2. *La Guacamaya*, 21 July 1902, p. 1.

61. *El Diablito Bromista*, 29 July 1906, p. 2.

62. See for instance the cartoons of *El Diablito Bromista* in the issues of 11 Aug. 1908 and 5 April 1908. An editorial piece in the 21 July 1907 issue of *El*

Diablito Bromista was entitled "Mexicans Alert! The U.S. wants to take over a piece of the national territory" (referring to the Magdalena Bay and Lower California). Similarly, in the 20 Oct. 1907 issue, the editorial title read "Unashamed Protection of the Foreign Worker." For other examples of this anti-U.S. nationalist thesis, see *El Duende*, 3 Dec. 1904, p. 1; *El Chile Piquín*, 26 Jan. 1905, p. 2; *El Diablito Bromista*, 25 Oct. 1903, p. 2.

63. *El Duende*, 25 Nov. 1904, p. 1. The term *la psicología* was coined in the 1890s after a judge ruled that transgressions against [censorship] laws should be determined by also taking into consideration "psychological theories" related to the effects of innuendo. Hence, a journalist should be held responsible not only for what he may have literally drawn or written, but also for what could be implied from his drawings or writings. See Victor Alba, "The Mexican Revolution," p. 127.

64. For one such homage, see, for example, *La Guacamaya*, 31 May 1904, pp. 1–2.

65. Tram conductors were a symbol of the technological "progress" brought about during the Porfirian regime. Perhaps reflecting as well the initial popular reaction and resistance to the introduction of this machine into the urban landscape, these trams were depicted in these papers as public enemies and as worse than "natural epidemics" in terms of the danger they represented and the accidents they had provoked. *La Guacamaya*, 5 Oct. 1906, p. 2. *El Diablito Bromista* criticized the many concessions given to the company running the trams when these vehicles constantly clashed and killed, 30 Aug. 1903, p. 2. See also *El Diablito Bromista*, 11 Oct. 1903; and *El Chango*, 9 June 1904, p. 1. *La Guacamaya*, 14 Jan. 104, p. 1.

66. *El Diablito Rojo*, 29 April 1901, p. 2.

67. *El Diablito Rojo*, 5 May 1901, p. 2. Shortly after this, *El Diablito Rojo* disappeared from publication, perhaps victim of the widespread repression against anti-Díaz publications that took place between 1901 and 1902, whereby more than forty-two papers were closed down (J. Cockcroft, *Intellectual Precursors*, p. 102).

68. *El-Diablito Bromista*, 14 Feb. 1904, p. 2.

69. *El Diablito Rojo*, 9 March 1908, p. 1.

---

6 Donald C. Hodges ◆ What Is Sandinismo?

The Sandinista Revolution of 1979 brought down the powerful Somoza family that had controlled Nicaragua since the mid-1930s. One of the reasons for the Sandinistas' success was their ability to communicate their revolutionary message to the common folk of Nicaragua. Their methods are discussed in this selection by Donald Hodges, who combines the scholarly credentials of a philosopher with a wide-ranging interest in Latin

From Donald C. Hodges, *The Intellectual Foundations of the Nicaraguan Revolution* (Austin, Texas, 1988), 184–96, 322–23. Reprinted by permission of the University of Texas Press.

*American social and political movements. A native of Texas who grew up
in Argentina, Hodges has many publications on the influence of Marxism
and other radical movements in Latin America.*

On a Sunday afternoon in December 1980, I watched the changing
sunlight on the giant red and black portrait of [Augusto César]
Sandino hanging from the cathedral in Managua's Plaza de la Revolución.
Next to me was a man who had lost both of his sons in the struggle against
[Anastasio] Somoza [Debayle]. "Poor little ones," he sobbed, "but we
got rid of the sonofabitch!" Then his tone abruptly changed: "But I am a
Sandinista; I am *not* a Communist."

His position was shared by others. Nicaraguans felt attracted to the
figure of Sandino but considered communism something alien. Many of
them denied that Sandino had any affiliation with Marxism. For the present
most people rightly believe that, unlike Cuba, Nicaragua is not a Communist country—although it may be on the road to becoming one.

As Tomás Borge, the minister of the interior, noted in a May 1981
interview, "The bourgeoisie accuses us of falling into totalitarianism. But
it forgets that here in Nicaragua we have freedom of the press; that we do
not use torture; that there is no *paredón* [wall against which prisoners are
executed by firing squads]; and that an opposition exists. . . . We do not
owe imperialism any explanation. But we will say to Latin Americans
that we are not going to become another Cuba." Although Cuba was the
crucible of the Nicaraguan Revolution, the latter differed from Cuba's
revolution in many ways: it recognized a plurality of political parties; it
tolerated ideological diversity; it had not officially executed anyone; it
had a collective leadership; and it favored a mixed economy. Borge also
commented on the differences in foreign policy, noting that "the Nicaraguan Revolution has its own opinions about Afghanistan and Poland."[1]

Although Sandinismo has been favorably received in Cuba, it has
been openly criticized by Soviet Marxists. They would like to see it displaced by the more orthodox Marxism of the Nicaraguan Socialist party
(PSN). Ironically, the Soviet Union recognizes both the Sandinista National Liberation Front [FSLN] and the PSN as legitimate representatives
of the Nicaraguan Revolution, whereas Cuba recognizes only the FSLN.

In Nicaragua I talked to Sandinistas who were not Marxist-Leninists
and to Marxist-Leninists who were not Sandinistas. But the leaders of the
Nicaraguan Revolution claim to be following both Marx and Sandino.
They are the ones who say that "Sandinismo is Marxism-Leninism applied in Nicaragua." They add that "Sandinismo is Christianity applied in
Nicaragua."[2] What they mean to convey is that Sandinismo is a compos-
ite of several revolutionary ideologies.

Paradoxically, there are Sandinistas who subscribe to the new Marxism and there are Sandinistas who do not. Actually, Sandinismo developed in two quite different ways, both under FSLN sponsorship. One was popular and folkloric, the other intellectual and systematic. The first consisted of Sandino's political legacy as recovered and transmitted by the FSLN, the "projects, attitudes and beliefs, mode of behavior and concrete actions of Sandino."[3] The result was a collective memory and heroic image of Sandino as a man of the people. Originally, his objectives and the reasons behind them were "transmitted from father to son among the peasant families that had become involved directly or indirectly in the Sandinista campaign."[4] Later, the FSLN disseminated these stories among other Nicaraguan families, stories transmitting a desire for social change and opposition to imperialism and dictatorship. Commitment to this popular version of Sandinismo required neither an acceptance of communism nor a knowledge of Marxism-Leninism.

The second form of Sandinismo reinterpreted and reformulated its popular content in light of the new Marxism. In legitimizing Sandino's thought, [Carlos] Fonseca transformed it into the ideological axis for adapting Marxism-Leninism to Nicaragua. Consequently, commitment to this advanced form of Sandinismo also signified an acceptance of communism.

For the FSLN the first or undeveloped version of Sandinismo served as a stepping-stone to the second or developed version. If we recall how Sandino's pre-Communist ideology helped prepare his Defending Army to accept the principles of communism, we have reason to believe that the FSLN deliberately adopted a similar policy. Not until after the victory over Somoza and the ensuing consolidation of revolutionary power did the FSLN embark on a massive campaign to raise the political consciousness of Sandinistas to a higher level.

In response to the U.S.-backed counterrevolutionary offensive in March 1982 and the declaration of a wartime national state of emergency, Sandinista leaders and the FSLN's official organ, *Barricada*, began stressing the obsolescence of folkloric Sandinismo and its supersession by Fonseca's intellectual version of Sandinismo.[5] They paid special attention to the vanguard role of Nicaragua's agricultural and industrial proletariat in carrying forward the revolution begun by Sandino. They also recognized the lessons Marx and Lenin had drawn from history as fundamental to the emancipation of this new social force, which had acquired historical importance only after World War II.[6] Because of the threat from abroad and the workers' increasing demands for socialism, the FSLN's leaders began saying that to be a fully developed Sandinista one also had to be a Marxist-Leninist.

By Marxist-Leninism they meant the new Marxism rather than the old. Unlike the Marxism of the PSN, the new Marxism allowed for a residue of Sandinismo that was not an extension of scientific socialism; it was a residue of revolutionary myths, the moral values of Christianity, the liberal commitment to human rights, and the patriotic values of Sandino. The ideology of this new Marxism or new-style Leninism, although at variance with scientific socialism, was one of the keys to making the revolution.[7]

There is general agreement that the revival of Sandino's movement dates from the efforts by Nicaraguan Marxists to rescue his political legacy from oblivion and to infuse it with a Marxist understanding of Nicaraguan reality. The three principal founders of the FSLN—Fonseca, Borge, and [Silvio] Mayorga—each learned his Marxism from the Nicaraguan Socialist party.[8] They turned to Sandino's writings in an effort to root their Marxism in a nationally based tradition.

But that is not the whole story. In speeches and writings by current members of the National Directorate, Sandinismo is presented in more than one light. Sometimes the Marxist components are stressed; on other occasions Sandino's contribution stands out. Two approaches are necessary because initially the revolutionary vanguard was motivated to act by one set of considerations and the masses by another. For the vanguard there could be no revolutionary movement and no intelligent strategy without a revolutionary theory; but neither could there be a revolutionary movement without Sandino's patriotic values and example. Thus concessions were made to the popular current within Sandinismo.

Fonseca's 1964 statement of the nature of Sandinismo, *Desde la cárcel yo acuso a la dictadura* (From prison I accuse the dictatorship), was an open appeal to the Nicaraguan people to join ranks against Somoza. It consisted of two parts: an indictment of the crimes and other illegal acts by the effective head of state, Somoza; and the sketch of a program for united popular action combining the principles of scientific socialism and a call to make ideological concessions for the sake of political unity.[9]

In an effort to broaden his popular support, Fonseca rejected a one-sided commitment to Marxism-Leninism. Publicly, he even denied being a Marxist-Leninist: "I am not a Marxist-Leninist and I didn't cease to be one at this moment!"[10] He could have been telling the truth, considering the ambivalence of "Marxism-Leninism," identified by the media with the alien doctrines emanating from the Soviet Union. As far back as 1961, he recalled, he had written a letter to the leader of Nicaragua's Conservative party setting forth his revolutionary, popular, and anti-imperialist views, views that should not be confused with Marxism.[11] Acknowledging that his pamphlet *Un nicaragüense en Moscú* had stressed the positive and humanitarian achievements of the Soviet regime, he claimed that this admission was not tantamount to accepting communism. He disagreed with the Communists, he explained, in holding that private property still had an important role to play in the future development of his country.

In his prison statement Fonseca urged Nicaraguans to embrace an ideology that would bring about their effective liberation. Such an ideology would not be exclusive. Declaring himself an open-minded Sandinista, he said, "In my thought I welcome the popular essence of the distinct ideologies of Marxism, of Liberalism, of Social Christianity."[12] He then described the popular essence and utility of each. Marxism is valuable not only for its approach to social problems but also for its capacity to organize people's lives with a view to changing the world. Liberalism is valuable for its defense of individual rights, for its power to move the rich to resist the government's corruption, and because the bourgeois-democratic revolution is based on a historic process that in Nicaragua is not yet finished. Social Christianity is valuable for its progressive uses of Christian doctrine and for saving Christianity from becoming a monopoly of conservative and counterrevolutionary forces. Fonseca concluded his review of the principal appeals for social change by calling for a broad front of Nicaragua's youth based on a common commitment, a national revolutionary ideology that must be the work of Marxists, Liberals, and Social Christians alike—an ideology like Sandino's.

Fonseca also envisioned the creation of a Sandinista party that would encompass most of the new generation. In the interest of common action against the dictatorship, this party would avoid quarreling with other opposition parties, such as the Nicaraguan Socialist party, the Independent Liberal party, and the Social Christian party.[13] Although one ought to criticize their errors, he observed, this should be done in a constructive spirit without resentment. The most urgent task, Fonseca indicated, was to build a united movement in which the various parties might maintain their independence and respective moral commitments. In effect, he anticipated two different kinds of political pluralism: that of a Sandinista movement combining the revolutionary features of Marxism, Liberalism, and Social Christianity; and that of a patriotic front including the corresponding political parties.

Both varieties of political pluralism were unacceptable to Nicaragua's textbook Marxists and sectarians of the PSN. In practice, Fonseca agreed with [José Carlos] Mariátegui that more than a scientifically based theory is needed to mobilize the masses for revolution, that revolutionaries must appeal to nonrational as well as rational motives, to the will to believe, and to basic human sentiments. A revolutionary must learn to make concessions to the people's lack of political awareness—that is the message of his prison statement.

But there was a limit, Fonseca believed, to the number and kinds of concessions that should be made. Five years later he criticized the Sandinista movement and himself for having temporarily succumbed to ideological opportunism. "Although the Sandinista Front of National Liberation raised an anti-imperialist banner, including that of the emancipation of the exploited classes, it vacillated in presenting a clearly Marxist-Leninist ideology."[14] As a result, the public was not given an opportunity to choose between the "real Marxists" of the FSLN and the "false Marxists" of the PSN. The FSLN could not resist the temptation to cater to the political backwardness of the masses; it underestimated the people's capacity to accept Marxism because of the bad name given to it by the PSN. These were the factors that had "led to vacillation and to the adoption of an ideology that on the national plane was founded on a compromise."[15] The mistake lay in presenting Marxism on a par with Liberalism and Social Christianity, Fonseca concluded, when it was precisely Marxism that had motivated the search for a form of ideological pluralism capable of overcoming differences and cementing the unity of the revolutionary forces.

This position was reaffirmed in Fonseca's November 1970 interview in Havana. In outlining the sources of Sandinista thought, he began by stressing the contribution of Marxism and its reinterpretation by Che Guevara. Marxist socialism rather than radical populism was taken as the guide to solving Nicaragua's pressing problems. Fonseca's only concession to political pluralism was the following: "Although we believe that the principles of scientific socialism must be the fundamental guide, we are willing to march together with persons who have the most diverse beliefs and are interested in overthrowing the tyranny and in liberating our country."[16]

This interview was a candid account of what Fonseca really believed. Among the principal influences on his thought he acknowledged the deep impression created by the overthrow of Jacobo Arbenz's popular government in Guatemala (1954), the assassination of the first Somoza by the revolutionary poet Rigoberto López Pérez (1956), and the example of the Cuban guerrillas fighting in the Sierra Maestra against the Batista dictatorship (1958).[17] The Cuban influence, he acknowledged, was the decisive one for Nicaraguan revolutionaries like himself. Inspired by the Cuban example, the veteran Sandinista general Ramón Raudales had dedicated himself in 1958 to the task of reviving the armed struggle that had been brutally interrupted in 1934. "One may say that Marxism catches fire in a broad sector of the people and of the Nicaraguan youth with the triumph of the Cuban Revolution."[18]

In his other political writings we find Fonseca acknowledging a major debt to Guevara—except that Sandino's name invariably precedes that of the Argentine guerrilla. I interpret this to have been a concession to Nicaraguan nationalism. In any case, Guevara's influence was paramount in the observations made in Fonseca's 1970 broadcast during the temporary takeover of a Managua radio station: "Socialist and national emancipation are united in the Sandinosta People's Revolution. We identify with socialism but we are not uncritical of the socialist experience. For the most part, socialism has fulfilled the expectations placed on it by history and humanity. The frustrations are not the rule but the exception."[19]

For the FSLN to have imposed a socialist ideology on rank-and-file Sandinistas, however, would have undermined its credibility while duplicating the work of the Nicaraguan Socialist party. Disagreements over long-range political goals and principles as well as philosophical differences concerning the nature of man and the meaning of human existence were expected to persist during the foreseeable future. Although a house divided cannot stand, ideological differences were minimized in the effort to reach agreement on immediate and more pressing objectives.

This point was reiterated in a 1972 interview with Ricardo Morales Avilés, a member of the National Directorate who died in combat a year later. Published as a pamphlet by the FSLN, the interview concluded with a series of questions and answers concerning political and strategical issues. Asked whether the unity of the revolutionary forces requires a single ideology, Morales replied that ideological contradictions exist not only between but also within revolutionary organizations, differences that can be eradicated only at the cost of internal disruption.[20] There are fundamental philosophical differences between Marxists and Christians; but that does not prevent them from studying national problems with the aim of establishing socialism in Nicaragua, from working together, and agreeing on the same strategical objectives and tactics. Although a Marxist approach to politics is fundamental to Sandinismo, Morales concluded, a Marxist worldview is not.[21]

The latter is essential to Marxism, but is it a necessary prerequisite for revolution? In a major address in December 1979, Humberto Ortega [Saavedra] indicated that it was superfluous.[22] Essential to the Nicaraguan Revolution were national values and the patriotic example of Sandino: "We found political, military, doctrinal, and moral elements in our people and in our history, not in foreign texts or theories of any kind."[23] Even the FSLN's theory was said to be Sandino's creation: "Sandinismo survived because it was the product of the concrete conditions of our country, because Sandino . . . made the people's needs his own, interpreted them, and with his struggle and actions created the theory we have recovered!"[24] Such statements reinforced the popular tendency in Sandinismo, which was alien to classical Marxism, while simultaneously deterring this current from becoming hostile to the FSLN's Marxist leadership.

Víctor Tirado also urged concessions to national values and traditions. He assimilated Marxist theory from the Communist party of his native country but learned to adapt it to the conditions of struggle in Nicaragua. In an interview in April 1979, he declared, "Some forces classify us as a Marxist tendency, as Communist. We have never affirmed that we are Marxists. We are a revolutionary front. Although among us are Marxists, there are also Christians. We take positions that are revolutionary and Sandinista." Asked to clarify what he meant by "Sandinista," he replied, "This is equivalent to nationalist. For to be able to give the anti-Somoza process a popular content we have to adopt national values. We shall not fail, since we raise the flag of Augusto César Sandino; we shall complete the work he was unable to consummate . . . with national values. That is why Sandinismo has popular appeal. To adopt international values would be something distinct because the people have no information about them." What concerned the FSLN, Tirado contended, was not whether its militants came from a Marxist party or had assimilated Marxist theory: "What interests us is that they are fully aware of *national values*, of Sandinista values."[25]

The program and objectives of the FSLN were certainly not Marxist, Tirado continued, nor was the struggle in Nicaragua over the question of capitalism versus communism. The issue was whether the people wanted dictatorship or democracy. The FSLN's objectives were democratic: overthrow of the tyrant; installation of a provisional government representative of all social classes; creation of a people's army in place of the elitist National Guard; formulation of an independent and nonaligned foreign policy; support for popular causes in Central America and the Caribbean; expropriation of the properties of Somoza and his inner circle; and application of a program of economic reconstruction.[26]

Tirado's statements recall Fonseca's earlier ones from prison in 1964. Only after victory, in his November 1979 speech on the third anniversary of Fonseca's death, did he affirm the Marxist dimension of Sandinismo. "Neo-Sandinismo"—Tirado's term for Sandino's political thought as refashioned by Fonseca and the FSLN—had its roots in the ideology, theory, and practice of Sandino as developed in the light of the Russian, Cuban, and Vietnamese revolutions.[27] Thanks to the Marxism of Lenin and Che Guevara, contemporary Sandinismo represented a unique blend of Nicaraguan nationalism and the contributions of revolutionary movements in other countries. "The original source of our revolutionary theory is national but never, listen well, never have we failed to take into account the experiences of Cuba, of the Soviet Union, of Vietnam, and of other peoples who struggled against oppression and exploitation. We take Sandino's thought as our starting point, but we have never ceased to consider the thought of Marx, of Lenin, of Che Guevara."[28]

Although an ally of the FSLN, the Nicaraguan Socialist Party bitterly rejects the FSLN's concessions to popular ideology. In its judgment, the figure of the heroic general stands in the way of a consistent struggle for socialism in Nicaragua, because his ideas represent a conception of the world incompatible with Marxism-Leninism.[29] Behind the scenes the PSN criticizes the Sandinista leaders for *not* being good Leninists. Guevara's brand of Marxism is also judged to be defective. Formally speaking, the PSN is right in claiming that the new Marxism diverges at various points from Leninist orthodoxy. But orthodoxy does not always lead to revolutionary effectiveness, and where it does not, as in Nicaragua, it, rather than Sandinismo, is incompatible with the revolutionary essence of Marxism-Leninism.

Fonseca's reformulation of Sandino's thought provided Marxism with a popular vehicle, which the PSN lacked, for making its influence felt on a national scale. The FSLN took to heart the maxim that there can be no leaders without followers, no revolutionary vanguard without significant concessions to the masses. Since Marxism-Leninism in Nicaragua had to retreat before a virulent and widespread anticommunism, an ideology that contradicted the premises of scientific socialism was required to mobilize the people. In rejecting the PSN's supervision, according to Tirado, Fonseca saved the FSLN from becoming a dogmatic sect alien to the history and experience of the Nicaraguan people: "Deeds have demonstrated the uselessness of the PSN's counsels."[30]

The PSN's distrust of Sandinismo is rooted in the anti-ideological strain of classical Marxism. Marx and Engels had resisted efforts to confuse their scientific outlook with the moral sentiments and prejudices of the workers. Idealistic, mystifying, and conventional appeals to morality were only grudgingly accepted and then only under pressure from representatives of the workers' movement.[31] Wrote Marx in March 1875, "What a crime it is to . . . force on our party again . . . obsolete rubbishy phrases, while . . . perverting the realistic outlook . . . by means of ideological nonsense about 'right' and other trash common among the democrats and French Socialists!"[32] Fonseca and the FSLN were not so cavalier. Under the influence of Guevara they developed their own revolutionary ethics, and Marxism was redefined as both a science and an unscientific postscript for waging the class struggle.

The history of contemporary revolutions, beginning with the October Revolution of 1917, had shown that Marx's grudging concessions to the ideological currents among the masses were far from sufficient. The Marxism of the Communist or Third International did not make up for this deficiency. Lenin's advocacy of a specifically Communist morality dissolved on analysis into a pseudoethics based exclusively on class interest and the worker's own self-interest.[33] Obligation, duty, self-sacrifice—the nonrational components of morality—were conspicuously absent. For Leninism, as for classical Marxism, the only rationale for risking human life in a revolutionary upheaval was that workers have only their chains to lose, because their lives are not worth living under the old system, and they have a world to win.

The new Marxism spawned by the Cuban Revolution challenged this preconception. In Nicaragua the FSLN made concessions to the people's prejudices and nonrational convictions from the beginning. The cult of Sandino performed an indispensable role in mobilizing the masses for a general insurrection, as did the FSLN's moral commitment to human rights and the concessions it made to the revolutionary current in Christianity. . . . The unique contribution of the Cuban and Nicaraguan revolutions was not only to adapt Marxism to the peculiar conditions of each country, but also to remold it as part of an indigenous movement independent of the local Communist parties. What Fidel Castro's revival of José Martí did for the July 26 movement in Cuba, Fonseca's recovery of Sandino's political legacy did for the struggle against imperialism and dictatorship in Nicaragua.

In its development of the new Marxism, the FSLN has shown political, strategical, and ideological flexibility. Its nonsectarian and pragmatic approach to making a revolution appears in its leaders' refusal to adhere rigidly to a supposedly "correct line," whether to a unitary assessment of political and historical events, or to a narrow and exclusive political-military strategy, or to a monolithic ideology. Although Marxist-Leninist parties also try to be flexible, their flexibility does not extend to matters of ideology.

Political flexibility should not be mistaken for lack of principle. Nonetheless, some Marxist-Leninist parties, including the PSN, have charged the FSLN with "opportunism." In their public statements the Sandinista leaders do in fact give the impression of having rejected "communism," however one interprets this emotionally charged and ambivalent term. As Bayardo Arce, the effective general secretary of the FSLN, said in a recent interview, "If you find a political project such as ours where 70 percent of the economy is in private hands, where you have twelve legally existing political parties, where all religion is freely operating, where you have radios and newspapers that freely operate pro and con . . . , that is Sandinismo, and that type of project certainly does not attract communists!"[34] After the revolution triumphed, he added, all sorts of people began calling themselves Sandinistas. That is why Sandinismo has become a synthesis of different and even opposed political and ideological currents not only of applied Marxism and Christianity: "I can also tell you that it is liberalism applied in Nicaragua!"[35]

Such statements are meant not only to be witty, but also to undercut hostile criticism of the FSLN. Actually, they are based on an esoteric or secret political line that is a distinguishing characteristic of revolutionary vanguards. Although the FSLN's propaganda has shifted in response to changing events and political pressures, its commitment to an economic, political, and cultural revolution in Nicaragua has remained unchanged. And because the FSLN's fundamental line continues firm, what is believed to be opportunism is not political flabbiness but revolutionary shrewdness aimed at winning political friends and neutralizing potential enemies. Despite [Bayardo] Arce's disclaimers, the Sandinista project of political pluralism and a mixed economy *does* attract "Communists."

Another and fundamentally different image of Sandinismo is widespread among supporters of the Nicaraguan Revolution in the United States. Several eminent scholars, including specialists on Central America, have so stressed the peculiar national characteristics of the Nicaraguan Revolution that it appears to offer a third path promising the best of both the capitalist and the socialist worlds. Conservative ideologues are mistaken, they claim, in believing that the presence of Marxists in the FSLN's leadership indicates that the revolutionary government will follow the pattern set by the Cuban Revolution. On the contrary, "although they logically felt [and feel] a bond of friendship and found [find] much in common with the only real revolutionary government in Latin America, the Nicaraguan revolutionaries, above all, were [and are] nationalists."[36] A similar portrait could be painted of Sandino.

Given this populist image of Sandinismo, the supposed perils of communism represented by the FSLN are dismissed because of their "patently bogus nature." Rather than an application of Marxism-Leninism to Nicaragua, the FSLN's Sandinismo is associated with a "cluster of highly nationalistic and political-economic reformist symbols with deep roots in the Nicaraguan psyche." Thus the impression is created that Sandinista ideology has a purely "populist origin and framework."[37] Such statements mistake the FSLN's appearance for reality.

Although the Sandinista leaders no longer disclaim their Marxism, as they once did, they present to the public an innocent version of what they mean by it. Said Humberto Ortega Saavedra in an address on September 1, 1980, "In Nicaragua the revolution triumphed with a clearly Marxist leadership, but not with a Marxistoid and bookish one that advertised itself as being 'Marxist-Leninist' and that understood by Marxism-Leninism something completely deformed and rigid. We did not understand Marxism in that way but as something else, as simply an instrument of analysis. . . . One has to study history and to find in history . . . the elements of this revolution."[38]

In characterizing Marxism as a mere instrument of analysis, Ortega sought to emphasize its scientific contribution. Who would object to that? Or to his professed concern for social justice? "I should have no fear in saying that we are in search of a just society, a society without exploiters and exploited. . . . If there are Christians like Gaspar García Laviana who gave their blood to make this revolution, then that is what counts!"[39] In short, the FSLN stands for an ideological revision of Marxism-Leninism fortified by Sandino's revolutionary legacy.

What, then *is* Sandinismo? It is an amalgam of Marxist theory and Sandino's revolutionary legacy under the auspices of the new Marxism. Like the new Marxism, Sandinismo has three principal dimensions: it offers an explanation of historical events; it arouses people to act with emotional appeals; and it serves as a guide to action. Marx's principles of scientific socialism hold sway in the area of historical explanation. Sandino's patriotic ideas and example prevail in matters of ideology. Sandinista practice is shaped by both of these components. In effect, Sandinismo is Sandino's revolutionary legacy impregnated with the new Marxism.

Notes

1. Tomás Borge, "Interview with Tomás Borge, 'We Will Not Take a Single Step Backward.' " *Intercontinental Press* (6 July 1981): 713–15.
2. Deirdre English, " 'We are Sandinistas': Conversations with Nicaragua's Embattled Leaders," *Mother Jones* (August–September 1985): 22–29, 51.
3. José Luis Balcárcel, "El sandinismo, ideología de la revolución nicaragüense," *Nicarauac* (Managua), no. 2 (July–August 1980): 112–19.
4. Ibid.
5. Michael Baumann, "Year at War Steels Mass Organizations: Sandinistas Put 'Borrowed Time' to Good Use," *Intercontinental Press* (27 December 1982): 884–88.
6. Ibid.
7. Balcárcel makes the mistake of reducing Sandinismo to an application of classical Marxism to Nicaragua. See Balcárcel, "El sandinismo," 117–18.
8. Tomás Borge, "Carlos, el amanecer ya no es una tentación," in *Nicaragua: la estrategia de la victoria*, ed. Fernando Carmona (Mexico, 1980), 103–22.
9. Carlos Fonseca, *Desde la cárcel yo acuso a la dictadura* (Managua: Secretaría Nacional de Propaganda y Educación Política del FSLN, no date).

10. Ibid., 7.
11. Ibid.
12. Ibid.
13. Ibid., 9.
14. Carlos Fonseca, *Nicaragua, hora cero* (Managua: Secretaría Nacional de Propaganda y Educación Política del FSLN, 1980), 27.
15. Ibid., 27–28.
16. Carlos Fonseca, "Con la revolucion siempre!" in *Nicaragua*, 139.
17. Ibid., 129–31.
18. Ibid., 133.
19. Carlos Fonseca, "Por la lucha armada, a la hermandad internacionalista," in *Nicaragua*, 166.
20. Ricardo Morales Avilés, *La dominación imperialista en Nicaragua* (Managua: Secretaría de Propaganda y Educación Política del FSLN, 1980), 39.
21. Ibid., 40.
22. Humberto Ortega, "La lucha de Sandino base de la revolución sandinista" in *La revolución a través de nuestra Dirección Nacional* (Managua: Secretaría de Propaganda y Educación Política del FSLN, 1980), 9.
23. Ibid., 11.
24. Ibid., 13.
25. Víctor Tirado López, "Crecera la ofensiva del FSLN dice el Mexicano Tirado López," interview by Guillermo Mora Tavares in *La batalla por Nicaragua: Cuadernos de Unomásuno* (Mexico City, 1980), 144.
26. Ibid.
27. Tirado López, "El pensamiento político de Carlos Fonseca Amador," in *La revolución a traves*, 20–21.
28. Ibid.
29. Donald Hodges interview with Luis Sánchez Sancho, general secretary of Partido Socialista Nicaragüense [PSN], Managua (26 December 1980).
30. Tirado López, "Pensamiento politico," 20–21.
31. Karl Marx, *Selected Works* (New York, 1933), Vol. 2, 606.
32. Ibid., vol. 2, 567.
33. V. I. Lenin, *The Lenin Anthology*, ed. Robert C. Tucker (New York, 1975), 667–68.
34. Interview with Bayardo Arce, in English, " 'We Are Sandinistas,' " 22.
35. Ibid., 23.
36. Thomas Walker, ed., *Nicaragua in Revolution* (New York, 1982), 20–21.
37. John A. Booth, *The End of the Beginning: The Nicaraguan Revolution* (Boulder, 1982), 216.
38. Humberto Ortega, "Diálogo abierto a la asamblea," *Revolución Sandinsta y Educación*, special issue of *Encuentro* (Managua), no. 15 (September 1980): 154–79.
39. Ibid., 174, 177.

Revolutionary Governments and Social Change

<hr>

7 Mary Kay Vaughan ◆ The Educational Project of the Mexican Revolution: The Response of Local Societies (1934–1940)

In the three decades after the overthrow of Porfirio Díaz, the Mexican government attempted to stimulate and to direct social change through-out the country. In this selection Mary Kay Vaughan, a preeminent specialist in the study of social change and educational institutions in Mexico, first explains how "revisionist" historians developed their argument that the Mexican revolution brought more harm than benefit to the peasant population in the 1920s and 1930s. According to the revisionists (or re-ductionists), the national government's rural schools provided literacy and basic learning in the countryside, but this centralized system also pushed the peasants into a modernized, consumer-oriented copy of urban society, typical of Mexico City and other large population centers.

Vaughan no longer accepts this perspective. As she explains, the central government often had to deal with active and capable groups of rural villagers who used their own traditional values to shape their educational experiences in the community schools. Two aspects of the revolution in Mexican education deserve special attention: 1) the intentions and actions of the national government; and 2) the response of the rural communities to the national government. What Vaughan finds among the villagers of the state of Puebla in the 1930s is close to the kind of peasant (and worker) assertiveness advocated a generation later by Brazilian social critic and educator Paulo Freire (see Selections 11 and 12).

Since the eighteenth century, most major national revolutions have fashioned blueprints for the creation of an "improved" society. To harness energies to a new human project, to create associations, loyalties, and values, revolutionaries have focused on education. The Mexican Revolution of 1910 was no exception. Regarding peasants as a homogenized

This essay was originally presented at the Conference on Latin American History of the American Historical Association in Washington, DC, on December 29, 1992. Published by permission of the author.

mass of sickly, lethargic, superstitious pariahs, reformers in the Secretaría de Educación Pública (SEP) sought to transform them through schooling into literate, sober, clean, scientific, market-oriented, and patriotic farmers. This they would do through action education, or "learning by doing": teaching through cultivating new crops; planting trees to fight erosion; raising bees and chickens; marketing produce and crafts; introducing new methods of hygiene, health care, child-rearing; and celebrating patriotic festivals. Theirs was a highly creative, ambitious project designed to assimilate, reconstruct, and invigorate the marginal and the deviant. It was also intended to pacify the dangerous, for these were peasants in full-scale rebellion.[1]

For many years, a self-congratulatory official history of revolutionary education prevailed as it has for most literacy crusades. Selfless reformers brought books, land, and hygiene to the peasant masses, homogenized by virtue of exploitation and oppression. In the 1970s, reproductionist historians challenged this view by highlighting the class dimensions of the educational project, its insensitivity to peasant culture, and the structural limitations inhibiting its realization within the context of a dependent, poor, capitalist country. The educational project was recast as one of middle-class management bent on manufacturing modernity. This reading formed part of a wave of revisionist analysis of the revolution. Revisionists focused on the central state as a successful manipulator of sociopolitical conflict on behalf of a "bourgeois" project.[2]

The reproductionist critique deepened when scholars such as Jean Meyer and Marjorie Becker examined peasant struggle against the state's modernizing project.[3] A dichotomy took shape of peasant against the state. The state emerged as merciless victor, a "steamroller" out to smash peasant culture and autonomy.[4] Although this approach made us conscious of state educators' intellectual construction of the "peasantry" as an object of transformation, it fashioned its own construction of the peasantry as a singularly resistant subject. "Resistance" literature, however, permitted a greater appreciation of peasant diversity and actuation when combined with proliferating studies in comparative peasant politics and Mexican regional history.[5]

Drawing from the regional studies of the Mexican Revolution undertaken by scholars in the last two decades, a recent postrevisionist analysis suggests a more complex relationship between state and society. Alan Knight argues that the Mexican revolutionary state in the 1920s and 1930s was no Leviathan capable of steamrolling society in the interests of its singular project. It was a fledgling institution subject to persistent contention in a context of intense sociopolitical mobilization around conflicting projects and goals.[6] Popular mobilization altered the agrarian structure, destroyed the hacienda system, pressured for labor union organization, and derailed the rabidly antireligious campaigns that intermittently obsessed revolutionary governments. The state was formed through contentious interaction with social forces who, in a moment of heightened politicization, articulated their interests in sometimes shrill and sometimes muted voices. Those in command of the state had no single project; it was devised and revised in interactive process.

Within postrevisionist reasoning, the central state could not impose its educational project. It had a Secretaría de Educación Pública intent on gaining control over older municipal and state primary schools and multiplying their number, but its own bureaucracy—its teachers—was volatile and fragmented. Moreover, teachers faced different constraints and opportunities at the regional and local levels, where those holding power limited federal state pretensions to school control. The juxtaposition of a weak central state and highly mobilized rural population enhanced the negotiating capacity of rural communities regarding education. Communities subjected the national schooling project to local scrutiny, contesting such issues as who would control schools and who would attend them, what was taught and learned, and what role the school would play in community life.[7]

In short, there was ample space at the regional and local levels to mediate and reshape the educators' notion of modernity. The study of this negotiating space questions the reproductionist model, where the state dominates the local community, and the resistance model, which renders the peasantry a heroic but clobbered victim. The construction of a negotiating space does not imply an oppositional victory for the objects of the state's social engineering. It does suggest a degree of activism and influence at the local level, shaped by prerevolutionary experience with literacy and schooling and characterized by contention and struggle in the revolutionary process. It seeks to delineate actors who participated in negotiations over schooling, their goals, motivations, definition of issues, and choice of tactics. The concept of negotiating space accepts the reality of structural constraints, political and economic, which shaped local options and effectiveness in altering the meaning of modernity as defined by the school. The Mexican revolutionary process concluded with the consolidation of an authoritarian state ruled by a single political party (the National Revolutionary Party [PNR], which in 1946 changed its name to the Party of the Institutional Revolution [PRI]) that orchestrated a rapid process of capitalist development after 1940.

This essay examines two negotiating encounters in the revolutionary educational project. Both took place during the period of socialist education (1934–1940), a period combining volatile public response to policy with expanding bureaucratic control by the central state. The encounters took place in the state of Puebla, which is situated on the central plateau and is part of the country's original colonial core where landlords and merchants dominated a mestizo and indigenous peasantry. During the revolution, peasants subordinate to large estates (haciendas) mobilized for land while those accustomed to commercial domination were more quiescent. Because a countryside as diverse as Mexico's was bound to engender multiple encounters over schooling, the two case studies are not presented for generalization but to delineate a conceptual approach to schooling in the Mexican Revolution as an interactive process between agents of the state and social subjects.

The Historical Moment in Educational Policy: Socialist Education, 1934–1940

Educational policy as a project of behavioral transformation for rural Mexico evolved between 1920 and 1940, subject to revision by successive groups of middle-class intellectuals representing different political coalitions and constituencies. Although national policy varied from one presidency to another, it was remarkably consistent. SEP aimed at creating primary schools for all rural Mexicans and implementing a homogeneous curriculum. The curriculum was designed to remake the traditional peasantry, supposedly rendered squalid, superstitious, and myopic by virtue of isolation or domination by priests, hacendados, and usurous merchants. The peasants were to expand their loyalty beyond the *patria chica* (local community) to the Mexican nation, their knowledge into the realm of science, and their production into the marketplace. In dialogue and policy, little effort was made to distinguish between the mestizo or predominantly European-origin peasantries and indigenous peoples. All suffered similar deficiencies and required the same transformation and incorporation. By homogenizing class and ethnicity, the educators overcame the racist aspects of Social Darwinism to champion the educability and transformability of non-European peoples.

   Disagreement among educators centered on questions of secularization and structural change. To what extent did modernization through education require the rooting out of religion itself, and should teachers and schools move beyond the classroom to mobilize communities against their structural oppressors—hacendados, merchants, and priests? Both questions were radically addressed in the policy of socialist education, introduced in December 1934, which decreed that teachers should attempt to destroy religiosity, or at least the superstition, excessive ceremonialism, and clerical submissiveness that accompanied it. Moreover, teachers should act to restructure power in the countryside as leaders or advisers of campesino and worker associations. Socialist education was never envisaged to socialize the means of production. It was radical enough, however, to provoke intense controversy and mobilization.

Scholars have long debated the response to socialist education.[8] For its critics, it was a totalitarian attempt to impose an exotic model.[9] Politically motivated, incompetently packaged by policymakers, dimly understood by teachers, socialist education degenerated into an orgy of antireligious rhetoric and excesses, offensive to national sentiment. It mobilized opposition and ended in failure. Indeed, recognizing widespread hostility to its antireligious offensive, President Lázaro Cárdenas (1934–1940) gutted this aspect of policy in 1936.

For its champions, socialist education marked the highpoint in a long struggle of Mexican teachers for social justice and national progress. It brought to the fore the deepest convictions and remarkable energies of a group of men and women fired by missionary zeal to sacrifice their youth, family life, material comfort and, in many cases, their own lives to overcome the forces of darkness and backwardness—promoting land reform, trade union rights, cooperative marketing, sanitation, science, and modern agriculture. Indeed, teachers acted as important allies to Cárdenas in his extensive program of land redistribution and promotion of workers' rights.[10]

Few studies have focused on how teachers at the regional level interpreted socialist education and how rural communities responded to and reshaped policy at its point of implementation.[11] The response to socialist education was more than a momentary reaction. It captured the cumulative interaction of communities with schools over a long period of time. Socialist education took place at a critical moment when peasant effervescence was on the verge of fizzling out under pressures of state consolidation. It was a negotiation informed by history with implications for the future: part of a set of conditions for entering the post-1940 process of economic growth and political stability, marked by institutional and electoral *continuismo*.

Framing the Teacher Articulation of Socialist Education

Since the creation of SEP in 1921 initiated the hiring of teachers for federal schools, the federal teachers' corps acquired regional characteristics, a function of nineteenth-century teaching traditions and teachers' recruitment, training, and mentoring in the revolutionary period. Their association with political movements and experiences in communities differed from state to state. In the period of socialist education, the space open to them for interpreting and implementing policy was shaped as well by three major actors: the Mexican president, the state governor, and rural communities. President Cárdenas could protect the teachers from a hostile environment or leave them to their own devices. He could make their project of transformation realizable by backing political movements for structural transformation and allocating resources such as land, credit, technical services, and infrastructural facilities. As Mexico's most radical president, he was inclined to sponsor such restructuring. He had to make his choices, however, within a context of resource scarcity. His goal of state consolidation often took priority over his commitment to democratic structural reform and determined how he would allocate scarce resources. The state governor could include the federal teachers in his building of a political machine within the emerging national party structure. Or he might attempt to exclude them as meddling representatives of external (central) power.

Puebla's federal teachers came from the modest middle class, rural and urban. Their ideological orientation derived from a strong liberal creed that had inspired the state's normal school and municipal primary schools in the nineteenth century. Through the leadership of Puebla normal school graduates like Rafael Molina Betancourt, who had worked with SEP, this faith in education as an attribute of modern, democratic citizenship easily transferred to the central government's project of social transformation through schooling.[12] Poblano teachers as a group did not practice the rabid antireligiosity of federal teachers' corps associated with radical governors in Tabasco, Sonora, and Michoacán: they were not "priest eaters" or "saint burners." They expanded, however, upon nineteenth-century notions of anticlericalism as a separation of church and state to embrace the fight against fanaticism as an expression of superstition and religious celebration as a waste of human energy and money.

The power of local rebellion in Puebla kept SEP from making deep inroads into rural areas until 1928 when the state governor, Leonides Andreu Almazán, invited federal teachers to help him consolidate a political machine built on the struggle for land (agrarianism) and trade unionism. The teachers' task was not easy in a countryside thick with pretensions to autonomy and was soon complicated by the introduction of socialist education, which evoked a hostile response from a strongly religious peasantry. In 1934, a more conservative political group linked to the Avila Camacho family took over the process of regional state consolidation.[13] Maximino Avila Camacho ran for governor in 1936 on an anti-Communist platform only barely disguising its attack on socialist education. Maximino Avila Camacho viewed federal teachers as obstructionists in his quest for control over regional politics.

For reasons of loyalty in the process of party and state-building, Cárdenas supported Avila Camacho and abstained from intervening in Puebla's internal affairs. Teachers had to fend for themselves in an often hostile environment: approximately seventeen teachers died at the hands of armed groups calling themselves "Cristeros." Nor did Cárdenas provide the poblano peasants with the material with which to become successful modern entrepreneurs, as SEP policy envisioned. Although he issued definitive titles to land for which poblano peasants had long fought, he did not give them the same level of infrastructural support he gave to agraristas in northern agricultural districts like La Laguna and the Yaqui Valley.

Framing Peasant Response to Educational Policy

The implementation of educational policy was hardly a singular function of the political space created by state personalities and institutions. Rural communities shaped teachers' options and determined how they conveyed the meaning of socialist education. In rewriting the educational script and reshaping its prescriptions for modernity, they were informed by their prerevolutionary experience with literacy and schooling. The role they assumed in the revolutionary restructuring of power and resources determined the pitch and tone of their voices, indeed, their discourse in relation to schooling. They were also constrained by the extent to which the central state or marketplace provided them resources commensurate with the transformation prescribed by the school.

In order to understand local response to socialist education we need to reconstruct revolutionary politics at the local level and the social environment that engendered it and was altered by it. Primary sources essential to this reconstruction include the bimonthly reports of school inspectors in the SEP archives, voluminous correspondence in the Acervos Presidentes and Gobernación files of the Archivo General de la Nación, material in state and municipal archives, and interviews with teachers, inspectors, and *vecinos* (neighborhood residents). By combining insights from analyses of peasant societies caught up in the midst of change with studies of peasant literacy, these primary sources can be used to reconstruct a social ecology of schooling, which shaped response to official educational policies. The constituent elements in a social ecology of schooling are economic, political, and cultural. Although these elements are local in their manifestation, they are interactive with processes in the larger society. They are historically embedded. Scholars of literacy and schooling emphasize the importance of the long term as a means of explaining momentary reaction. The ecology of schooling is by definition dynamic—responsive to sudden jolts, such as revolutionary upheavals or civil wars, or more gradual processes of change, such as market penetration.

The dominant school of thought in social histories of peasant literacy and schooling is still fundamentally modernization theory. It is best articulated by Eugen Weber in *Peasants into Frenchmen* and at base supported by François Furet and Jacques Ozouf in their study *Lire et écrire*.[14] Following Weber, literacy is not vital to agrarian societies because spiritual salvation does not require reading. Rather, literacy is something that cities, as agents of states and markets, impose on rural society. The greater the presence of the state, the greater the inroads of the modern market in rural life, the more rural people perceive the utility of knowing how to read and write. In modern Western history, literacy skills are often bound up with state schools designed to shape individuals to a nonrural world, to integrate them into a national framework, into its state and its markets.[15]

This thesis of imposed integration has some validity for rural Mexico at the end of the nineteenth century. On the eve of the revolution, rural Mexico was "in full mutation," to capture an image painted by French historian François Javier Guerra.[16] Since 1880, a process of rapid modernization had seriously, although differentially and unevenly, undermined the relative autonomy of peasant communities. Railroads altered the landscape by making it commercially desirable and accessible. Land expropriation by haciendas, taxation, commercialization, and inflation threatened the integrity of subsistence communities, sent people migrating in search of work, and frequently subverted long-standing hierarchies of power, order, and meaning. *Mestizaje*, or acculturation of indigenous communities, proceeded apace, so that according to the 1910 census, only 15 percent of Mexicans spoke no Spanish.[17] It was also a period of school expansion: the number of primary schools in Mexico roughly doubled, from five thousand in 1878 to ten thousand in 1907. The fact that literacy did not increase as rapidly as schools in this period—19 percent of the population over twelve was literate in 1895 compared with 29 percent in 1910—attests to the unevenness of the process of integration and the resistance, ambivalence, and impoverishment it provoked in rural communities.[18]

The thesis of imposed literacy underestimates the active role of rural people in relation to schooling. What is now coming to light in our studies of nineteenth-century Mexico is the notion that peasant participation in state formation—in the bloody civil wars and defense against two foreign invaders—was linked to at least two visions of schooling realized at the regional and local levels—a liberal ideology that saw schooling as the source of modern, secular citizenship, and a Catholic ideology that emphasized schooling for both literacy and a reaffirmation of the faith, embattled by the triumph of the liberal state.[19] This selection examines a very Catholic state whose public primary schools were inspired by liberal, republican ideology.

While visions realized at the local and regional levels account for the plethora of schools in the countryside in late nineteenth-century Mexico, their presence or impact should not be exaggerated: schools were poorly and irregularly attended. Economic and social factors conditioned the development of cultures of schooling. Furet and Ozouf point to material wealth as an important determinant of rural schooling: Can a community or an individual family sustain investments in schooling?[20] These were important considerations in Mexico: the larger and more solvent the community, the more likely it was to have a school for boys and, increasingly, one for girls; the larger the number of solvent families, the higher the enrollment.

Social factors of class, gender, and ethnicity conditioned schooling. Peasant communities are hierarchical, and, with economic change in nineteenth-century Mexico, social differentiations within them often increased. Poor families' reluctance to educate children derived in part from an awareness that their children would be discriminated against in schools by teachers and students alike.[21] Relations with nonpeasant powerholders influenced schooling as well. For instance, if the school benches were occupied by the children of hacienda administrators, children of the peones were likely not to be there.

Many who appeared to be excluded because of class in fact chose not to send their children to school. Skepticism as to the value of schooling pervaded peasant ranks and sometimes entire communities: schooling was often regarded as a waste of time, an exercise in the moral evil of idleness. Many saw the school as a dangerous, unregulated place to send children.[22]

Educating women might be perceived as particularly dangerous, for it implicitly threatened the patriarchal organization of rural life.[23] Men dominated politics, religion, property, and market relations, where literacy skills were useful. Girls were valued for their domestic work and their marriageability. Their mothers taught them the skills they needed in the secluded sphere of the hearth. Under what conditions did the exclusion of girls from schooling begin to break down in rural Mexico, as it clearly did at the end of the nineteenth century? Whether or not girls were being incorporated into the culture of schooling on the eve of the revolution and how they were incorporated (into single-sex, coeducational, public, or private schools) are strongly linked to the pace of their incorporation after 1910.

Ethnicity also influenced school attendance. Indigenous peoples had no uniform response to schooling in Spanish. As open agrarian communities engaged in long-standing interaction with the state and marketplace, many indigenous towns on Mexico's central plateau were friendly to schools. Tlaxcala and Morelos, both states of dense pre-Hispanic settlement, had the highest literacy rates in central Mexico. In "regions of refuge," such a the Sierra Norte de Puebla, the strength of cultural autonomy and economic self-sufficiency discouraged interest in Spanish literacy.[24] As is explained below, however, some Nahuatl-speaking villages actively entered the civil wars and acquired a liberal faith in schooling. Guy Thomson has hypothesized that those communities likely to join the liberal National Guard were no longer self-sufficient.[25] Thus communities in the process of losing their resource base might make strategic use of schooling and literacy. Still another variation occurred in northern Mexico among indigenous tribes like the Yaqui and Tarahumara, who were fighting to preserve their autonomy from the advancing state and marketplace. For them, state schools on their own territory were often a symbol of conquest, an admission of defeat in a moment of heightened, unresolved struggle.

The modernization-as-imposition thesis underestimates the effectiveness of local power in reshaping school programs prescribed by the state, controlling the functioning of the school, and defining the teacher's rights and responsibilities to the community. As Ben Ekloff has shown in his study of peasant literacy in nineteenth-century Russia, although teachers came to moralize, sanitize, and nationalize the Russian peasants, villagers preferred to select from the school program the knowledge and skills they wanted.[26] Men wanted to learn how to read and write in order to cope with new landownership after emancipation. In Mexico, as in Russia, the social custom of selecting from the official curriculum was well established: a smattering of reading, writing, counting, and patriotic history sufficed for those interested in schooling in most communities. Moreover, Mexican primary schools were ensconced in ritual ensuring local control and accountability. Regulating the schools, administering supplies, presiding in judgment over teacher and students at final examinations was part and parcel of municipal office.[27]

Finally, as Andrés Lira Gónzalez has shown in his study of Mexico City's Indian communities in this period, many teachers were more important to communities outside the classroom than inside it.[28] In places where literacy was still a scarce but increasingly useful commodity, the male teacher doubled as secretary of the town council or more informally served as scribe attending to matters of bureaucracy, recordkeeping, and contracts. Like the priest, he was called on to mediate local disputes. Above all, he was responsible for the patriotic festival.[29] Just as religious ritual had legitimized community cohesiveness in the colonial period, in the nineteenth century secular festivals became in many places as important to community life as they were to state legitimization. The teacher, the school, and its pupils were key actors in this local ritual.

Whether strong or weak, prerevolutionary cultures of schooling influenced postrevolutionary educational encounters. A clamoring for access to the privileges of the few was a major goal of insurgent groups. Prior exclusions of women, large numbers of campesinos, and indigenous peoples, however, influenced the pace and nature of educational *inclusion* in the revolution. Similarly, in many instances, prerevolutionary customs of local control over schooling helped to empower the peasantry in facing federal school programs. The efficacy of exercising these customary rights was heightened in a revolutionary process juxtaposing a mobilized rural population against a weak central state. Their exercise could take the form of subtle resistance. Restricting the amount of time children spent in school shrank the curriculum. If a mother pleaded that she had to work when the teacher wanted to show her a new recipe, the mother shaped the contours of the school's program of behavioral transformation. More directly, villagers frequently drove unpopular teachers out of town. Resistance could explode into organized mobilization as it did against the antireligious aspects of socialist education. But behavior that may appear resistant might be tactical negotiation: not necessarily the rejection of a modernization project, but attempts to adjust it to local needs, possibilities, values, and customs in a period in which a mobilized rural population reclaimed spaces, fought over power and resources, and shaped the role of the state in their lives.

In Puebla, where the response to late nineteenth-century modernization was mediated by a dense precapitalist socioeconomic matrix, a strong network of municipal primary schools coexisted with low literacy rate. In 1910, outside the city of Puebla, 23 percent of men over twelve years of age and 16 percent of women knew how to read and write in Spanish compared with 33 percent and 24 percent, respectively, at the national level.[30] Because of the strength of its peasant sector, Puebla was a perfect target for SEP's transformation project. Literacy gains in rural Puebla in the revolutionary period between 1920 and 1940, however, were somewhat disappointing: male literacy rose to 38 percent while female literacy inched up to 22 percent. These compare with 1940 national literacy rates of 50 percent for men and 42 percent for women. The schooling encounters in two regions of revolutionary Puebla described in the following sections were chosen for variations in prerevolutionary school culture, market and state integration, ethnic composition, revolutionary mobilization, and central state intervention in the reallocation of resources and power.

Tecamachalco

Consisting of nine counties and twenty-five thousand people in 1930, the ex-district of Tecamachalco was representative of Mexico's grain-producing central plateau.[31] Despite the penetration of the railroad, economic growth was sluggish in prerevolutionary Tecamachalco. Haciendas and ranchos dominated subsistence-oriented, largely mestizo villages. Literacy was low: 23 percent for men in 1910 and 18 percent for women.

In 1900, Tecamachalco had boys' schools in larger villages organized around the liberal vision. Girls' schools, which taught reading, writing, arithmetic, and patriotic history, were beginning to open. In any town, the school was an important institution of local power supervised by municipal officials, rancheros, hacienda administrators, small merchants, and well-to-do peasants. The school's instructional function was perhaps more critical in the elaboration of the patriotic festival than it was in the classroom.[32]

During the Mexican Revolution, villagers here rose up to recover land, water, and political office. Their force eliminated the hacendados, most of whom were absentee, and marginalized many rancheros (mid-sized farmers). By 1930, one third of the male population were land reform recipients. Demand for greater access to schooling was uneven. In the 1920s, literacy rose among boys and girls in villages where agrarian reform coincided with relative wealth before the revolution and a prerevolutionary culture of schooling. Poorer agrarista [local peasants who called for redistribution of hacienda lands] communities less familiar with schooling held back.

In the 1920s, literacy was acquired through locally controlled private or municipal schools. In the 1930s, when federal schools entered, youth literacy fell by 13 percent despite an expansion in school supply. Deschooling was part of a negotiating process driven by political, cultural, and economic factors.

Politically, the 1930s were years of intensified struggle as state consolidation brought local autonomy to an end. Campesino groups fought over newly acquired resources and hegemony in emerging regional and national associations. Maximino Avila Camacho's attempt to reinstate the marginalized rancheros in his state political machine heightened the level of conflict. The violence deterred school attendance, especially for young girls, who were vulnerable to rape and assault.

Political dispute often centered on the school. Agraristas sought to control the teacher, sent from afar by SEP. They argued with the teacher over who would manage the plot of land set aside for school support in government land-reform grants. They insisted on their right to use the school's space for political meetings and ejidal business.

Villagers ran into cultural conflict with SEP's transformational paradigm. Deeply religious, many parents removed their children from the "godless" socialist school in 1935. Many contested federally mandated coeducation. Only recently accustomed to schooling girls separately, they were not ready to expose them to boys and male teachers. Women resisted teachers' campaigns to reconstruct their households. They saw their homes as private, inviolable spaces and found most of the teachers' recommendations impractical and unconvincing.

The state had allocated small bits of land to Tecamachalqueños, but neither water nor infrastructural support. As drought, freezes, and rising prices ravished the area, many men migrated, leaving their animals and fields in the hands of women and children. These conditions reduced not only school attendance but the capacity of novice teachers to introduce new agricultural techniques and the willingness of farmers to listen to them.

During these years, communities reshaped the federal school program. While official policy demanded schools with workshops, gardens, cooperatives, and home visits, the communities created the prerevolutionary school with its emphasis on reading, writing, counting, and patriotism. All references to religion were struck from the curriculum. A couple of years of irregular attendance were sufficient to meet family needs and possibilities. The villagers defined the school's space. They closed the doors of the home, limited the teachers' access to the ejido, and recreated the prerevolutionary civic role for the teacher as the organizer of patriotic festival subordinate to local powerholders and handler of documentation between village and state.

Between 1910 and 1940, male literacy rose from 23 percent to 38 percent while female literacy rose from 18 percent to 22 percent. After 1940, school attendance for boys and girls began to rise. Party formation and state consolidation institutionalized emergent peasant leadership. Infused with the state's discourse linking progress and schooling, agraristas, along with rancheros and merchants, assumed their civic responsibility for schooling and negotiated their terms of control with teachers. The culture of schooling widened. State subsidization helped poorer communities and families to sustain schools. Violence subsided, making it safer to attend school. The completion of the highway between Puebla and Tehuacán increased trade. In the 1940s, government infrastructural support arrived when several communities benefited from the opening of the irrigation works at Valsequillo and others constructed deep water wells.

In the negotiations between Tecamachalqueños and SEP over schools, both parties were altered. The villagers molded the school's project to tolerate aspects of traditional culture formally abhorred by policymakers. Villagers disciplined teachers into serving their interests and respecting local rights and customs. But the school's modernizing project did alter village life and behavior. Between 1940 and 1960, literacy and schooling became more possible and necessary, given the intersection between rising standards of living, increasing mobility, and interaction with cities. Attendance rose, as did the number of years spent in school and acceptance of a modernizing curriculum. This was not a simple, knee-jerk response to market imperatives. The school had introduced new notions of national culture, mobility, consumption, knowledge, and social interaction, which drew people into the modernizing process. Through the negotiations of the 1930s, the villagers appropriated not only the school but the modernizing process, and they in turn were appropriated by it.

Zacapoaxtla

In 1930, the Zacapoaxtla region, in Puebla's Sierra Norte, embraced six counties with twenty-six thousand people.[33] Here, the revolution's literacy crusade achieved little. Male literacy rose from 22 percent in 1900 to 30 percent in 1940. Women's literacy edged up from 11 percent to 15 percent.

Compared to Tecamachalco, the Sierra Norte was incorporated late into the Spanish state. A mountainous region lacking in resources attractive to the early colonizers, it served as a zone of refuge for Nahuatl, Totonac, and Otomi peoples, whose societies approximated the "closed corporate communities" typologized by Eric Wolf in contrast to the more open towns of Tecamachalco.[34] Although briefly Christianized and superficially administered by Spanish officials, the communities' autonomy and resources were unthreatened until creole and mestizo settlers arrived at the end of the eighteenth century looking for land and markets.[35]

As non-Indian penetration coincided with the upheavals of independence, foreign invasion, and civil war, Zacapoaxtla's Nahuatl communities used the politics of state formation to salvage as much autonomy as possible. On the district's southern tier at the entry to the Sierra, where productive land was scarce and communities were most accustomed to interaction with the state, villages allied with the Liberals, who had promised tax exemption and land through participation in National Guard units. The municipality of Xochiapulco was created from an expropriated hacienda to reward National Guard heroes who had defended Puebla against the French in 1862. In the district's center, around the town of Zacapoaxtla, villagers followed creole merchant elites into the conservative movement in hopes of avoiding liberal privatization of their communal lands. To the north in the remote municipality of Cuetzalán, indigenous peoples, unaccustomed to outsiders, rebelled against encroachment and eschewed permanent alliance with either liberals or conservatives.[36]

In the late nineteenth century, Ladino [modernized mestizo] commercial elites in Zacapoaxtla and Cuetzalán consolidated control over the indigenous.[37] They allowed them their smallholdings but processed and traded the Indians' coffee and sugar, sold them finished goods and aguardiente at high prices, and carved out their own small estates. Politically, these headtowns dominated Indian villages. Set up for boys in some places, schools were non-Indian institutions. The teacher often doubled as the town secretary, the headtown's agent in the village. Because Ladinos handled relations with the outside world, the indigenous people felt little pressure to learn to read and write in Spanish. In 1900, only 23 percent of the region's people spoke Spanish.

Domination involved reciprocity.[38] Many communities kept enough land for subsistence and maintained their own institutions of government, religion, and socialization. In times of need, they turned to the elites for protection. The merchant families cemented control through use of renascent Catholicism. They sponsored the building of churches and shrines, organized pilgrimages, and fostered the integration of indigenous music, dance, and drama into their religious festivals.

Zacapoaxtla's southern tier towns were less integrated into this nexus. Here, the Zacapoaxtlan elites had some of their few haciendas. As they expanded these, they reduced many villagers to peon, sharecropper, tenant, or poacher status.[39] Churches were primitive, untouched by the religious Renaissance. Schools were better attended. On the southern tier's western rim, Xochiapulco was a radical thorn in the side of coservative Zacapoaxtla. In Xochiapulco, schools were part of a cult of yeoman liberalism. The most important holiday was not religious but patriotic: the Fifth of May, commemorating the day when the Xochiapulqueños etched themselves into the records of world history defending Mexico against the foreign invader. Literacy in Xochiapulco was ideologically rather than market-driven. In 1900, the municipality had the highest percentage of literate men (44 percent) in Puebla outside the capital city. As elsewhere in the Zacapoaxtla region, female literacy was very low in Xochiapulco (13 percent).[40]

Unlike Tecamachalco in the revolution, Zacapoaxtla produced no unified popular insurgency demanding resources and power. Xochiapulqueños joined Madero and in the 1920s began to press for the breakup of hacienda lands.[41] They allied with Rafael Molina Betancourt, a Zacapoaxtlan who, from his position in SEP in Mexico City, brought federal schools into the region in 1923. In Xochiapulco, literacy shot upward. Girls attended school. But elsewhere, neither the schools nor the agraristas made much headway until 1929, when Governor Almazán exiled the region's political boss, General Gabriel Barrios, and moved to destroy his power base by sponsoring agrarian organization. Rafael Molina Betancourt and his brother Fausto, a SEP inspector in Zacapoaxtla in the early 1930s, created a rural normal school in Xochiapulco to train teachers in SEP's transformational ideology and to mobilize villagers for land reform.[42]

Their pedagogical expansionism was soon contained. When the Avila Camacho group took control of state politics in 1933, they reversed the pro-agrarian policy and shored up the Zacapoaxtlan elites. Out of loyalty to Maximino Avila Camacho, Cárdenas did not intervene to support the more radical alternative of the teachers and the Xochiapulqueños. Agrarianism and socialist education gained support in southern tier towns, but in Zacapoaxtla and Cuetzalán, elites quashed both. They rallied villagers against "godless" socialist education. Coeducation deeply disturbed people who had had no experience schooling women. Religiosity, permeating a ceremonial social order, was lived culture. Traditional elites understood this better than teachers, who abstracted superstition and religious fiestas as discrete anachronisms to be discarded. SEP never seriously considered the strength of ethnicity. For this omission, it paid a price. In Cuetzalán, *cristero* bands, led by ex-officers of the deposed General Barrios, burned schools and terrorized teachers to the cry of "Viva Cristo Rey!"[43]

Teachers were domesticated by local elites, lack of sufficient external backup, and the power of indigenous cultural integrity. Not until the 1960s did villagers north of the southern tier begin to send children to school in significant numbers. Zacapoaxtla, however, was not a rout for SEP. Teachers remained a political force that derived a persistent solidarity and legitimacy from their trade union and SEP. Their local bases were the southern tier agraristas. These supports grounded a discourse of change and social justice, which attracted different indigenous groups as they coped with the opportunities and constraints of post-1940 economic growth. Teachers forged the political opposition in Zacapoaxtla and on several occasions brought their faction to municipal power introducing reforms, which mitigated but never abolished the region's servile social relations.[44]

Conclusion

This essay describes a way of examining the rural educational crusade of the Mexican Revolution distinct from the reproductionist thesis—which, in exaggerating state power, confuses intent with outcome—and the resistance thesis—which posits a schematic opposition between the abstract entities of state and society. I have looked at how the targets of state social engineering responded to architectural blueprints in a period of political mobilization and weak central state control.

In this analysis of the parameters and substance of local agency in these encounters, the history of a particular institution (the school) and practice (literacy) emerged as an important variable and one that has been recognized by several scholars, including François Furet, Jacques Ozouf, and Brian Street.[45] In contrast to Furet and Ozouf, who think that the French Revolution made little difference in rural education, I contend that revolutionary mobilization was an important variable in Mexico. It determined who could take advantage of and appropriate the state's school project. Education was not in itself liberating or ameliorating: it could only be used for such purposes.

Moreover, the educational project could inhibit the very liberation or amelioration it proposed. Recognition of peasant cultural integrity and difference was never the educators' strong suit. In the case of the Nahuatl villagers of central and northern Zacapoaxtla, contesting the educators' paradigm in defense of culture actually contributed to the prolongation of their prerevolutionary domination. Cultural issues proved critical in educational negotiations.

Finally, this approach to understanding revolutionary education is not an argument in favor of society as history's mover as opposed to the meddling, intrusive state. In the case of Tecamachalco, the state sponsored, legitimized, and equipped new groups to participate in an economic transformation that made schooling more accessible and useful. In the case of Zacapoaxtla, the central state remained marginal as a transformer of conditions and agency of empowerment to new groups. It allowed old ones to continue controlling the negotiation of economic processes and thus to delay the appropriation of schooling by dominated groups.

Notes

1. Key studies of the Mexican Revolution's educational project are John Britton, *Educación y radicalismo en México*, 2 vols. (Mexico: Sepsetentas, 1976); Victoria Lerner, *La educación socialista, Historia de la Revolución Mexicana*, Vol. 17 (Mexico: Colegio de México, 1987); Ernesto Meneses Morales, *Tendencias educativas oficiales en México*, 3 vols. (Mexico: Centro de Estudios Educativos,

Universidad Iberoamericana, 1982–1988); D. L. Raby, *Educación y revolución social* (Mexico: Sepsetentas, 1976); Ramon Eduardo Ruiz, *Mexico: The Challenge of Poverty and Illiteracy* (San Marino, CA: Huntington Library, 1963); Mary Kay Vaughan, *The State, Education and Social Class in Mexico, 1880–1930* (De Kalb: Northern Illinois University Press, 1982); Josefina Zoraida Vázquez, *Nacionalismo y educación en México* (Mexico: Colegio de México, 1970).

2. For a reproductionist analysis of Mexican revolutionary education, see Vaughan, *The State, Education, and Social Class in Mexico*. A classic statement of revisionist historiography is Arnaldo Cordova, *La ideología de la Revolución Mexicana: La formación del nuevo regimen* (Mexico: Ediciones Era, 1972). See also, among many others, essays in *Caudillo and Peasant in the Mexican Revolution*, ed. David Brading (Cambridge: Cambridge University Press, 1982).

3. Marjorie Becker, "Black and White and Color: Cardenismo and the Search for a Campesino Ideology," *Comparative Studies in Society and History* 29 (1987): 453–65; Jean Meyer, *La cristiada*, 3 vols. (Mexico: Siglo Veintiuno, 1973).

4. See Alan Knight, "Revolutionary Project, Recalcitrant People: Mexico 1910–1940," in *The Revolutionary Process in Mexico: Essays on Political and Social Change, 1880–1940*, ed. Jaime E. Rodríguez O. (Los Angeles: UCLA Latin American Center Publications, 1990), 247–50.

5. Resistance literature related to the peasantry is associated with the work of James Scott, *The Moral Economy of the Peasantry, Rebellion and Subsistence in Southeast Asia* (New Haven: Yale University Press, 1976); *Weapons of the Weak: Everyday Forms of Peasant Resistance* (New Haven: Yale University Press, 1985); and *Domination and the Arts of Resistance: Hidden Transcripts* (New Haven: Yale University Press, 1990). Comparative studies of the peasantry include Eric Wolf, *Peasant Wars of the 20th Century* (New York: Harper and Row, 1969); Jeffrey Paige, *Agrarian Revolution: Social Movements and Export Agriculture in the Underdeveloped World* (New York: Free Press, 1975); Teodor Shanin, *Peasants and Peasant Societies* (London: Basil Blackwell, 1971); Joel Migdal, *Peasants, Politics and Revolution: Pressures toward Political and Social Change in the Third World* (Princeton: Princeton University Press, 1974). On Mexico, see, among others, John Tutino, *From Insurrection to Revolution, Social Bases of Agrarian Violence, 1750–1940* (Princeton: Princeton University Press, 1986); Friedrich Katz, *Riot, Rebellion, and Revolution: Rural Social Conflict in Mexico* (Princeton: Princeton University Press, 1988); on Mexican regional history, see, among many others, Brading, *Caudillo and Peasant*.

6. See Alan Knight, "The Mexican Revolution: Bourgeois? Nationalist? Or Just a 'Great Rebellion'?" *Bulletin of Latin American Research* 4, no. 2 (1985): 1–37; "Interpretaciones recientes de la Revolución Mexicana," *Memorias del Simposio de Historiografía Mexicanista* (Mexico: Comité Mexicano de Ciencias Históricas, Gobierno del Estado de Morelos, Instituto de Investigaciones Históricas, UNAM, 1990), 193–210.

7. See Elsie Rockwell, "Schools of the Revolution: Enacting and Contesting State Forms (Tlaxcala 1910–1930)," in *Everyday Forms of State Formation: Revolution and the Negotiation of Rule in Modern Mexico*, ed. G. Joseph and D. Nugent (Duke University Press, forthcoming), for a novel and suggestive study of teacher/community interaction around schools in this period of the revolution. See also Mary Kay Vaughan, "The Construction of Patriotic Festival in Tecamachalco, Puebla (1900–1946)," in *Rituals of Rule, Rituals of Resist-*

ance, ed. W. Beezley, C. E. Martin, and W. E. French (Wilmington, DE: Scholarly Resources, 1994).

8. Important works on education in the 1930s are Britton, *Edcación y radicalismo en México*; Lerner, *La educación socialista*, and "Historia de la reforma educativa, 1933–1945," *Historia Mexicana* 29 (1979): 91–132; Josefina Vázquez, "La educación socialista en los años treinta," *Historia Mexicana* 18 (1969): 408–23; Ernesto Meneses Morales, *Tendencias educativas oficiales en México, 1934–1964* (Mexico: Universidad Iberoamericana, 1988), 52–231; and Raby, *Educación y revolución social*. See also Engracia Loyo, "Lectura para el pueblo, 1921–1940," *Historia Mexicana* 33 (1984): 298–345.

9. See, for example, Jorge Mora Forero, *La ideología educativa del regimen cardenista* (Mexico: El Colegio de Mexico, 1976), and "Los maestros y la práctica de la educación socialista," *Historia Mexicana* 29 (1970): 133–62.

10. See Raby, *Educación y revolución social*; and Arnaldo Cordova, "Los maestros rurales en el cardenismo," *Cuadernos Políticos* 2 (174): 77–92.

11. An exception is Raby, *La revolución social*. Many regional level studies of socialist education have now been published, including Becker, "Black and White and Color"; Salvador Camacho Sandoval, *Controversia educativa entre la ideologia y la fe: La educación socialista en la historia de Aguascalientes* (Mexico: Consejo Nacional para la Cultura y Las Artes, Serie Regiones, 1991); Mary Kay Vaughan, "La actuación política del magisterio socialista en Puebla y Sonora (1934–1939)," *Critica* 32–33 (1987): 90–100; "The Implementation of National Policy in the Countryside: Socialist Education in Puebla in the Cárdenas Period," in *La ciudad y el campo en la Historia de México*, ed. Ricardo Sánchez, Eric Van Young, and Gisela Van Wobeser (Mexico: Universidad Nacional Autónoma de México, 1992), 893–904; Pablo Yankelevich, *La educación socialista en Jalisco* (Guadalajara: Departamento de Educación Pública, Jalisco, 1985).

12. See Vaughan, "La actuación política del magisterio socialista en Puebla y Sonora"; and "Women School Teachers in the Mexican Revolution: The Story of Reyna's Braids," *Journal of Women's History* 2, no. 1 (July 1990): 143–68.

13. On Puebla politics from 1928 to 1940, see Julio Glockner Rossainz, *La presencia del estado en el medio rural: Puebla (1929–1941)* (Puebla: Universidad Autónoma de Puebla, Centro de Investigaciones Filosóficas, 1982); Jesús Marquez Carrillo, *Los origines de Avilacamachismo. Una arqueología de fuerzas en la constitución de un poder regional: el estado de Puebla, 1929–1941* (Tesis de Licenciatura, Universidad Autónoma de Puebla, 1983); Wil Pansters, *Politics and Power in Puebla: The Political History of a Mexican State, 1937–1987* (Amsterdam: Center for Latin American Research and Documentation, 1990); and Rogelio Sánchez López, *La institucionalización: Una historia de los derrotados: Puebla, 1929–1932* (Tesis de Licenciatura, Universidad Autónoma de Puebla, Taller de Marco Velazquez sobre la Revolución mexicana en el estado de Puebla, 1992).

14. Eugen Weber, *Peasants into Frenchmen* (Palo Alto, CA: Stanford University Press, 1976), 110–14, 303–38; François Furet and Jacques Ozouf, *Reading and Writing: Literacy in France from Calvin to Jules Ferry* (Cambridge: Cambridge University Press, 1982), 149–50.

15. Weber, *Peasants*.

16. François Javier Guerra, *Le Méxique de l'ancien régime à la révolution*, 2 vols. (Paris: Editions l'Harmattan, 1985), 269–71.

17. Barry Isaac and Hugo Nutini warn us that census figures on indigenous speakers severely underestimate the latter. Hugo G. Nutini and Barry Isaac, *Los pueblos de habla nahuatl de la región de Tlaxcala y Puebla* (Mexico: Instituto Nacional Indigenista, 1974), 295.

18. See Vaughan, *The State, Education*, 39–66; and "Primary Education and Literacy in Nineteenth Century Mexico: Research Trends, 1968–1988," *Latin American Research Review* 24, no. 3 (1990), 42–55.

19. See Vaughan, "Primary Education and Literacy"; Guerra, *Le Méxique*, Vol. 1, 59–62, 160–62, 206. On the liberal schooling tradition carried into the revolution in the state of Tlaxcala, see Rockwell, "Schools of the Revolution," 7–20. For studies of peasant participation in state formation and their appropriation of "modern" ideologies, see Alan Knight, "El liberalismo mexicano desde la Reforma hasta la Revolución: Una interpretación," *Historia Mexicana* 35 (1985): 59–85; Florencia Mallon, "Peasant and State Formation in Nineteenth Century Mexico: Morelos, 1848–1858," *Political Power and Social Theory* 7 (1988): 1–54; "The Conflictual Construction of Community: Gender, Ethnicity and Hegemony in the Sierra Norte de Puebla," paper presented at the University of Chicago Seminar in Latin American History, May 1990; Guy P. C. Thomson, "Popular Aspects of Liberalism in Mexico, 1848–1888," *Bulletin of Latin American Research* 10, no. 3 (1991): 265–92; "Bulwarks of Patriotic Liberalism: The National Guard, Philharmonic Corps and Patriotic Juntas in Mexico, 1847–1888," *Journal of Latin American Studies* 22 (1989): 31–68.

20. Furet and Ozouf, *Reading*, 153–63, 234–35.

21. Vaughan, *Women School Teachers*, 149; Rockwell, "Schools of the Revolution," 31–32, 36.

22. Robert Redfield, *Chan Kom, The Village That Chose Progress* (Chicago: University of Chicago Press, 1950), 137–38; Furet and Ozouf, *Reading*, 243; Weber, *Peasants*, 318–23.

23. Furet and Ozouf, *Reading*, 243; Vaughan, "Rural Women's Literacy and Education in the Mexican Revolution: Subverting a Patriarchal Event?" in *Creating Spaces, Shaping Transitions: Mexican Women of the Countryside, 1850–1990*, ed. Heather Fowler Salamini and Mary Kay Vaughan (University of Arizona Press, forthcoming).

24. The term is taken from Gonzalo Aguirre Beltrán, *Regions of Refuge* (Washington, DC: Society for Applied Anthropology, 1979), 1.

25. Thomson, "Popular Aspects of Liberalism in Mexico," 286–88.

26. Ben Ekloff, "Peasants and Schools," in *The World of the Russian Peasant: Post Emancipation Culture and Society*, ed. Ben Ekloff and Stephen P. Frank (Boston: Unwin Hyman, 1990), 115–30.

27. Rockwell, "Schools of the Revolution," 7–25; Vaughan, "The Construction of Patriotic Festival," 5–13.

28. Andrés Lira Gónzalez, "Indian Communities in Mexico City: The parcialidades de Tenochtitlán and Taltelolco, 1812–1919," Ph.D. diss., State University of New York, Stony Brook, 545–60. Frederick Starr's visit to Mexican villages in the 1890s suggests the same multiplicity of roles for the teacher, see, for example, Starr, *In Indian Mexico* (Chicago: Forbes, 1908), 260.

29. See Alan Knight, "Intellectuals in the Mexican Revolution," *Los intelectuales y el poder en Mexico*, ed. Roderic A. Camp, Charles A. Hale, and Josefina Zoraida Vázquez (Mexico and Los Angeles: El Colegio de México and UCLA Latin American Studies Center, 1992); Vaughan, "The Construction of

Patriotic Festival," 5–13; Thomson, "Bulwarks," 31–68; Luz Elena Galvan, "La soledad compartida: Una historia de maestros, 1908–1910," Ph.D. diss., Universidad Iberoamericana, 200, 219–22.

30. Literacy figures are taken from *Censo general de la república mexicana verificada el 18 de octubre de 1900* (Mexico: Dirección General de Estadística, Ministerio de Fomento, 1900); *Tercer censo de la población, 1910* (Mexico: Dirección General de Estadística, Ministerio de Romento, 1918); *Quinto censo de la población: 15 de mayo de 1930* (Mexico: Dirección General de Estadística, Secretaría de Economia Nacional, 1930); *Sexto censo de la población, 1940* (Mexico: Dirección General de Estadística, Secretaría de Economia Nacional, 1940). I have analyzed Puebla statistics in "Economic Growth and Literacy in Late Nineteenth Century Mexico: The Case of Puebla," in *Education and Economic Development since the Industrial Revolution*, ed. Gabriel Tortella (Valencia: Generalitat, 1990), 89–111.

31. In the late nineteenth century, states were divided into administrative regions known as districts, which were abolished in the revolution. I have used this nineteenth-century space as a unit for analysis.

32. All the information related here about Tecamachalco is taken from the following sources: SEP inspector reports in the Archivo Historico de la SEP; material from the Archivo Municipal de Tecamachalco; correspondence in the archives of presidents Abelardo Rodríguez, Lázaro Cárdenas, and Manuel Avila Camacho, contained in Acervos Presidentes in the Archivo General de la Nación; and interviews with teachers who worked in Tecamachalco in the 1930s. For full citations see Vaughan, "The Construction of Patriotic Festival," and "Rural Women's Literacy and Education in the Mexican Revolution."

33. As in the case of Tecamachalco, Zacapoaxtla was by 1930 an ex-district. In 1900, it included five counties as Xochiapulco had separated from it to form part of the district of Tetela. As Xochiapulco continued to be a key actor in Zacapoaxtlan history, however, I have included it in my definition of the Zacapoaxtla region.

34. See Eric R. Wolf, "Closed Corporate Communities in Mesoamerica and Central Java," *Southwestern Journal of Anthropology* 13 (1957): 1–18.

35. See Bernardo García Martínez's exhaustive history, *Los pueblos de la Sierra, El poder y el espacio entre los indios del norte de Puebla hasta 1700* (Mexico: El Colegio de México, 1987); on eighteenth-century settlement, see Guy P. C. Thomson, "Montaña and Llañura in the Politics of Central Mexico: The Case of Puebla, 1820–1920," in *Region, State, and Capitalism in Mexico. Nineteenth and Twentieth Centuries*, ed. Wil Pansters and Arij Ouweneel (Amsterdam: CEDLA, 1989), 60–65.

36. Thomson's work elucidates these three options. See "Montaña and Llañura," 65–72; "Popular Aspects of Liberalism in Mexico," 279–87; "Agrarian Conflict in the Municipality of Cuetzalán (Sierra de Puebla): The Rise and Fall of "Pala" Agustín Dieguillo, 1861–1894," *Hispanic American Historical Review* 71, no. 2 (1991): 205–58; on Xochiapulco, "Bulwarks," 31–68. On Xochiapulco, see also Mallon, "The Conflictual Construction of Community"; and Donna Rivera Moreno, *Xochiapulco: una gloria olvidada* (Puebla: Gobierno del Estado, 1991), 41–141. On the civil wars of Zacapoaxtla, see Ramón Sánchez Flores, *Zacapoaxtla, Relación historica* (Puebla, 1984), 115–219.

37. I use the term "Ladino" to refer to those non-Indian elites who served as intermediaries between the indigenous and the outside world: they were for the

most part creole in Zacapoaxtla and Cuetzalán but included some mestizos. On elite-indigenous relations, see Thomson, "Agrarian Conflict," 251–58; Sánchez Flóres, *Zacapoaxtla*, 99, 127, 229–45; Nutini and Isaac, *Los pueblos de habla nahuatl*, 157, 162, 169, 175, 309, 360–61, 392; Moisés Saenz, *Escuelas Federales en la Sierra de Puebla: Informe sobre la visita a las Escuelas Federales en la Sierra de Puebla, realizada por el Subsecetario de Educación, Profesor Moisés Saenz* (Mexico: Secretaría de Educación Pública, 1927), 82–83; Archivo Municipal de Zacapoaxtla, Libro Num. 3, Actas de translación de dominio de terenos adjudicados. Años de 1885, 1887, 1888, 1886; Fondo Comun Auxiliar, 1916–1917 (hereafter cited as AMZ). On schools and literacy, see Vaughan, "Economic Growth and Literacy," 100–102; AMZ, Instrucción Pública, Expediente 33, Actas levantadas por los jurados de examen y calificación de los niños de las escuelas públicas de esta Municipalidad, February 1988.

38. On reciprocity with the context of domination, see Scott, *The Moral Economy*, 35–55.

39. See Archivo General de la Nación, Acervos Presidentes, Fondo Lázaro Cárdenas, Expediente 403/190 (hereafter cited as AGN/FLC); Archivos de la Comisión Agraria Mixta, Puebla, Expediente 2211, El Molino; Expediente 935, Las Lomas; Expediente 867, Jilotepec (hereafter cited as ACAM). See also Pierre Beaucage, "Antropologie économique des communautés indigènes de la Sierra Norte de Puebla (Méxique). 2. Les Villages de haute montagne," *Canadian Review of Sociology and Anthropology* 10, no. 4 (1973): 290–96.

40. On Xochiapulco schools and festivals, see Archivo Municipal de Tetela, Caja 75, Instrucción Pública, 1883, Expediente 54, February 1, 1883; Thomson, "Bulwarks," 31–33; David LaFrance and Guy P. C. Thomson, "Juan F. Lucas: Patriarch of the Sierra Norte de Puebla," in *The Human Tradition in Latin America: The Twentieth Century* ed. William Beezley and Judith Ewell (Wilmington, DE: Scholarly Resources, 1987), 6–8.

41. ACAM, Expediente 187, Atzalán, Apulco.

42. On federal schools in the region in the 1920s, see, among others, AHSEP, Expediente 48.80, Departamento de Educación y Cultura Indígena; Moisés Saenz, *Las escuelas federales*, 68–72; 88–90; AMZ, Instrucción Pública, 1927; on the normal school as promoter of agrarianism and educational crusade, see AGN-FLC, Expedientes 151.2/1181, 544.5/650; interviews with Faustino Hernandez, Puebla, March 13, 1987, Eduardo Ramírez Díaz, Puebla, February 15, 1987; Porfirio Cordero, November 11, 1986; León Ramírez, Puebla, July 8, 1987; Alfonso Fabila, *Sierra Norte de Puebla: Contribución para su estudio* (Mexico: SEP, 1949), 201–6.

43. On opposition to socialist education, see, among others, AHSEP, Dirección de Educación Rural, Expedientes 206.4, 316.7; AGN-FLC, Expediente 151.2/1181.

44. Interviews with Francisco Torral, Zacapoaxtla, March 4, 1993; Rafael Alcantara, March 5, 1993; Filadelfo Vazquez, March 4, 1993; Henry Torres Trueba, "Nahua Factionalism," *Ethnology* 12, no. 4 (1973): 463–74; Louisa Paré, "Caciquismo y estructura del poder en la Sierra Norte de Puebla," in *Caciquismo y poder politico en el Mexico rural*, ed. Roger Bartra (Meico: Siglo Veintiuno, 1978), 38–43, 49–62; Nutini and Isaacs, *Los pueblos de habla nahuatl*, 284–88, 293, 391–92; Beaucage, "Antropologie économique des communautés indigènes de la Sierra Norte de Puebla (Méxique.) 1. Les Villages de basse montagne," *Canadian Review of Sociology and Anthropology*, 10, no. 2 (1973): 122–31.

45. Furet and Ozouf, *Reading*, 67–68, and on French Revolution, 82; Brian Street, *Literacy in Theory and Practice* (Cambridge: Cambridge University Press, 1984), 129–80.

---

8 Virginia Garrard Burnett ◆ God and Revolution: Protestant Missions in Revolutionary Guatemala, 1944–1954

The revolutionary government of Guatemala instituted programs to reach the isolated and impoverished Indian peoples in the rural areas of that nation. In carrying out these programs the representatives of the government attempted to build a rural education system that paralleled in some ways the work already begun by Protestant missionaries. Virginia Garrard Burnett of the University of Texas at Austin has done extensive research on the spread of Protestantism in Guatemala. In the article below she gives special attention to the relationship between Protestant missionaries and the government under Presidents Juan José Arévalo (1945–1950) and Jacobo Arbenz Guzmán (1950–1954). Students should examine the circumstances behind the changes in the relationship between the government and the missionaries after Arbenz gained the presidency.

"Our institutions," remarked a North American Protestant missionary in Guatemala in 1910, referring to his denomination's missions, schools and clinics, "can do more than gunboats."[1] From the time of the Liberal reform of Justo Rufino Barrios, most of Guatemala's Liberal rulers had agreed. Valued by nineteenth-century Liberal rulers for their development projects, their usefulness in the struggle against Catholic clericalism, and, most importantly, for the packaging of North American values, beliefs, and culture in which they wrapped the Word of God, Protestant missionaries worked in Guatemala with the blessing and encouragement of the government from the late nineteenth century until 1944. That year, the "last caudillo"—the old Liberal dictator Jorge Ubico—was ousted from power and replaced by a reformist junta, marking the beginning of Guatemala's decade-long flirtation with progressive revolutionary government.

The change of government precipitated a transformation in the relationship between the Protestant churches and the state. Initially, this

From Virginia Garrard Burnett, "God and Revolution: Protestant Missions in Revolutionary Guatemala, 1944–1954," *The Americas* 46, no. 2 (October 1989): 205–23. Reprinted by permission of *The Americas*.

transition was a propitious one, as the revolutionary government and the missions developed a symbiotic relationship in which each institution drew from the strength of the other. As the revolution gained momentum under the Juan José Arévalo and particularly under the Jacobo Arbenz regime, however, the government came to regard the Protestants not as ambassadors of civilization, but as agents of imperialism. This perception not only drove a wedge between the Guatemalan state and the foreign missions, but it also shattered the fellowship of local congregations. The era would leave a lasting legacy of political conservatism on Protestant work in the country, as well as a lingering sense of displaced nationalism among native Protestants. The purpose of this paper, then, is to examine Protestantism in Guatemala in the context of that country's revolution.

Protestant work in Guatemala dates from March 15, 1873, when the Liberal caudillo Justo Rufino Barrios issued a Decree of Freedom of Worship, establishing freedom of religion in the republic, and opening it to foreign missionaries. The purpose of the decree was twofold. The first was to strike a blow at the Roman Catholic church, the philosophical and institutional bedrock of the opposition Conservative party. The second goal of the decree was to attract immigrants from the modern—and Protestant—countries such as Germany and the United States that Barrios, a devoted Positivist, sought to emulate.[2]

In November 1882, a Presbyterian pastor named John Hill arrived in the country as the personal guest of Barrios. Hill established the nation's first permanent Protestant mission and effectively forged a lasting bond between Liberal government in Guatemala and North American Protestantism. From 1882 to 1920, five major missions took root in the republic: the Presbyterian church, the Central American Mission (CAM), an evangelizing "faith mission" based in Texas, the Quakers, the Church of the Nazarene, and the Primitive Methodist church, a fundamentalist offshoot of the United Methodist church. By 1940, several small American-based Pentecostal sects had established themselves in Guatemala as well. The missionaries who came to Guatemala with these missions enjoyed a special and proprietary relationship with Barrios and the Liberal leaders who succeeded him into the twentieth century. Valued by Liberals for their work in establishing schools and clinics and in promoting North American values—from free enterprise to Western dress—the missionaries enjoyed a privileged status in the republic as informal ambassadors of the religion and culture of the United States.[3]

The 1920s and 1930s saw a decline of Liberal dominance and, with it, a diminishing of missionaries' strength and privilege. Mission work hesitated during a period of political chaos in the 1920s and then faltered during the regime of Jorge Ubico, which lasted from 1931 to 1943. Though of Liberal persuasion, the insular, egocentric Ubico was personally at odds with the foreign religious ventures. For a time, he constrained the missionaries' religious work. When the exigencies of the Good Neighbor Policy, however, forced Ubico to take a new look at the American missions, he eventually saw value in their secular programs in education and medicine. On these pragmatic grounds, Ubico chose to support them during his last years in office.[4]

The revolution that ended the strongman rule of Ubico in 1944 marked the end of Liberal rule and threatened to destroy the traditional relationship between the Guatemalan state and foreign Protestant missions. The new government, ruled first by a provisional junta and then by Juan José Arévalo, a civilian president elected in December 1944, was based on broad reformist ideals which Arévalo dubbed "spiritual socialism." Essentially, Arévalo's program of reform consisted of a bold nationalism combined with a concern for the working class that aimed to build up Guatemala's economic resources without foreign capital and to provide what he called a "square deal" for the common man. Specifically, this program would translate into a number of pieces of innovative legislation. In 1948, Arévalo signed a progressive labor code that allowed for the unionization of urban workers and of laborers on large agricultural plantations. He also established a national Social Security Institute. The revolutionary government would make overtures toward reforms in land tenure in the nation. Finally, Arévalo would seek to elevate the general standard of living of the population by implementing a far-reaching program to promote literacy nationwide.[5]

In the first days after Ubico's departure, however, the American missionaries had been unsure of how amenable the revolutionary government would be to the Protestant cause.[6] Yet despite its nationalistic leanings, the new administration seemed to harbor no ill will toward the foreign missions. The missions were reassured when the new government presented its new constitution, which resoundingly reaffirmed the same kinds of religious legislation that the old Liberal leaders had advocated.[7] The Constitution of 1945 declared the "profession of all religions (to be) free, without any preference," and specified that no religious "groups or their members . . . and ministers of cults (could) intervene in politics or in questions to the organization of labor."[8]

Despite the fact that the new constitution gave no one religious faith the right to take precedence over another, the Protestants found their relationship with the new Arévalo regime to be nearly as close as it had been with the old Liberal governments of earlier years, for the missions' secular projects complemented the government's goals in national development. Although the Protestants were a minuscule group—a survey taken in 1940 showed less than 2 percent of Guatemalans were Protestant, and the missionary force numbered well under one hundred—their cultural impact far exceeded their numbers.[9] "Spiritual socialism"had no place for the missions' theological offerings, but Arévalo was nonetheless eager to incorporate the Protestants' secular efforts into his own program of national development. By the end of 1945, the Presbyterian mission could happily report to its home mission board: "The Mission's relations with the government have been of the most cordial nature. Apparently new missionaries are welcome and (are) necessary for the establishment of the new democracy."[10] Shortly thereafter, the president publicly demonstrated his support of mission work by allowing a Lutheran pastor to present him a copy of the Lutheran catechism at a public labor rally.[11]

The revolutionary government's interest in Protestant work was pragmatic, for planners in the Arévalo administration correctly recognized that Protestant missions could be useful in the regime's ambitious plan for a national literacy program. Because of their belief that the ability to read the Bible was central to salvation, Protestants had pioneered the cause of universal literacy in Guatemala since the 1890s. Eager to tap their experience, Arévalo named Antonio Guerra, a prominent Presbyterian layman, to head the Ministry of Education's literacy program and requested that he act as a liaison to coordinate activities between the government and Protestant churches.[12]

Responding to government requests, the evangelical synod, an interdenominational committee made up of representatives of the five major denominations, created a joint literacy campaign in 1945, to coordinate the disparate and sometimes overlapping programs which various denominations had started in earlier years. The evangelical synod established a literacy committee (Comité de Alfabetización) made up of representatives of each denomination to oversee the campaign and assessed each denomination for money and personnel to support the campaign, to be supplemented by a small grant from the Presbyterian church in the United States.[13] The project's goal was to teach four hundred people to read every six months.[14]

The Central American Mission, the Friends, the Nazarenes, and the Primitive Methodist church all contributed to the literacy campaign, but the Presbyterians dominated the effort. In early 1945, the synod named Presbyterian missionary Paul Winn to coordinate the program.[15] With the synod's backing, Winn started up more than a dozen rural schools for children and adults in isolated parts of the country. The schools were ungraded and designed for students of all ages, and were run in close conjunction with the government-sponsored literacy programs. The evangelicals established schools only where a government-run reading program did not already exist, so that there would be no duplication of effort.[16] The evangelical schools taught reading using the method designed by an American missionary in the Orient by the name of Charles Laubach; the Guatemalan government eventually adopted the method for use in its own literacy program.[17] The evangelical literacy campaign also worked with the government in providing reading materials for the newly literate. Missionaries who worked among the Quiché and Mam peoples published syllabic reading charts in those languages, while the government provided most of the literature in Spanish. The government oversaw the content of readings materials in both Spanish and indigenous languages.[18] To complement the formal readers used in the schools, Winn and his wife began publication of a monthly magazine for new readers called the *Publicación Pro-Alfabetización* or simply, *PAN*. *PAN*, which was published between 1946 and 1951, included short stories, anecdotes, Bible passages, brief lessons in health and hygiene, and occasional political slogans, all in a colorful large-print format.[19]

By late 1946, the evangelical literacy campaign and the government reading programs were intimately integrated. The slogan of the synod campaign was highly nationalistic: "For God and Country—That Which I Have, I Give to You."[20] The Presbyterians helped to coordinate a government literacy census among the Mam during the summer of 1946, while the government used the missionaries' Mam alphabet to try to create a common alphabet for the Indian languages of Guatemala.[21] At the same time, the CAM noted that a large number of its own converts in rural areas served as teachers in the government schools.[22]

The rural schools proliferated in the western highlands, in Huehuetenango, Quezaltenango, San Marcos, Chimaltenango, Totonicapán, and Sololá, El Quiché, and Suchitepequez, while active programs also operated in Jutiapa and in the Alta and Baja Verapaces.[23] Church-sponsored literacy projects thrived on the large fincas on Guatemala's Pacific coast, where the synod sold *PAN* and other reading materials to local *finqueros* to distribute among their workers.[24]

Beyond the literacy efforts, a second concern which many of the Protestant missionaries shared with the Arévalo government was a common interest in labor movements.[25] Breaking with the precedent set by Ubico, the Arévalo administration had supported the development of labor organizations since its first days in power. In 1948, the government's concern for the rights of labor culminated in a progressive labor code, which permitted the formation of unions for urban workers, the right to strike, and the privilege of collective bargaining—rights which also extended to rural laborers on the larger plantations in the country.[26] Initially, the Protestant missionaries saw the new administration's interests in unionization and collective bargaining to be in keeping with conventionally accepted ideas of the rights of labor in the United States.[27]

The missions lent more than passive support to the labor movement. In 1944, with some prodding from its National Assembly back in the United States, the Presbyterian church officially went on record to advise its blue-collar members to join a union and to support the government's collective-bargaining policy.[28] On its own initiative, the evangelical synod began an active literacy campaign among banana workers on the United Fruit Company's plantations in Tiquisate in 1945.[29] In 1947, the Tiquisate campaign began to focus its efforts specifically on members of the new banana workers' union, which had formed after the promulgation of the new labor code.[30]

As late as 1950, an independent missionary from the United States began a ministry of what he called "industrial evangelism," a program which specifically targeted agricultural workers. The missionary worked among UFCO workers and the newly unionized workers of large coffee plantations in the Verapaces, earning him the distrust of commercial producers, particularly the mammoth U.S.-owned United Fruit Company. In 1951, however, the "industrial evangelist" left Guatemala at the forceful urging of UFCO.[31]

Mission activity during the Arévalo years had other critics as well, particularly from religious sectors. The missions' close relationship with the Arévalo government served to exacerbate an existing hostility between the Protestants and the Roman Catholic church. The Catholic hierarchy, under the leadership of the ultra-conservative Archbishop Mariano Rossell y Arellano, had initially hoped that Arévalo's program of "spiritual socialism" would reverse the anticlerical tone of the Liberal period.[32] It had soon become clear, however, that the new constitution of 1945 retained the same kinds of religious legislation as the one which had preceded it. It was also evident that Arévalo, a religious skeptic—although his mother had reportedly converted to Protestantism after listening to a CAM radio broadcast—was as anticlerical as any of the old Liberal leaders.[33]

Such factors convinced the Roman Catholic church hierarchy that the new regime was virtually indistinguishable from any of its predecessors since Justo Rufino Barrios in matters of church and state. If anything, many members of the church hierarchy, some of whom were sympathetic to the Spanish falangists, despised this regime even more because of its socialist tendencies. The year that Arévalo took office, a caustic but widely read Catholic weekly called *Acción Social Cristiana*, began to denounce the new government, which it claimed was made up of "Liberals, Masons, and Communists" as an enemy of the church.[34] The journal, which was modeled after the Spanish falangist chronicle *Cristianidad*, was not an official voice of the church, but it did reflect the opinions of the most conservative elements in the local hierarchy, including the archbishop, who were forbidden by the constitution to express any overt political sentiments.[35] Despite this prohibition, through such journals as *Acción Social Cristiana* and pastoral letters, the Catholic church would become a leader in mobilizing internal opposition to the revolutionary governments of Arévalo and, later, Jacobo Arbenz.[36]

Particularly distasteful to the ultra-conservative Catholics were the Protestants, whom they opposed on not only religious but also political and nationalistic grounds. As early as 1944, *Acción Social Cristiana* accused the Protestants of being "the opening wedge of communism" in Guatemala. Another article in 1945 was more specific; entitled "Protestantism: Fountainhead of Communism?," this selection attempted to draw a connection between the American missionaries, the "Dean of Canterbury," Moscow, and Vicente Lombardo Toledano, the Marxist head of the national labor union in Mexico. In 1947, yet another article described the "accord or allegiance between Protestantism and communism" and suggested that "the avalanche of missionaries could be Communists taking advantage of excessive freedom of religion" to take over the country.[37]

Although these attitudes were by no means universal, *Acción Social Cristiana* did have an impact outside the Catholic hierarchy. In 1945, a series of related articles written by Catholic laymen appeared in local newspapers which unfavorably equated radical social change with the Protestant faith. An article appearing in the newspaper *La Hora* in 1945, argued that "only Catholicism can withstand communism," and pointed to Franco's Spain as a model of democracy. Another defined the right to hold private property as a specific tenet of the Catholic faith. This polemic thus recast the Protestant missions in their familiar role as a counterweight to the Catholic church's political influence.[38]

By the waning years of the Arévalo regime, however, the cordial ties between the government and the missions had begun, almost imperceptibly, to fray. By 1948 Arévalo's reforms had alienated the traditional bases of power in the country—landowners, businessmen, and factions of the army—to such an extent that the president was forced to rely increasingly on other sectors, most notably leftists within his administration, for support. Although as late as 1949 a Presbyterian pastor could report to his sponsors that "the Government maintains a sympathetic attitude toward our missions and missionaries," missionaries had begun to worry privately that the leftward leanings of the government could translate into an anti-Americanism that would threaten their missions and work.[39]

The missionaries' fears were realized in 1950, when the election of Jacobo Arbenz to the presidency brought the fragile alliance of the Protestant missionaries and the revolutionary government to a hasty end. Arbenz, a stridently progressive army colonel, found the idea of foreign missionaries utterly inimical to his fiery brand of nationalism. The North American missionaries, for their part, were alarmed by the pronounced leftist posture of the new government, for the Arbenz administration sought to channel the nationalistic spirit of reform kindled during the Arévalo administration into a wholesale restructuring of Guatemalan society. During his inaugural address, Arbenz had pledged to accomplish three objectives during the course of his administration. The first was to convert Guatemala into an economically independent country. The second was to end Guatemala's feudal patterns of labor relations and land ownership and to modernize the country along capitalistic lines. Finally, Arbenz vowed to raise the standard of living of Guatemala's poor.[40]

Although Arbenz's agenda for reform was theoretically similar to Arévalo's, in practical terms it was considerably more radical. Moreover, although Arbenz himself was not a Communist, he relied heavily on the advice of Communists in his Cabinet, giving them an influence that they had never enjoyed during the Arévalo years. Under his Communist advisers' guidance, Arbenz would introduce unprecedented legislation to divest the nation's largest landholders of their vast plots of unused lands and redistribute it to the tillers of the soil. Since the largest landowner in the country by far was the North American-owned United Fruit Company (UFCO), Arbenz's demands for land reform and his overall agenda for social change carried strongly nationalistic overtones.

It was not surprising, then, that shortly after taking office Arbenz began to slow the tide of Americans coming into the country by tightening up requirements for entry and residence visas. Not long before Arbenz's inauguration, the veteran Presbyterian missionary Paul Burgess wrote to his board in New York that missionaries of all denominations were having considerable difficulty in obtaining residence visas from the Ministry of Foreign Relations. Burgess, however, who had worked in Guatemala for nearly forty years, was sanguine. "This is not necessarily an anti-missionary attitude on the part of the Government," he reassured his board, "for employees of the UFCO and other commercial enterprises find it even harder to secure these visas. It may be part of the 'Red' influence in the present government or just the inferiority complex of a little country expressing itself before the great United States."[41]

As time went on, however, it became apparent that the foreign missionaries were indeed a target of the Arbenz administration, as the government set in action a series of new regulations that made it increasingly difficult for Protestant missionaries to work in Guatemala. Believing North American missionaries to be more the agents of cultural imperialism than of God, Arbenz sought to severely restrict their entry into the country. The Ministry of Foreign Relations tightened the criteria for missionaries to obtain entry visas, demanding they be able to "pay all expenses during the time [they remained in the country] and pledge not to molest the state in any way." Some potential missionaries were required by the Foreign Ministry to undergo review by the National Police. Applicants from the Central American Mission (CAM) fell under the particular scrutiny of the Ministry of Foreign Relations, perhaps because of the mission's claims of "apoliticism" and its close ties to conservative groups in the United States. Successful completion of the visa application process, however, was no guarantee of approval; by 1952, the administration routinely denied admission to North American missionaries without explanation. Eventually, the Arbenz government made visa application such a trying and labyrinthine process that the influx of missionaries into the country slowed to less than a dozen a year by 1953, less than half what it had been during the Arévalo years.[42]

Even if the government had not created these obstacles, the Protestant work would have slowed on its own. Watching with growing concern as Guatemala inched to the left under Arbenz, missionary boards in the United States began to withhold funds from their missions and to make plans to withdraw their personnel from the country. Their fears deepened in June 1952, when the government announced its watershed Agrarian Reform Law, whch effectively expropriated with compensation the unused lands of the vast plantations owned by the United Fruit Company and other large plantations. Protesting the attempt to expropriate the lands, the United States began to build a case for Communist infiltration of the Arbenz government. At the same time, violence in the countryside began to mount, as peasants, who were eager for land and unwilling to wait for the formal redistribution process, began to take land by force.[43]

While the missionaries were probably never in any physical danger, the government's increasingly radical agenda posed a growing obstacle to Protestant work during the early 1950s. The problem with the expropriation of the fruit company's land had fueled hostility between the United States and Guatemalan governments, and the burden fell upon foreigners who worked in the country. After the passage of the Agrarian Reform Law, Arbenz mandated legislation designed to lessen the institutional strength of the American missions. In 1953, the president backed a law sponsored by the teachers' union that required that 40 percent of the faculty at all private schools be assigned by the government. The National Congress vetoed the law, but had it passed, it would have cut at the heart of the Protestants' extensive educational program.[44]

By early 1954, the Protestant missionaries had lost the only lasting tie they had with the revolutionary government, the rural schools. In an effort to end the foreigners' prominence in the national literacy program, the Arbenz government enacted a law requiring teaching aptitude certificates, which in effect eliminated the evangelicals' teaching staffs. The missionaries reported that officials enforced the new laws rigorously in the Protestant schools, even though by one missionary's reckoning, "not even one" teacher in the government schools possessed such a certificate.[45] To the missionaries, the apparently arbitrary enforcement of this law on mission schools was clear evidence of the present government's nationalistic anti-Americanism.

By the end of Arbenz's first year in office, the American missionaries, reflecting the opinion of American policymakers and businessmen in the country, were nearly united in their opposition to the regime. Although they had initially hoped that the Arbenz regime would increase social justice in Guatemala, the missionaries were convinced by late 1951 that the Arbenz government was Communist and, as such, was both a religious and a political threat to their work. Although few missionaries shared the opinion expressed in *Verbum*, the official mouthpiece of the archbishop, that land distribution was unnecessary and was merely a political device to attract illiterate voters, most agreed that the government's means of land reform were unacceptable.[46] To the Protestant missionaries, moreover, the national sympathy for communism was a special source of anguish, for it represented a rejection of the package of American ways and Protestant beliefs that they had preached for so many years.

Yet the missionaries did not take the challenge passively. The CAM rang forth the battle cry to "answer the barrage of Communist literature with Christ-centered propaganda produced in quantity and quality."[47] The Presbyterians sponsored a general seminar on communism for the missionaries of the other denominations at the annual conference of the evangelical synod in 1951.[48] Missionaries of all denominations thundered bold denunciations of communism from their pulpits, insisting that all true and just government must come from God, rather than from godless ideologues.[49] In a few instances they attacked government programs directly, such as on the Sunday after the Agrarian Reform Law went into effect, when the pastor of the Central Presbyterian Church in the capital preached a sermon explaining how the right to private property was integral to Christian life.[50]

Below the level of national politics, a more immediate threat to mission work lay with the local congregations, where bitter schisms arose between those who supported the government's revolutionary programs and those who did not. While foreign missionaries opposed the government programs more or less as a bloc, many of their parishioners were among the most active advocates of the radical reform. The greatest advocates of the radical reform were those who stood to benefit the most from it—the poor, the landless, and the illiterate. Since people of the lower classes made up the largest proportion of the Protestant membership, it was not surprising that the radical reform would find considerable support in the Protestant churches. Moreover, the fact that converts had already committed a major deviance from accepted social norms by joining a Protestant church in the first place often meant that indigenous Protestants were more open to radical change than were their Catholic counterparts. To many of the Protestants, the process was logical: having thrown off religious oppression, it was now time to strike out for political freedom.

Pragmatically speaking, Protestant Guatemalans were in a much better position to become involved in radical politics than were their Catholic brethren. Articles in the Catholic journals *Verbum* and *Acción Social Cristiana* which warned against communism in all its guises and prohibited, on threat of excommunication, voters from casting their ballots in local elections for "Communist candidates"—a term which included most leftists—influenced the thinking of many Catholics.[51] Protestants, on the other hand, who lacked the direction of a single authority, could and did interpret their churches' more ambiguous positions on political involvement to their own satisfaction. Another practical factor which made native Protestants open to reform, and land reform in particular, was that they had fewer material vested interests than their Catholic neighbors. In Indian villages, most men were members of the local Catholic religious brotherhoods, or *cofradías*. These brotherhoods frequently opposed government programs on the grounds that land reform would jeopardize their *cofradía* landholdings. Protestants, who had no *cofradía* interests at stake, had little to lose and much to gain by supporting the reforms.[52]

These factors were at least in part responsible for the fact that Indian Protestants tended to be more actively involved in the radical reform than their Ladino counterparts. For example, in Chinautla, in the department of Guatemala, Presbyterian laymen formed the leadership of the *unión campesina*, which managed the distribution of lands under the Agrarian Reform Law of 1952.[53] Indigenous Protestants also figured prominently in the agrarian reform movement in the Indian villages around Lake

Atitlán, where local elections placed Protestants in public office for the first time.[54] Protestants formed the core of leadership of local agrarian committees and peasant leagues in highland villages around Quezaltenango.[55] Protestants also figured in the Confederación de Trabajadores de América Latina (CTAL), a Communist organization which faithful Catholics had been forbidden to join by the church hierarchy.[56]

The prominence of Protestants in the agrarian reform pitted them against local indigenous leaders belonging to Catholic Action, a Catholic religious-political organization that had started in Guatemala in the 1930s. Especially active in the Indian regions of Quiché and Totonicapán, the movement had gained ground during the early days of the Arévalo administration, when, for the first time, departmental officials could be elected rather than appointed. Catholic Action candidates had won local elections with some success until the 1949 presidential election, when the church had expressed strong opposition to Arbenz's selection. By 1951, Catholic Action had taken on the trappings of an anti-Communist crusade. Thus, when Protestants competed for—and won—positions in local government at the expense of Catholic Action candidates, the traditional religious struggle, even during the revolutionary years, once again assumed its customary political outlines.[57]

Indigenous Protestants, however, were by no means united in their support of the radical reform, and controversy over the government program shattered the fellowship of many congregations. In some situations, the issue caused a permanent rift between congregations and their pastors, while elsewhere the controversy caused fratricidal division among church members. An example of this occurred in the Presbyterian Quiché mission in Cantel, on the eastern border of Sololá. In that parish the fellowship in the congregation began to disintegrate when a number of members of the church became active in the land distribution program. Conservative members of the church criticized their activist brethren for dabbling in political matters, while radicals berated their brothers for their complacency.[58]

Tensions began to mount in 1953, when radical members of the congregations became active in the local peasant committee. In the last months of the year, the syndicate allegedly began to harrass some conservative members of the congregation with threats of death. The conservative Presbyterians responded with a blistering public campaign against the Presbyterian *sindicalistas*. Posting printed placards around the town denouncing the *politicastros evangélicos* (the Protestant shysters), the conservatives upbraided the radicals for the moral shame they had brought to the church through their political work and exhorted them "not to use the smokescreen of religion for their vile politics." By the first months of

1954, the Cantel mission had split into two separate churches. The radical Protestants formed a new mission called Gethsemane, while the conservative and apolitical Presbyterians remained part of the old congregation and continued to meet in the church building.[59]

It is important to note that American missionaries generally tried to remain neutral in this and similar struggles elsewhere, despite the fact that the revolutionary nationalism posed a specific threat to the missionaries' own work and were usually contrary to their own personal political views. Indeed, the patriarch of the Presbyterian mission, Paul Burgess, himself no political radical, wrote a sympathetic report to describe the concerns of the radical dissidents in the Cantel Church to readers in the United States. "We thot [sic] it only fair," he explained, "to share some of the experiences of the brethren in Christ who have chosen to remain Presbyterians while being enthusiastic agrarians."[60]

Many missionaries, particularly among the Presbyterians, seemed to have been guardedly empathetic to the concerns of the radical members of their flocks, although few were sympathetic ideologically. In 1954, the Presbyterians asked congregations in the United States to "pray for the Government of Guatemala. Many are sincerely seeking to remedy age-old evils in our society. Finding sympathy and help in Communist circles, they naturally think the beast is not as evil as he is pictured."[61] Another evangelical observer noted, "A number of people in Guatemala, including university students and some Protestants, have been exposed to Communism and attracted by it . . . especially with its basic appeal for social justice."[62]

A few missionaries were determined to maintain or even expand their work during the Arbenz years, even as the political climate became increasingly threatening. The evangelical synod's literacy campaign had continued to operate on the United Fruit Company's plantations around Tiquisate since the mid-1940s, despite the fact that large-scale strikes paralyzed the area in 1948 and 1949 and even after the plantations became the focus of the expropriation issue in 1952 and 1953.[63] As late as 1954, the interdenominational journal *Guatemala News* reported "a great campaign to put the Word into the hands of the new settlers in the Tiquisate region. [Bibles will be given] to the settlers and workers of the United Fruit Company."[64]

Indeed, at least one mission was openly sympathetic to the radical government, even at the height of the Arbenz reforms. This was the Missouri Synod Lutheran church, which, having opened its first mission in Guatemala in 1947, was unfamiliar with the traditional political orientation of the Protestant missions. Between 1950 and 1953, the Lutheran church in the United States sent at least five seminarians to Guatemala, specifically to work in conjunction with several government-sponsored development programs.[65] Their most ambitious program, begun during the summer of 1951, was in Zacapa, where seminarians worked along-side the Ministry of Agriculture's Instituto Agropecuario Nacional to try to improve agricultural production in a ten-*aldea* area. By 1952, the program had expanded to include classes in agricultural techniques and social welfare. The Lutheran church also conducted several social programs in Guatemala City. The largest of these was a social welfare agency opened in 1952 to improve the standard of living among the burgeoning masses of the urban poor in the capital.[66] This program was apparently not tied in directly to any specific government-sponsored development project, but did operate with the government's blessing.

Because of these programs and of the Lutheran church's relatively liberal political stance, the relationship between the Lutheran church and the Arbenz administration seems to have been reasonably close. Evidence of a congenial relationship lay in the fact that Lutheran missionaries during the revolutionary period experienced none of the problems with visas and immigration that plagued the missionaries of the other denominations. In fact, the Ministry of Foreign Relations in the Arbenz years seems to have often processed the papers of Lutheran applicants with remarkable dispatch.[67]

Yet the Arbenz government remained somewhat suspicious of the Lutherans. While the Ministry of Foreign Relations did not demand the same stringent visa qualifications that it asked of other groups, the ministry did require other kinds of certification from the mission. The Ministry of Foreign Relations insisted that the Lutheran missionaries agree to the stipulation that they return to the United States at any time that the government might judge that they had acted "to the detriment of the country."[68] It also demanded that the home mission board send each missionary the rather tidy sum of 250 quetzales per month, so that they would not be an economic burden to the country.[69]

In short, the Arbenz administration's relationship with all foreign missions, even the Lutherans, was an uneasy one. Mutual suspicion, fueled by the decaying relations between the United States and Guatemala, destroyed whatever possibilities might have existed for large-scale cooperation. The uncertainty of the 1951–1954 period took its toll on the Protestant work, and few missionaries mourned when the CIA-backed forces under Carlos Castillo Armas forced Arbenz to step down in June 1954. Most missionaries, however, backed the Castillo Armas coup only passively. Although they were relieved to have the leftist government out of power, they were unsure how the new reactionary regime would regard mission work, especially since so many indigenous converts had been actively involved in revolutionary programs. As one missionary summed up his concern for the future of the work in his annual Christmas letter in 1954: "The Communists are out now," he wrote. "But they left the yarn in such a snarl that we can hardly continue the old pattern of weaving."[70]

The revolutionary years, in summary, were a time of mixed fortunes for Protestant work in Guatemala. During the Arévalo administration, the institutional work of the missions flourished. The early Arévalo years reflect the traditional and symbiotic relationship between Protestant missions and the Guatemalan state. As such, the early Arévalo government valued Protestant missionaries as foils for Catholic power and for their developmentalist projects. Although relations between missions and the government began to sour slightly in the late 1940s, as Arévalo came to rely increasingly on leftists for advice, the administration, by and large, continued the pro-Protestant policies of the earlier governments.

Relations between the Protestant churches and the state worsened significantly with the election of Jacobo Arbenz to the presidency. Arbenz's highly nationalistic agenda for reform and the crisis over the expropriation of the United Fruit Company's lands alienated most North American missionaries, who eventually concurred with the U.S. State Department's evaluation that the Arbenz government was infiltrated by Communists. The Arbenz administration, for its part, aggravated the deteriorating relations with the Protestant missionaries by restricting missionaries' visas and applying legislation designed to weaken their influence.

Not all Protestants, however, were alienated during the Arbenz period. Some foreign missionaries, particularly those with the Lutheran Mission, became actively involved in the government's most liberal reform projects. Such support, however, like that of individual Catholic priests, was the exception rather than the rule during the Arbenz administration.

A more significant trend that emerged during the revolutionary period was that native Protestants, having experienced a spiritual transformation, hoped to participate in the nation's political transformation. These politicized Protestants often rose to positions of leadership in local land reform projects and peasant organizations, giving them an influence that far outweighed their numbers. The upheaval of these years, in terms of national politics, and within the Protestant flock, would ultimately cause the missions to redefine their work and identity in Guatemala. By 1955, the foreign missions found that they no longer had the symbiotic relationship they had enjoyed with the old Liberal regimes, nor were there the shared social concerns that had linked them to the Arévalo administration. Forced to reinterpret their political stance, the missions would adopt an anti-Communist posture that endeared them to the new counterrevolutionary government. The Protestant missions, however, never completely regained the status they had enjoyed during the balmy days of Liberal rule.

Notes

1. Guatemalan Mission to Presbyterian Board of Foreign Missions (hereinafter cited as PBFM), 3 May 1910, PBFM letters 1903–1911.

2. Gobierno de Guatemala, *Recopilación de las leyes emitidas por el gobierno de la República de Guatemala*, tomo 1, June 1871–July 1881 (Guatemala: Tipográfia de "El Progreso", 1881), p. 174; see also Paul Burgess, *Justo Rufino Barrios* (New York: Dorrance & Co., 1926), p. 109–110; J. Lloyd Mecham, *Church and State in Latin America: A History of Politico-Ecclesiastic Relations* (Chapel Hill: University of North Carolina Press, 1966), p. 319; Hubert J. Miller, *Iglesia y estado en el tiempo de Justo Rufino Barrios* (Guatemala: Universidad de San Carlos, 1976).

3. Mildred Spain, *And in Samaria: A Story of Fifty Years' Missionary Witness in Central America 1890–1940* (Dallas: Central American Mission, 1940), p. 161; James M. Taylor, *On Muleback Through Central America* (Knoxville, Tenn.: James M. Taylor, Publisher, 1913), p. 50; see also David Stoll, *Fishers of Men or Founders of Empire? The Wycliffe Bible Translators in Latin America* (Cambridge: Cultural Survival, 1982).

4. Archivo General de Centro América in Guatemala City (hereinafter cited as AGCA), Ministério de Gobernación, Carta #100 Jorge Ubico to Ministério de Gobernación, 18 November 1931); Ministério de Relaciones Exteriores, "Inscripciones de extranjeros," 542; see also Kenneth J. Grieb, *Guatemalan Caudillo: The Regime of Jorge Ubico* (Athens: University of Ohio Press, 1979).

5. Thomas M. Leonard, *The United States and Central America 1944–1949: Perceptions of Political Dynamics* (Tuscaloosa: University of Alabama Press, 1984), p. 84; Stephen Schlesinger and Stephen Kinzer, *Bitter Fruit: The Untold Story of the American Coup in Guatemala* (Garden City, NY: Anchor Press, 1983), p. 37; Thomas and Marjorie Melville, *Guatemala: The Politics of Land Ownership* (New York: Free Press, 1971), pp. 27–32; Richard Immerman, *The CIA in Guatemala: The Foreign Policy of Intervention* (Austin: University of Texas Press, 1982), pp. 43–57; Leo A. Suslow, "Aspects of Social Reform in Guatemala 1944–1949," Latin American Seminar Reports #1, mimeographed (Hamilton, NY: Colgate University, 1949).

6. "Report of the Education Committee," *Guatemala News*, 35 (4):6–7.

7. *El Noticiero Evangélico*, 29 (255):3.

8. Mecham, p. 320; Georgina R. Allcott, "An Historical Survey of Evangelical North American Mission Boards in Guatemala," (Master's thesis, Columbia Bible College, 1970), p. 29.

9. The census figure comes from a biased source, the Catholic weekly *Acción Social Cristiana*, 30 December 1948. The figure seems accurate, however, when compared with the statistics which appear in Kenneth Grubb's *Religion in Central America* (London: World Dominion Press, 1937).

10. Minutes of the Annual Meeting of the Presbyterian Mission, 1946, Iglesia Evangélica Nacional Presbiteriana in Guatemala City (hereinafter cited as IENP).

11. Clarence T. Kuehn, "The History of the Lutheran Church-Missouri Synod in Guatemala until June 1949," (Master's thesis, Concordia Seminary, 1950), p. 42.

12. Antonio Guerra, interview held 21 January 1985.

13. *Boletín de la Iglesia Central Presbiteriana*, 23 March 1947; *Harvester*, 56 (1):4; *Harvester*, 27 (3):6–11; *Central American Bulletin* (hereinafter cited as *CAB*), #266 (1946):3.

14. *El Mensajero Evangélico*, 41 (5):23.

15. Minutes of Meeting of the Guatemala Station, 3 January 1945, IENP.

16. Doyle Brewington to Paul Burgess, 24 March 1945, IENP; PBFM to Guatemala Mission #302, 3 January 1946, p. 3, IENP.

17. *CAB* #266 (1946): 3; *Harvester*, 26 (12–13):10, "Resultados de la campaña de alfabetización por el comité del sínodo," *El Cristiano*, 42 (472):5–6.

18. Minutes of the Annual Meeting, October 1945, p. 1, IENP.

19. *El Mensajero*, 41 (2):18; see also Pro-Alfabetización Nacional (hereinafter cited aas PAN) 1945–1961; PAN 3 (2):3.

20. PAN 3 (2):3.

21. *El Noticiero Evangélico*, 30 (276):9–10; "A Mission's Contribution to the Indian Problems of Guatemala," *Guatemala News*, 39 (3–4):3.

22. *CAB* #266 (1946):3.

23. PAN 2 (8):1, 4; *El Mensajero Evangélico*, 41 (7):23–25; *El Mensajero*, 39 (10):5; *El Mensajero*, 39 (9):4.

24. Paul Winn to Virginia Garrard, letter 12 February 1985.

25. See Archer C. Bush, "Organized Labor in Guatemala 1944–1949" Latin American Seminar Reports #2 (Hamilton: Colgate University, 1950); R. L. Woodward, Jr., "Octubre: Communist Appeal to the Urban Labor Force of Guatemala 1950–1953, *Journal of Inter-American Studies*, 4 (1962): 363–374.

26. Schlesinger, pp. 38–39; Melville, p. 31.

27. T. N. Harer to PBFM, 27 August 1944, IENP.

28. "Minutes of the Annual Meeting of the Guatemala Mission: Report to the General Assembly of the Presbyterian Church, May 1944, IENP.

29. Schlesinger, p. 42.

30. *El Noticiero Evangélico*, 29 (263):110–11.

31. Paul Burgess to PBFM, 3 November 1950, IENP.

32. Anita Frankel, "Political Development in Guatemala 1944–1945: The Impact of Foreign, Military, and Religious Elites," (Ph.D. dissertation, University of Connecticut, 1969), p. 194; see also Mary Holleran, *Church and State in Guatemala* (New York: Columbia University Press, 1949).

33. *Aclaraciones del Excmo. y Revmo. Sr. Arzobispo Metropolitano, sobre la recta y firme postura de la iglesia de Guatemala con relación al presente momento político y protesta por las insidiosas calumnias de partidos políticos contra el clero de nuestra país* (Guatemala: Imprenta Sensur, 1950), in Hubert J. Miller, "Catholic Leaders and the Guatemalan Revolution Under the Jacobo Arbenz Administration," unpublished paper, presented at SCOLAS Conference, San Antonio, TX, April 1988.

34. *CAB* #279 (1948):16.

35. "Los católicos disocian del pueblo de Guatemala," *La Hora*, 27 January 1945; Frankel, p. 193.

36. Frankel, pp. 169–170, 192.

37. *Acción Social Cristiana*, 11 October 1945: *Acción Social Cristiana*, 22 May 1947.

38. Maria Cobos Batres, "Solo el catolicismo podría salvarnos," *La Hora*, 5 June 1945: "Los catolicos disocian del pueblo de Cristo," *La Hora*, 27 January 1945.

39. Narrative Report of the Guatemala Station, 1949, IENP; Leonard, pp. 75, 80–96.

40. Leonard, pp. 75–106.

41. Burgess to PBFM, 20 September 1950, IENP.

42. Burgess to Ruth Wardel, 18 November 1950, IENP; AGCA, Ministerio de Relaciones Exteriores, "Ingresos de religiosos," p. 565.

43. For various evaluations of the Arbenz regime see: Manuel Galich, *¿Por qué lucha Guatemala? Arévalo y Arbenz: Dos hombres contra un imperio* (Buenos Aires: Elmer Editor, 1956); Daniel James, *Red Design for the Americas: Guatemalan Prelude* (New York: John Day Company, 1954); Ronald M. Schneider, *Communism in Guatemala 1944–1954* (New York: Frederick A. Praeger Publishers, 1958); José Aybar, "Dependency and Intervention: The Case of Guatemala in 1954," *Hispanic American Historical Review*, 59 (4): 737–758; Jim Hardy, *Gift of the Devil: A History of Guatemala* (Boston: South End Press, 1984). For a specific but uncritical description of UFCO activities in Guatemala see Stacy May and Galo Plaza, *The United Fruit Company in Latin America* (Washington, DC: National Planning Association, 1958).

44. Annual Report, La Patria School, 1953, IENP.

45. Northern Presbytery Annual Report, 1954, IENP.

46. Miller, pp. 6–7.

47. *CAB* #318 (1953):10.

48. Minutes of the Executive Committee, 12 September 1951, IENP.

49. *Boletín de la Iglesia Central Presbiteriana*, 5 July 1953; 6 December 1953; 1 June 1952.

50. Ibid., 8 June 1952.

51. *Verbum*, 25 September 1949, pp. 1–2, in Miller, "Catholic Leaders," pp. 10–11.

52. Ricardo Falla, "Evolución político-religiosa del indigena rural en Guatemala (1945–1965)," *Estudios Sociales Centroamericanos*, 1 (1):27–47.

53. Falla, 27–47; see also Ruben E. Reina, *Chinautla: A Guatemalan Indian Community* (New Orleans, MARI Publication #24, 1960).

54. Falla, pp. 32–33.

55. Stoll, *Fishers*, p. 48.

56. Mariano Rossell y Arellano et al., *Carta pastoral colectiva del episcopado de la provincia eclesiástica de Guatemala sobre la amenaza comunista en nuestra patria* (Guatemala: Tipografía Sánchez y de Guise, 1945), in Miller, p. 10.

57. Miller, p. 8.

58. "Carta Abierta, Cantel Enero 1954, 'A los politicastros evangélicos: David Ordóñez Colóp, Gabriel Sam Chuc, Obispo Salaníc Salaníc, Felipe Santiago Colóp García, Juan Itcep & otros, con motivo de la manifestación de los 'revoltosos' no REVOLUCIONARIA del 13 de diciembre próximo pasado.' " IENP: "Presbyterian Agrarians," *Guatemala News*, 44 (6):3–5.

59. Ibid.

60. "Presbyterian Agrarians," *Guatemala News*, 44 (6):3–5.

61. *Guatemala News*, 45 (1):3.

62. Stanley Rycroft, "Guatemala a Symbol," *World Dominion*, November–December 1954, p. 354.

63. Schlesinger, p. 42.

64. *Guatemala News*, 43 (1):3.

65. AGCA, Ministério de Relaciones Exteriores, "Ingresos de religiosos," 565, 16 August 1952; 16 July 1951; 22 July 1950; 4 September 1953; 24 July 1952.

66. Ibid., 16 July 1951; 24 July 1952; 16 August 1952.

67. Ibid., 22 July 1950; 16 July 1952; 24 July 1952; 16 August 1952; 4 September 1953.

68. Ibid., 16 July 1951.

69. Ibid., 16 August 1952.

70. Christmas letter from the Paul Burgess family, 1954, IENP.

---

9 Ruth and Leonard Greenup ◆ Education for Perón

Argentina of the 1940s was a country caught in deep internal struggles complicated by rumors of fascist intrigue and the very real diplomatic rivalry between the United States and Nazi Germany during World War II. Ruth and Leonard Greenup were young reporters working the Argentine beat during this time of turmoil and uncertainty. The newly married couple worked for the Buenos Aires Herald, *an English-language newspaper that covered Argentina from provincial cattle shows on the Pampas to the political machinations in the nation's capital. While the following selection tends to exaggerate the influence of Nazi Germany, it also conveys through a first-person account the chilling story of an authoritarian military regime's campaign against the country's long-established and widely respected education system.*

A school teacher, nearly sixty years in his grave, is one of the most controversial figures in present-day Argentina—most respected by democrats and most hated by the elements which have been in power since the June 1943 revolution.

Domingo Faustino Sarmiento left a heritage bitterly opposed to totalitarian rule; therefore, it is his name that has been most often used as a banner in the struggle against military government. It also explains why the educational system, and in particular the universities, have fought against [Juan Domingo] Perón and his ilk.

Sarmiento was a president, but first and foremost he was an educator. Proof of this is that he built a thousand new primary schools in Argentina

From Ruth and Leonard Greenup, *Revolution Before Breakfast: Argentina, 1941–1946* (Chapel Hill: University of North Carolina Press, 1947), 187–208. Reprinted by permission of the publisher.

at a time when there were fewer than two million inhabitants. He also brought teachers from the United States to instruct the young men and women who were to teach in the new buildings. Sarmiento believed that literacy and a knowledge of the world would help make his people great.

He did more to educate the Argentines than any other man. In 1869, before he became minister of education, seventy-seven out of every one hundred persons were unable to read or write; but in 1895, when his efforts were beginning to bear fruit, nearly half the population could read and write; and in 1943 the Ministry of Education estimated that only 16.6 percent of all persons above the age of fourteen were illiterate. In South America this is a remarkably low figure. Only Uruguay can compare with it.

There have been other great educators in Argentina, but most of them took their inspiration from Sarmiento. He is indirectly responsible for the fact that in recent decades Argentina spent more money for education than all the other countries of South America together; that until recently there were two school teachers in Argentina for every soldier; that until the military coup of 1943 Argentina was one of the few countries that spent more money on its educational system than on its army, navy, and air force.

The educational system in Argentina has not changed a great deal since the days of Sarmiento, except that the schools have become larger and more numerous. The basic standards that Sarmiento set for education of the people have not changed much—perhaps not enough. The standard requirement for compulsory attendance is for three years in the schools supported by the federal government and two years in schools financed by the provinces. The primary schools still maintain six grades, and there are far too few secondary schools to take care of students who could and should advance beyond the primary schools. In 1942 the Ministry of Education estimated that out of the approximately two million students in all the nation's schools, only one out of eleven reached high school and one out of forty-two attended an institution of higher learning. An indication of "improvised" education is seen in a 1944 report stating that the rich Argentine nation had only four thousand buildings constructed especially for schools. The national educational authorities were renting eleven thousand of the fifteen thousand structures used in the country as schools and even by renting still did not have enough room to give each child a desk.

As for instruction, teaching is still by rote and recitation and is largely "academic," with little emphasis on preparing the students for any life other than a "cultural" or strictly professional one. There is scant industrial or specialized instruction, which is a serious lack at a time when

Argentina is changing from an entirely pastoral era to a mixed economy of agriculture and industry.

But the fact that Sarmiento was responsible for the present educational system and the construction of one fourth of the buildings expressly raised for primary schools does not account for the hatred felt for him by the totalitarian forces—the ones who have arrested teachers for merely reciting speeches he made nearly a century ago.

To them it is the ideas of Sarmiento that are dangerous—in particular his belief in democracy and his open admiration of the United States. These concepts of Sarmiento lived on in the schools. That is why peace fled the classroom with the advent of military government in Argentina, and desks and chairs, the blackboards and buildings marked the field of battle for the opposing ideas of Sarmiento and Juan Domingo Perón. Ideas fought ideas, and sometimes blackboard erasers went into combat with tear gas bombs. The struggle was as unequal as bare hands against a saber. With brute force the military regime and its followers were able, at any chosen moment, to muzzle the democratic spokesmen in the primary and secondary schools. Through mass discharges and suspensions of teachers and threats against others they extracted lip service for their creed in the classroom. And they implanted authoritarian doctrines through at least one special "orientation" school for teachers, which is, fortunately, inoperative at the moment.

The only pillar of the educational structure that consistently has repulsed the totalitarians is the university hierarchy. The university students constitute one of the few elements which viewed the 1946 presidential elections as a battle between fascism and democracy. That is why Perón and the *peronistas* hate the universities and are "reforming" them.

It was not surprising that the military men who seized power in Argentina should attempt to revamp Sarmiento's educational system into a new mold for the young. They had seen the carefully indoctrinated youth of Germany and Italy become enthusiastic and useful slaves of fascism in those countries. And the Argentines set out in more or less efficient fashion to duplicate the performance. Teachers were told what to teach and which things to ignore—which of the great Argentine statesmen should be passed over lightly in history classes, and which others should be held up and glorified in the eyes of Argentine youth. As in Germany, the emphasis was shifted from the great but unspectacular values of culture, philosophy, art, and the sciences to glorification of military history and super-citizenship.

Not by accident did we learn of the perversion of education in Argentina and the heroic struggle of the university students against it. Ruth and I never had a chance to forget it, because of Albert, a gay, intelligent nineteen-year-old who liked to drop in on us and talk. We liked to have him come. Albert always brought a little gift—sometimes just a few chocolates, fifty centavos worth of cakes, or some garden flowers for Ruth.

But one night he came flourishing a bottle of French champagne. The dust was still on the bottle, and it was years old.

"Albert, you shouldn't have done this," I protested mildly. I didn't think a student could afford such luxuries.

Albert grinned, waved my protest aside as if even champagne wasn't good enough for his friends.

"But we're going to celebrate," he said. "Besides, the father of one of my friends gave it to me because of what we did to the German chargé d'affaires today. He was invited to speak before our law class.

"Well, it was like this," Albert continued, "when our professor brought the German into the classroom we clapped our hands and cheered. The German liked it. He smiled at us and bowed. Then, we started clapping our hands together harder and harder and yelling, 'Bravo, bravo.' After we had kept this up about ten minutes, the professor motioned for us to be still. But we kept right on applauding and applauding. Finally, the German sat down, but we kept on cheering him. We didn't stop for the whole hour and he never did get a chance to say a single word."

Ruth and I were impressed so much by the cleverness of Albert and his classmates that we asked him if he would take us to visit his school, the University of La Plata, on our next day off and Albert agreed.

When we arrived at the law school building the following week, we were greeted at the door by a committee of students who ushered us into a conference room, where we were seated in high-backed leather chairs around a big oval table. All of the law students were dressed in correct dark business suits and their mustaches were neatly trimmed. Clean-shaven Albert looked strangely like a plump brunette cherub among his somber classmates. They were older and more serious-looking than university students in the United States.

I didn't see any bobby soxers and asked about the status of women in the university. The students told me that there were a few women in the university but not the large proportion of coeds found in the United States.

One young man, whom Albert introduced to us as the president of the La Plata Federation of Students, informed us that unlike in the United States, the students of Argentina were a real political force. They were either Fascists, conservatives, democrats, socialists, or Communists. They took their politics as seriously as Yankee students took their college football.

As for rights, Argentine students were far ahead of their colleagues in the United States. Compulsory class attendance, for instance, had been abolished many years ago, and students found nonattendance an extremely practical way of eliminating professors who were inefficient or whose politics they didn't approve. For example, if one of the law professors started teaching Fascist doctrines, students who disagreed could simply stay away from his classes. He couldn't go on teaching to an empty room forever, so the students would eventually have a professor more to their liking. They even had a voice in choosing the dean of the law school.

Another boy explained that the school was now in the midst of a student election with the party lines sharply drawn between Fascist and democratic students. The issue in the coming election was not who would be the campus beauty queen but whether Argentina should remain neutral or join the Allies. They then explained their alliance with students of other universities throughout the country and told how it had helped to bring about better conditions for students, as well as greater influence in national politics.

After our conference with the students, Albert took us in to meet his dean, a gentle little man, who served us coffee in his office. Ruth asked him to comment on the legality of President [Ramón S.] Castillo's state of siege. The question obviously distressed him and instead of replying he went to one of his book shelves and took out a manual on democracy he had written several years earlier for distribution among the armed forces. Then we asked him if he would discharge a professor for criticizing President Castillo or his policies. The dean promptly replied that his professors were free to criticize—that is, as long as they confined their criticisms to the policies of the government officials and did not attack the men personally.

The law school dean told us that many professors were also senators and representatives and that one of the surest ways to become president of Argentina was to become a college professor first.

Ruth and I left the University of La Plata that afternoon feeling ashamed of ourselves and other Americans because we knew so little of the fine institutions of learning in that land.

The revolution came two months later.

I had not particularly noticed the schoolchildren before then. I knew, of course, that they all wore white cotton pinafores, which made the rich and poor look alike. And I had sometimes been amused to see little girls wearing fingernail polish and lipstick. Otherwise, I hadn't thought much about the schoolchildren of Argentina.

But almost overnight, it looked as if the country had been taken by an army of white pinafores. I guess I noticed them for the first time at the big Flag Day celebration just a couple of weeks after the military coup.

There were thousands of them out that day. Row after white row walked through the streets, and behind and in front of them marched the soldiers. Many of the students were only seven or eight years old. It was a cold, windy day, and I wondered how any mother could be foolish enough to let her child out of the house in a thin cotton uniform, bareheaded and without gloves. They shivered and their hands and faces turned blue with cold while they listened through the long nationalistic speeches.

The next day, a friend complained that her children had been given a holiday from school but were ordered to attend the celebration. Their teachers were required to be there to take the roll, and the principals were there to watch the teachers.

After that, no one could overlook the school children in their white pinafores. They were in every newsreel paying homage to one general or another. They lined the streets in parades and threw flowers at General [Pedro Pablo] Ramírez, later at General [Edelmiro] Farrell and still later at Colonel Perón. But they were always there, as ever-present as the blue and white Argentine flag.

Ruth and I used to go to all kinds of demonstrations after the military government came to power. We watched anti-United States meetings, nationalist students' rallies, and the government holiday celebrations. The children were at all of them.

Ruth came home from visiting a friend one day with an alarming report. The friend's eleven-year-old daughter had wanted to show off before a visitor so she sang the June 4 revolution song—every word of it. Then she told Ruth that she "just loved to march." We knew then what was happening in the schools.

We knew one Argentine teacher—whose family had cherished liberty for generations. Her mother had been taught by some of the American teachers brought to Argentina by Sarmiento and she recalled the experience with obvious pride. The daughter also hated the military dictatorship but was attending every parade and demonstration. It was that or her job, and she needed the money. But out in the fresh air dictatorship wasn't so bad, she said. In the schools it was worse. She told us of the wholesale dismissal of every teacher in her school with a Jewish name. "Couldn't it have been for some other reason?" I asked.

"No," she replied, "only because they were Jews. Among them were some of the best teachers we had. Some had been at the school for ten and fifteen years."

But long before these dismissals began, the totalitarian teachings and the pattern of the Argentine school system had already become apparent.

One of the first acts of the new government was to modify the hitherto autonomous Universidad Nacional del Litoral. The pretext for so doing was that the school was "communistic," and to make sure that students would be taught no more "advanced (democratic) ideas" the well-known pro-Nazi Jordan B. Genta was named the *interventor*. To the astonishment of his students, he informed them that he had been sent there by God for the good of the country.

This self-proclaimed apostle, however, was greeted with boisterous irreverence by university students all over Argentina. Albert and his colleagues staged a demonstration in La Plata, the highlight of which was turning loose a pig bearing the name of Genta in big letters.

It was Genta's faith in [Adolf] Hitler, rather than in God, which forced his removal by the minister of education, Colonel [Elbio] Anaya. So great was the rejoicing in Santa Fe, the home of the university, that citizens rang church bells throughout the city.

The students' triumph was short-lived, however. Anaya's courage cost him his job. Genta was rewarded for his services at Litoral by an appointment as *interventor* in the National Teachers' College, where he was in a position to do far more damage to the democratic cause without being in the public eye. And to replace Anaya as minister of education, the government selected Dr. Gustavo Martínez Zuviría. Under the pen name of Hugo Wast he had written the most vicious anti-Semitic books in all South America. His works against Jews and democracy were in almost every Latin American bookstore, and his claim that fascism was the only means of world salvation was well known to most of the Argentines.

Just a short time before Zuviría's appointment, a group of some 150 prominent Argentines, many of them educators and professional men, had signed a manifesto asking for the restoration of constitutional government and for Argentina to break with the Axis. The new minister of education issued a decree ordering the immediate dismissal of all university professors who had signed the document.

This statement of the government's intention to remain friendly with the Axis and at the same time to liquidate academic opposition caused great indignation in educational circles. Various university presidents resigned immediately rather than permit the expulsion of their pro-democratic teachers. Among them was Dr. Alfredo Palacios, the president of the University of La Plata and the grand old man of Argentina. A Socialist senator for many years, Palacios had been responsible for more liberal labor and social legislation than any other man. No man in public life was more respected by the people. Palacios's stand was that he would resign the presidency rather than oust six of his professors for signing the manifesto, although he planned to continue teaching in the university.

When Dr. Palacios presented his resignation to the five-member faculty council, all but one of the others resigned rather than accept the post.

The fifth council member, who then became president, was promptly burned in effigy by the students and at least once his image, labeled "Quisling," was found hanging by the neck from the highest flagpole.

The purge continued. The University of Buenos Aires lost seventeen professors, including such noted figures as Samuel Bosch, Rafael Augusto Bullrich, Mariano R. Castex, and Bernardo A. Houssay. Twelve leaders of the University of Córdoba were discharged; the University of Litoral lost eight; the University of La Plata, six; the Ministry of Public Instruction, six; and the National Council of Education, one. Houssay and Castex immediately fled to Uruguay to escape arrest, as did several other of the manifesto signers.

Zuviría was only beginning his strangulation of education in Argentina. He outlawed the powerful Federación Universitaria Argentina, the national association of university students, branding it "communistic."

The democratic federation retaliated with a nationwide student strike. We saw a lot of Albert and his friends during those days, and they told us of the arrest of many of their classmates. Students who had part-time jobs in the government were warned that if they supported the strike they would lose their jobs. If the father of a university student worked in a public office, he was visited by a government official and told that unless his son returned to the classroom he would be discharged. No pressure was too big or too little to be brought on the students. Some of the student leaders were called in by government officials and offered soft jobs at high salaries if they would fall in line with the new regime. Albert was offered a job at $125 a month—which is a princely sum for a student—if he would use his influence to get his friends back to classes. Albert refused. About that time, the students began to take up collections for a clandestine paper. Albert stopped smoking so he could use cigarette money to help buy newsprint and pay printers. He walked instead of riding a bus, thereby saving two and a half cents.

As was to be expected, a few of the students liked the new government and found it profitable to inform on their democratic classmates. But Albert and his friend Arturo took effective steps to muzzle one group of pro-Fascist students who lived together in a large house in La Plata after learning they had made overtures to the army leaders. One evening Albert and his cohorts mailed a large quantity of leftist literature, as well as several dozen copies of the student underground newspaper, all addressed to students in that house.

Then they watched cautiously while the postman delivered the package. After allowing a reasonable time for the students to open it, Albert telephoned the La Plata police with the anonymous tip that a group of

Communists were living at the address of the Fascist students. Then Albert and his friends sauntered over to that neighborhood to watch their project bear fruit.

The police were prompt, and a few moments later Albert saw them dragging out half a dozen young men who were loudly protesting, "But we're Fascists. We're not Communists, we're Fascists!" The young men and the literature were taken together to the central police station. It took about three days for the students to establish proof that they were actually Fascists and therefore entitled to continue their studies unmolested. By planting such evidence, Albert had shown a keen understanding of government policies regarding education. Every repressive measure was taken under the guise of fighting communism, even though communism is a negligible influence in student life in Argentina.

We learned something of what Zuviría ordered teachers to stress and ignore in their classrooms from a friend who worked part time as a teacher and part time as a journalist. He had been warned by his superiors to ignore certain sections in the primary school history books and in particular to skip lightly over the section dealing with the life and works of Sarmiento. He had been ordered to emphasize and glorify [Juan Manuel de] Rosas, the Argentine dictator and bloody tyrant of a century ago.

Meanwhile, a mother reported to us how her daughter in kindergarten was being indoctrinated even before she knew how to read and write. On the child's return from school one afternoon, the mother asked what she had learned that day. "Oh, we learned about the other countries," she answered. "And what did you learn about them?" the mother asked?

The little girl promptly recited, "We learned that the other countries are our friends, but the United States is our enemy!"

From his exile in neighboring Uruguay, Dr. Gumersindo Sayago, one of the professors ousted from the University of Córdoba for signing the manifesto, charged that in primary schools and high schools an "unfortunately large number of totalitarian teachers install a false concept of sovereignty by exalting the hate of the foreigner, especially the North American."

It was about this time that Zuviría issued his swan song on the task of education in Argentina: "The country must be Christianized in harmony with its history and constitution. The birthrate, rather than immigration, must be increased. . . . The doctrines of hate and atheism must be eradicated. . . . The revolution was carried out under our one and only flag and under the sign of the Cross."

To help along his "Christianizing" process, Zuviría made two important appointments in the educational field. José María Rosa, Jr., was named director of the Board of Education in the province of Santa Fe, and Julio Sanguinetti was given a similar post in the province of Buenos Aires. Both had been previously identified with the Axis-financed press.

Another appointment was that of an army officer to the chair of educational philosophy in a normal school. He was given the job after Zuviría and his associates decided that the teacher who had held the post for many years, a Jew, should not be entrusted with a position in which it was possible to mold the opinion of future teachers. Thus the army officer was induced to take the position. The students shortly began to ask their new teacher questions. Unqualified as he was, he could never answer them. One day he became infuriated by their questions, began pounding his desk and shouting, "Will you stop asking me questions! I don't know anything about the subject. I'm only here because it is my duty!"

An Argentine educator friend of ours told us at a cocktail party one night of his own experiences with the military government. The man, a school inspector, had been one of the first to lose his job under the new regime because he had always been an outspoken friend of the United States and of democracy. His greatest hero was Henry Wallace.

He described how he had become friendly during the previous summer's vacation with a navy man and how they always exchanged warm *abrazos* when they met on the street, in true Latin fashion. On their last meeting, some weeks past, the naval man proudly informed our friend that he had just been appointed second in command of a battleship.

The previous day, he had been surprised to get a telephone call from the navy officer. "Can you help me out?" he was asked. "But I don't know anything about battleships," the school man confessed. "Oh, it isn't that," he was told. "I've been named the head of a division in the Department of Education and I don't know anything about it."

Our friend reached for another San Martín cocktail and beamed as he recalled his reply. "I just said, 'Well, I don't think I should. You know what is happening to collaborationists in France these days.' "

Meanwhile, Zuviría, an ardent Catholic, continued to cultivate the church in a move to get its wholehearted support for the new government. And on December 31, 1943, the day that all political parties were dissolved, the government issued a sensational decree—Catholic religious instruction for all public schools. The decree stated that the Department of Religious Instruction, under Zuviría, had been created for the purpose of controlling the teaching of the Roman Catholic religion.

Parents could request that their children be excused from religious instruction, the government promised. In practice, however, this was seldom considered advisable. A father holding a government post, or being in any way connected with the government, automatically put his job in jeopardy by making such a request.

An overwhelming majority of Argentines are Catholic, but religion has been separated from the schools for generations. The decree met with mixed reception from Catholics, some of them believing that religious instruction should be confined to the church and the home. But those who held such sentiments seldom dared express them, as government statistics later showed. The Ministry of Justice and Public Instruction announced that 91.1 percent of the pupils under the ministry's jurisdiction had chosen to take the courses of religious instruction, and the remaining 8.9 percent favored moral instruction. The percentages of pupils who had been exempted from religious instructions in eight of the provinces were: Buenos Aires, 2.05; Catamarca, 0.00; Córdoba, 0.60; Corrientes, 0.05; Entre Ríos, 4.36; Salta, 0.40; San Juan, 0.09; and San Luis, 0.10 percent.

Ruth and I watched education go farther and farther down the totalitarian path, with practically every issue of a Buenos Aires newspaper printing short filler items about teachers being discharged for "communism," for obstructionist tactics, for "indiscipline," or equally obscure offenses. At the end of the first year of the revolutionary government, the National Board of Education announced it had dismissed 348 teachers and others considered "unworthy of the honor of being teachers in Argentine schools or forming part of the administrative staff of the board." Of the total, sixty-four were discharged for "Communist activities," fifty-four for "immorality," and forty-six for "disorderly conduct."

Argentina's rupture of relations with the Axis came early in 1944. Many Argentines believed that their schools would soon be allowed to revert to the liberal tradition of Sarmiento. Support for their optimism came with the removal of Zuviría, the most frankly pro-Nazi member of the cabinet, less than a month later.

But later events proved them too trusting. President Ramírez was almost immediately ousted, and Perón soon came to the fore as the Argentine "strong man." The hated Zuviría was replaced in the highest educational post in the land by Dr. Alberto Baldrich, a political adventurer who had been known as a Communist but had since "matured" into a nationalist and rabid anti-*yanqui*. Baldrich had recently distinguished himself by expropriating certain American interests while serving as federal commissioner of the province of Tucumán. The street car company had been taken over, and Tucumán street cars were seen proudly flying the Argentine flag on the trolley rope and displaying posters which read, "This Car Argentine."

In his new post, Baldrich received a full-page tribute from the Nazi-financed *El Federal*, on the first anniversary of the revolution. The newspaper, which had appeared under the name of *El Pampero* until the rupture of relations with the Axis, said that the universities were now in good hands. Also praised by *El Federal* was Dr. José Ignacio Olmedo, the head of the National Council of Education. *El Federal* rejoiced over the fact that Olmedo had been given the responsibility for molding Argentine children into the nationalistic ideology.

Dr. Olmedo came up to the newspaper's expectations by ordering all teachers of children from the third through the sixth grades to hold special classes for three days during the revolution celebration and giving the teachers a list of nationalistic slogans which they were ordered to keep on their blackboards during the period. Among these were:

"Our Fatherland exists by the free determination of its people and by the victorious strength of its sword."

"We are a free and constitutional nation, therefore have the inalienable right of carrying out a great function in America."

"It is not enough to be an Argentine, you must know how to prove it."

"To be Argentine does not constitute a peaceful, contemplative or literary position. To be Argentine is a dynamic and essentially active condition."

Special slogans were issued for the girls. Among them were:

"One son more is a new sentinel of sovereignty."

"The new Argentina wants healthy, strong and heroic women."

"The Argentine woman must know how to fulfill her natural obligation with zeal."

A short time later found Baldrich enlarging his scope to advise soldiers in the *Gaceta Oficial* that "when the sword of the military is unsheathed it is not merely a piece of shining metal but a materialization of the spirit in which is present nothing less than the Fatherland itself. For this reason, to have a Fatherland and to be its soldier is one and the same thing."

The same warlike note was reflected in the July 1944 issue of the Bulletin of the Ministry of Justice and Public Instruction, which stated, "The State is an order that is at once warlike and cultural . . . it is a society that is by definition an army whose arms are prepared for battle and whose souls are prepared for flight (dying)."

Only four days after his appointment as minister, Baldrich ordered all pupils to write a composition based on the principles expounded by General Farrell at a special Pan-American Day address during which the president complained that "Argentina is not understood" by the other countries of the Americas.

When one pupil, Martha Grinberg, a fifth-year student, received her copy of the Farrell speech, she tore the copy into small pieces before the other students and her teacher.

When the incident reached the attention of Baldrich, he promptly expelled Martha from school and announced that she also would be prohibited from attending any other school in the Argentine republic. Furthermore, the principals had been entirely too lenient with Martha, and for that, they were ordered suspended from their posts for fifteen days.

Martha was soon to be joined by other grade school pupils.

Bernardo Wolnivch, a Uruguayan and sixth-grade pupil, was expelled from his school and prohibited admission to others for being an "unworthy and bad foreigner." Bernardo had at the end of a patriotic ceremony torn his national rosette from his pinafore, thrown it to the ground, and spat on it.

Similar measures were taken against Bernardo Schievitch, a pupil of an adults' school, who, upon being reproached for not having attended a patriotic ceremony, replied that he could not be "forced to love" his country's flag.

Juan Moroz, an eight-year-old Russian, also was expelled when it was reported that he had "used offensive words with regard to the person of His Excellency the President of the Republic." A like fate befell Moses Levy, age fifteen, when it was charged that he caused a disturbance during a ceremony held in homage to the Argentine flag. Another boy, Antonio de Simón, was expelled for derisive whistles during a lecture on Flag Day.

During this period, Argentina was in a diplomatic quarantine, unrecognized by most of the countries of the world. Soon President Farrell's government began to make a few token gestures toward democracy, and with these came the "resignation" of Dr. Baldrich.

These moves apparently fooled no one inside the country, least of all the nationalist students. For days before the Día del Estudiante celebration, sound trucks paraded the streets announcing the Marcha de Antorchas, or torchlight parade, sponsored by the pro-Nazi Sindicato Universitario Argentino, much smaller than the democratic Federación Universitaria Argentina, but noisier.

On the day of the parade the streets were flooded early with pamphlets attacking such men as Doctor Palacios and other democratic leaders, but the students waited for dusk to fall before beginning their march from the closed Congress building to Plaza de Mayo. Their torches cast a red glow over the crowds as they marched in almost military formation down the avenue shouting such slogans as *"Maté sí, whisky no,"* and *"Sanciones, ha! ha! ha!"* The reference to sanctions was made at a time when there was much talk of the United States imposing economic sanctions against Argentina for her failure to live up to her treaty commitments.

The nationalist students stopped along the line of march to throw stones into the plate glass window of the democratic newspaper *Crítica*. To our astonishment we found an American friend in this crowd, carrying a torch and shouting nationalist slogans in Spanish. When the police took away the youth who had hurled the stone, our friend followed behind them and later reported to us that the young man had been quietly turned loose on a side street a block away. After a pause in front of the Axis-controlled newspaper *Momento Argentino* to pay tribute to it for its support of "neutrality," the students massed in the beautiful plaza, directly in front of the Government House.

What I saw in the plaza was both impressive and sinister. The nationalist students had rigged up a tremendously large Argentine flag. It was draped vertically with a big condor of metal on top of it. Then there were smaller flags, also hanging vertically. Hundreds of blazing torches and mounted police with glittering trappings all around made us feel as if we had stepped somehow into the middle ages. The smoke from the torches cast a stinking haze through the whole plaza. It was one of the weirdest sights I had ever seen.

The speeches followed the usual Nazi line, favoring neutrality, the Perón-Farrell government, and opposing cooperation with the democracies.

About this time Doctor Palacios, who had been under constant police supervision since he resigned as president of the University of La Plata, made his escape by night across the River Plate to small but intensely democratic Uruguay.

Albert woke us up early the next morning to tell about it. Doctor Palacios, as we knew, was one of the most easily recognized men in Argentina. His handlebar mustaches, broad-brimmed black hat, and long-flowing black cape made him an easy figure for the police to watch, and he was followed everywhere he went. It had been impossible for him to leave the country as his house had been under observation at all hours.

Then, according to Albert, one of the educator's favorite students had an idea which was communicated to the proper channels, and the necessary preparations were made. One night the student went to call on his old professor. Some time later, "Doctor Palacios" was seen leaving the house and the plainclothes police naturally followed the figure in the black cape and wide-brimmed hat. Meanwhile, the real Doctor Palacios inconspicuously left by the back way to take the secret route to Uruguay.

Behind him, he left a letter of resignation which further damaged the prestige of the military government.

"Educators," said Doctor Palacios, "are the soul of the nation; they study its problems, scrutinize its ways, and strengthen its sentiments. . . . But now I cannot teach with dignity because I have not liberty. I do not see any way of filling the chair, under police vigilance. . . . I am leaving the country with great grief. . . . Taking away our liberty means denying our traditions."

In late 1944 and early 1945, the military regime began to show unmistakable signs of shifting towards the democratic processes in education. It was the eve of the Mexico City Conference when the Farrell-Perón government was anxious to appear in a good light abroad and thus win long-delayed recognition from the other American governments.

In February 1945, the cabinet met and voted to reinstate all university professors who had lost their jobs for signing the pro-Allied manifesto eighteen months earlier. Special pains were taken to point out that the dismissals had taken place during the regime of President Ramírez. The government press office announced that President Farrell had "interrupted his convalescence" to attend the meeting.

Perón, also seeking a seat in the "democratic" bandwagon, called on the minister of public instruction that same day, and the minister later revealed that Colonel Perón had urged him to call university elections and thereby restore autonomy to the universities.

The decree was then issued ending intervention at the Universities of Buenos Aires, Córdoba, Tucumán, Cuyo, and Litoral. Elections were called for March to select university governing councils, which in turn would select the deans and delegates to the supreme councils.

The elections were held, and the democratic forces again gained control. The honeymoon lasted for some six months—from shortly before the Mexico City Conference where Argentina obtained continental recognition to after the San Francisco Conference where it was given a seat with the United Nations.

Argentina's delegates to San Francisco hardly had time to return to Buenos Aires, unpack their suitcases, and sit down to *bifes*, however, before the conflict between the democratic educational forces and the totalitarian government was resumed.

This time the students took the offensive, and for the first time in twenty-seven years, all the universities in the country were closed in a twenty-four-hour nationwide strike to demonstrate the opposition of the entire student population—leftists and rightists alike—to the military regime and to demand the return of democratic, constitutional government.

Some thirty thousand students of all political complexions were called out by the university federation. The students were mainly incensed by the government's international double-dealing.

For even though Argentina had joined the United Nations and declared war on the Axis, pro-democratic forces attempting to celebrate the fall of Berlin had been fired on by the police.

And when the Japanese surrender came, some two hundred uniformed troops, led by their noncommissioned officers, invaded the streets of Buenos Aires shouting, "*Viva* Hitler! *Viva* Mussolini! *Viva* Perón! Down with Democracy! Death to the Jews!" and "Long Live Germany!" When bystanders refused to proclaim their support of Perón, they were beaten. At the end of two days' rioting, four persons had been killed and more than a hundred wounded, many of them students.

Secondary school teachers of the nation then proposed a period of mourning and the suspension of classes for two days to show their "repudiation of the vandalistic deeds committed by totalitarian and retrograde movements." The government immediately dismissed by decree the twenty-four high school teachers, including fourteen women, who had signed the original manifesto. But most of the high schools remained closed, and those that did open were shunned by teachers and students alike.

The greatest wave of terrorism and retaliation in recent Argentine history followed the giant "March of the Constitution and Freedom," a pro-democratic demonstration, in September 1945. The abortive military uprising led by General Arturo Rawson in Córdoba a few days later gave the authorities an excuse to reimpose the state of siege and punish their critics.

Within twenty-four hours, educational and cultural leaders were crowded into jail cells all over Argentina. Among them were all six presidents of the country's universities, along with many deans and professors. Three of the presidents, those of the Universities of Buenos Aires, Córdoba, and Litoral, had signed a declaration asking the military government to surrender its powers to the Supreme Court. The head of Litoral University had been even more blunt. He had signed his name at the top of a list of some one hundred professors petitioning the Supreme Court to withdraw its recognition from the regime.

The university students answered with a nationwide program of civil disobedience. They barricaded themselves inside university buildings in the heart of the capital, as well as in the universities located in the provinces. Embattled students in the engineering school of the University of Buenos Aires were only a few feet away from Colonel Perón's stronghold, the Secretariat of Labor and Social Welfare.

As soon as the students of the University of Buenos Aires took over the engineering, law, and social science buildings, large squads of armed police attempted to storm the buildings. When the students still held out, thirty armed men walked across the street from the direction of the Secretariat of Labor and fired on the students, wounding two.

A day later, masses of police, accompanied by the local fire brigade, surrounded the University of La Plata. First they broke down the great door and then hurled tear gas bombs while the firemen turned fire hoses on the students trying to hold them back. From classroom to classroom the battle raged. With tear gas and truncheons the police fought against students armed with the only weapons they could find—chairs and benches, blackboards and school books. When the battle ended, eleven students, including women, had such severe police saber cuts in the head that they had to be rushed to first aid stations. And of the 250 students and professors arrested, at least 50 were injured.

Police in the capital were just as ruthless as they had been in La Plata. They broke into the University of Buenos Aires buildings, and arrested between fifteen hundred and two thousand university students and professors, including two hundred female students and professors' wives. The women were thrown into cells with prostitutes.

Similar drastic action was taken to evict students barricaded inside other universities.

A people aroused by the needlessly harsh treatment of its students was one of the factors which swept Colonel Perón temporarily from power in October 1945. It is significant that one of the first acts of the new two-man cabinet was to issue a decree reopening all Argentine universities.

But Colonel Perón and his cohorts were able to regain power and brought back with them their totalitarian ideas of education.

The university students, however, continued to oppose Perón strongly through the campaigning for presidential elections. His election was a severe blow to them. The votes—cast in freedom and counted honestly—knocked out a main prop from student opposition to military government, their argument that the regime was "unconstitutional." It also gave Perón a free hand to enforce his will on the universities. Promptly the students announced they would return to their classrooms, "enriched by the experience" of fighting Perón and that there would be no more student strikes such as that in September 1945.

Some men might have been content with this declaration that the students were abandoning their greatest weapon, but not Perón. On May 4, a month before his inauguration as president, the government again sent "*interventores*" into all six of the nation's universities, with orders to eliminate "politics" and to recommend "reforms" in their teachings.

Perón still had not completely silenced the opposition to him in the universities, but, in his Five-Year Plan, presented to Congress in October 1946, he sounded the death knell for free education. Under the plan, the new president would control the educational system; Perón would appoint a National Council of Education to choose teachers and select the curricula, and he would also name the president of each one of the universities.

It was obvious that teachers and professors who defended anti-government attitudes must either be "converted" to the cause or lose their jobs and in some cases their freedom; and those students outspoken against their "constitutionally elected" president could expect expulsion and possibly arrest. Their disappearance from the top rung of the nation's educational ladder would hardly be noticed, for soon there would be plenty of students with the officially correct views moving up from the secondary schools to replace them.

Perón's "purge" of both educators and students in the universities proceeded rapidly in late 1946 and early 1947. Several hundred university professors hostile to Perón's doctrines were dismissed or resigned voluntarily in protest. Scores of students barred from Argentina's universities for their continued opposition to the government sought higher learning in neighboring Uruguay and Chile. Others with smaller financial resources were forced to abandon their university training.

When Perón leaves office five years hence—if he does—it seems likely that his type of instruction will by then have snuffed out the flame of educational freedom which had been lighted by Sarmiento but a few decades ago.

The next few years will open up new opportunities for thousands of young Argentines. There is great need of technicians and skilled workers to supervise operations of men and machines. Perón's Five-Year Plan called for a vast expansion of industry, and it also outlined a system of state schools to prepare Argentine youth for a place in the industrial Argentina. Many students will be encouraged to abandon the classics, in favor of the monkey wrench, blueprints, and industrial charts.

Our friend Albert will not like this. There will be limited room for him in the new Argentina. For with the shining new gadgets in the laboratories will go regimented flag-waving, overdoses of supernationalism, and deification of the leader. All this will be repulsive to Albert, who reached intellectual maturity before the revolution of 1943. But Albert has a little brother. He already knows how to march, and he has learned to like it. He has many years remaining in the classroom. And it is in his school days—not Albert's—that there will be education for Perón.

10 Joseph S. Roucek ◆ Pro-Communist Revolution in Cuban Education

Joseph Roucek has worked and written extensively in the fields of sociology, political ideology, and the sociology of education. A native of the former Czechoslovakia, he has concentrated much of his research on eastern Europe, but Fidel Castro's revolution drew his attention to Cuba. Castro became a controversial figure in the United States because of his determination to establish a form of communism in Cuba. Education played a crucial role in this process, and Roucek's essay provides evidence of Communist ideas in Cuba's schools. Students should note the emphasis Castro placed on teacher training and literacy campaigns and consider how these programs fit into his government's overall plans to change Cuban society.

In October 1963, the international crisis that centered on, and arose out of, events on the Caribbean island of Cuba, was the culmination of a series of events which had kept Cuba in the world's headlines for the previous four years—ever since the revolutionary regime headed by Dr. Fidel Castro had established itself in power in December 1958. The understanding of this crisis is quite difficult because this matter has been subject to widely differing interpretations, and many aspects of the regime's history are intensely controversial.[1]

The relationship between Castro and the Communists has been the most disputed aspect of the Cuban revolution. On the one hand, there are those who claim that Castro has been a Soviet agent since 1948; on the other hand, there are those who claim not only that Castro is not a Communist but that his movement and communism are "natural enemies." The fact remains, however, that the July 26 Movement was a movement, not a party, and that it lacked homogeneity and a developed apparatus. But Castro, once in power, badly needed the assistance which the trained cadres of the Communist party could provide. He also needed a coherent ideological basis for his regime. Thus his movement and the Rebel Army were allowed to wither away, the former being replaced increasingly by the Communists and the latter by the large, amorphous militia. After Castro decided to collectivize agriculture, his dependence on the Communists

From Joseph S. Roucek, "Pro-Communist Revolution in Cuban Education," *Journal of Interamerican Studies and World Affairs* 6, no. 3 (July 1964): 323–35. Reprinted by permission of the *Journal of Interamerican Studies and World Affairs*.

increased as he was embarking on a revolution for which the movement had not fought and in which many of its members did not believe. After the suspension of the sugar quota by Washington and the nationalization of U.S. property in July 1960, the Cuban economy became increasingly dependent on Soviet bloc trade and aid, and Soviet bloc arms started arriving in quantity that summer. This induced Castro to make his famous speech on December 1, 1961, announcing that he was a Marxist-Leninist and had always been "a sort of Marxist-Leninist."

In this process of transforming Cuba into a Communist satellite, education has played a leading role—as it has in all pro-Communist satellites.

Castro's Base of Power

On July 26, 1953, an attack on the army barracks of Santiago de Cuba was led by a young lawyer named Fidel Castro. After having been sentenced to fifteen years' imprisonment, he was released after eleven months under a general amnesty decreed by President [Fulgencio] Batista. He took refuge in Mexico, later landing in Oriente Province on December 2, 1956, with a small group of armed followers. Hiding in the hills, they carried on guerrilla warfare against government forces. On January 1, 1959, the Batista administration collapsed and the bearded revolutionists, headed by Fidel Castro, made their triumphal entrance into the capital on January 8; there soon followed a series of trials and executions of Batista's followers that shocked the world.

Castro's strength, interestingly enough, depended originally on Cuba's middle class, attracted to him by resentment against the discredited traditional political parties; hence, the revolutionary leadership even today is composed mostly of young middle-class elements.[2]

Side by side with the large middle class, Cuba had an energetic and progressive-minded industrial working class, rooted in the sugar and tobacco industries. But the rebel army came mostly from a third section of the Cuban population—not yet touched by social and economic progress—the *montunos*, the mountain folk eking out a living from casual jobs. The plight of this section has been cleverly exploited by Castro's appeals. Furthermore, almost a quarter of Cuba's population is black or mulatto; they support, for the most part, Castro's regime with enthusiasm, feeling that they are now sharing equally in the great effort to educate and employ all Cuban people.

Of the many changes that have influenced the basic form of Cuba's life, two are most profound and irrevocable. One is the land reform which has broken up large holdings and created communal farms where many peasants work, though the state owns them. The other is the explosion of schools and education, under the direction of the crew-cut, young minister of education, Armando Hart.[3] *"Everyone* seems to be in school."[4]

Castro has made a shrewd pitch to youth and opinion-shaping intellectuals of Cuba, and Latin America. His regime has been especially interested in the making of *Fidelistas*, the status assigned to those who have reached adulthood since the revolution and had gone through the educational machinery; those twenty-five years of age and over are considered "doubters." Castro's "indoctrinated" generation is a product and staunch supporter of the "new Socialist Cuba." Dr. Castro, a premier in his middle thirties, has opened a new field to Cuba's youth involving them directly in the life of the nation; they participate in the monolithic, slogan-filled politics, shoulder guns, drive heavy equipment, and receive wide publicity in the press. The framework has been provided by reorganizing completely the pre-Castro system of education. Scores of brand-new schools have been built all over the island. The government provides thousands of scholarships and the students wear special uniforms which set them apart as *becados*. The schools have also assumed the task of regimentation; students march in military step to and from classrooms, and even sports take place under strict discipline.

Educational Changes under Castro

On assuming power in January 1959, the new minister of education proclaimed immediately the intention of reorganizing education at all levels so that the latter would mirror the political, economic, and social changes of the revolution.[5] The following formal objectives were proclaimed: 1) quantitative and qualitative development of educational services; 2) decentralization of administrative and technical functions; 3) establishment of a modern system of educational planning to synchronize all plans and services; 4) technical improvement of all branches of education; and 5) general educational reform. Decree No. 2099, published on October 13, 1959, provided for regulatory powers of the minister of education over all education. Since then, private schools have all been nationalized or closed.

In the same year, educational departments were set up de facto in each province and municipality to handle the problems of elementary, secondary, and vocational education. The Central Planning Board (Junta Central de Planificación, JUCEPLAN) created twenty-four regional zones for overall government purposes, including regional departments of education. A Commission of Educational Planning operates directly under the minister and has authority over all educational operations. The structure of elementary and secondary education has been converted to a six-year elementary, three-year basic secondary, and three-year upper secondary. Elementary education was declared compulsory.

Students, after completion of elementary grades, take examinations (given by the Ministry of Education) in order to enter a national basic secondary school. The three-year basic secondary program is a prevocational period during which the student's abilities are observed and then channeled into one of several upper secondary programs (including university preparatory, commercial, technical, art, home economics, and teacher-training programs). Each municipality is to have at least one school offering basic secondary education. In addition, there are technological, agricultural, and industrial schools (*escuelas tecnológicas, agrícolas e industriales*) of three years. Upper secondary schools (*escuelas secundarias superiores*) comprise preuniversity schools (*institutos preuniversitarios*); schools of surveying (*escuelas de agrimensural*) annexed to the preuniversity institutes; schools of commerce (*escuelas de comercio*); schools of fine arts (*escuelas de bellas artes*); agricultural and industrial technical schools (*institutos tecnológicos, agrícolas, e industriales*); and elementary teacher-training schools (*escuelas de maestros primarios*). The upper secondary programs are, in general, three years in length, while the teacher-training program takes four years.

Several steps were taken to reorganize teacher training. After the new regime assumed power, numerous teachers (especially those employed since 1952, when the previous government had come to power) were dismissed; some six hundred secondary-school teachers were released and some immediately re-employed for the rest of the academic year. But both groups were permitted to take competitive examinations in September 1959, leading to possible tenure-bearing positions, and new laws provided a pension for secondary- and elementary-school teachers with more than twenty years of experience. Special schools (the Home Economics School and the Normal School for Kindergarten Teachers) were abolished; specialized elementary-school teachers (such as of home economics and physical education) were to teach all subjects and, eventually, plans were announced that all future elementary-school teachers were to be graduates of the new Escuela de Maestros Primarios. At the same time, the government ran training and orientation courses to prepare them as "integral" teachers (teachers of all subjects).

In 1960, the Higher Institute of Education (Instituto Superior de Educación) was founded for the purpose of determining teaching qualifications, qualifying teachers for specific teaching assignments, acting as the government liaison office in matters of international education exchange, and organizing educational conferences, seminars, and other professional activities.

A Volunteer Teacher Corps (Cuerpo de Maestros Voluntarios) was created of upper secondary-school students prepared through emergency teacher-training courses; university students were trained through similar emergency training, and for vocational and technical schools, workers without previous training as teachers were placed as instructors in such schools. In 1961, a group of one thousand applicants with basic secondary-school backgrounds, was selected and granted scholarships to attend a first-year course at the Vocational Initiation Center for Elementary School Teachers (Centro de Iniciación Vocacional del Magisterio Primario) in the Sierra Maestra mountains. Members of the group were to have three years of pedagogical-cultural education in schools located in rural communities and one year of practice teaching. In addition, three- to six-month special training courses were initiated in April 1961, in order to qualify immediately as teachers those students who were nearing completion of their normal-school education.

Schools for secondary-school teacher preparation (Escuelas del Profesorado Secundario) were founded in 1959 in the universities, with programs of from four to five years in length. (Formerly, regular university graduates could be appointed to teaching positions; these new schools required teachers to be trained in an integrated program, including general culture, special subjects, and methodological principles.) Schools for Fine Arts Inspectors were also created, and graduates of an emergency course (one- or two-year programs) were assigned to People's Farms and Agrarian Cooperatives to foster artistic recreation in rural communities. Plans were also made for Farms for Youth (Granjas Juveniles) for students from rural communities who would pursue general secondary and technical courses and receive free room, board, and medical facilities.

Politically involved in the struggle for power during 1956–1958, the universities of Havana, de las Villas at Santa Clara, and Oriente were closed; the private University of Villanueva was shut down briefly but reopened early in 1958.

Under Castro, the University de las Villas was the first to reopen, in February 1959, with fourteen hundred students; the University of Oriente reopened in March 1959, but both campuses had been purged of alleged collaborators. The University of Havana, occupied by the military between January 1 and May 1959, was the last to reopen. But there were troubles between the university and the students with regard to procedures for purging professors; the Federation of University Students (FEU) took control. Elaborate reforms were initiated, including reorganizing the curriculum, rewriting university statutes, clarifying obligations of the professors, and giving greater voice to students in the administration and operation of the university.

Law II of January 14, 1959, invalidated courses taken at and degrees given by the University of Villanueva and other private universities between November 1956 and January 1, 1959; but resentment over this step led to modification of the decree in May. Students of private institutions, who had received degrees between November 1956 and January 1959, however, were not allowed to practice their professions for one year. Eventually, though, all universities—with the exception of the three public institutions—were closed, and credits and degrees earned by students were subject to review by government boards. The three remaining institutions (Universidad de la Habana, Universidad Central "Marta Abreu" de las Villas, and Universidad de Oriente) had their faculties and fields of studies reorganized and renamed, and radical changes were introduced in the content of courses and textbooks. In January 1960 the Mixed Commission (students and professors) of the University of Havana approved an article for the university statutes requiring university students to give a year of service to the government after the completion of their courses in order to qualify for degrees.

The glaring shortage of professors and doctors inspired the government's interest in importing such specialists from Communist countries, especially for the Faculty of Medicine of the University of Havana. More than fifteen hundred of Cuba's physicians had fled Cuba, although as a group they were some of the early supporters of the Castro government. Their principal complaint was that most doctors were unwilling to tolerate restrictions placed on free professional practice. The government dissolved the Cuban Medical Association and tried to make all physicians join the Sindicato Unico de Trabajadores de la Medicina (Union of Medical Workers). The regime also exerted pressure on physicians to volunteer for service with the militia and harassed physicians who refused to join by depriving them of gasoline rations. Earnings of physicians remaining in Cuba are believed to average about $500 a month; most work fixed hours under the direction of the Ministry of Health.[6]

A reorganized Ministry of Health took control of all but a few of the nation's hospitals, and medical care was offered to all, without direct charge. Most physicians are now connected either with the Ministry of Health or employed by mutual-aid societies; those who wish to continue private practice may do so. Medical education is being accelerated at Havana University School of Medicine and a second medical school has been established at Santiago. (In pre-Castro days, Havana graduated about eighty physicians each year; the medical course lasted seven years.)[7]

Operation of the Educational System

While pupils and students learn how to read and write and to master modern technology, in contemporary Cuba they also receive a steady diet of Marxist-Leninist theories and slogans—which they must absorb above all else. Within the Marxist-Leninist framework, an important element in indoctrination is the concept of "revolution." The word "revolution" is regarded differently in Latin America from the way it is in the United States, where it has become a "bad" word. In Latin America, "revolution" is a magical word which carries very favorable connotations. It symbolizes hope that things will be better. Though once Latin America saw old-style revolutions played by generals like musical chairs, in recent years, South America has seen also new-style social revolutions—witness Mexico and Bolivia. Here, revolution is clearly a remedy of desperation. In many Latin American countries, unless reforms are soon made, revolution is definitely on the horizon. In fact, in one sense, the only question in Latin America is: "what kind of revolution will there be?—a Sovietized social revolution, such as the Communists were able to accomplish in Cuba, or a gradual, peaceful, social revolution leading to a better world for Latin America's people?"

Everywhere in Cuba, Cubans are confronted by portraits of communism's saints, Marx and Lenin. The Soviet leaders obviously exert enormous influence on the Castro regime, although Cartier-Bresson found that "the Russians, who live clannishly in their own installations, have left little imprint on the ordinary Cuban people."[8] There is no question that Cuba is a Communist, or "Socialist," country, as Castro prefers to call it. Yet it is far from being a duplicate of the USSR or Communist China.

On ideological issues, Premier Castro strives to be neutral between the USSR and China; at the same time, he declares that Cuba is firmly "Marxist-Leninist." The Cuban Communist party—the United Party of the Socialist Revolution in Cuba—appears to be considerably advanced in its organization. The party permeates most public and private activities of the island. Dr. Castro also claims that each country must work out its own Marxist-Leninist system to suit local conditions. Certainly Cuba has done that; the flavor and atmosphere of Cuban communism must be unique in the Communist world.

The government subsidizes all sports and encourages youngsters to join political organizations such as the Young Pioneers of the Union of Communist Youth. Complementing these are the schools of revolutionary instruction, open to everyone, where the student is thoroughly coached in the intricacies of Marxism-Leninism. Many textbooks come with explanations that have raised more than one eyebrow. A geography manual by Capt. Antonio Núñez Jiménez, head of the Academy of Sciences, tells readers, for instance, that prior to Premier Castro's advent "Cuba could only trade with the United States."[9] It describes the peninsula of Florida to the north as "a giant fang which wants to bury itself in the back of our small island." "But," it adds, "in the future, when imperialism will disappear, the image will not be that of a fang but of a friendly arm stretched toward our nation." Such remarks coincide fully with the revolution's belief about what education should be, and Education Minister Armando Hart has been quoted as saying "the nonpolitical teacher has come to an end."

Castro's regime is especially proud of its experiment in raising a new crop of "elite" youngsters by providing them with special scholarships (an experiment resembling [Soviet Chairman Nikita] Khrushchev's "boarding schools"). Thus, today, some seventy thousand *becados* are living in Havana's suburbs in expropriated hotels or in the former homes of the rich and middle class, now most of them "ninety miles" away in exile. Fresh farm boys are housed there, on a nine-months' schedule, learning, from 8 A.M. to 5 P.M. daily, classical ballet (!), music, Marxism, general subjects, and French (taught by a Swiss). The girls study languages, the arts, or a few home economics courses seven hours a day, and also receive two hours of Marxism-Leninism after supper.[10] All *becados* live away from home and are shielded from parental influence, but they can visit their families on vacations. Non-Marxist education is not available. Amid the palms and putting green of the swank old Havana Club, in Cubanacán, a new Fine Arts Center is rising, designed to become another Lincoln Center, where 1,550 "qualified" students from all over Latin America are studying modern dance, drama, ballet, fine arts, and music.

The Drive Against Illiteracy

In 1961–62, most *becados* "volunteered" for the patriotic task of aiding in the government's plan to conquer illiteracy. The year 1961 was declared the Año de la Alfabetización, as well as Año de la Educación. Illiteracy had been estimated in 1958 at nine hundred thousand or approximately 22 percent of the population aged fifteen and above—one of the lowest rates among the Latin American republics. The National Commission for Literacy, established by the new government to organize the campaign, is composed of technical officials of the Ministry of Education, delegates from university schools of education, and lecturers in teacher-training schools. It was reported that since April 1959, 817 literacy centers had begun operating with 2,751 teachers and more than 16,000 students.

An "Army of Education" of one hundred thousand students over twelve years of age was organized in 1961 to go into the interior to teach illiterates. Regular schools were closed on April 15 for this purpose, several months earlier than usual, and were not reopened for the 1961–62 school year until February 1962 (several months later than usual). Students selected for the "Army of Education" were organized into uniformed brigades and given special indoctrination courses, whose content was to be passed on to the peasants in the course of the literacy campaign. Two manuals were issued by the Ministry of Education: *Venceremos*, a primer for students; and *Alfabeticemos*, an instruction guide for teachers on how to overcome illiteracy and at the same time to indoctrinate students in the "ideological objectives of the revolution."

The campaign must have been costly, since the Cuban teenagers (*brigadistas*), clad in Cuban blue jeans and equipped with lamps made in China, were let out of school for eight months. The government claims that as a result of this campaign practically everyone in Cuba has learned to read and write and that "the peasants at least felt that somebody in the city cared about them, and the youngsters came back burning with a zeal to do something about the countryside. Everywhere, you see follow-up classes, which take the newly literate up to the third grade."[11]

On the other hand, today, by the thousands, Cubans young and old are trekking to Prague, Moscow, Leningrad, etc., to learn fishing, technology, Russian, and, of course, Marxism-Leninism. Most, if not all, return convinced that communism is the only way of life. At the same time, this Communist "Republic of Improvisation," in its Puritanical zeal, has come up with some unusual solutions for social problems. Many alumnae prostitutes are, for instance, in school learning to sew and to type. Their "rehabilitation" course, scheduled for six months, has now been stretched (Socialist realism!) to two years.

The Web of Control

The educational structure, as in all Communist countries, is inseparably related to the whole "way of life" of the Cuban people. Most Cubans live according to the orders and directives of the Committee for the Defense of the Revolution, really thousands of small committees organized down to the block level, whose most active members belong to ORI, an organization made up of both Castro's supporters and Communists. They know everything about everyone's life and can give and take away favors. The committee does social work, distributes clothing, gives vaccinations, and fights juvenile delinquency. Above all, however, its task is to defend each block against counterrevolution. Its job was, originally, vigilance. Now, these defenders—mostly middle-aged housewives—shoulder fourteen duties in all for the regime. Issuing ration books is just a start; they also see that children on the block are vaccinated; that everyone learns to read and write; that the local butchers dole out meat fairly; that "culture" is encouraged; and that neighbors are indoctrinated with good revolutionary principles. It runs "indoctrination" sessions in kitchens, garages, and on porches.[12] (These resemble an American Bible class—except that the text, read line by line aloud and then discussed, is a dreary tome on Cuban socialism, written by old Communist Blas Roca in the 1940s. The last chapter, which praised Batista, with whom Roca collaborated, has been expunged.) "Criticism and self-criticism" sessions are frequent and big occasions at these "reunions." (Even Cubans admit that the new Cuba is cursed with the fact that everyone is always at some meeting.)

The cultural orientation is directed by the powerful Council on Culture, which promotes art all the way down to folk dancing on state farms. Castro is also making a big pitch to intellectuals; painters, for example, glory in their freedom to paint abstract art, something not tolerated in other Communist countries. In fact, a touring exhibit of Cuban modern art was banned in East Germany.

This type of organized and directed life is strengthened by all other available means of social control. On communal farms, for instance, all Cubans work together and eat in mess halls. The press is full of propaganda and imprecations. Messages are crude and couched in stereotyped Marxist lingo. Numberless posters plaster billboards and walls, featuring social and political ideas or boasting of production figures (instead of promoting usable goods). One of the most popular ones shouts: "A country that studies is a country that wins!"[13]

Adult education is also promoted by Soviet technicians, who are especially engaged in instructing farm boys in the workings of imported machinery (mainly tractors, jeeps, and trucks). They do not mingle a great deal with Cubans, except, like U.S. soldiers abroad, with kids who ask for their cigarettes.[14]

Special attention has been paid to Cuba's women, who, today, are more than occupied and always attending meetings. As *milicianas*, they usually carry guns and guard buildings, although housekeeping is difficult in present-day Cuba with food and clothing shortages and the necessity of waiting in lines for scarce goods after working long hours. Where are the maids? Off to school learning typing and other trades. Girls vying to be queen of the 1963 "Socialist Carnival" were chosen not only for looks but also for "good revolutionary conduct." At Castro's rallies, in fact, the loudest cheers and chants still seem to come from the ladies.

Castro's facility in communicating with his followers has also been made easier by the numerous radio stations and receivers, not to mention television. In 1958, Cuba had 94 radio stations and about 94,000 radio receivers (ranking second after Argentina, with one receiver for every five inhabitants); there were also 11 television stations, and 365 receivers—and certainly this number has climbed under Castro's regime. The extensive use of films and the press as mass media on behalf of the regime is evident. In 1959, Cuba possessed 510 motion-picture houses and 58 periodical publications, including daily newspapers and reviews, with an average of 129 copies per 1,000 inhabitants (a figure exceeded in Latin America only by Argentina and Uruguay).[15]

At the same time, Castro has had difficulties with his followers in higher educational institutions, especially the University of Havana. In January 1962, Dr. Juan Marinello, president of the Cuban Communist party, was named rector of the University of Havana, and the goal of training 25,000 engineers and technicians in their specialties and in Marxist-Leninist principles was set for the next eight years. New programs for university degrees in all fields now include a required subject entitled "Historic and Dialectical Materialism" taken throughout the first year and a half of study. But Dr. Marinello was dismissed as rector on November 10, 1963. "His removal [was] viewed by specialists . . . as further evidence of Premier Fidel Castro's dispute with his orthodox allies,"[16] and of Castro's desire to tighten his control over governmental and party bureaucracies. Dr. Marinello was replaced by Dr. Juan Mier, deputy minister of education, whose appointment eliminated the last vestiges of student autonomy. Even under Communist leadership, students had retained some voice in the appointment of the university's faculty and administration. Previously, the premier had exhorted students at the university to greater dedication and sacrifice; he had bitterly denounced those who choose easy administrative posts rather than the technical and scientific jobs needed for Cuba's reconstruction. In the beginning of November 1963, in fact, Castro contended that while two thousand students had applied for diplomatic careers only two hundred had entered graduate courses in agronomy. Later, another leader, Joel Iglesias, was removed as head of the Union of Communist Youth, Cuba's counterpart to the Soviet KOMSOMOL [Communist Youth League]. There had been complaints of poor leadership and ineptness against Iglesias, the youngest man to accompany Castro to the Sierra Maestra. Iglesias was replaced by Miguel Martín, who had been active in organizing militia units near Santa Clara.

Overall Trends

The attraction of Cuba's experiment may perhaps be judged from the fact that fifty-nine U.S. college students defied the State Department, broke government regulations, and went to Cuba as guests of Castro in 1963.

> Laura Berquist concludes: "Castro isn't the new Bolívar, the savior he grandiosely seems to think he is. But in the four turbulent years, under the severest U.S. pressures, including an invasion, his regime has made amazing strides—in racial integration, health, housing and education. The price tag—the loss of civil liberties, the party-line press, the police-state trappings does not appeal to *me*, but many Cubans feel otherwise."[17]

Yet, most Cubans are also not as Marxist brainwashed as one would think. As Cartier-Bresson reports: "They are struggling to industrialize and they are worried about the future. They live with the stern Marxist morality because they must, but they are allergic to organization and to the usual Communist emphasis on conformity of any kind. . . . Nobody will easily convert them into hard Communist zealots."[18] Castro's government is realistic about this and has not tried to push the concept of absolute discipline too far (in spite of the numerous early executions). For instance, the basic Cuban passion, the lottery, is still tolerated, but it has become a tool of the revolution and the government simply takes a bigger percentage. And prostitution remains, in spite of all government claims to the contrary. Education, like all other things Cuban, inevitably feels similar conflicts.

Notes

1. Theodore Draper, *Castro's Revolution, Myths and Realities* (New York, Praeger, 192) has devastatingly exploded the myth that Castro, at the time of his victory, was leading a "peasants' and workers' " revolt. On the other hand, William Appleman Williams, *The United States, Cuba, and Castro* (New York, Monthly Review Press, 1962), plunges into the Cuban controversy, his chief target being Draper. A pro-Castro view is also represented by C. Wright Mills, *Listen, Yankee!* (New York, Ballantine, 1962). Earl E. T. Smith, *The Fourth Floor: An Account of the Castro Communist Revolution* (New York, Random House, 1962), shows the ineptitudes of Washington's foreign policies.
2. Royal Institute of International Affairs, *Cuba: A Brief Political and Economic Table* (New York, Oxford University Press, September, 1958); Draper, *Castro's Revolution*, pp. 42–48; Lino Novas Calvo, "La tragedia de la clase media cubana," *Bohemia Libre*, No. 13, January 1, 1961.
3. For documentary pictures of the new schools, see: "This is Castro's Cuba Seen Face to Face," photographs by Henri Cartier-Bresson, *Life*, LIV, 11, March 15, 1963, pp. 28–42.

4. Laura Berquist, "My 28 Days in Communist Cuba," *Look*, XXVII, 7, April 1963, pp. 15–27.

5. The best available survey, summarized here, of educational changes can be found in: U.S. Office of Education, Division of International Studies and Services, *Educational Data: Cuba*, No. 67, OE-14034-67 (Washington, D.C., Government Printing Office, November 1962). My request for material sent to the Ministerio de Educación, Havana, brought a reply from Mario Riva Patterson, director of "Ciudad Libertad," of April 16, 1963, and the following publications: Ministerio de Educación Primaria, *Jornada de la limpieza y la salud*, Havana, 1962; Comisión Nacional de Alfabetización, *Informe al pueblo de Cuba del resultado de la campaña nacional de alfabetización*, n.d.; Ministerio de Educación, *Realizaciones de la Revolución, Alfabetización nacional*, 1961; and Armando Hart, "La Revolución y los Problemas de la Educación" (mimeographed); Ministerio de Educación, *Informe de Cuba a la Conferencia sobre Educación y Desarrollo Económico y Social* (convocada por la UNESCO, la CEPAL y la OEA del 4 al 19 de marzo de 1962 en Santiago de Chile y respuesta de Cuba a la declaración de Santiago de Chile), Havana, 1962.

6. "Cuba: Physicians and Patients," *MD Medical Magazine*, VII, 2, February 1963, pp. 75–76.

7. Most famous of all Cuban physicians was the illustrious Carlos J. Finlay (1833–1915), for many years the symbol of tropical medicine, and the first to incriminate a specific mosquito in the transmission of yellow fever.

8. Cartier-Bresson, "This Is Castro's Cuba," p. 31.

9. "Pro-Castro Youth Toe Mark," *Christian Science Monitor*, April 8, 1963.

10. "Cubans Show School Setup," *Christian Science Monitor*, January 31, 1963.

11. Berquist, "My 28 Days," pp. 15–27, 20.

12. Ibid., p. 20.

13. Cartier-Bresson, "This Is Castro's Cuba," p. 42.

14. For documentary evidence of the presence of Soviet technicians, see ibid., pp. 28–42.

15. UN, *Statistical Yearbook*, 1961, pp. 638, 642.

16. Henry Raymont, "Pro-Moscow Red Loses Cuban Post," *New York Times*, November 11, 1963.

17. Berquist, "My 28 Days," p. 20.

18. Cartier-Bresson, "This Is Castro's Cuba," p. 42.

IV Problems of Institutionalization

*The Challenges of Bureaucratization
and Centralization*

11 John W. Donohue ◆ Paulo Freire—
Philosopher of Adult Education

When Paulo Freire's book Pedagogy of the Oppressed *appeared in English translation in 1968, it stimulated a rush of interest in the United States. The original Portuguese version was already widely read throughout Latin America. In 1972, John Donohue was present for one of Freire's early appearances in the United States at New York's Fordham University. Trained as a Jesuit and formerly a professor of education at Fordham, Donohue covered Freire's visit for* America, *a Catholic journal devoted to social and political issues. Donohue's article captures the essence of Freire's ideas along with a brief portrait of the Brazilian educator's engaging personality at a time when his pedagogy and persona were beginning to attract a large international following.*

The faculty lounge on the twelfth floor of Fordham University's Lowenstein Center has a spectacular view up and down Manhattan Island and the diluted neo-Bauhaus decor favored by waiting rooms in big airports. But not much of either was visible one evening late last February because people occupied all available chairs and any open spots on the gold-and-ochre carpet. They had come, however, not to admire the

From John W. Donohue, "Paulo Freire—Philosopher of Adult Education," *America* 127 (September 1972): 167–70. Reprinted by permission of *America* and the author.

lighted city outside or the standard abstract paintings inside but to hear Paulo Freire, the Brazilian philosopher of education, who is one of the two or three Catholic Christians since the Renaissance to have achieved a sizable and non-parochial reputation as an educational pioneer.

Pedagogy of the Oppressed (1968), which expounds Freire's method of adult education, is widely described as a revolutionary design for an ideal world. That method has been used successfully in Brazil, Peru, and Chile, and Freire's work is now the subject of doctoral dissertations in theology as well as in education. If his name is not yet so well-known in the United States, at least it's familiar enough, especially among radical critics of contemporary education, to have drawn that full house to the Fordham lounge.

Although there was some determined crawling about that evening for advantageous positioning of tape recorders, this crowd was eager and good-natured. For the most part, though, it wasn't middle-aged in fact and not at all so in spirit. There were some older people, including casually dressed priests and nuns, but it was predominantly a gathering of young men and women whose uniform was that of the counterculture. But if the more exotic among them, like one bearded figure lost in the brown and yellow folds of an ankle-length Moorish robe, had come expecting to be told how to run a revolution, they were probably disappointed because the lecture remained at a rather severely abstract level.

Yet surely no one was disappointed with the person and presence of Paulo Freire himself. For one thing, with his heavy head planted close to his shoulders and his steel-gray beard, he looked like a bespectacled Socrates in a business suit—but a chain-smoking, Brazilian Socrates who remarked companionably about the cup of coffee at his elbow: "Without coffee it is difficult for me to talk."

When he did talk, it was with a calm directness that established a quick rapport with his audience. No doubt this ability to create a sense of friendly intimacy is characteristic of Freire, whose admirers are apt to refer to him possessively as "Paulo." That relaxed atmosphere also prompted the less inhibited listeners to help out with the exposition. Did Freire, searching for the phrase to describe a particular social fact, murmur in some perplexity, "Struggle class? Class struggle?" Then a burly, garrulous West Side activist, who had been distributing leaflets earlier in the evening, would boom encouragingly, "Both!"

Interventions of this sort seemed to gratify Freire, who likes to insist that students and teachers must always learn together. "*We exist* explains *I exist*," he told the young people at Fordham. "I cannot be if you are not. I cannot know alone. For me to know, it is necessary for you to know." It is perhaps because Freire's English is uncertain that his ordinary sentences are apt to come out sounding like significant epigrams. "I do not believe too much in speeches," he said as he began that evening. "More and more I believe less." And he added, looking around serenely, "I *love* to emphasize obvious things."

What he emphasized in fact were the major themes that appear and reappear in his speeches and books that include, besides *Pedagogy of the Oppressed*, a 1967 predecessor, *Education as the Practice of Liberty*, that has been translated into Spanish but not yet into English. Before trying to sort out these ideas, we ought to stop for a moment over Freire's personal history because it has strongly conditioned his life's work. In this, he's like John Dewey, a thinker from whom Freire has learned a great deal. For Dewey once said of himself that what he had learned from books "has been technical in comparison with what I have been forced to think upon and about because of some experience in which I found myself entangled."

While still a child, Freire found himself entangled in experiences that were instructive but bitter. He was born in 1921 in Recife, in northeast Brazil, where three fifths of the 25 million people were still illiterate when Freire introduced his methods there ten years ago. In a foreword to the English version of *Pedagogy of the Oppressed* (Herder and Herder, 1970), Professor Richard Shaull of Princeton Theological Seminary writes that Freire's family was reduced to real poverty during the worldwide economic depression that started in 1929. This distress is said to have inspired the eleven-year-old Paulo Freire to make a vow that he would dedicate his own life to relieving the hunger and servitude of the poor.

If that vow helped turn Freire to the work of education, it was probably a natural taste for philosophizing that led him first to studies in the history and philosophy of education, areas in which he taught at the University of Recife where he took his degree in 1959. Shortly afterward, in the 1960s, reform movements were stirring various zones of Brazilian life. They were represented in government, for example, by Joâo Goulart, who became president in September 1961, despite the army's lack of enthusiasm for him. And it was during these years that the Brazilian Bishops Conference sponsored a Basic Educational Movement (MEB) that launched a nationwide effort to eliminate illiteracy while simultaneously heightening the peasants' social and political awareness (see Am., "The Church and Conscientização," 4/27/68) through the pages of a primer called *Viver e lutar* ("To Live Is to Struggle").

About this time, Freire, by now the father of a growing family, began to devise his own methods of adult education along with a philosophical rationale for them. His aims were like those of the Brazilian bishops' program, that is to say, teaching the poor both to read and to appreciate the possibility of improving their wretched circumstances.

Freire believes that one way in which the oppressed are kept domesticated is through the mass media's propaganda. He proposed, therefore, to use images of another sort precisely to awaken and liberate the poor. So it is not surprising that when the generals, outraged by all these subversive goings-on, overturned Goulart in the spring of 1964, they also suppressed the MEB and jailed Freire for seventy days. After his release he was, as Shaull puts it, "encouraged" to leave Brazil. He went first to Chile, where he spent five years refining his theory and applying it to the literacy campaigns instituted by Eduardo Frei's Christian Democratic government. Later, Freire spent some time at Harvard's Graduate School of Education and came to be appreciated by people like Jonathan Kozol, currently the chief spokesman for the free school movement in this country. Nowadays, Freire lives in Geneva and works for the World Council of Churches' Office of Education. But jet travel makes it possible for him to carry his message round the world to meetings and seminars like those held at Fordham last winter.

This message has two parts, theory and practice, that Freire would insist must not be separated, since each is incomplete by itself. When he was working in Chile in 1966, the Ministry of Public Education there produced a set of materials implementing his pedagogical ideas. It was called a "psychological-sociological method of teaching adults" and included a teachers' manual, a series of graded readers and a packet of twenty-five charts designed both to teach the alphabet and to develop people's "consciousness of their own value as human beings." This last is the famous *conscientização*, a capacious term signifying the kind of reflective understanding of problems that will issue in effective action. Although Freire himself points out that he neither invented nor popularized this expression, it is now as closely linked to his thought as democracy was to Dewey's.

That whole Chilean teaching apparatus carried a subtitle, *la raíz y la espiga*, which, for our purposes here, we might translate as "the root and the flowering." Then, prescinding from what the Chilean ministry may have intended, we can take "root" as a symbol for Freire's theory and "flowering" for the practice flowing from that philosophy and say something about each.

On first acquaintance, *Pedaogy of the Oppressed* is apt to strike informed readers as a Cook's tour through the master-concepts of the writers who have influenced Freire. The footnotes in *Education as the Practice of Liberty* are a better guide to those influences than the references in

Pedagogy, but, in any case, the origins of Freire's leitmotivs are so clear that they cannot be missed, even in the latter book.

To begin with, Freire fully accepts the Greek (and Christian) concept of man as a being essentially defined by the powers of reflective thought and free choice. For him, as for Aristotle, knowledge and liberty are the true goods of the soul. We are most human when we are free and most free when we can choose. Freire, as his work and writings show, is dominated by the desire to make these humanistic values fully available to every one. He is consequently critical of both capitalist and Communist societies because he believes that neither allows for the maximum self-development and growth in freedom of all men and women.

One need not be a Christian, of course, to have this kind of generous concern for universal humanistic education. Dewey enunciated it in a celebrated sentence from *School and Society*: "What the best and wisest parent wants for his own child, that must the community want for all of its children." Mao Tse-tung put a similar ideal into a Marxist perspective when he claimed that the revolution would provide education for that 90 percent of the Chinese people whose "sweat and blood" had created a culture in which they had no share. In Freire, however, this basic orientation has distinctively Christian roots. That might not be immediately clear from *Pedagogy*, which quotes Marx, Lenin, Mao, [Fidel] Castro, Che Guevara, [Gyorgy] Lukács, and [Frantz] Fanon (as well as Camilo Torres and John XXIII), but not the Gospel.

Nevertheless, if one peers just a bit below the surface of this text, one discovers certain characteristically Christian emphases, and these are made explicit in some of Freire's speeches and published letters. He surely wants a radical reordering of society but thinks this is possible only if there is cooperative dialogue between the haves and the have-nots. That, in turn, requires friendship, for there can be no dialogue between antagonists. Freire's rhetoric of reform deals, consequently, not with fire and sword and the breaking of chains, but with some recognizably Christian concepts and metaphors. "Men in communion liberate each other," he writes in *Pedagogy*. "Salvation can be achieved only *with* others." And he advises teachers of the poor to respect and trust each of their students and not attempt to impose middle-class culture upon them.

What the fortunate of this earth really require is a radical change of heart, and Freire likes to describe this in terms of the Easter imagery of rebirth. "The man who doesn't make his Easter, in the sense of dying to be reborn, is no real Christian," he said in a talk in Rome two years ago. "That is why Christianity is, for me, such a marvelous doctrine." In fact, he set the whole work of revolution within a religious dimension when he wrote to a young student of theology: "The Word of God is inviting me to recreate the world, not for my brothers' domination, but for their liberation" (*Catholic Mind*, September 1972).

For in this harsh, real world, the men and women who make up the mass of silent oppressed are unable to realize their human potential for free intelligent activity because their natural and social environments are so brutal. These are the people of the Third World, which, as Freire told his Fordham audience, is not so much a geographical as a theological and political concept. It is the world of all the voiceless, suffering poor, whether these be Arab *fellahin* or Peruvian campesinos or migrant workers in the United States. Since they all need liberation, Freire is convinced that his theory and method, although generated by his Brazilian experiences, have universal validity and applicability.

The existence of these oppressed populations is, of course, a fact, but Freire's Marxian conceptualization of that fact is oversimplified. He divides society too neatly into just two categories: an oppressive minority running affairs for its own profit and the oppressed majority who are not allowed to think or choose for themselves. But, as reviewers have pointed out, this distinction is inadequate because some of the oppressed are themselves dominators and exploiters of the others. Freire does recognize this but is not sufficiently impressed to alter his analysis.

Instead, the analysis goes on to indict a device that Freire believes the oppressors employ to keep down the oppressed. This is what he calls the "banking concept" of education because it aims to deposit in passive recipients only those ideas and attitudes that the ruling class judges proper, while discouraging independent thinking. Freire finds this notion only too generally accepted. "People think schools are temples where they can find a chaste, untouchable knowledge," he complained at Fordham. "Fantastic!"

He would replace this banking concept by a "problem posing" education in which "men develop their power to perceive critically *the way they exist* in the world *with which* and *in which* they find themselves." That is to say, knowledge must grow out of experiences that are genuine transactions with reality. And this, of course, is the central thesis of Dewey's instrumentalism, which sees man caught up in an evolving universe that constantly confronts him with problems. These difficulties stimulate real thinking, and true (or *good*) ideas are those solutions that work in practice. But the banking concept would also be rejected out of hand by a much older tradition, as a student of educational history like Freire knows. Plato, Aristotle, and Thomas Aquinas all insisted that the chief agent of authentic learning is the student himself and that the most the teacher can do is to cooperate in that process.

Freire cherishes this idea of the teacher as cooperating. He puts it into the context of Martin Buber's thesis that education best takes place in an I-thou setting of authentic dialogue between two persons who respect each other and learn together—"The encounter," as Freire says in *Pedagogy*, "of men in the world in order to transform the world." Put this vaguely, the notion may induce skepticism in veteran teachers. It is easier to appreciate, however, if one remembers that Freire is thinking particularly of adult education. Those who teach adults should have, he says, the attitude of comrades, not masters, for they will fail if they are patronizing, manipulative, or authoritarian.

Their job is to cooperate in a process of liberation that has two phases: understanding and action. First of all, students and teachers must reflect upon the actual world in which they find themselves. For, as Freire put it in that Rome talk: "Even a peasant is a man, and any man wants to explain the reality around him." But this moment of speculative knowledge is not enough. It must be followed by practical efforts to improve the human condition through shared enterprise in science, art, technology, and the solving of problems in human relationships. It all comes down to what Emmanuel Mounier, the French Christian personalist, once said: "A thought which does not lead to a decision is an incomplete thought." Not fake, to be sure, but incomplete. Freire does not quote these words, but he does acknowledge Mounier as an influence, and he does constantly emphasize the importance of what he calls "praxis." For as he wrote to that theology student, one cannot try to change man without touching the world in which he lives.

These are the centerpieces of Freire's thought, and one might wonder why such familiar concepts have so great an allure and why they interest young people who usually detest classic teachings. It may be, of course, that a pragmatic theory seems more novel in Latin America than in the United States. Moreover, Freire is in that powerful tradition of revolutionary reform for which not only [Georges] Danton and Marx but the American Constitutional Convention spoke. He likes, in fact, to infuse even standard concepts with a radical flavor. Thus "theory" becomes the phase of denunciation of evils, and "practice" the phase of announcing changes, while the two together constitute utopianism or working for a better world. To tell the truth, Freire's fondness for philosophizing sometimes leads him to overweight a simple idea with an enormously elaborate speculative framework. His complicated explanation of "the codification of generative themes" in the pictures he used to teach reading and spark discussions is one case in point. Passages like this would have benefited from a good dose of British analytic salts.

But such passages do not suffocate Freire's essential themes, which he organizes into something more than a mere amalgam of other men's ideas. In *Education as the Practice of Liberty*, he adverts once to [Alfred North] Whitehead's criticism of any education that merely transmits "inert ideas." It is fair to say that the influences Freire has absorbed are in him far from inert. He is himself well aware of what he has done, and elsewhere in the same work he makes a revealing selection of a line from Dewey's *Democracy and Education*. It comes from a passage in which Dewey ruminates on the nature of creative thinking and remarks that the materials [Isaac] Newton used were not original ideas but familiar, even commonplace ones. "Only silly folk," Dewey continues in the sentence Freire quotes, "identify creative originality with the extraordinary and fanciful; others recognize that its measure lies in putting things to uses which had not occurred to others." This is a good account of what Freire has done. The appeal of his theory consists precisely in the ensemble he has made from his sources and his putting this to work in the service of a noble ideal. For perhaps the most powerful attraction Freire's writings have is in the authentic humanitarian passion that vitalizes and unifies them. Besides, as young reformers know, Freire has practiced what he preaches. That practice is the flowering stalk rising from the root of his theory, and it illustrates and clarifies the philosophy. The materials published by the Chilean ministry are a reliable guide to this pedagogy, for Freire has recommended them to students of his methods.

Those methods aim, as we have already noted, to do more than teach reading to adult illiterates. They are also designed to get these people thinking about the actions they might take to cure the physical and social ills besetting them. The very first line of the first reader announces firmly: "This book will be our friend." A serious friend, though, who examines chapter by chapter the conditions of life, often hard enough, as it is known to peasants and workers. At times, indeed, the primer assumes a school-teacherly moralizing tone. The discussion of *El Alcohol*, for instance, bluntly describes this commodity as poison and says it is a mistake to suppose it makes one strong. On the contrary, the bull and horse, the lion and elephant all have great strength and endurance, and they drink only water.

But Freire would himself probably prefer to have people arrive independently at these sobering reflections after pondering over them together. Discussions of that sort are stimulated by the colored slides and charts used by teachers trained in Freire's methods. The charts, for example, are bold, vigorous drawings illustrating aspects of village or work life or recording the development of technology with sketches of hunters, woodsmen, carpenters, field workers, ditch diggers, millers, and water carriers.

For usually the first problems to be solved by the poor of developing countries are technological ones—bringing water to the village or improving agriculture.

Generally a single word is also emblazoned on these cartoons so that those studying them will learn letters, syllables, and words, while being prompted at the same time to reflect upon the picture's theme. Those themes are poignant enough. *Fábrica*: the factory in the background behind a fence of cruelly pointed iron bars with a barefooted waif perched on its ledge while two melancholy men study the sign, "No Openings." *Camino*: peasants trudging along a road or riding a burro while a sleek car whizzes by. *Guitarra*: not being played but just ogled in its splendid isolation in a shop window by people who cannot afford guitars. *Yugo*: a farmer about to yoke a very disheartened-looking ox. Another picture has no label but shows a peasant plowing under a dramatically fierce sun. *Sindicato*: a meeting of workers. *Casa*: these workmen coming home at evening.

You cannot sift through these twenty-five charts without getting some sense of what Freire has done. He combines the concrete imagination of great pedagogical innovators like [Friedrich] Froebel and [Maria] Montessori with the utopian vision of the great prophets of social reform. One can lose one's footing, of course, on each of these ideal heights, which is why John F. Kennedy defined himself as an idealist without illusions. But while such caution is eminently logical, still in the real and often illogical world the boundaries between ideals and illusions are sometimes ragged.

It is clear from *Pedagogy of the Oppressed* that Freire knows, for instance, that once the poor have gotten on a bit they frequently assume the least admirable characteristics of the bourgeoisie. Nevertheless, he remains convinced that this dismal development can be avoided by a truly human education, and so he also remains deeply hopeful and therefore deeply Christian.

"There is only one way for me to find peace," he said at the close of that 1970 talk in Rome, "to work for it, shoulder to shoulder with my fellowmen. . . . I am not yet completely a Catholic, I just keep on trying to be one more completely, day after day. . . . I just feel passionately, corporately, physically, with all my being, that my stance is a Christian one because it is 100 percent revolutionary and human and liberating, and hence committed and Utopian . . . love that cannot produce more freedom is not love."

12 Kevin Healy ◆ Animating Grassroots Development: Women's Popular Education in Bolivia

The history of education is replete with names of pedagogical theorists whose words have filled volumes but whose ideas have seldom had a lasting impact on the actual processes of learning and teaching. Paulo (or Paolo) Freire is an exception. As Kevin Healy's article reveals, Freire's ideas have directly influenced an innovative education program for peasant women in Bolivia. Healy is a professorial lecturer in the Program of Social Change and Development at the Johns Hopkins School of Advanced International Studies. Much of the following essay is based on his personal observations in the rugged highlands of Bolivia.

B elow the blue vastness of mountain sky, a dozen women in bowler hats and brightly striped shawls sit, fanned out in a tightly drawn semicircle, watching intently as the last in a series of illustrated posters is flipped over. Preceded by color drawings of a woman harvesting potatoes, washing clothes, cooking supper, and pasturing sheep, the final poster—labeled "Community Meeting"—depicts a woman pouring soup into bowls for a group of men huddled in conversation around a table. Standing to one side and pointing to the poster, the discussion leader asks, "What is going on here in this one? What does it mean?"

"It is our true situation," says a woman near the center of the fan. "We work, but no one sees us as we are."

"Yes, my identity papers say I am a 'mother,' but we are all farmers, too," adds another.

"It is like the campesina we talked about in that other picture, the one pasturing animals," says a third. "It is always the mothers and their daughters who are expected to look after the sheep. Who are the real sheep here anyway?"

One after another, these women are taking their turn at the educational game known in the Bolivian altiplano as *rotafolio*. This particular session in the courtyard of a village church in the department of Oruro had focused on the daily hardships and conditions of peasant women, but *rotafolio* is a mobile civics course whose posters can open windows on a myriad of other subjects—from literacy, to ethnic identity, to the effects on small farmers of inflation and debt in the national economy. The tech-

From Kevin Healy, "Animating Grassroots Development: Women's Popular Education in Bolivia," *Grassroots Development* 15, no. 1 (Special 20th Anniversary Issue, 1991): 26–34. Reprinted by permission of *Grassroots Development*.

nique is not new; its origins can be traced to the illustrations in Paolo Freire's *Education as Practice for Liberty*, the influential Brazilian educator's how-to book on adult literacy training that outlines techniques for unveiling the relationship between people and their culture, suggesting how poor people can learn to shape their own lives by "naming" and transforming their social, economic, and cultural reality. Inspired by that book and Freire's pioneering volume *Pedagogy of the Oppressed*, nongovernmental organizations (NGO) throughout the hemisphere during the past two decades have fashioned *rotafolios*, puppet shows, sociodramas, and a multitude of other educational devices into a tool kit for grassroots organizing.

For the past eight years, the Capacitación Integral de la Mujer Campesina (CIMCA) has been refining these techniques and using them to inspire social change in Oruro, a desolate region thirteen thousand feet above sea level whose treeless, windswept plains—dotted with adobe villages—stretch between two Andean cordilleras. With one of the highest infant mortality rates in the hemisphere, winters of bone-numbing cold and periodic droughts, life for the predominantly indigenous population is not easy in the best of times. But the national economic crisis of the 1980s has devastated the region, reducing sheep herds to scraggy flocks, shriveling markets for small farmers' cash crops, and throwing thousands of tin miners out of work. For the past decade, more Aymara and Quechua men of the area have been emigrating in search of work, leaving their mothers, wives, and sisters behind to eke out a living from small family farms.

Out of these seemingly barren conditions, CIMCA has emerged as a beacon for women's rights and ethnic empowerment, inspiring the people of Oruro to uncover latent resources in their communities that would enable them to shape their own future and the future of their children. As CIMCA's director, Evelyn Barrón, points out,

> Women are the great untapped resource of Latin America. Things are beginning to change in Oruro because we clearly cannot afford to waste the energies of more than half the people. If women are limited to looking after kids, tending livestock, and passing out food baskets from overseas aid programs, we will never touch the roots of rural poverty. Our story is still evolving, but we are getting our chance because almost everything else has failed.

CIMCA believes that the rural poor must organize to develop, but it also believes that effective organizations require active memberships. This notion is widely held in development circles, but only partially practiced. By waking up people through popular education, CIMCA has not only planted the seeds of organizational reform throughout Oruro, it has also begun to produce the problem-solving leaders and self-confident memberships those organizations must have to attack the real needs of their communities. The journey toward this goal has been a long one, and its progress has been measured in fits and starts.

The Birth of CIMCA

CIMCA was founded in 1982 by a dynamic pair of Bolivian educators, Evelyn Barrón and Rita Murillo, who out of desperation decided to tilt at the windmills of development orthodoxy in Bolivia. Barrón is the guiding spirit of that quest. She was born in a small, southern valley town two days by bus from Oruro. With the self-assurance instilled by a mother who was the town's mayor and a father who was a lawyer, Barrón left home as a young woman determined to make her mark. She enrolled at the national university in La Paz, earning a degree in social work, and in her twenties became director of the women's bureau of a national government program to promote rural community development. After seven years of record harvests for red tape, she began to wonder if the agency was for serving small farmers or for employing urban professionals to tell farmers what to do.

Barrón eventually left her position and went to work in the projects office of Caritas Boliviano, a nonprofit development agency of the Catholic church, where she met Rita Murillo. They worked together for several years, but came to believe that the agency's distribution of surplus U.S. grains through local mothers' clubs too often led to a development dead end. People were not starving, but nutrition levels remained substandard, and women were not learning how to improve production to feed their families. At about this time, Barrón and Murillo became acquainted with the writings and thoughts of Paolo Freire, who believed that charity undermined self-esteem among the poor and left them at the mercy of their benefactors. Too often it was a barter in which basic necessities were exchanged for apathetic silence.

These ideas were not well received among their colleagues, so the two women left to join Catholic Relief Services, which also funneled food aid to the poor but was staffed by several professionals interested in starting community development projects. Believing that success depended on local participation, Barrón and Murillo took charge of a training program designed to get women more actively involved in their communities. When the agency's priorities shifted, however, the two decided to found their own organization, CIMCA, and set out to test their beliefs in Oruro, an area of dire need that had few NGOs and minimal public resources.

No More White Elephants

The effort might never have gotten off the ground without a grant from the IAF (Inter-American Foundation), which was interested in encouraging Bolivians to find new models for sparking development among rural women. One of the attractive features of CIMCA's proposal was its decision to minimize administrative overhead and maximize operational flexibility. From the beginning, Barrón and Murillo were determined to invest their energies and capital in people rather than offices or buildings. From her experience with the national community development program and two NGOs, Barrón knew that there were plenty of public facilities and church meeting halls that were unused or underused because they never became integrated fully with local communities. CIMCA would put these white elephants to work rather than enlarge the size of the herd by building a centralized training center.

Anyone visiting for the first time the one-room CIMCA office in the modest two-story house in a rundown section of the city of Oruro might wonder if CIMCA was an organization only in name. Looking at the battered desk, the handful of chairs, the piles of educational pamphlets with indigenous faces on the covers, the clerk occasionally interrupting her typing to answer the phone, it seems that nothing much is happening. But if one looks at the departmental map of Oruro hanging on the wall, studded with brightly colored tags marking the communities along the route of CIMCA's van, a different conclusion rapidly comes into focus. To find CIMCA—its leaders, its trainers, its impact—one must travel into the campo.

During the organization's early years, CIMCA's van was everywhere, pulling into one altiplano community after another out of the blue. The staff of trainers would pop out, engage curious onlookers in conversation, and persuade them to call a community meeting where interest could be sparked in women's issues and popular education. After a meeting was convened, Barrón would introduce herself and the staff and explain what they hoped to accomplish. "We all know that economic development projects are needed," she would start,

> but they are not enough. We need to see the true nature of our problems. If only a handful of people get rich from a project while the rest stay poor, is that development? I have been in communities where campesinos have learned how to increase their yields, and made lots of money, but turned around and bought a truck rather than put some of it aside to educate their children. Perhaps you, too, have seen families take milk out of the mouths of their children to sell at the state dairy. This is giving value to things instead of people. What kind of development is it when women learn only to sew and knit and mind their own business?

Isn't the world their business, too? Shouldn't they have a say about what happens to their families, their communities, their country?

Often the meeting never got beyond the spectacle of outsiders putting on a show. But CIMCA usually found a candidate or two eager to attend a regional training session to learn how to become an *educadora popular*, a popular educator capable of promoting community development. And if the show seemed to energize everyone, CIMCA would single out the community for more intensive training by assigning a staff member to live there for a time and hold informal classes in popular education.

This scattershot approach had its drawbacks. Recruits came from every corner of the department, making it difficult to schedule regular follow-up visits to see how new *educadoras populares* interacted with their communities. When follow up did occur, the results were often discouraging. Distilling years of experience, Barrón and her colleagues had focused their training on achieving an immediate impact by improving community health and nutrition. Training sessions fed this information to trainees through the latest in popular education techniques to hold student interest. When CIMCA staff visited newly trained promoters at home, however, they discovered that few families had changed their behavior. They were still selling their best sources of protein, such as eggs and meat, and were not growing the variety of vegetables needed for a balanced diet.

More alarming still, CIMCA found that many of their newly trained *educadoras populares* had abandoned their work, and often their villages, to get married. In selecting trainees, Barrón and her colleagues had emphasized young, single women who could read and write. Older women were thought to be too resistant to change and less energetic and imaginative in inspiring others to change. The evidence soon suggested that perhaps the young were too changeable, unable to persevere when confronted by prospective husbands who saw popular education as an unnecessary diversion from starting and raising a family.

Yet CIMCA was also running into trouble even in the handful of pilot communities singled out for intensive promotion by core staff members. Ubaldina Salinas, CIMCA's best promoter, had been assigned for several months to the village of Querarani. Enthusiasm ran high when CIMCA's van had made its first visit, but when Salinas returned to set up a women's training workshop, no one came to the first session. Each time she rescheduled, she met the same stony silence. Finally, CIMCA recalled Salinas to reassess the assignment. She reported that the men were not letting their wives attend the sessions—not because they were threatened, but because they were not included. Faced with the choice of withdrawing or adapting, CIMCA sent Salinas back and opened up the sessions to all interested members of the village. That was the beginning of Querarani's development, planting the seeds of a future harvest, whose bounty would become apparent only later.

In the meantime, the crisis left an indelible mark on CIMCA, raising questions about its grassroots development strategy. Should CIMCA trainees be promoting community organizations for women parallel to those dominated by men? Would this fracture and weaken communities that were already unable to defend their interests adequately in Bolivian national society? CIMCA decided to take a pragmatic course. It would continue to work with organizations such as mothers' clubs, but it would also try to strengthen and reform community peasant organizations by proving for initiatives that would broaden their membership base and lead to women's empowerment.

One such opportunity seemed to open in the province of Moza. Moza's small farmers produced potatoes that were renowned throughout Oruro, but lack of organization left them unable to bargain for better terms from the middlemen who trucked the crop to market and received the lion's share of the profits. CIMCA decided to work with a new association of potato growers in fifteen communities, helping them consolidate their organizations by starting a project to encourage women to take a more active leadership role. Andean women play a key role in cultivating the crop, so it seemed obvious that their involvement was crucial for introducing new techniques to raise yields. CIMCA also hoped the time was ripe to show that women should participate in deciding how to raise profits through direct marketing. This attempt backfired, however, when ambitious male leaders grew impatient with the popular education process and tried to seize control of project assets by pushing Barrón and CIMCA's other trainers out of the zone. Suspecting that the leadership of the association had viewed women's training as a goose for laying golden eggs from outside funding, and realizing that local women were not far enough along to defend their own interests, CIMCA decided to withdraw from the zone.

The loss of young women promoters, the failure to change family diets, the temporary setback in Querarani, the withdrawal from Moza all had a common thread running through them. Barrón had long believed that development projects could not work without community participation. For women to participate fully, basic attitudes had to be changed not only in society but among women. Barrón concluded that

> our early efforts fell short not because there was no need to improve
> nutrition or for families to raise their incomes, but because our women
> trainees did not truly value themselves, or have a sense of their own

dignity. Realizing this forced us to get at the motivational factors, those deep-seated beliefs that form a person's self-image and place in society.

For CIMCA to have an impact, it would have to begin at the level of the women it hoped to energize by first encouraging them to identify their own needs. Instead of providing answers, CIMCA would teach people how to ask questions.

Crystallizing a Pedagogy

Paulo Freire called the process of awakening people to the power of their own questioning *conscientização*. In encouraging the women and men of Oruro to begin that journey toward greater awareness of self and to understand how that could become a model for transforming the inertia of rural society into productive motion, CIMCA has also changed during the past eight years. From an ad hoc, improvisational approach, CIMCA has gradually evolved a structured multiphased program that has begun to come full circle, enabling the organization to begin addressing the complex of issues, including health and nutrition, that for a time it was forced to put aside. There are three stages to this training process.

The first stage of training takes place at a centrally located site near participants' home communities. This has two advantages: it ensures that graduates become part of a mutual support network to sponsor local development, and it facilitates the scheduling of follow-up monitoring by CIMCA staff. In 1989, CIMCA held nine microregional workshops.

Enrollment in each of these workshops is limited to about forty people for optimal participation. The three trainers are drawn from CIMCA's core staff of four and from another half-dozen professionals and previously trained paraprofessionals who are available on a part-time basis as needed.

The first day, trainees are divided into small groups and taken outdoors for short walks and asked to make observations on what they see in the village around them. Those who overcome their shyness usually note little that is remarkable, finding only what is to be expected. On the last day of training, they will repeat this process and report back to the whole group on how their perceptions have changed from learning to see and question the hidden and constraining assumptions underlying the routines of daily life.

During the intervening two weeks, participants are exposed to a variety of situations designed, as CIMCA puts it, "to help one lose one's fear." Foremost among these fears is the fear of speaking. Cooking, eating, sleeping, dancing, singing, and working together, and looking after one another's children, creates a kind of family bonding that helps make it safe to talk freely. But it is the *rotafolio* that deepens the talk into dialogue.

CIMCA's *rotafolios* are the products of eight years of workshops, distilling testimonies from the whole range of women in Oruro. They are drawn by Germán Treviño, a graduate of the school of plastic arts in Oruro who has been working with CIMCA since 1984. He emphasizes that the power of the illustrations depends on "truly conveying what the *compañeras* tell us about their experiences. Sometimes it requires changing the *rotafolio* a half-dozen times before they are satisfied. The women do not want caricatures so I have to study their faces carefully." Years of studying faces for clues to the stories he has heard the women tell, Treviño says, has changed his opinions about the situation of rural women, which he never thought about before, allowing him to see their problems for the first time and to identify their humanity with his own.

This process of identification is what makes the drawings such an effective tool for consciousness-raising. *Rotafolios* are intended to be linked together to form a fan around a central theme. Together, they provide the elements of a puzzle that workshop participants will solve as they discuss an unfolding succession of narrative situations. Gradually, participants will come to identify it as the story of their own lives. Many years of workshop experience attest to the validity of the story line contained in each set of *rotafolios*, but participants must discover and resolve that story for themselves. To emphasize that trainees are in control of the process, and to ensure maximum participation among literate and illiterate alike, drawings are often no longer labeled. The point of the story emerges from the telling, but its outcome is foreshadowed from the very beginning in the strong and resolutely human faces of the indigenous women in the drawings. As one CIMCA trainee described her experience, "Before I came here, I thought I was supposed to be poor. Now I realize that is not so, and I will not let it be so for my children."

CIMCA has developed three sets of *rotafolios* about altiplano women, and these form the core of the first set of workshops. Trainees are asked to analyze the condition of peasant women at all stages of the life cycle—from birth, through childhood, adolescence, and marriage, into old age. In the altiplano, it is common for people to commiserate with the parents of a newborn girl, implying that they have received a burden rather than a reward. In tracing the path of that burden as it is borne from grandmother to mother to daughter, the *rotafolios* eventually arouse a smoldering anger among the workshop participants at the experience of discrimination they all have in common.

Are we peasant women the victims of discrimination?

If we are the victims of discrimination, how do we perceive it? As women? This is one of the forms of discrimination a woman suffers, for being a woman, and it is called GENDER DISCRIMINATION.

For being peasants? Another form of discrimination occurs when women of the city scorn women of the countryside. This is called ETHNIC DISCRIMINATION.

For being poor? There is also discrimination against peasant women for belonging to the lower, exploited class. This is called CLASS DISCRIMINATION.

And is it true that we discriminate against ourselves?

And for whom is it important to maintain this situation? Will not dividing and maintaining divisions between men and women weaken popular movements?

Do we continue as we are? . . . or do we say . . . "Bring an end to the problem!"

How? Like this?

Or like this?

And if we manage to bring an end to this situation, who will benefit? The woman is responsible for the education of children and on her depend the new generations.

"The community . . . Why?" Women can bring positive ideas to the solution of the needs of their community.

"The nation? Why?" Popular movements strengthen themselves with the participation of women.

There are *rotafolios* to show that anger. Pictures of campesinas breaking the chains binding their wrists, ripping off the bandanas covering their eyes, tearing the padlocks from their mouths, and crashing through brick walls. What is interesting about this anger is that it is not directed toward men but toward gender roles. In the *rotafolio* of a woman smashing a wall, a man stands beside her, urging her on. Other *rotafolios* suggest what a freer society might look like, showing men sharing responsibility for collecting firewood, pasturing sheep, or tending an infant. The *rotafolio* of a girl remaining behind to herd sheep while her brother saunters off—books in hand—to school is eventually answered by one of a husband and wife watching their son and daughter study together.

The channel for change outside the family is directed toward community organizations. Another set of *rotafolios* focuses on the ayllu, a traditional system, based on lineage, for allocating the distribution of village labor and resources, and the *sindicato*, an association of all households in the community that serves as a local government and is the primary vehicle for addressing common needs, such as building and maintaining roads, schools, and water systems. Women are usually allowed to attend *sindicato* meetings only when their husbands are ill or have migrated in search of work, or if they are heads-of-household. The only leadership position open is "secretary of women's affairs," which often exists in name only at the regional level.

CIMCA's *rotafolios* offer a platform for questioning this arrangement and suggest how it might be reformed. The *rotafolio* labeled "Community Meeting," which shows a woman serving soup to a group of busy men, is followed by others showing a woman nervously addressing a group of seated men, working diligently beside other villagers on a community project, and finally sitting behind the table making decisions with the other community leaders.

Before the last phase of CIMCA training is over, trainees take turns tracing copies of *rotafolios* that they will take back to their communities for a nine-week practicum working with a local organization. During this time, a CIMCA trainer will make a return visit to see how things are going.

Those *educadoras populares* who have shown special promise are invited to attend a second set of workshops, which draw together people from throughout the province. Insights about family and community problems that were learned in the first workshops are now applied on a regional and national level. Introduced to the concept of "marginality," trainees examine how economic and ethnic discrimination helps perpetuate poverty. In small groups they analyze how indigenous people, even though they are the majority, are shunned by the national media, how they are expected to shed their traditional clothing, stop speaking Aymara and Quechua, change their surnames, and cut their braids if they want to fit into mestizo culture. While learning to make and use puppets, play a variety of educational board games, and act in sociodramas, trainees probe the humiliations they or their friends and relatives have experienced while migrating to the city to look for work.

These exercises follow the same course traced by the *rotafolios*, channeling anger at the recognition of systematic discrimination toward a search for effective remedial action, for examples of ethnic pride that can be a catalyst for economic and social development. Again, much of the focus falls on the *sindicato*, which is much more than a community presence. With elected bodies at the zonal, departmental, and national levels, *sindicatos* have spearheaded the movement toward land reform, rural schooling, the end of military rule, and the return to constitutional democracy. CIMCA's hopes for the *sindicato* as a vehicle for socioeconomic change are shared by numerous other NGOs and development practitioners in Bolivia.

But CIMCA tempers its hopes with a critical eye. *Rotafolios* explore the dangers of corrupt leadership practices, co-optation by political parties, and the prevalence of machismo attitudes that exclude women from active participation and positions of authority. CIMCA's workshop prepares women for the rise to positions of leadership in the *sindicato* movement and for the struggle to hold leaders accountable to their memberships, regardless of gender. As one recent CIMCA graduate, Flora Rufino, remarked,

> First by joining, then by leading group discussions, I have learned how to talk with, not at, people. Now I can speak clearly and forcefully in public. I have the skills to keep minutes or run a meeting, and I know how to analyze issues in ways that allow the community to inform itself about national as well as local problems. CIMCA has challenged me to question, and that has taught me how to think.

Critical thinking is the basis of problem solving, and the third stage of CIMCA training concentrates on technical subjects, such as community health, nutrition, animal husbandry, and agronomy. Launched in 1988, this program brings CIMCA full circle. With a cadre of popular educators who have a firm sense of self and society and are highly motivated (one, for example, put a clause in her wedding vows obligating her spouse to support her work as an *educadora popular*), it was only natural that they would demand to learn the kinds of skills that CIMCA had first come to the campo, years before, hoping to teach.

The workshop brings together men and women from throughout Oruro. Professional trainers offer seminars in a variety of disciplines, and there are field trips to ongoing rural development projects being sponsored by other NGOs. These visits are a learning opportunity for everyone; CIMCA's trainees arrive full of questions, not only about how to prepare seedling nurseries, for instance, but armed with suggestions on how local women might be included more actively in the project.

Sometimes the entire workshop is held at a site specializing in a certain skill. The Centro Agropecuario del Desarrollo Altiplano (CADEA), a previously underutilized agricultural and livestock research station operated by the government in Oruro, is a prime example. CADEA's agronomists and extensionists are delighted with the arrangement. "We have had some problems reaching campesino groups," explains one researcher,

> but CIMCA has a well-developed methodology, including the *rotafolio*, for getting communities to apply what they are learning. Sometimes teaching a technical course can be frustrating, like shouting into the bottom of a well, but with CIMCA you know they have the ability to draw the knowledge up so it reaches campesinos' fields.

CIMCA Reaches Out

After eight years of tireless effort in Oruro, CIMCA has moved beyond using other people's white elephants to helping NGOs and public agencies better use their own infrastructures. Overcoming the deeply entrenched barriers to reaching and mobilizing rural women is perhaps the single hardest task in development, and word-of-mouth communication about CIMCA's effective training methods has spread quickly throughout the department, and beyond. Grassroots organizations and NGOs from as far away as La Paz and the neighboring department of Potosí are lined up to seek CIMCA's counsel. The European Community, which funds a rural development program in Bolivia staffed by more than 170 employees, recently asked CIMCA to train the campesinas in its projects. The UN Food and Agricultural Organization has asked CIMCA to support small-scale irrigation projects. Even universities are sending their students and instructors to sit in on CIMCA workshops and observe the magic firsthand.

Perhaps the most dramatic turnaround involves Caritas Boliviano, the agency Barrón left behind on her journey to start her own development organization. As recently as the mid-1980s, CIMCA's stinging *rotafolios* on the negative impact of food aid on rural communities was eliciting complaints from the agency's departmental director. During the past year, however, the relationship with Caritas has become increasingly cordial. Frustration with the limited impact of the Caritas program led its local director to ask CIMCA to introduce training in popular education to the sixty mothers' clubs in the province of Totora, laying the foundation for a health education program to be jointly managed by the two agencies. A similar effort is under way at the request of a local bishop to revitalize a moribund network of mothers' clubs in the province of Corocoro.

CIMCA may eventually become the primary trainer of other NGO trainers in Oruro, but it has not lost sight of its goal to help make *sindicatos* more democratic by catapulting campesinas into leadership positions at all levels of this multitiered structure. As a result of CIMCA's persistence, the walls of gender discrimination are beginning to crack. Its trainees have moved beyond attending and speaking out at local, provincial, and regional *sindicato* congresses, to win elective posts. Nearly twenty have been elected to leadership councils in the various provinces of Oruro. The crowning achievement, however, was the election of four campesinas to offices on the executive committee of the departmental federation representing several hundred thousand small farmers.

The foundation for this accomplishment was laid at a CIMCA workshop for fifty women community leaders several months prior to the congress. After the course was completed, CIMCA staff divided the region by cantons and provinces and monitored the performance of trainees at *sindicato* meetings. Forty of the women were then invited back to a second workshop to polish their skills and plan election strategy.

The most revealing sign that something fundamental had changed occurred after the election, when one of the winners was appointed secretary of women's affairs. Rising to address the several hundred delegates, most of them men, seated before her, she declined the job, saying, "How long do we have to make believe this is a real position? You give us a seat at the table, but you go on making decisions in the back room. We are as capable as any man of filling a responsible position."

Embarrassed, the male leaders overseeing the transition of power announced she would be the new secretary of *sindicato organización*, an office that has traditionally wielded considerable clout.

Although CIMCA's pre-election workshop set the stage for this broadening of representation, the antecedents of the story reach all the way back to the community of Querarani, the scene of one of CIMCA's early false starts. After CIMCA acceded to community demands and held training workshops that included men as well as women, villagers created the Asociación Familiar Campesina (ASFACA) to start local development initiatives. ASFACA has an unusual leadership structure that fills each office with a man and a woman, who are also husband and wife. The idea is in harmony with the traditional dualism of Andean culture that predates the arrival of the conquistadors, but as an expression of power sharing, it emerged directly from CIMCA's workshop. (This suggests that to prevent women's empowerment from being stillborn, it is important to find roots for the concept in traditional culture so that transformation of that culture occurs from within rather than becoming one more alien idea imposed from the outside.)

Since its emergence, the Asociación has started a literacy program in Aymara; worked with an international donor, CARE, to install a potable water system, with individual standpipes for each home; planted communal vegetable gardens to diversify family diets; and purchased a tractor families can lease to till their farms. With the income from the tractor rental, the Asociación is buying a generator to bring electricity to the village. Last year, a man and a woman from Querarani joined the other three women trained by CIMCA as newly elected officials on the executive committee of Oruro's departmental federation of *sindicatos*.

Querarani is harvesting the fruits of *conscientização*. And the men and women of this isolated Andean village are not alone. CIMCA was recently featured alongside select projects from Asia and Africa in the four-part series *Local Heroes, Global Change* being televised in the United States, Japan, and Western Europe to examine models for a new direction in development. Evelyn Barrón has been invited to seminars abroad to share her experience in empowering rural women. The ideas set in motion by Paolo Freire are being felt worldwide, and CIMCA's voice is on the cutting edge of the dialogue. Working with the people of Oruro, CIMCA is helping create participatory institutions at the base of society to ensure that "democratization" becomes more than a hollow word.

The Impact of International Institutions: Ideas and Images from Abroad

13 Alan Wells ◆ The Americanization of Latin American Television

The penetration of U.S. television programs and practices into Latin America began in the 1950s and 1960s. Alan Wells was one of the first serious students of this process. A native of England where he worked in the paper and plastics industry as a youth, Wells pursued an academic career in the United States. Drawing from his training as a sociologist and his sensitivity to international issues, Wells's Picture Tube Imperialism? *was published in 1972. His bold analysis of the status of U.S. influences on Latin America's nascent television industry is also notable for its understanding of the environment in which learning—both in school and out—takes place.*

The presence of major corporations in Latin American television has been documented. The American Broadcasting Company–Paramount and the National Broadcasting Company were the two most active U.S. corporations in Latin American television in the 1950s and 1960s. It is not assumed here that such foreign enterprises necessarily constitute barriers to the region's development merely because they are not indigenous. This is the crude anti-capitalist or anti-imperialist position for which there is little scientific evidence. Nor is it agreed, as [Marshall] McLuhan has argued, that the television medium itself is in any way inherently damaging. Instead it will be argued that program content, the linkages with advertising and U.S. consumer manufacturers, and the strong commercial nature of the operations in general, are each contributing factors which fashion the medium into a powerful conduit for widespread consumerism. This is not offset by producerism imperatives in the medium—

From Alan Wells, *Picture Tube Imperialism? The Impact of U.S. Television on Latin America* (Maryknoll, NY, 1972), 118–25. Reprinted by permission of the author and Orbis Books.

the promotion of skills and consumer tastes suitable for goods that are widely attainable—nor by increased productive capacity. Given this consumerism/producerism imbalance, the medium in itself is probably detrimental to the internal development of the region, although many other factors, including the existence of bonanza enterprises, undoubtedly mask its effect on the economy as a whole.

The initial purveyors of commercial television often claim that their operations will produce significant social and economic benefits. But like the exhortations of the would-be opium merchant, their claims are not always recognized by foreign countries at their face value, even though the disadvantages of the medium are not so readily apparent until after the enterprise is in full swing; that is, if the disadvantages are ever recognized at all. Nonetheless, since the "benefits" are not totally convincing, it is sometimes necessary to use considerable persuasion in order to attain market entry. [Harry] Skornia, for example, concludes that the pressure tactics employed by U.S. firms in England were instrumental to the establishment of commercial channels in that country "over the objections of large segments of both political parties, and without the British public having any real opportunity to participate in the decision."[1] Trade journals, advertising agencies, and broadcasters, he concludes, are openly proud of such manipulative "successes."

The Triumph of Commercial Television

Unlike in Europe in the early days of the medium, in Latin America public television has not gained any substantial foothold.[2] Thus all the countries have predominantly private and commercial forms of operation, even where the government has either been active in the past or is still active in broadcasting. The Mexican government, for example, showed an early interest in the medium. But today Mexico has only one public station— that of the Instituto Politecnico Nacional—among its twenty-four programming stations.[3] Chilean broadcasting was originally government owned and noncommercial, but the Universidad Católica operations in both Santiago and Valparaiso are now commercial stations with ABC Worldvision affiliations. The Venezuelan Ministry of Communications runs one educational and cultural station, Televisora Nacional, but the remaining five are all commercial with U.S. corporate interests in each. Peru has a similar public station under the Ministry of Education, and the Brazilian government owns Televisão Nacional, the only noncommercial station of the thirty-three operating in Brazil. Radio-Televisora Nacional in Colombia and T.V. National in Guatemala are both government stations which nonetheless carry private advertising commercials. (In Colombia the government leases one national channel and one limited to Bogota to commercial programmers.) Thus public noncommercial television has not taken hold even in the countries where the government operates stations. In the remaining countries, television is entirely commercial and is privately owned.

The nature of this broadcasting has a direct impact on the two factors that have been isolated as crucial to development, producerism and consumerism.

Television and Consumerism

There are North American interests in each country in the region, although their extent varies from country to country. Influence, however, is apparently wider than financial holdings alone. Two Latin Americans have expressed this in their report to the United Nations Economic, Social, and Cultural Organization (UNESCO) as follows:

> Throughout the continent the television stations are directly or indirectly dependent upon the major United States networks—and the greater the need for the latest technical equipment and trained technicians, the closer those links are. In Latin America the United States has a monopoly of the supply of the new technology, the basic film material, the technical experts, and, of course, the large-scale capital needed to increase the size of the local investment.[4]

Their last sentence, as they probably realize, is an exaggeration. Latin Americans are themselves active in financing the medium and some native interests, for example, Goar Mestre's operations, are even international in scope. The indirect influences are nonetheless very real. These include the importation of programming materials and the widespread imitation of U.S. practices by indigenous program producers. This is clearly apparent in local programming and advertising practices.

Programming

The programs shown on overseas television, particularly in Latin America, are often of U.S. origin whether or not the United States has station or network interests in the country. In 1965, for example, program sales of U.S. television programs abroad were alone worth nearly $80 million.[5] In the same year it is estimated that the U.S. television industry as a whole earned $125 million in overseas sales (programs, equipment, and other services). These earnings are thought by [W.] Dizard to be highly significant for the following reason: "For some parts of the television industry—notably the production of television films—the overseas market means the difference between profit and loss on its operations."[6] As in the United States, old movie films in Latin America are also sold to television stations. These and their similarly old television counterparts are sold for widely fluctuating prices. Such reusable products have often already recouped their costs on the domestic market or been written off as losses, so business is very lucrative and (arbitrary) pricing becomes a matter of good will and contract skills. With the rapid worldwide expansion of stations and audiences, the film companies have to date enjoyed a "sellers' market."

As mentioned previously, the major U.S. networks also have production company interests in Latin America. Even so, approximately 80 percent of the hemisphere's current programs—including "The Flintstones," "I Love Lucy," "Bonanza," and "Route 66"—were produced in the United States.[7] Within the limits imposed by foreign governments, including their ability to set quotas on imported programs, the network interests usually stimulate such United States imports. Thus, for example, when the Central American CATVN network was formed, ABC International announced that the stations "would carry film shows from United States firms; this included ABC-TV, which itself owned and exported such programs as 'The Untouchables.' "[8] ABC's interest in the larger LATINO network to the South probably gives similar prerogatives.

The suitability of these programs (which constantly depict North American life-styles and folklore) for poor Latin American countries is open to serious question. As an avid educational television proponent and intra-industry rival, Skornia is harsh in his questioning of their suitability: "Isn't the world we live in today so literally *one world* that we can no longer be indifferent to poverty, hunger, and misery anywhere on the globe? And what effect on starving people do our programs have—featuring waste, dissipation, violence, and luxury?"[9]

One possible answer to his question would be that the effect of this type of programming is to encourage an elite sector to live in North American style without the sacrifices necessary for indigenous development, while the masses are shown—but cannot enter into—the modern cosmopolitan world. The content of such programs undoubtedly influences the viewer toward consumerism, without upgrading his productive skills or increasing his willingness to save and sacrifice.

Although there is an extensive and viable research literature on the misanthropic effects of various types of television programs, the major companies either ignore or discredit the findings. The usual ploy is that the viewer will not learn from, or imitate, the contents of an "entertainment" program—a fallacy clearly exposed by McLuhan. The governments of several developed countries—including France, Germany, and Japan—now regulate program content to deemphasize crime and violence and to enforce safeguards for the young. The Federal Communications Commission (FCC) is far less potent in the United States, and even its mild brand of regulation is resisted by U.S. corporations abroad, where, of course, the commission itself is not authorized to act.

Programming, then, is generally similar to that in the United States, even when the material is produced indigenously. It is geared to the "audience" and "market," and its object is primarily to entertain the viewer and to sell the goods it advertises.

Advertising Practices

The overseas programming prerogatives of the networks extend to, and often coincide with, those in advertising: "For example, ABC can sell *Batman* to an advertiser and then place *Batman* along with designated commercials on any Worldvision country where the advertiser wants it to appear."[10] Advertisements carried in this way are usually for the goods of sophisticated, or at least large-scale international, corporations which are predominantly North American. They sometimes use the same advertisement for their product that is used in the United States after it has been dubbed in Spanish. The product, however, is destined for the Latin American elites, not the mass middle class as in the United States. Even when the advertisements give accurate consumer information of the products (which they patently do *not* in the United States), they do not usually serve any viable *mass* needs when transferred intact from the United States to an underdeveloped country.

The scheduling of advertisements throughout the region usually follows the U.S. pattern. Thus the programs are frequently and consistently interrupted for commercial spots. The options demonstrated by Japanese and some European commercial stations—that is, placing advertisements *between* programs or scheduling them all at the end of the day's broadcasting—are not exercised in the region. The emphasis is thus heavily on sales. Indeed, ABC International's LATINO chain (and CATVN, which is now treated by the corporation as an integral part of it) is not described in the trade as just an interconnected programming network. Instead, it is billed as "basically a sales tool, offering advertisers discounts as well as the convenience of a multi-station buy through a single source."[11] This clearly favors the international corporation ("discounts" given to large buyers run as high as 25 percent, and only the large enterprise needs such "multiple buys") over the emergent indigenous manufacturer. Thus, the style of advertising appears to promote cosmopolitan sectorism; that is, it serves the interest of international consumer-goods manufacturers who cater to local "modernist" elites.

Television and Producerism

Although the emphasis of the medium in Latin America is clearly on the sale of "modern" sector goods, it cannot be assumed that it has no part in facilitating producerism. But if we discount the impact of the limited educational programming, producerism is not being consciously or directly promoted. Rather, the rewards for sectoral inequality are being displayed, but the means to attain a more widespread material culture are not. The producerism effects that remain therefore stem from minor information services and the indirect effects of the programming.

In the media study conducted by [P. J.] Deutschman and his associates, respondents were questioned about the usefulness of the media for providing information relevant to their tasks as (technical) change agents. They rated television and radio equally, but both media rated very low: "The mean rating fell about midway between 'little' and 'some' useful information."[12] Meteorologists and air traffic controllers found reports on the weather useful, and public officials used news broadcasting to gauge public reactions to their agencies' activities (actually what they were probably getting was the *stations'* reaction); this is not a direct indicator of public reaction, but merely one of the possible sources of influence on it.[13]

The same team of researchers also reported on some of the indirect influences of seemingly innocuous "entertainment" types of program:[14] A personnel director, for example, claimed to use television dramas as case studies in his training program on personnel problems. Street and office scenes shown in television films were found of value (but surely a limited one) to a city planner in Nicaragua and a Colombian office manager. A bank manager helped defend his enterprise by following television programs on fictional bank robberies; and police in Panama, Peru, and Honduras picked up police methods from watching crime dramas. (No doubt the local criminal elements also learned a little from such programs.) But these indirect effects that may have minimally improved efficiency are clearly minor when compared to the producerism potential of the medium, and they are almost certainly far outweighed by its consumerism effects.

Notes

1. Harry J. Skornia, *T.V. and Society* (New York: McGraw-Hill, 1965), pp. 11–12. The British affair is given full treatment in W. W. Wilson, *Pressure Group: The Campaign for Commercial Television* (London: Martin Secker and Warburg, 1961).

2. This applied to the seventeen countries in my sample. Cuba, which I have excluded from this consideration throughout, has been an obvious exception in the postrevolutionary years.

3. Station information given below was gathered from sources in Alan Wells, *Picture Tube Imperialism? The Impact of U.S. Television on Latin America* (Maryknoll, NY: Orbis, 1972), Table IX, chapter 5, and UNESCO, *World Radio and Television* (Paris: UNESCO, 1965).

4. Luis P. Estrada and Daniel Hopen, *The Cultural Value of Film and Television in Latin America* (Paris: UNESCO [Mimeo], July 1968), p. 6. This, they claim, leads to the lamentable stagnation of the region's arts and the "Americanization" of Latin culture. They are not directly concerned with television's implications for consumer styles and economic growth.

5. According to the Motion Picture Association, the 1965 telefilm sales overseas amounted to $76 million in 1968. They reached $80 million in 1968. See Erik Barnow, *The Image Empire* (New York: Oxford University Press, 1970), p. 309.

6. W. Dizard, *Television: A World View* (Syracuse: Syracuse University Press, 1966), pp. 3–4.

7. J. Frappier, "U.S. Media Empire/Latin America," *North American Congress on Latin America Newsletter*, vol. 11, no. 9 (January 1969), pp. 1–11. In the summer of 1970 the following U.S. programs were broadcast in Colombia: "That Girl," "Marcus Welby," "High Chaparral," the "Jerry Lewis" and "Carol Burnett" shows, and the "Untouchables."

8. Skornia, *T.V.*, p. 187.

9. Ibid., p. 191.

10. R. Tyler, "Television Around the World," in *Television Magazine* (October 1966), p. 33, cited by Frappier, "U.S. Media Empire."

11. *Advertising Age* (January 29, 1968), p. 53.

12. P. J. Deutschman et al., *Communication and Social Change in Latin America* (New York: Praeger, 1968), p. 65.

13. Ibid., p. 65.

14. Ibid.

14 Gerald K. Haines ◆ The Projection
of a Favorable American Image in Brazil

*Television was only one medium by which persuasive information and
images were broadcast to the general public in Latin America. Gerald K.
Haines explores U.S. efforts to orchestrate the flow of media messages in
Brazil in the late 1940s and early 1950s in the context of the early Cold
War—the struggle between the United States and the Soviet Union for
power and influence around the world. This struggle was often concentrated in Europe and Asia, but the United States was sensitive to the spread
of communism in the Western Hemisphere and, as Haines emphasizes,
used the mass media in an attempt to persuade Brazilians to reject communism and accept U.S. values and ideals. Of particular importance was
the work of agencies such as the United States Information Service (USIS),
a branch of the State Department.*

American decisionmakers in the postwar era sincerely believed in the
exceptional superiority of the United States not only politically and
economically but also culturally. They accepted the notion that the center
of world culture had shifted, with World War II, to the United States.
Firm believers in peace, prosperity, and progress as the inevitable bless-
ings of Western civilization, they saw the United States as the ordained
instrument of providence, civilization, and progress. Many held to the
traditional view that culture evolved from primitive, irrational forms into
modern liberal-rational entities. They believed that American cultural
values and assumptions reflected the ultimate triumph of rationality and
progress.[1] Viewing much of their relations with Latin America, indeed
with the entire Third World, as a problem in the dynamics of cultural lag,
they had little doubt as to the desirability of spreading American ideals
and values abroad.[2]

With the advent of the Cold War, policymakers in both the Truman
and Eisenhower administrations adopted cultural diplomacy as an explicit
weapon in their arsenal to fight communism. Cultural policy became in-
extricably linked to foreign policy objectives. By the 1950s, national security justifications came to dominate all cultural programs. During this
period the U.S. cultural program greatly expanded and emerged as a combination of national interest, anticommunism, and bureaucratic activism.[3]

From Gerald K. Haines, *The Americanization of Brazil: A Study of U.S.
Cold War Diplomacy in the Third World, 1945–1954* (Wilmington, DE, 1989),
159–83.

Secretary of State John Foster Dulles put the U.S. position succinctly in a telephone conversation with President Eisenhower: "Cultural affairs [were] a very good way of doing things [for] you have to pat them a little bit and make them think that you are fond of them."[4]

This was a major change from earlier policy. Traditionally, U.S. cultural relations were primarily in the hands of private interests. The government played little or no role in the process. Cultural relations were to sensitize the elite sectors of other nations to similarities and differences between peoples in order to promote understanding, trade, and international peace. World War II and the Soviet-U.S. confrontation that followed concentrated power in the cultural field in the government.[5]

With the conclusion of World War II, President Truman transferred the information and cultural programs of the Office of War Information (OWI) and the Office of the Coordinator of Inter-American Affairs (OCIAA) to the Department of State. These programs had been largely liquidated by 1946.[6] The department continued, however, a greatly reduced effort to present "a full and fair picture of the United States" to the rest of the world under its International Information and Educational Exchange program and later under the United States Information Service (USIS). In December 1947 the new National Security Council (NSC) called for a carefully coordinated cultural and informational program "to influence foreign opinion in a direction favorable to United States interests and to counteract the effects of anti–United States propaganda." Convinced that the Soviet Union had declared psychological war on the United States, the NSC ordered the Department of State "to develop a vigorous and effective ideological campaign."[7]

In 1948, Congress enacted the Smith-Mundt Act to counteract Soviet propaganda and to sell America to the world. In response to growing Cold War tensions, President Truman directed Secretary of State [Dean] Acheson in the spring of 1950 to prepare a vigorous "Campaign of Truth" as a U.S. offensive in response to Communist lies.[8] Department of State planners had already designed and implemented a multifaceted program of cultural, educational, and informational persuasion for the worldwide struggle between democracy and communism. Drawing on the experience of the OCIAA and the OWI, which during World War II had managed an extensive and successful propaganda program, the Department of State used traditional cultural interchange methods such as the exchange of persons, books, art, and music and the new mass media approach to cultural relations to get the U.S. message across and to strengthen the international bonds against communism. The mass media approach, using the press, radio, television, and motion pictures, meshed perfectly with American predilections for technological solutions to political and economic problems. It held unprecedented possibilities for mass education and, given its populist, mass audience approach, was attuned to immediately altering opinions and attitudes.[9]

In response to its increasing responsibilities in the area of psychological warfare and to congressional urging to expand overseas information services and programs, the Department of State established the International Information Administration (IIA) in 1952. Now the United States had a full-fledged propaganda program.[10] Responsibility for the effort, however, was still split between the Department of State, the Technical Cooperation Administration, and the Mutual Security Agency. President Eisenhower's Advisory Committee on Government Organization, headed by former OCIAA Coordinator Nelson Rockefeller, recommended in April 1953 the consolidation of the information programs under a new foreign information agency.[11] It also pleaded for the commitment of greater financial resources to take on the Communists in the battle for minds.[12]

Another Eisenhower committee, the President's Committee on International Information Activities, also argued that the information program lacked funds and central direction and recommended that the United States take the offensive in a global propaganda campaign. The committee reflected the prominent American belief that the Communist movement was a tool of Soviet power bent on world domination. The United States had to respond to Communist propaganda with the "dissemination of truth."[13]

Following the advice of his committees Eisenhower created the United States Information Agency (USIA) on July 31, 1953. The USIA was to be an instrument of foreign policy employed in combination with diplomatic, military, and economic policy. The new agency's primary purpose was to persuade foreign peoples that it was in their own interest to follow the lead of the United States in opposing Communist expansion and promoting peace and prosperity. While it was to avoid a propagandistic tone and present a straightforward picture of the life and culture of the people of the United States, including not only scholarly and artistic fields but also "the spirit of America" from athletics to political oratory, it was not required to present all facets of American life. In short, it was to present an appealing picture of the United States and to interpret and explain American objectives and policies in a favorable light.[14] Its job was to sell the United States to the world just as a salesman's job was to sell a Buick or a Cadillac or a radio or television set.[15]

Because of Brazil's strategic importance and dominant position in Latin America, it became a focal point for U.S. cultural and informational programs. U.S. planners concentrated on "the traditional spirit of friendship between Brazil and the United States." With an almost missionary zeal USIS officials attempted to develop individualistic and democratic traits in the Brazilians, to get them to "think things through in patterns similar to our own in politics, economics, and social welfare."[16]

In general, U.S. planners sought to increase the general knowledge and appreciation by Brazilians of the United States, its culture, and foreign and domestic policy. Convinced that intellectual and cultural understanding were the handmaidens of economic and political cooperation, policymakers in both the Truman and Eisenhower administrations set about cultivating the cultural goodwill of the Brazilian people. Furthermore, they tried to persuade Brazil to follow the lead of the United States in its opposition to communism and to counter Communist propaganda with an "instructive, enlightened information program." Both Truman and Eisenhower tried to demonstrate the mutual interests of Brazil and the United States in democratic institutions and to spur the Brazilians to protect their freedom by "cleansing their system of Soviet-controlled or influenced communist and peronist elements." All was to be done without giving the impression that the United States was interfering in any way with the internal affairs of Brazil.[17]

In addition, Washington continually stressed its concern for Brazilian development and attempted to persuade the Brazilians that they could best ensure the success of their economic development proposals through close cooperation with the United States and with private enterprise. The U.S. government should not attempt to force America's culture or its economic system on Brazil, the planners maintained, but it was essential to tell the Brazilian leaders and mass audience the story of how free enterprise and the American way of life had been successful in contrast to what prevailed behind the Iron Curtain. By the time of the Korean War, U.S. objectives in Brazil had expanded to include combating neutralism and stressing the value of playing an active role in the conflict between the "free and slave world." Strong support for American and UN efforts to organize the world for peace was the "only hope for survival of Western Christian civilization."[18]

Calling for the aggressive promotion of this program and an expanded effort to meet the Communist threat, USIS officials in Brazil in 1950 pictured the possible activities of an effective cultural and information program as almost limitless. According to Sheldon Thomas, the public affairs officer in Brazil, "vast areas remain to be explored; large segments of the population should be reached much more frequently; media actively should be supplemented with personal contacts; and the emotional reflex of the average citizen should be conditioned to a fine degree." Thomas felt certain that by employing the best techniques of American advertising, ingenuity, originality, and persistence, all the American goals in this area could be met with "spectacular results." He warned, however, that the

U.S. reservoir of goodwill in Brazil was only half full. They would have to act quickly to preserve and expand pro-American feelings.[19]

Analyzing Brazilian attitudes toward the United States, the planners generalized that the two nations had a long history of friendly relations, that most middle-class Brazilians had a traditional and deep-rooted liking for Yankees, and that since World Wars I and II Brazil had drifted away from France and the rest of Europe toward a closer association with the United States. Other favorable factors affecting relations, according to these American analysts, included Brazil's recognition of the United States as the leading world power; its admiration for American achievements in the fields of industry, science, agriculture, and medicine; common Western traditions and democratic ideals; the influence of the Catholic church; and close business associations. The United States was Brazil's best customer; it supplied Brazil with many basic materials and equipment, and the Rotary Club and American Chamber of Commerce were very active in Brazil.[20]

On the negative side of the ledger, however, was the fact that a large percentage of the Brazilian population was illiterate, undernourished, and socially submerged. Coupled with a provincial suspicion of foreigners was a degree of envy, resentment, and bitterness toward Americans and toward the United States as an exploiter nation. Widespread ignorance of American cultural achievements and the feeling that the United States was essentially materialistic and lacking in culture, general apathy toward world events, growing nationalism, and general corruption, demagogy, and incompetence all contributed to an atmosphere, according to the USIS report, that promoted instability, anti-Americanism, and a receptive ground for Communist propaganda.[21]

Moreover, U.S. officials believed that Brazil was dangerously apathetic toward the Soviet Union and its satellites. According to American embassy officials in Brazil, the government there displayed a remarkable tolerance toward Communists entrenched in strategic positions and generally saw no real or immediate danger in Soviet Russia. Anti-American forces would grow and conditions worsen, the embassy warned, unless the program in Brazil was considerably strengthened. Any curtailment of the U.S. cultural and informational programs would necessitate additional expenditures at a later date in an effort to regain the ground that would be lost. For USIS planners, the United States was in a life-and-death struggle against the advancing adversaries of democracy.[22]

Attempting to counter the reportedly growing anti-American trend and expanding on Truman's information program, policymakers in the Eisenhower administration stepped up the American cultural and propaganda effort in Brazil. Various sectors of Brazilian society, such as the media, the military, government workers, business and political leaders, the literate middle class, labor, the church, and educators, were singled out for special attention and identified as target groups.[23] To get the American message across to these target groups and to stimulate pro-American sentiment in Brazil, both the Truman and Eisenhower administrations initiated a vast array of traditional cultural exchange programs and new mass media informational programs. They believed that they were contesting for the very souls of the Brazilians.

As early as 1950 the two nations signed a bilateral cultural convention that allowed each country to establish in the other's territory cultural institutes, information offices, libraries, and film centers and to increase its educational exchange programs and exhibits. Using this convention as well as the education exchanges authorized under the Smith-Mundt Act of 1948 as a legal basis, the United States greatly increased its cultural activities in Brazil.[24] For example, officials of the United States Information and Education Service (USIE, another State Department program) established a variety of exchange programs, including a foreign leader program to bring future Brazilian leaders to the United States. Concentrating on educators, working journalists, artists, intellectuals, scholars, and students since, according to U.S. reports, they frequently harbored anti-American prejudice, U.S. policymakers hoped to win them over by "providing a genuine understanding of the United States and its people, its democratic form of government, and its social and political institutions." This could best be accomplished by visits, training grants, and scholarships for study and travel in the United States. These elites would, as a result of their stay, be imbued with a politically helpful pro-American orientation and would take back to Brazil a favorable image of the United States.[25]

U.S. officials wanted not only to promote American culture and values and anti-Communist attitudes but also to wean the Brazilians away from the "European influence," notably French, that dominated Brazilian culture. According to Deputy Public Affairs Officer Francis J. McArdle, Brazilians were well aware of the technical competence of the United States but distressingly unaware of American activities in and contributions to the theater, music, literature, and art.[26] The exchange programs were acclaimed a major success by U.S. officials as Brazilians visited and studied in the United States. It seemed a splendid investment, as the Brazilians developed a deep appreciation for the United States and its institutions.[27] William A. Wieland, the public affairs officer in Brazil, observed that the returning Brazilians were, in most cases, ardent champions of American democracy.[28]

Despite such laudatory statements the exchange program encountered a number of problems. Many American academicians complained that the long-term educational and informational benefits of such a program were being subordinated to short-range propaganda objectives. Even programs such as the Fulbright scholarships were designed to indoctrinate as well as educate. Educators were uneasy about "the propaganda motives" behind these programs. Education was now part of a "total American effort to build a free world."[29] Returning Brazilians also expressed their shock at the widespread ignorance they had encountered regarding Brazil. Upon arriving in the United States one Brazilian student was asked such questions as "How many revolutions do you have in Brazil per year? Do you like being governed by [Juan] Perón?" and told "I must learn Spanish and visit Brazil." The high cost of travel and the expensive living standard in the United States also caused problems. U.S. officials in Brazil constantly complained that only rich Brazilians could really afford to go to the United States and that people from the arts were usually excluded.[30]

Although both the Truman and Eisenhower administrations continued to build an official cultural and information program, they also paid homage to the ongoing tradition of private initiative in the cultural area and public-private cooperation.[31] For example, when the USIS learned of a visit by Leonard Bernstein to Brazil, it not only advertised his appearance as guest conductor with the Symphony Orchestra of Rio de Janeiro but also arranged to distribute copies of his recordings to various Brazilian radio stations and featured him in an issue of its publication *Em Marcha*. Similar arrangements were made when the distinguished American poet Robert Frost attended a writer's congress in São Paulo in 1954. American officials were especially delighted when the black U.S. labor leader Hilton E. Hanna visited Brazil. Not only did he read his speech in Portuguese, but he also "answered questions about racial prejudice in the United States with ease," citing the activities of other black leaders throughout the United States.[32]

U.S. officials in Brazil were acutely sensitive to Brazilian racial attitudes. Although they realized that racial discrimination existed in Brazil, they played up its reputation for racial tolerance and suppressed publicity regarding the refusal of well-known hotels in Rio de Janeiro and São Paulo to admit Joe Louis and Katherine Dunham during their tours of Brazil.[33]

Despite such problems, the United States continued its cultural offensive. To counter Soviet attempts to picture the United States as a nation of materialists interested primarily in industrial rather than cultural riches, the Department of State encouraged American businessmen, university professors and students, labor groups, and private organizations to take part in cultural and artistic achievements. Although the U.S. government did not directly finance projects such as the exchange of paintings between the Museum of Modern Art in New York and the Museum de Arte Moderna in São Paulo or the performance of the American National Ballet company in Rio, or American theatrical companies performing "Porgy and Bess" at the São Paulo Exposition, U.S. officials promoted such activities at every opportunity. Such events illustrated the high achievement of cultural life in the United States, they argued. Even the search for American basketball coaches by the Brazilian Basketball Confederation caught the attention of USIS planners. Encouraging this purely American sport in Brazil would help to improve relations, reasoned William V. Denning of the International Educational Exchange Service.[34]

U.S. officials even sent Mother Goose pinups to cement relations between the two nations. These cardboard cutouts of Mother Goose characters, the cynical American vice counsel at Bahia, Robert S. Henderson, wrote, "would undoubtedly impress Brazilian children with a sustaining faith in the principles of democracy through the examination of Little Bo Peep." Henderson questioned, however, their value in influencing the opinion makers of Brazil.[35] By 1953, nineteen different federal agencies and numerous private groups were engaged in exchange programs in Brazil.

Cultural exchange programs were only part of the overall U.S. effort to promote mutual understanding and to get the American message across. Under its USIS program the Department of State established a number of cultural and information centers and libraries and attempted to alter radically the nature of Brazilian education. The centers conducted seminars for teachers of English, supplied popular U.S. magazines, organized lectures, passed out pamphlets on such subjects as "Communism," "How to Run a Union Meeting," "Organizing a Democratic Trade Union," "First Aid," and "Personal Hygiene," and in general promoted American culture.[36]

The binational centers and information libraries also organized discussions relating to American literature, history, music, and art. Under a book translation program the U.S. government encouraged commercial publishers to translate appropriate American books into Portuguese. Such books as Eleanor Roosevelt's *This I Remember*, George Orwell's *Animal Farm*, Lewis Mumford's *Condition of Man*, Henry David Thoreau's *Walden*, Margery Miller's *Joe Louis: American*, Catherine Owens Pearce's *Mary McLeod Bethune*, Herman Melville's *Moby Dick*, and Dorothy Thompson's *The Truth about Communism* soon appeared at U.S. Information centers throughout Brazil.[37] To ensure that U.S. publishers were able to recover the proceeds of their sales in Brazil, since the Getúlio Vargas government restricted foreign exchange transactions, the

Eisenhower administration also guaranteed convertibility and negotiated an Informational Media Guaranty Agreement with Brazil.[38]

Despite careful review of the types of material included in the libraries, the Department of State's book program came under increasing domestic attack during the 1950s, as Senator Joseph R. McCarthy accused the department of promoting Communist propaganda. Although McCarthy's attack was rambling and never specific, the International Information Agency (IIA) reacted quickly by issuing a policy directive in early 1953 that "no materials by any Communists, fellow-travelers, etc., will be used under any circumstances by an IIA media or mission."[39]

The IIA directed its libraries to withdraw any material detrimental to American objectives. Assistant Secretary of State for Public Affairs Carl McArdle wrote that any materials "which are receptive to international Communist propaganda have no place in the program." IIA libraries were not reference libraries but rather were intended to disseminate favorable information about the United States.[40]

In Brazil this resulted in the removal of such books from the shelves as I. F. Stone's *Secret History of the Korean War*, Shirley Graham's *Paul Robeson, Citizen of the World*, and Howard Fast's *The American* and *Patrick Henry and the Frigate's Keel*. The U.S. embassy in Rio also temporarily removed the books of Gilberto Freire, the noted Brazilian sociologist, from its libraries but quickly restored them to the shelves because of possible adverse comment.[41] Despite McCarthy's attack, U.S. publications flooded Brazil.[42]

Books were only part of the program. In addition to helping establish university chairs in American studies in São Paulo and Rio de Janeiro and promoting the use of American textbooks in classrooms throughout Brazil, U.S. educational experts sought to change the old attitudes and habits of the entire Brazilian education system. Attempting to wean the Brazilians from their long-established traditional European system, which stressed a classical education for the elite in the social sciences, humanities, and law, the American educators emphasized the need for professional training in such fields as engineering, agricultural science, medicine, physics, and chemistry. What was needed, according to these educators, was more practical education—technical training in industrial arts programs, vocational courses, management, and business administration. These courses would create both a trained labor force and a new managerial class. This American concept of practical education, the experts stressed publicly, would greatly benefit Brazilian development. Privately, they believed that the adoption of the American system would also greatly aid U.S. businesses operating in Brazil and help the anti-Communist campaign.[43]

Sensitive to criticism that they were "soft on communism," Department of State officials pointed proudly to their activities abroad that effectively countered the Soviet "hate America" propaganda effort. In Brazil the anti-Communist campaign focused on influencing the mass media—newspapers, magazines, radio, television, motion pictures—as well as the government information agency, Agencia Nacional.[44] Here was a chance to achieve immediate positive results by putting to use the burgeoning U.S. communications technology.[45]

Viewing the Brazilian press as the major molder of public opinion, U.S. policymakers wooed local publishers, editors, columnists, and reporters. USIS personnel and embassy officials provided the Brazilian press with personal copies of the department's wireless file, books, periodicals, and other background materials in an attempt to influence the content of Brazilian newspapers and magazines. Seeing each newspaper as a potential outlet for "our cause," U.S. officials distributed materials to over five hundred Brazilian newspapers and magazines. Concentrating on the major newspapers in the Assis Chateaubriand chain (which owned twenty-nine dailies, five magazines, twenty radio stations, and two television stations), the papers controlled by pro-American publishers such as Carlos Lacerda, Pereira Carneiro, and Paulo Bittencourt, and the Agencia Nacional, the USIS provided background materials, wire service information, photographs, and cartoons depicting the United States in a favorable light. In addition, the embassy press office wrote and distributed under pseudonyms a variety of anti-Soviet and anti-Communist articles. Reasoning that USIS material would be received more favorably and avoid cries of "Yankee propaganda" if it were not attributed to the U.S. government, the embassy press office wrote newspaper columns and series under the pseudonyms Claude McKnight, Barry W. Richards, Walter J. Taylor, and George Dexter. These columns were designed to unmask the true nature of communism and Soviet expansionism. Exercising extreme caution in the distribution of these series, the embassy forwarded copies to the various consulates as classified matter. U.S. consuls then placed them personally with key Brazilian reporters and publishers. All was done without any attribution to USIS. Such articles as "The Sinking of a Nation," which described the various steps the Communists and Soviets used in seizing Hungary; "Nations That Disappear," which portrayed Soviet expansionism; and "The Press in the Satellite Countries," which showed the absolute domination of information media by the Cominform, ran as featured articles in such papers as *O Globo* and in such popular magazines as *O Cruzeiro*.[46]

The Korean War brought an increased effort to sway the Brazilian press. Numerous articles promoting international cooperation to stop aggression and peace through strengthening the free world were placed with key newsmen. The Americans expanded their efforts to reach the Brazilian masses with photographs of the U.S. actions in Korea (especially of attempts to care for Korean children war victims), cartoons depicting [Joseph] Stalin helping to crush South Korea, comic strips promoting American heroes such as Superman and Captain Marvel rescuing everyday citizens from the Communist menace, and serialized books such as *Death Comes from the Kremlin* and *One Who Survived*.[47]

Treating the case of Julius and Ethel Rosenberg, public information officials carefully followed Washington guidelines to provide a matter-of-fact treatment of the case and to stress the scrupulously fair process of the trial. The USIS-inspired editorial that ran in *O Globo*, *Jornal Do Brasil*, and *Ultima Hora* condemned the death penalty but argued:

> If North American justice is criminal for condemning to death convicted and confessed spies—of most important atomic papers—tried under free procedures before a large public and with the participation of several defense lawyers, some of whom were designated by the North American Communist Party itself, what is Communist justice, which sends citizens to their deaths because of simple party quarrels, in secret trials, under accusations of merely subjective and strictly political value?[48]

The embassy press section followed up this editorial by providing the Brazilian press with a series of articles entitled "Watch Out for Spies." Written by U.S. Press Section Chief Robert Gonzaga, the series was based on the House Committee on Un-American Activities document "100 Things You Should Know about Communism" and focused on the infiltration of Communist spies into both public and private organizations. Gonzaga placed the articles by direct arrangements with [Assis] Chateaubriand, and they bore no attribution to the USIS when *O Globo* featured them on its front page.[49]

To counteract magazines perceived as Communist such as *Para Todos*, *Orientacão*, *Horizonte*, and *Emancipacão*, which were geared to the Brazilian middle class and intellectuals and railed against "America's decadent imperialism, war mongering, and rotten capitalist society," the USIS in Brazil began producing the monthly magazine *Em Marcha*. Patterned after the old OCIAA publication *Em Guardia*, the elaborately illustrated, sleek new magazine was edited primarily to interest opinion-forming groups and through them to reach the broader public. It emphasized the traditional friendship between the United States and Brazil, promoted mutual interests, and attempted to allay Brazilian fears of economic exploitation. It combated the Soviet line by exposing "Communist lies with factual material representing the American point-of-view."

As envisioned by USIS representatives in Brazil, *Em Marcha* was to present an overall picture of American concepts, institutions, culture, and "the democratic way of life." Carrying such features as "Figuras da America" (which profiled Brazilian leaders one month and U.S. leaders the next), "Elections in a Democracy," "Partners in Progress," "Brazilians in the United States," and columns on U.S.-Brazilian military cooperation and free enterprise, the magazine, according to U.S. officials, was a positive approach in the propaganda war for freedom and democracy.[50] First published in February 1952, *Em Marcha* received a number of glowing reviews from Brazilian critics. Embassy officials considered the new venture a major success, for it got the American message across to leader groups who would, in general, not be receptive to the more blatant approach carried out by the embassy in newspapers.[51]

The Brazilian press was not the only concern of American officials. U.S. policymakers viewed Brazilian radio and television as extremely important elements in their information program, since more than 60 percent of the nation's population was illiterate. The Brazilian Institute of Public Opinion estimated that there were over 3.5 million radios in the country and that an average of four people listened to each radio set. This put the audience at 14 million listeners. In addition, in rural areas and in the *favela* (urban slum) sections a loudspeaker system was employed to broadcast programs. Radio was thus the only mass medium capable of reaching all the identified target groups.[52]

As for television, it was in its infancy but growing rapidly. The embassy estimated that there were fewer than twenty-five thousand sets in Rio de Janeiro and twenty thousand in São Paulo in 1952. Nevertheless, seeing television's potential, American officials encouraged their Brazilian counterparts to adopt the regulations and standards used by the U.S. Federal Communications Commission. This would not only facilitate the export of television equipment to Brazil by such U.S. firms as RCA, GE, Zenith, and Philco, but, with American technical help and training in this new medium, it also would promote U.S. methods and the American message.[53]

Using techniques similar to those developed to influence Brazilian newspapers and magazines, U.S. embassy personnel produced radio and television scripts and even complete programs for broadcast in Brazil as part of their "Campaign of Truth." Concerned that if the origins of the programs were known they would be labeled propaganda and immediately suspected, the embassy made every effort to avoid any such identification. Approaching Chateaubriand, U.S. officials made arrangements for the programs to be sponsored as a public service by Emissoras

Associadas (the radio station chain owned by Chateaubriand) in its "desire to contribute to Brazilian progress and the strengthening of freedom and democracy."[54] They used local writers and actors to provide "a sensitivity to local political and social trends" and the correct accents, and employed Brazilian production techniques, "although inferior to U.S. methods," to earmark the shows as a local product and thus help remove any taint of "foreign propaganda."

U.S. planners, however, controlled every script. Over 60 percent dealt with anticommunism and were specifically tailored for the Brazilian market. For example, the radio program "Nos Bastidores do Mundo" (Our World behind the Scenes) was a daily five-minute news commentary that explained to the people of Brazil the meaning of world events seen in the light of U.S. foreign policy. Written in the vernacular of the man-in-the-street, the program was aimed primarily at the lower middle class and laboring groups. Its objectives included presenting the United States favorably, countering misconceptions deliberately spread by the local Communist party, and exposing Communist falsehoods and Kremlin claims to the allegiance of Brazilian workers. It also strove to create a climate of confidence in the free world and to encourage a spirit of self-help and self-reliance. The commentary was written daily by the U.S. embassy radio editor, a Brazilian citizen, Al Neto, who soon became one of the most popular people in Brazil. More than three quarters of all Brazilian stations carried his daily broadcast.[55] Another program, "O Destino e a Esperanca" (Destiny and Hope), was a fifteen-minute, thrice-weekly dramatic serial centering on a São Paulo factory worker who goes to the United States in an exchange program to work in a New Jersey plant. A Brazilian veteran of World War II, he is married to an American woman. The hero tells the story of his life among American working men. Thus the hero, a Brazilian, tells of the common experiences and concerns of the American and Brazilian working classes.[56]

Concerned about Communist propaganda that focused not only on Yankee imperialism and the exploitation of Brazil but also on U.S. racial prejudice, embassy officials attempted to design and produce programs dramatizing the life, struggle, and success of American blacks such as Marian Anderson, Joe Louis, Jackie Robinson, Ralph Bunche, and Mary McLeod Bethune. U.S. writers provided scripts for local productions that portrayed blacks in sympathetic roles and made black spirituals and American jazz recordings available to Brazilian radio stations. The embassy also attempted to eliminate phrases such as "for the first time" from news releases when American blacks performed or appeared at cultural events in the United States. For example, in describing combat activities of the U.S. 25th Division in Korea, the embassy commented on its heroism and efficiency and then, toward the end of the news item, simply stated that the division was composed of both black and white troops. No mention was made of the fact that this was the first integrated division in the U.S. Army. Carried by many Brazilian newscasts, the embassy considered this item very successful.[57]

Embassy officials believed that the shortwave Voice of America programs were far less effective. Not only had local stations greatly improved their own news presentations, but Brazilians preferred the BBC (British Broadcasting Corporation). Its signal was cleaner, and many Brazilians believed that the BBC presented better balanced, more varied, and less biased programs. One typical Brazilian critic said: "Last night I heard a BBC broadcast in which the English government policy in Tehran was severely criticized. I never hear anything of the sort from the Voice of America. According to the VOA the United States had never erred in its foreign policy or anything else." Furthermore, VOA broadcasts came during an hour of a popular Brazilian soap opera.[58]

Despite such criticism, U.S. officials in Brazil as well as in the United States considered the Voice of America as presenting "the truth" and looked upon it as "insurance" against Communist propaganda. They reasoned that it had influence among the leadership classes even if it were not a popular mass program.[59] In fact, an embassy radio survey of 1952 found that the most listened to American programs were privately sponsored shows such as "Hit Parade" and "Jack Benny." In the long run these programs probably had a more lasting effect on the Brazilian people than any of the USIS-produced programming.[60]

Efforts "to get the American message across" in the motion-picture field suffered a similar fate. Despite the wide distribution of well-intended, well-produced films and film strips on communism, health, travel, science, the arts, and the Korean War, films produced by the major American studios gained the most attention and popularity in Brazil. "Twelve O'Clock High," "Sands of Iwo Jima," "Neptune's Daughter," "Donald Duck," and "Tom and Jerry" filled Brazilian theaters. Twentieth Century Fox, MGM, Paramount, Universal, Warner Brothers, and Walt Disney dominated the Brazilian motion-picture market. Still, U.S. officials quietly attempted to prevent distribution in Brazil of films considered harmful to the American image. Of special concern were films portraying American gangsters or showing racial discrimination in the States.[61] U.S. officials in Brazil complained that Hollywood films were often harmful, wiped out much of USIA's effectiveness, and presented a distorted picture of the United States. All Americans were gangsters, millionaires, or cowboys. Bedroom farces distorted American values, and American women were portrayed as either gold diggers or career women.[62]

Nonetheless, over 70 percent of all films shown in Brazil in 1952 were American.[63]

Although the governments of both Eurico Gaspar Dutra and Getúlio Vargas attempted to stem the flow of American films into Brazil, and there was the usual criticism that Yankee films were corrupting the youth of Brazil, the public continued to flock to see American pictures. Reluctantly, U.S. information officials sought to capitalize on the success of the American motion-picture industry by running documentaries in the major theaters along with the feature attractions. They also cautioned that popularity was not the only standard for judging the success of their information programs. The films shown at military barracks and public schools were effective, USIS officials claimed, in implanting the idea in youthful minds of Brazilian-U.S. collaboration, friendship, and anticommunism.[64]

In 1950 the American anti-Communist campaign received a boost when the Brazilian National Defense Council made a secret decision to intensify its anti-Communist efforts and ordered the Agencia Nacional to approach USIE officials for help. The U.S. embassy was only too eager to assist. It supplied Portuguese-language pamphlets, books, film strips, and motion pictures to the official government propaganda agency. When the Agencia Nacional launched the strongly anti-Communist radio programs "Agencia Informative Europa Livre" (Information Agency for Free Europe) and "Paisagens de Vila" (The Villagers) under direct orders from the Vargas government, the USIE radio unit systematically supplied the programs with material. U.S. Counselor for Public Affairs Herbert Cerwin evaluated the programs as "rather amateurish by American standards" and not truly effective as a propaganda vehicle. They were, however, according to Cerwin, "a welcome initiative and indicated that the Brazilian Government is conscious of the Communist threat."[65]

In addition to promoting American culture, the American way of life, and anticommunism, U.S. officials in Brazil carefully monitored the cultural efforts of other nations. The Soviet Union and its satellite states received the most attention. Embassy officials such as the counselor for public affairs, the cultural attaché, the information officers, the legal attaché, the labor attaché, and the motion picture, press, and radio officers all reported on newspapers, pamphlets, books, and trips suspected of being subsidized by the USSR and its satellites. Although releases from the Soviet news agency Tass were not distributed in Brazil after the Dutra administration broke diplomatic relations with the Soviet Union in 1947, embassy officials noted that Radio Moscow was still clearly heard in most of Brazil. They also believed that the Czechoslovakian and Polish legations distributed large quantities of Soviet-sponsored Communist propaganda in an attempt to influence Brazilian students, industrial and rural workers, and intellectuals.[66]

The Soviet Union and the Communist bloc states were not the only countries monitored by the U.S. embassy. It carefully noted and analyzed the activities of all foreign nations in Brazil. The embassy reported to Washington that the French, for example, set up an information service in Brazil that distributed press materials and supplied publishers such as Diarios Associados with newsreels and photographs and maintained a strong cultural exchange program with Brazil. Great Britain not only beamed BBC broadcasts into Brazil but also signed a long-term cultural agreement with the Vargas government in 1950; the British News Service actively promoted BBC film, radio materials, newsreels, and the distribution of its wire service, and Britain also established cultural institutions in Brazil and promoted Brazilian-British friendship and cooperation.

Analyzing these efforts, U.S. embassy officials believed that, although the Brazilian elite considered France as the natural spiritual and cultural mentor of Brazil and French cultural influence was still present, younger Brazilians no longer had such strong attachments. They were more American-oriented. As for the British, according to the embassy, although the Brazilians respected them for their honesty and reporting abilities, England was now looked upon as a faded symbol of an empire in decline.[67] Although U.S. policymakers were primarily concerned with the Soviet Union and its propaganda campaign, they did not want to see any foreign power become too influential in Brazil, politically, economically, or culturally. They desired a cultural Monroe Doctrine.[68]

In comparing the cultural and informational programs of the other countries in Brazil, Ambassador Herschel Johnson, writing in 1952, stated that the United States was far ahead and, except possibly for BBC radio broadcasts, provided by far the most balanced, most effective information and cultural programs. This effort was extremely valuable in getting the American message across and counterbalancing not only Soviet but also other foreign power propaganda programs, according to Ambassador Johnson. Most American policy leaders agreed with Johnson's assessments.[69]

In summary, during the early Cold War period, policymakers in both the Truman and Eisenhower administrations believed that a Soviet-directed global Communist movement that spread anti-American sentiments and suspicion was undermining U.S. influence not only in Brazil but also in Latin America and the rest of the world. Viewing the Communist propaganda program as a major threat to the United States, both administrations developed and promoted a vast, hard-hitting, anti-Communist, and pro-democracy "Campaign of Truth." Drawing on the World War II experience of the OCIAA and the OWI, policymakers instituted a massive cultural and informational program designed to win over the Brazilian populace. They used both traditional cultural interchange methods and, increasingly, the mass media to influence the Brazilians. A steady flow of U.S. visitors, information, and educational materials flooded Brazil. All proclaimed the advantages of a free way of life, of the American way. By the 1950s, U.S. policymakers viewed their cultural and informational programs in Brazil as important tools in the ideological confrontation between the United States and the Soviet Union. Ironically, just as in the economic arena, despite continuing rhetoric encouraging private initiative and private action, the U.S. government increasingly came to dominate all aspects of this cultural and informational program.

Viewed as a major success in fostering closer Brazilian-U.S. relations, feelings of cooperation and mutuality, and a better understanding of U.S. society and values, the cultural and information program in Brazil grew quickly in size during the early 1950s. Begun under the auspices of the Department of State in 1947, by 1952 it threatened to overwhelm the American embassy in Rio de Janeiro, and by 1954 it became a totally separate agency, the United States Information Agency, committed to persuading the Brazilians that it was in their interest to follow the lead of the United States in world affairs and in economic, political, social, and cultural development. While attempting to win the psychological battle with the Soviet Union, U.S. officials also sought to displace traditional European influence throughout Brazil with American values, trends, and standards.

Avoiding a propagandistic tone, this informational program attempted to portray U.S. objectives and policies in a favorable light and to counter false Communist charges. In the final analysis, however, although the official U.S. cultural and information programs in Brazil were widespread, targeted to numerous Brazilian groups, and undoubtedly effective, they constituted only a very small part of the total impact the United States had on Brazilian society. U.S. private corporations advertising for popular consumer products and American films, fashion, architecture, music, sports, and life-style inundated Brazil. Brazilians thirsted after things American. Adopting the American model of consumption, they wanted consumer items ranging from blue jeans to soft drinks, from rock and roll to automobiles and televisions. The Brazilian language reflected this growing unofficial American presence. Brazilian Portuguese, like American English, has an enormous ability to absorb vocabulary from almost any source. Slang from American movies and comic strips merged with English terms in sports, science, technology, and the press to provide Brazilians with terms such as *sex appeal*, *show*, *far west*, *films*, *bar*, *nylon*, *shorts, gangsters, duplex, DJ,* and *rock and roll.* For better or for worse, by accident or by design, the North American presence in Brazil grew in intensity and sophistication in the early 1950s.[70]

Notes

1. Frank A. Ninkovich, *The Diplomacy of Ideas: United States Foreign Policy and Cultural Relations, 1938–1950* (Cambridge: Cambridge University Press, 1981), pp. 70–72.

2. See Ninkovich, *Diplomacy of Ideas*, p. 30; and Manuel J. Espinosa, *Inter-American Beginnings of U.S. Cultural Diplomacy 1936–1948*, Department of State Publication 8854, International Information and Cultural Series 110 (Washington, DC: Government Printing Office, 1976).

3. See Charles A. Thompson and Walter H. C. Laves, *Cultural Relations and U.S. Foreign Policy* (Bloomington: Indiana University Press, 1971); and Morrell Heald and Lawrence S. Kaplan, *Culture and Diplomacy: The American Experience* (Westport: Greenwood Press, 1977).

4. John Foster Dulles to Eisenhower, February 26, 1953, Telephone Series. John Foster Dulles Papers, Dwight D. Eisenhower Library, Abilene, Kansas.

5. See Ninkovich, *Diplomacy of Ideas*, p. 176.

6. For a description of the OCIAA see Donald W. Rowland, *History of the Office of the Coordinator of Inter-American Affairs* (Washington, DC: Government Printing Office, 1947). For a review of the effectiveness of this early U.S. program in Latin America, see Gerald K. Haines, "Under the Eagle's Wing: The Franklin D. Roosevelt Administration Forges an American Hemisphere," *Diplomatic History* 1:4 (Fall 1977): 373–88. The OCIAA was abolished in 1947.

7. See NSC 4, December 9, 1947, Record Group (RG) 273, National Archives (NA); NSC 7, March 30, 1947, RG 273, NA; and NSC 20/1, August 18, 1948, RG 273, NA.

8. See "Program for Strengthening U.S. International Information," *Papers Relating to the Foreign Relations of the United States, 1952–1954* 2:2, 1600 (hereafter cited as *FRUS* followed by year). See also Howland Sargeant, "Helping the World to Know Us Better," Department of State *Bulletin* 19 (November 28, 1948): 672; U.S. Congress, House, Hearings on HR 3342, *U.S. Information and Educational Exchange Act of 1947*, 80th Cong., 1st sess., 1947, and U.S. Congress, Senate, Hearings on Senate Resolution 243, *Expanded International Information and Education Program*, 81st Cong., 2d sess., 1950.

9. Ninkovich, *Diplomacy of Ideas*, pp. 116–19; Jeremy Tunstall, *The Media Are American* (New York: Columbia University Press, 1977), p. 9.

10. See Department of State, Departmental Announcement No. 4, "Establishment of the U.S. International Information Administration (IIA)," January 16, 1952, *FRUS, 1952–1954* 2:2, 1591–95, 1627.

11. See memorandum for the president by the president's Advisory Committee on Government Organization, April 7, 1953, *FRUS, 1952–1954* 2:2, 1691–97.

12. Ninkovich, *Diplomacy of Ideas*, p. 132.

13. "Report to the President by the President's Committee on International Informational Activities," June 30, 1953, *FRUS, 1952–1954* 2:2, 1795–1899. See also Edward Barrett, *Truth Is Our Weapon* (New York: Funk and Wagnalls, 1953), p. 9; and U.S. Department of State, Office of Intelligence and Research,

Communist Offenses against the Integrity of Education, Sciences, and Culture (Washington, DC: Government Printing Office, 1951).

14. Theodore C. Streibert was the first director of USIA. For an outline of the USIA program and goals see memorandum from Streibert to Eisenhower, October 27, 1953, *FRUS, 1952–1954* 2:2, 1754–5, 1765. See also "Summary of USIA Operations, January 1, 1954–June 30, 1954," Report of NSC, August 18, *FRUS, 1952–1954* 2:2 1777–79.

15. See Leo Bogart, *Premises for Propaganda* (New York: Free Press, 1976), p. xv. See also Barrett, *Truth Is Our Weapon*, pp. 8–10; and Robert E. Elder, *Information Machine: The United States Information Agency and American Foreign Policy* (Syracuse: Syracuse University Press, 1968), p. 4.

16. See Ninkovich, *Diplomacy of Ideas*, p. 53; and Espinosa, *Inter-American Beginnings of U.S. Cultural Diplomacy*, pp. 15–23.

17. Sheldon Thomas, draft report to Joseph B. Tisinger, February 1, 1950, DS 511.32/2-150, RG 59, NA; "Country Plan for Brazil," March 20, 1953, DS 511.32/3-2053, RG 59, NA.

18. See the "Country Plan for Brazil," March 20, 1952, DS 511.32/3-2052, RG 59, NA; and "Country Plan for Brazil," April 28, 1953, DS 511.32/4-2853, RG 59, NA. For earlier plans see dispatch 1217 of December 22, 1949, DS 511.32/12-2249, RG 59, NA; and Thomas, draft report to Tisinger, February 1, 1950, DS 511.32/2-150, RG 59, NA.

19. Thomas, "USIE Psychological Offensive in Brazil," November 8, 1950, DS 511.32/11-850, RG 59, NA. See also William A. Wieland, "USIS Program in Brazil," March 19, 1953, DS 511.32/3-1953, RG 59, NA.

20. Ibid.

21. Ibid.

22. Ibid.

23. Ibid.; "Country Plan for Brazil," March 20, 1952, DS 511.32/3-2052, RG 59, NA; F. R. Lineaweaver (U.S. consul, Recife), "USIE Semi-Annual Evaluation Report," May 31, 1950, DS 511.32/8-350, RG 59, NA.

24. See Dean Acheson to U.S. embassy in Rio, October 17, 1950, DS 511.32/10-1750, RG 59, NA. For the text of the Smith-Mundt Act see PL 402, 80th Cong., 2d sess., 64 *Statutes at Large* 987.

25. Ninkovich, *Diplomacy of Ideas*, p. 43.

26. Francis J. McArdle, dispatch to the Department of State, June 10, 1953, DS 511.32/6-1053, RG 59, NA.

27. See, for example, U.S. Consul George T. Colman, "Brief Report on Returned Leader Grant," May 29, 1954, DS 511.323/5-2954, RG 59, NA.

28. Wieland, "IIA Prospectus for Brazil," April 30, 1953, DS 511.32/4-3053, RG 59, NA.

29. See Welson S. Compton, Administrator of IIA, extract from "Report on International Information Administration—1952" to the secretary of state, December 31, 1952, *FRUS, 1952–1954* 1:2, 1648; and Ninkovich, *Diplomacy of Ideas*, pp. 148–49.

30. See Thomas (public affairs officer), "Comments on the Department's Exchange of Persons Program," January 18, 1950, DS 511.323/1-1850, RG 59, NA; and Colman, "Educational Exchange: Evaluation Report," August 31, 1954, DS 511.323/11-1254, RG 59, NA. See also Raymond C. Smith to embassy, "Student Grants in Artistic Fields," September 3, 1954, DS 511.323/9-354. RG 59, NA.

31. Ninkovich, *Diplomacy of Ideas*, p. 168.

32. See Wieland, "Exchange of Persons Program," October 13, 1953, DS 511.32/ 10-1353, RG 59, NA; Dulles to American embassy, "Frost Visit," June 30, 1954, DS 932.119-SA/6-3054, RG 59, NA; and Colman, "Visit of Hilton E. Hanna," December 1, 1953, DS 511.323/12-153, RG 59, NA. During World War II the OCIAA had actually sponsored the visits of many American artists and film stars to Brazil. See Haines, "Under the Eagle's Wing," p. 386.

33. See Henry S. Hammond (labor attaché), "Anti-Racial Discrimination Law," July 13, 1951, DS 832.411/7-1351, RG 59, NA. See also Orlando Soares, *Desenvolvimento econômico-social do Brasil e Eua* (The socioeconomic development of Brazil and the United States) (São Paulo: Colecão Nôvos Tempes, 1976), pp. 24–53.

34. See William V. Denning to Edward Krause (director of athletics, University of Notre Dame), December 16, 1953, DS 511.32/12-1653, RG 59, NA. On the museum exchanges see Nelson Rockefeller to Acheson, November 2, 1950, DS 511.32/11-250, RG 59, NA; and Acheson to Rockefeller, January 18, 1950, DS 511.32/1-1850, RG 59, NA. See also Edward W. Barrett to Herschel Johnson, April 28, 1951, DS 511.32/4-2851, RG 59, NA; and Tapley Bennett to John Cabot, "São Paulo Exposition," May 15, 1953, DS 832.191/SA/5-1553, RG 59, NA.

35. Robert S. Henderson, "Mother Goose Pinups," July 17, 1953, DS 511.32/ 7-1753, RG 59, NA.

36. The U.S. libraries and binational centers often complained that many of these popular magazines were stolen from the mail and requested diplomatic pouch service for delivery. They also requested that subscriptions to such scholarly journals as *Saturday Review of Literature, Harper's, Music Educator's Journal,* and the *NEA Journal* be canceled, as nobody read them. See Andy G. Wilkison (director of library services), "Magazine Distribution Plan," June 5, 1950, DS 511.32/ 6-550, RG 59, NA; Robert C. Johnson, Jr. (American consul, Bahia), "Cultural Center Request for Changes in Subscriptions to Magazines," October 10, 1950, DS 511.3221/10-1050, RG 59, NA; and Robert C. Johnson, "Bi-National Centers: Transmission of Magazine List," January 31, 1952, DS 511.32/1-3152, RG 59, NA. For a list of the pamphlets see *FRUS, 1952–1954* 2:2, 11620–28. See also Dorothy Greene, *Cultural Centers in the Other American Republics* (Department of State Publication 2503, Washington, DC: Government Printing Office, 1946).

37. See Alan K. Manchester (cultural affairs officer), "Request for Books under Book Translation Program," January 3, 1952, DS 511.3221/1-352, RG 59, NA; Herbert Cerwin (counselor of embassy for public affairs), "Division of Overseas Information Centers: Book Translation Program Plans for Brazil," March 13, 1952, DS 511.3221/3-1352, RG 59, NA; and Acheson to embassy, June 25, 1951, DS 511.3221/6-2551, RG 59, NA.

38. See Ellis M. Goodwin (first secretary of embassy), "Effects of the Dollar Shortage on Commercial Imports of American Publications," September 5, 1952, DS 511.32/9-552, RG 59, NA; memorandum by Sterling Cottrell, "Informational Media Guaranty Program," November 22, 1954, DS 511.11-2254, RG 59, NA; and Streibert, "Informational Media Guaranty Program," November 16, 1954, DS 511.32/11-1654, RG 59, NA.

39. See memorandum from Bradley W. Connors (assistant administrator for policy and plans of the U.S. International Information Agency) to Walter K. Scott (deputy assistant secretary of state for administration), February 20, 1953, *FRUS, 1952–1954* 2:2, 1671–73. See also Joseph R. McCarthy to Dulles, April 7, 1953,

FRUS, 1952–1954 2:2, 1697–98. McCarthy never produced a detailed list of which publications he considered to be written by Communists. See Bogart, *Premises for Propaganda*, pp. xvi–xvii.

40. McArdle to Herschel Johnson, March 17, 1953, *FRUS, 1952–1954* 2:2, 1685–86.

41. See memorandum by Wieland, May 22, 1953, DS 511.32/5-2253, RG 59, NA. See also "Bookburning" folder, John Foster Dulles papers, Dwight D. Eisenhower Library, Abilene, Kansas.

42. For a sample of this propaganda material and a listing of a variety of leaflets, pamphlets, books, and posters, see Dulles, circular to certain diplomatic and consular offices, and bulky file, February 15, 1952, DS 511.00/2-1552, RG 59, NA. See also U.S. Consul V. Lansing Collins, Jr., "Annual Review of USIE Activities, Distribution of Publications in Pôrto Alegre," January 14, 1950, DS 511.32/1-2650, RG 59, NA.

43. See Adolf Berle, "Mission of American Professors and Specialists to Brazil," May 18, 1945, DS 832.017/5-1845, RG 59, NA; Brazilian Division memorandum, "Activities in Brazil," May 8, 1946, records of the Office of American Republics Affairs, Brazil, RG 59, NA; William Pawley, dispatch to secretary of state, June 25, 1947, DS 832.12/6-2547, RG 59, NA; Allen Dawson, "Activities to Be Carried on by the Inter-Departmental Committee on Scientific and Cultural Cooperation in Brazil," May 8, 1947, records of the Office of American Republics Affairs, Brazil, RG 59, NA; McArdle (deputy public affairs officer), "Educational Exchange Programs," June 8, 1954, DS 511.323/6-854, RG 59, NA; and "IIA Prospectus for Brazil," various dates, DS 411.323, RG 59, NA. See also John V. D. Saunders, "Education and Modernization in Brazil," in Eric N. Baklanoff, ed., *New Perspectives of Brazil* (Nashville: Vanderbilt University Press, 1966), pp. 109–41; and Robert J. Havighurst and J. Roberto Moreira, *Society and Education in Brazil* (Pittsburgh: University of Pittsburgh Press, 1965).

44. See "Positive Content in IIA Programming to the Other American Republics," January 26, 1953, DS 511.00/1-2653, RG 59, NA.

45. Ninkovich, *Diplomacy of Ideas*, p. 116.

46. See Edward Miller to Herschel V. Johnson, January 19, 1951, Miller Files, Lot File 53D-26, RG 59, NA; Cerwin (public affairs officer), "USIE Press Operations in Brazil," May 25, 1951, DS 511.32/5-2551, RG 59, NA; Thomas (public affairs officer), "New Series of Feature Articles," March 16, 1950, DS 511.3221/3-1650, RG 59, NA; Thomas "Articles in Brazilian Publications," August 21, 1950, DS 511.322/8-2150, RG 59, NA; Thomas, "Pamphlet Series Entitled *Countering Soviet Propaganda*," November 29, 1950, DS 511.3221/11-2950, RG 59, NA; Thomas, "USIS Press Campaign," November 10, 1950, DS 511.32/11-1050, RG 59, NA; and Cerwin, "Placement of Material on World Peace Council," July 16, 1951, DS 511.32/7-1651, RG 59, NA.

47. Wieland, "Comic Strips," February 13, 1953, DS 511.3221/2-1353, RG 59, NA; and Wieland, "Embassy Operations Memorandum," January 27, 1953, DS 511.322/1-2753, RG 59, NA.

48. See Dulles, circular to certain diplomatic posts, December 11, 1953, 511.00/12-1153, *FRUS, 1952–1954* 2:2, 1668–70; and Wieland, "Rosenberg Case," December 11, 1953, DS 511.322/12-1153, RG 59, NA.

49. See Cerwin, "Three Articles Entitled 'Watch Out for Spies' Frontpaged by *O Globo*," October 8, 1952, DS 511.322/10-852, RG 59, NA. The Brazilian armed

forces picked up the articles and reprinted them as a pamphlet, much to the delight of the U.S. press section. See Cerwin, "Publication by Brazilian Armed Forces of 'Watch Out for Spies,' " October 14, 1952, DS 511.322/10-1452, RG 59, NA.

50. See Cerwin, "Production of *Em Marcha*," July 3, 1952, DS 511.32/7-352, RG 59, NA; and Cerwin, "Embassy's Magazine *Em Marcha*," July 10, 1952, DS 511.32/7-1052, RG 59, NA.

51. Cerwin, "Production of *Em Marcha*," July 3, 1952, DS 511.32/7-352, RG 59, NA; Cerwin, "Reviews of Magazine *Em Marcha*, June 30, 1952, DS 511.322/6-3052, RG 59, NA; Cerwin to Howland Sargeant (assistant secretary of state), February 11, 1952,DS 511.3221/2-1152, RG 59, NA.

52. See Cerwin, "Brazilian Potential Market (Radio, Newspapers and Magazines)," June 26, 1951, DS 511.32/6-2651, RG 59, NA; Wieland, "USIS Program in Brazil," March 19, 1953, DS 511.32/3-1953, RG 59, NA; and Cerwin, "Radio," May 15, 1951, DS 511.324/5-1551, RG 59, NA.

53. See John Logan Hagan (economic officer), "Standardization of Television in Brazil," January 28, 1953, DS 932.44/1-2853, RG 59, NA; Thomas, "Policy Guidance on Use of Television in USIE Programs," March 27, 1950, DS 511.324/3-2750, RG 59, NA; Charles K. Ludewig (American consul, São Paulo), "Status of Television in São Paulo," August 31, 1950, DS 932.44/8-3150, RG 59, NA; William P. Rambo (American vice consul, Rio), "Television Development in Brazil," June 16, 1950, DS 932.44/6-1650, RG 59, NA; Acheson to embassy, August 30, 1950, DS 932.44/8-3050, RG 59, NA; Cerwin, "Television," June 16, 1952, DS 511.32/6-1652, RG 59, NA; and Cerwin, "Television," September 3, 1952, DS 511.324/9-352, RG 59, NA.

54. Cerwin, "Radio," October 15, 1952, DS 511.324/10-1551, RG 59, NA.

55. See James Scott Kemper (U.S. ambassador to Brazil), "Evaluation of the Program Effectiveness of United States Internatioinal Broadcasting," April 7, 1954, DS 511.324/4-754, RG 59, NA; Cerwin, "USIE Semi-Annual Evaluation Report," August 23, 1951, DS 511.32/8-2351, RG 59, NA; Cerwin, "USIE Radio Programs," July 16, 1951, DS 511.324/7-324 through 7-1651, RG 59, NA; and Cerwin, "Local Radio Operations," May 15, 1951, DS 511.324/5-1551, RG 59, NA.

56. See Cerwin, "Radio," October 15, 1951, DS 511.324/10-1551, RG 59, NA.

57. See Cerwin, "Packaged Radio and Television Programs Dealing with the American Negro," February 27, 1952, DS 511.324/2-27952, RG 59, NA; Lee M. Hunsaker (assistant public affairs officer), "Projected Transcribed Radio and Television Series," March 4, 1952, DS 511.324/3-452, RG 59, NA; and Robert Johnson, Jr. (American consul, Bahia), "USIE Semi-Annual Evaluation Report, December 1, 1950, to May 31, 1952," June 27, 1951, DS 511.32/6-2751, RG 59, NA.

58. Cerwin, radio survey on the Voice of America, the Al Neto program, and "A Vida Que O Mondo Leva" (The life that the world leads), November 20, 1952, DS 511.324/11-2052, RG 59, NA. See also Cerwin, "Report on Field Trip through Northern Brazil," July 25, 1951, DS 511.32/7-2551, RG 59, NA.

59. See "IIA Prospectus for Brazil," April 30, 1953, DS 511.32/4-3053, RG 59, NA. See also Bogart, *Premises for Propaganda*, p. xii.

60. For the survey see Cerwin, "Radio Survey," November 20, 1952, DS 511.324/11-2052, RG 59, NA.

61. See *FRUS, 1952–1954* 2:2, 1625–26.

62. Bogart, *Premises for Propaganda*, p. 90; William J. Bushwaller (assistant cultural attaché), "Recent Motion Picture Developments," April 17, 1953, DS 832.452/4-1753, RG 59, NA.

63. See Robert Lobel, "Motion Pictures—Current Developments," May 19, 1950, DS 832.452/5-1950, RG 59, NA.

64. See Thomas (public affairs officer), "USIE: Effectiveness of Program," December 29, 1950, DS 511.32/12-2950, RG 59, NA; Stewart Anderson, "Motion Pictures—Current Developments," January 27, 1950, DS 832.452/1-2750, RG 59, NA; Acheson to embassy, April 29, 1950, DS 511.325/4-2750, RG 59, NA; Thomas, "Special Showing of USIS Films," May 29, 1950, DS 511.325/5-1950, RG 59, NA; and Lineaweaver (U.S. consul, Recife), dispatch, August 3, 1950, DS 511.32/8-350, RG 59, NA. For Brazilian attempts to limit U.S. film imports see Bushwaller, "Recent Motion Picture Developments," April 17, 1953, DS 832.452/4-1753, RG 59, NA; Bushwaller, "Motion Picture Developments," May 20, 1952, DS 832.452/5-2052, RG 59, NA; and John G. McCarthy (president, Motion Picture Association of America) to Miller, September 30, 1952, DS 832.452/9-3052, RG 59, NA. Brazil provided U.S. filmmakers with their largest market in Latin America and was second in importance out of all the countries in the world, according to McCarthy. See also "Brazilian Restrictions on Motion Pictures," February 15, 1952, DS 832.452/2-1552, RG 59, NA; and Bushwaller, "Developments since Signing of Motion Picture Decree," December 11, 1952, DS 832.452/12-1151, RG 59, NA. With regard to U.S. government–sponsored films see Cerwin, "Film *With These Hands*," October 30, 1952, DS 511.325/10-3052, RG 59, NA. (This film portrayed U.S. family life and attempted to show how Americans, like Brazilians, had great affection for children and family. It was designed especially to appeal to Brazilian women.) Cerwin, "*Soldiers of Freedom*," April 24, 1952, DS 511.325/5-2252, RG 59, NA. (The Portuguese version of this film showed the destructive work of communism and the community of interest of free people.)

65. Cerwin, "Anti-Communist Programs," October 8, 1951, DS 732.001/10-851, RG 59, NA; Cerwin, "Anti-Communist Radio Programs," October 11, 1951, DS 732.001/10-1151, RG 59, NA; telegram from Herschel Johnson to Acheson, December 14, 1950, DS 511.325/12-1450, RG 59, NA.

66. See Cerwin, "Country Plan for Brazil," March 20, 1952, DS 511.32/3-2052, RG 59, NA, for a summary of Communist activities.

67. See Wieland, "USIS Country Plan for Brazil," April 28, 1953, DS 51.32/4-2853, RG 59, NA; Thomas, "USIE Films for Television," August 9, 1950, DS 511.325/8-950, RG 59, NA; George E. Miller (American consul, Recife), "Monthly Report on Information and Cultural Activities," January 13, 1950, DS 511.32/1-1350, RG 59, NA; William A. Krauss (public affairs officer, São Paulo), "Exposition Commemorating the Centenary of the English Public Library," September 29, 1950, DS 832.19 1-SA/9-2950, RG 59, NA; and telegram from Herschel Johnson to Acheson, September 12, 1952, DS 511.32/9-1252, RG 59, NA.

68. See Ninkovich, *Diplomacy of Ideas*, p. 89.

69. See Herschel Johnson to Acheson, September 12, 1952, DS 511.32/9-1252, RG 59, NA.

70. See John F. Santos, "A Psychologist Reflects on Brazil and Brazilians"; and Earl Thomas, "Emerging Patterns of the Brazilian Language," in Baklanoff, ed., *The Shaping of Modern Brazil*, pp. 264–300. See also Robert Wesson, *The United States and Brazil: Limits of Influence* (New York: Praeger, 1981), p. 145.

15 Elaine C. Lacy ◆ Autonomy versus Foreign Influence: Mexican Education Policy and UNESCO

Because of its proximity to the United States, Mexico has often felt the brunt of external cultural influences. In spite of its sensitivity to these foreign influences and a history of strong revolutionary nationalism that reached its peak in the 1930s, the Mexican government welcomed the United Nations Educational, Scientific, and Cultural Organization (UNESCO) in the 1940s and 1950s. Historian Elaine C. Lacy of the University of South Carolina at Aiken describes the circumstances surrounding Mexico's acceptance of UNESCO's influence in the development of a literacy program during these years.

Mexico is currently undergoing remarkable changes, especially in several key areas of government and the economy. Mexican President Carlos Salinas de Gortari ushered in an era in which Mexico's revolutionary aims and rhetoric have been modified in favor of policies that would have been unthinkable only a decade ago. His development strategy, for example, provides for privatization of Mexican holdings, allows increased foreign ownership in the Mexican economy, and calls for a free-trade agreement with Mexico's old nemesis to the north, the United States. Some may view these actions as the first steps in a movement away from the almost aggressive nationalism and economic sovereignty that grew out of the Revolution of 1910. But Mexican nationalism is more complex than it appears. Mexico abandoned its nationalistic stance in some areas, including education, long ago. This study examines Mexico's educational policy making in the post-World War II era, and discusses the reasons for dismissal of autonomy in this vital area.

The revolution and civil war which swept through Mexico between 1910 and 1917 was in part a nationalistic response to foreign domination of the country's resources and economic infrastructure. In its struggles to rebuild the war-torn nation, the revolutionary government which took office in 1917 exhibited a fierce spirit of nationalism bordering on xenophobia. The constitution of 1917 included nationalism and antiforeign sentiment among its major themes. Since that time, Mexican governments bolstered nationalism to foster national unity and as a way to protect Mexican sovereignty, and nationalism acted as a symbol of the central

From Elaine C. Lacy, "Autonomy versus Foreign Influence: Mexican Education Policy and UNESCO," *SECOLAS Annals* 23 (March 1992): 53–59. Reprinted by permission of the author and *SECOLAS Annals*.

political party's legitimacy. Mexican art, architecture, music, dance, and literature glorified all things Mexican, including the country's Indian heritage, while foreign culture and influence were officially rejected. José Vasconcelos, minister of education and presidential candidate in the 1920s, spoke for many Mexican intellectuals in calling for a uniquely Mexican culture, saying he was "tired, [and] disgusted with all this copied civilization."[1]

The high point of Mexican nationalism occurred during the administration of Lázaro Cárdenas, president from 1934 to 1940. The Cárdenas government went its own way in foreign policy decisions, took steps to protect and preserve the country's indigenous heritage, and dramatically established Mexican sovereignty by expropriating all foreign oil companies operating in Mexico. The expropriation damaged U.S.-Mexican relations and led to a boycott of Mexican oil on the world market, but for most Mexicans, Cárdenas was a hero.

Mexico's leaders since 1920 have stated their determination to solve Mexican problems with Mexican solutions. This mindset is evident in the history of government education policies. José Vasconcelos, who constructed the first postrevolutionary education ministry in 1921, eschewed foreign education models, considering them inappropriate for Mexico because they did not address the Mexican reality.[2] He lamented the encroachment of U.S. ideas into Latin American educational systems in general, particularly criticizing Cuba for utilizing the U.S. educator John Dewey's methods. He said Cuba had "surrendered her soul to the same people who control her sugar and manipulate her politics."[3] Vasconcelos hoped to create a Mexican school that would promote Mexico's "own brand of culture." His successors in the late 1920s also believed that education should promote an appreciation of all things Mexican, and attempted to gear Mexican education, especially in rural areas, to local needs.[4]

Further, the Mexican government's Six-Year Plan of 1933, which guided all public programs including education, openly stated that the Mexican government shunned "foreign doctrines." The plan called for "socialist" education for Mexico's schools, but even here Mexican planners insisted that socialist education was not a foreign doctrine but came out of the Mexican experience.[5]

This nationalist mindset continued into the early 1940s. According to an official statement of education policy by the Manuel Avila Camacho government in 1941, the Mexican school would be used to form a nationalist spirit, would be "devoid of all foreign influence," and would "reject foreign ideologies."[6] Jaime Torres Bodet, education minister under Avila Camacho (1940–1946) and again under [Adolfo] López Mateos (1958–1964), argued in 1944 that Mexico must not be a slave to imported academic disciplines. Mexican education must teach Mexicans to "appreciate our own national soul."[7]

Beginning in the post-World War II era, however, Mexico's official posture regarding federal education showed signs of change. The government moved from a determined rejection of foreign impulses and began to follow the lead of international agencies, in particular the United Nations Education, Scientific, and Cultural Organization (UNESCO), in education policy formation. Within a short time, Mexico's educational policy appeared to be determined almost entirely by UNESCO's pronouncements.

UNESCO came into existence in late 1945. Its mandate was "to contribute to peace and security by advancing the mutual knowledge and understanding of peoples by encouraging education and the spread of culture, and by protecting, increasing, and sharing in every appropriate way the world's cultural and scientific heritage."[8] UNESCO, as an offshoot of the United Nations, also worked for the spread of democracy and democratic ideals in underdeveloped areas of the world.

Supported by dues from member states and funds from the United Nations, international lending institutions, and private donors, UNESCO offered and continues to offer a variety of educational services. These include educational research, international conferences and training sessions, on-site assistance and training for member states, provision of grants and loans for education projects, and planning, staffing and implementation of special education projects.

Mexican educational policy first openly reflected the influence of UNESCO during the Miguel Alemán Valdéz administration (1946–1952). By the next presidential term many aspects of UNESCO's and the Mexican government's education objectives were virtually identical. The initial UNESCO education program of the 1940s, termed Fundamental Education, was aimed primarily at adults in underdeveloped areas of the world. It incorporated literacy training into a broad educational program designed to help people in backward areas understand their immediate problems and to provide them with the skills to help themselves. These skills would aid them in improving their way of life, productivity, health, and political, social, and economic organization. Objectives also included the spiritual and moral development of participants.[9]

In 1944, the Mexican government initiated a national literacy campaign. Reflecting UNESCO's influence, the literacy drive by 1948 combined literacy training with practical instruction related to social and economic improvement of the home and community.[10] Under President Adolfo Ruiz Cortines (1952–1958), literacy programs were tied to training in health care, agricultural improvement, and citizenship. The government, parroting UNESCO, said citizens must first come to understand their own situation, and be provided with initiative and skills to solve their own problems as well as those of their community.[11] Moreover, training in citizenship was to "promote devotion to democracy and a firm loyalty to its ideals."[12]

Further cooperation between the Mexican government and UNESCO is seen in the creation in 1950 of the first regional training center for Fundamental Education, the Centro Regional para Educación Fundamental en América Latina (CREFAL) in Pátzcuaro, Michoacán. Land for the center was donated by former Mexican President Lázaro Cárdenas. The original purpose of CREFAL was to train teams from various Latin American nations, including Mexico, in the principals of Fundamental Education, which they would take back and apply in their own countries. A further objective was the production of educational materials, which were tested in rural Mexico before application elsewhere. Teams from CREFAL went into the countryside and engaged in not only literacy instruction but a wide range of community improvement activities such as road building, agricultural activities, care of livestock, community health care, and construction of homes and community centers.[13] With Mexico's rural communities acting as laboratories for formation of instructional techniques and methodology, CREFAL helped the Mexican government meet rural educational objectives.

In the spring of 1956, UNESCO held a Regional Conference on Free and Compulsory Education for Latin America in Lima, Peru. The purpose of the gathering was to give impetus to the development of primary education in Latin America, and to urge formal educational planning, which should be related to economic and social development. In response, Mexican President Adolfo López Mateos in 1959 inaugurated the Eleven-Year Plan, which focused on the improvement of primary education in Mexico, an area neglected since the 1930s. As a result of the plan, the government constructed thousands of new schools and trained thousands of new teachers. In early 1960, Victoriano Veronesse, general director of UNESCO, visited Mexico and gave the plan high praise.[14] Not only did the program represent Mexico's first real educational plan, an activity recommended by UNESCO at the Lima conference, but the plan focused on improving primary education.

UNESCO programs continued to shape Mexico's education policies in the 1960s. At a UNESCO-sponsored international conference in Montreal in 1960, educators were urged to integrate literacy training and adult education into a program of "permanent education."[15] Adults should not merely receive basic instruction but should consider it a first step toward lifelong training. In 1965, UNESCO's international conference of educators met in Tehran, Iran. By this time, the concept of Functional Literacy replaced Fundamental Education as one solution to world underdevelopment. Functional Literacy combined literacy training with vocational training for achieving development goals. For the first time, international educators recognized the link between literacy training and socioeconomic development.

In 1966, Mexico's minister of education in the [Gustavo] Díaz Ordaz administration (1964–1970), Agustín Yáñez, gave the Mexican government's definition of literacy as that proposed at the Tehran conference. Literacy training, he argued, should form only a part of general education; it determines economic development, and should lead to permanent education.[16] Once again Mexico's government echoed UNESCO's objectives.

Mexico's education policy continued to follow UNESCO's lead into the 1970s and 1980s. At regional education ministers' conferences held in Latin America in the late 1960s and early 1970s, recommendations included giving priority to technical and vocational education, reforming secondary education, and gearing science and technological training to the demands of development.[17] The Conference of Ministers held in Mexico City in 1979 emphasized the democratization of education. The general director of UNESCO stated at that conference, "There can be no democratizing of education 'unless the whole population, including the least privileged groups, participated in its functioning, thus making it serve the interests of the entire community.' "[18] In addition, from UNESCO's Conference on Adult Education, which met in Nairobi, Kenya, in late 1976, came the recommendation that adult education foster a critical understanding of contemporary world problems. Further, governments should include provision for adult education in national development plans, and adult education activities should be adapted to the needs and aspirations of social groups or local communities.[19]

True to form, Mexican President Luis Echeverría Alvarez (1970–1976) undertook a series of educational reforms that created new secondary and college-level institutions, promoted and reorganized technical education, and created open, flexible Functional Literacy programs for those over age fifteen. President José López Portillo (1976–1982) launched a National Education Plan which focused on the universalization of primary education. The plan also promised improvement of the relations between technical education and the nation's productivity requirements. In the area of adult education, UNESCO's influence is apparent in López Portillo's creation in 1982 of a new department within the federal Ministry of Education, Instituto Nacional para la Educación de Adultos (INEA). Another new division of the Education Ministry, which falls under the aegis of

INEA, is the National Literacy Program (PRONALE), which includes among its methods the concept of structural analysis, that is, a fostering of critical understanding of current problems and aspirations.

Why would Mexican education planners relinquish autonomy in this critical area of national development? Several factors may account for such governmental actions in the face of leaders' continued insistence on Mexican self-determination and strong nationalistic tendencies.

In the post-World War II era and through the early 1980s, Mexico formally adopted import substitution industrialization as an economic development model, and scarce educational funding was concentrated in higher and technical education to prepare a trained work force. At the same time, governmental leaders continued to espouse Mexican revolutionary aims, in which universal education and literacy training played a major role. This would indicate the need to improve primary and adult education, especially in rural Mexico. But the post-1945 leaders in Mexico were more pragmatists than idealogues, and when presented with the opportunity for funding and assistance from an international organization, at no cost to the federal government, they welcomed it. This freed up funding for them to devote to what they surely considered an area of more rapid return on investment, technical and higher education.

The role of Mexican Minister of Education Jaime Torres Bodet in UNESCO's influence in Mexico must not be overlooked as well. Torres Bodet, who served as a foreign diplomat before being selected for the education post in 1941, served as delegate to world UNESCO conferences in the 1940s. He served as general director of UNESCO between 1948 and 1952, during the birth of CREFAL. Torres Bodet, considered one of three great educational leaders in Mexican history, no doubt influenced Mexican presidents in their decision to follow UNESCO's lead.

The nature of Mexican–United States relations also likely played a role in Mexican leaders' decisions to engage in hemispheric meetings of ministers of education and to adopt policies devised therein. The United States did not participate in UNESCO's regional meetings, and Mexico, often at odds with its neighbor to the north, perhaps looked at its alignment with other Latin American education leaders as another way to achieve regional solidarity and still devise educational policy without relying on the United States.

The study of Mexico's reliance on UNESCO provides evidence regarding the nature of Mexican nationalism. First of all, it is selective; economical and political factors dictate its nature. Secondly, as one Mexican observer argues, Mexican nationalism is more survival instinct than ideology.[20] It allows various governments to maintain control, foster unity, and demonstrate Mexican autonomy. But at times these governments find it more pragmatic to ignore certain aspects of nationalism.

This selectivity helps explain Mexico's recent economic and political metamorphosis. Mexico's inability to solve its massive economic and social problems led to Salinas's move away from the nationalistic and protectionist development model that characterized Mexican growth since the revolution. In its quest for modernization and sustained national growth, Mexico's government is more pragmatist than ideological. As many observers have suggested, the revolution may currently be unraveling, but as seen in the case of education policy formation, in some respects the process began in the immediate post-World War II era.

Notes

1. José Vasconcelos, *La raza cósmica: misión de la raza Iberoamericana* (México: Calpe Mexicana S.A., 1948), 9–10.
2. Vasconcelos, *A Mexican Ulysses: An Autobiography* (Bloomington: Indiana University Press, 1963), 160–161. During the nineteenth century, Mexico tended to adopt foreign ideas and cultural modes, including educational models. The English Lancastrian schools, which first appeared in Mexico in the 1820s, endured until the late nineteenth century. Vasconcelos's rejection of such foreign models illustrated the desire of educational leaders after 1920 to satisfy local needs and national aspirations with local solutions.
3. Vasconcelos, *El proconsulado*, 570–571, in William Rex Crawford, *A Century of Latin American Thought* (New York: Praeger, 1961), 261–262. Vasconcelos's immediate successors, however, tried Dewey's "learning by doing" methods in rural Mexico but soon abandoned the project for lack of success.
4. See Ramón Ruiz, *Mexico: The Challenge of Poverty and Illiteracy* (San Marino: Huntington Library, 1963), 28, 38; George F. Kneller, *The Education of the Mexican Nation* (New York: Columbia University Press, 1951), 63.
5. *Plan sexenal del gobierno del Partido Nacional Revolucionario* (México: s.p.i., 1934); Alberto Bremauntz, *La educación socialista en México* (México: Imprenta Rivadenera, 1943), 247.
6. *La Nación*, 18 October 1941, in Ernesto Meneses Morales, *Tendencias educativas oficiales 1934–1964* (México: Centro de Estudios Educativos, 1988), 250.
7. Jaime Torres Bodet, *La escuela mexicana* (México: Secretaría de Educación Pública, 1944), 14–15, 49.
8. Preamble to the UNESCO Constitution, in Raymond E. Wanner, "UNESCO: An Introduction to Its Education Program," *Comparative Education Review* (October 1982): 420.
9. UNESCO, *Fundamental Education: Common Ground for All Peoples. Report of a Special Committee to the Preparatory Commission of the United Nations Educational Scientific and Cultural Organization. Paris 1946* (New York: Macmillan Company, 1947), 2, 8–9. See also Thomas J. La Belle, *Nonformal Education and Social Change in Latin America* (Los Angeles: UCLA Press, 1976),

102; Manuel A. Godina Velasco, "La Alfabetización y La Educación de Adultos en México," *Educación* 5 (May–June 1977): 31.

10. Mexico, *Memoria de la Secretaría de Educación Pública que presenta al H. Congreso de la Unión el titular de la misma C. licenciado Manuel Gual Vidal, 1948–49* (México: Secretaría de Educación Pública, 1949), 386.

11. An Education Ministry publication of 1955 stated, "The results of the [literacy] campaign have demonstrated that to know how to read and write is not enough to become capacitated to improve oneself and to effectively serve the community." *Acción educativa del gobierno federal 1952–1954* (México: Secretaría de Educación Pública, 1954), 65. See also *Un Nuevo Camino* (México: Secretaría de Educación Pública, 1955), n.p.

12. Secretaría de Educación Pública, *Programa alfabetización* (México: Secretaría de Educación Pública, 1954), 10.

13. Lincoln Allison Pope, *Informe de experiencias en el CREFAL*, unpublished report prepared for CREFAL, Pátzcuaro, Michoacán, 23 November 1953.

14. Meneses Morales, *Tendencias educativas oficiales en México 1934–1964*, 539.

15. Godina Velasco, "La Alfabetización y La Educación de Adultos en México," 31.

16. "El alfabeto: cimiento de la Educación Popular," *La Prensa*, 21 August 1966.

17. José Blat Gimeno, *Education in Latin America and the Caribbean: Trends and Prospects. 1970–2000* (Paris: UNESCO, 1983), 30.

18. Gimeno, *Education in Latin America and the Caribbean*, preface.

19. Torsten Husen and T. Neville Postlethwaite, eds., *The Informational Encyclopedia of Education* (Oxford: Pergamon Press, 1985), 5344.

20. Alan Riding, *Distant Neighbors: A Portrait of the Mexicans* (New York: Random House, 1984), 26.

Suggested Readings

The following bibliography contains titles for additional reading on the main topics considered in this volume. This listing is far from exhaustive, and students are encouraged to consult the footnotes and bibliographies in the works cited below. This bibliography uses the following abbreviations:

HAHR   *Hispanic American Historical Review*
JIAS   *Journal of Inter-American Studies and World Affairs*
JLAS   *Journal of Latin American Studies*
LARR   *Latin American Research Review*

Education and Social Change

For challenging discussions of the role of education in Latin American society, see two books by Thomas La Belle, *Nonformal Education and Social Change in Latin America* (Los Angeles, 1976), and *Nonformal Education and the Poor in Latin America and the Caribbean: Stability, Reform, or Revolution?* (New York, 1986), and the study by Martin Carnoy and Joel Samoff, *Education and Social Transition in the Third World* (Princeton, 1990). Among the general studies of individual countries are Ramón Eduardo Ruiz, *Mexico: The Challenge of Poverty and Illiteracy* (San Marino, CA, 1963); Rolland Paulston, *Society, Schools, and Progress in Peru* (New York, 1971); and Hobart A. Spaulding, Jr., "Education in Argentina, 1890–1914: The Limits of Oligarchical Reform," *Journal of Interdisciplinary History* 3 (Summer 1972): 31–71.

Social change is one of the most studied and most debated subjects in the social sciences and humanities. Anthropologists Clifford Geertz, in *Local Knowledge* (New York, 1983), and Michael Taussig, in his *The Devil and Commodity Fetishism in South America* (Chapel Hill, 1980), explore the learning experiences of peasant peoples in a variety of settings. Economist Albert O. Hirschman has much to say about the nature of social change in *Journeys Toward Progress* (New York, 1963), *Essays in Trespassing: Economics to Politics and Beyond* (New York, 1981), and *Getting Ahead Collectively* (New York, 1984). Political scientist Kalmon Silvert wrote several pioneering books in this area—especially *The Conflict Society: Reaction and Revolution in Latin America* (New York, 1961) and *Man's Power* (New York, 1970). Claudio Veliz edited two books of relevance to social change: *The Politics of Conformity in Latin America* (New York, 1967) and *Obstacles to Change in Latin America* (New York, 1970). Veliz has also written an important interpretive study, *The Centralist Tradition in Latin America* (Princeton, 1980).

Earlier works in this area that retain considerable value include Seymour Martin Lipset and Aldo Solari, eds., *Elites in Latin America* (New York, 1967); Irving Louis Horowitz, ed., *Masses in Latin America* (New York, 1970); Harold E. Davis, *Latin American Social Thought: An Historical Introduction* (Baton Rouge, 1972); John J. Johnson, *Political Change in Latin America* (Stanford, 1958); and Frank Tannenbaum, *Ten Keys to Latin America* (New York, 1962).

The Nineteenth Century

Two useful introductions to this period are E. Bradford Burns, *The Poverty of Progress* (Berkeley, 1980), and David Bushnell and Neill Macaulay, *The Emergence of Latin America in the Nineteenth Century* (New York, 1988). More specialized studies include Frank Safford, "In Search of the Practical: Colombian Students in Foreign Lands," *HAHR* 52, no. 2 (May 1972): 230–49, and *The Ideal of the Practical: Colombia's Struggle to Form a Technical Elite* (Austin, 1976). On Mexico see Dorothy Tanck de Estrada, "The 'Escuelas Pías' of Mexico City, 1786–1820," *The Americas* 31 (July 1974): 51–71, and Mary Kay Vaughan, "Primary Schooling in the City of Puebla: 1821–1860," *HAHR* 67, no. 1 (February 1987): 39–66. Vaughan's "Primary Education and Literacy in Nineteenth-Century Mexico: Research Trends, 1968–1988," *LARR* 25, no. 1 (1990): 31–66, provides commentary on numerous studies in both English and Spanish. On nineteenth-century Brazil see E. Bradford Burns, *A History of Brazil* (New York, 1980), and Richard Graham, *Britain and the Onset of Modernization in Brazil, 1850–1914* (Cambridge, 1972). Argentine education has received much attention in recent years: John E. Hodge, "The Formation of the Argentine Public Primary and Secondary School System," *The Americas* 44 (July 1987): 45–65, and two studies by Mark Szuchman, "Childhood Education and Politics in Nineteenth Century Argentina," *HAHR* 70, no. 1 (February 1990): 109–38, and *Order, Family, and Community in Buenos Aires, 1810–1860* (Stanford, 1988). See also Alison Bunkley's biography, *The Life of Sarmiento* (Princeton, 1952), and Sarmiento's classic, *Life in the Argentine Republic in the Days of the Tyrants* (New York, 1960, reprint of 1868 edition). On educational reform in Colombia see Jane Loy, "Primary Education During the Colombian Federation: The School Reform of 1870," *HAHR* 51, no. 2 (May 1971): 275–94. Gertrude Yeager supplies insights into the place of women in education in "Women's Roles in Nineteenth-Century Chile: Public Education Records, 1843–1883," *LARR* 18, no. 3 (1983): 149–56. A synthesis of nineteenth-century trends is available in Spanish: Carlos Newland, "La educación elemental en Hispanoamérica: desde la independencia hasta la centralización de los sistemas educativas nacionales," *HAHR* 71, no. 2 (May 1991): 335–64.

Many of Latin America's leading educators of the nineteenth century were also intellectuals included in W. Rex Crawford's venerable, if somewhat dated, *A Century of Latin American Thought* (New York, 1961). Rafael Caldera's *Andres Bello* (London, 1977) is a brief biography of an international leader in the field.

Universities in Ferment

Valuable overviews are provided by Joseph Maier and Richard Weatherhead, eds., *The Latin American University* (Albuquerque, 1979), and Arthur Liebman, Kenneth N. Walker, and Myron Glazer, *Latin American University Students: A Six Nation Study* (Cambridge, MA, 1972). Richard J. Walter's *Student Politics in Argentina: The University Reform and Its Effects, 1918–1964* (Austin, 1968) remains a classic study. Several recent works on Chile have added considerable depth in this area: Iván Jaksić, "Philosophy and University Reform at the University of Chile: 1842–1973," *LARR* 19, no. 1 (1984): 57–86; Iván Jaksić and Sol Serrano, "In the Service of the Nation: The Establishment and Consolidation of the Universidad de Chile, 1842–1879," *HAHR* 70, no. 1 (February 1990): 139–71; and Gertrude M. Yeager, "Elite Education in Nineteenth-Century Chile," *HAHR* 71, no. 1 (February 1991): 73–105. For a biography of the Peruvian political figure who emerged from that nation's student movement, see Fredrick Pike's *The Politics of the Miraculous in Peru: Haya de la Torre and the Spiritualist Tradition* (Lincoln, NE, 1988). On Haya's chief radical rival of the 1920s, see Harry Vanden, *National Marxism in Latin America: José Carlos Mariátegui's Thought and Policies* (Boulder, 1980). In addition to Don Mabry's study, *The Mexican University and the State: Student Conflicts, 1910–1971* (College Station, TX, 1982), see Michael E. Burke, "The University of Mexico and the Revolution," *The Americas* 35, no. 2 (October 1977): 252–73, and Elena Poniatowska, *Massacre in Mexico* (Columbia, MO, 1992).

E. Bradford Burns's "The Intellectual Infrastructure of Modernization in El Salvador, 1870–1900," *The Americas* 41, no. 3 (January 1985):

57–82, is a readable study of a crucial period in the history of that nation's university and education system in general.

Two important works on recent tendencies in higher education are Donald Winkler's *Higher Education in Latin America: Issues of Efficiency and Equity* (Washington, DC, 1990) and Dole Anderson, *Management Education in Developing Countries: The Brazilian Experience* (Boulder, 1987). The second concerns an effort to transfer the U.S. business school model to Brazil.

Revolution

The subject of revolution has provoked much research and writing, as well as a great deal of controversy. The Mexican revolution is a good place to begin. John Hart's *Revolutionary Mexico: The Coming and Process of the Mexican Revolution* (Berkeley, 1987), Ramón Eduardo Ruiz's *The Great Rebellion* (New York, 1980), and Alan Knight's *The Mexican Revolution* (Cambridge, 1986) combine factual depth and analytical insights to portray the revolution from a variety of perspectives.

For more specialized studies in the area of education and social change see: James D. Cockcroft, *Intellectual Precursors of the Mexican Revolution, 1900–1913* (Austin, 1972); Mary Kay Vaughan, *The State, Education, and Social Class in Mexico, 1880–1920* (DeKalb, IL, 1982); Deborah J. Baldwin, *Protestants and the Mexican Revolution: Missionaries, Ministers, and Social Change* (Urbana and Chicago, 1990); and two by John A. Britton, "Indian Education, Nationalism and Federalism in Mexico, 1910–1921," *The Americas* 32, no. 1 (January 1976): 445–58, and "Urban Education and Social Change in the Mexican Revolution, 1931–1940," *JLAS* 5, no. 2 (1972): 233–45.

Two books on socialist education by contemporary observers must be used with an awareness of the authors' sympathetic attitude toward their subject: George I. Sánchez, *Mexico: A Revolution by Education* (New York, 1936), and George C. Booth, *Mexico's School-Made Society* (Stanford, 1941).

The Guatemalan revolution of 1944 and the Nicaraguan revolution of 1979 were major events in Central America's recent past. The best introduction to Central American history is Lee Woodward's *Central America: A Nation Divided* (New York, 1985). Another valuable source of references is John A. Booth, "Socioeconomic and Political Roots of National Revolts in Central America," *LARR* 20, no. 1 (1991). Jim Handy's *Gift of the Devil: A History of Guatemala* (Boston, 1984) concentrates on the revolution and its long-term consequences. Kay Warren includes much commentary on the impact of education in her *The Symbolism of Subordi-*

nation: Indian Identity in a Guatemalan Town (Austin, 1978). Education
and social change in Sandinista Nicaragua are discussed in Robert Arnove,
Education and Revolution in Nicaragua (New York, 1986), and in several essays in Thomas Walker, ed., *Nicaragua: The First Five Years* (New
York, 1985), while the molding of a revolutionary commitment is explored in Omar Cabezas, *Fire from the Mountain* (New York, 1985).

The Cuban revolution has given rise to a vast literature. Historical
background can be found in John M. Kirk's *José Martí: Mentor to the
Cuban Nation* (Tampa, 1983), a succinct intellectual biography of an ar-
ticulate advocate for social change for late nineteenth-century Cuba. Louis
Perez traces the roots of Cuba's social and economic problems through
the early twentieth century in his *Cuba under the Platt Amendment* (Pittsburgh, 1986). On the abortive attempt at a social revolution, see Luis E.
Aguilar, *Cuba 1933: Prologue to Revolution* (New York, 1974). The spread
of Communist influence in education and in other areas is discussed in
several important works; among them: Jorge Domínguez, *Order and Revolution* (Cambridge, MA, 1978); J. R. O'Connor, *The Origins of Socialism
in Cuba* (Ithaca, 1970); Jaime Suchliki, *University Students and Revolution in Cuba* (Coral Gables, FL, 1969); and Tad Szulc, *Fidel: A Critical
Portrait* (New York, 1986).

The interaction of education, society, and politics in Cuba in the 1960s
and 1970s attracted much attention from both scholars and journalists in
the United States. Richard Fagen's *The Transformation of Political
Culture in Cuba* (Stanford, 1969) was a pioneering study. For press reac-
tion see Laura Berquist, "My 28 Days in Communist Cuba," *Look* 28
(April 19, 1963): 15–27, and E. R. John, "American in Cuba; Visit to
Ciudad Camilo Cienfuegos, a School-City," *The Nation* 202 (March 14,
1966): 297–99. Students can find several additional articles listed in *The
Readers' Guide to Periodical Literature, The New York Times Index*,
INFOTRAK, and other reference guides for this period.

Problems of Institutionalization

The emergence of large institutions for the purposes of mass education is
a common characteristic of the twentieth century in not only Latin America
but also most of the world. The writing on this subject is quite voluminous. The works mentioned here are intended as only an initial listing.
Supplementary works can easily be identified by consulting the bibliographies in these works and standard library reference tools.

General books that emphasize institutionalization and its problems
are Philip H. Coombs's *The World Crisis in Education* (New York, 1985),
Val Dean Rust's *Alternatives in Education: Theoretical and Historical*

Perspectives (Beverly Hills, 1977), and Martin Carnoy, *Education as Cultural Imperialism* (New York, 1974).

More specialized studies of various aspects of institutionalization include: Shirley Brice Heath, *Telling Tongues: Language Policy in Mexico, Colony to Nation* (New York, 1972); Michael W. Foley, "Organizing, Ideology, and Moral Suasion: Political Discourse and Action in a Mexican Town," *Comparative Studies in Society and History* 32, no. 3 (July 1990): 455–87; John A. Britton, "Teacher Unionization and the Corporate State in Mexico, 1931–1945," *HAHR* 59, no. 4 (November 1979): 674–90; Rod Camp, *Intellectuals and the State in Twentieth Century Mexico* (Austin, 1985), especially chapters 8 and 9; and Mike Tangeman, "Once a Bastion of Communism, a Mexican State University (Puebla) Is Now Racked by Economic, Political Upheaval," *Chronicle of Higher Education* 36, no. 34 (May 9, 1990): 39–40. On similar topics in Brazil, see Barbara Weinstein, "The Industrialists, the State, and the Issue of Worker Training and Social Services in Brazil, 1930–1950," *HAHR* 70, no. 3 (August 1990): 379–404; Scott Mainwaring, "The Catholic Church, Popular Education, and Political Change in Brazil," *JIAS* 26, no. 1 (February 1984): 97–121; and Robert Havighurst and J. Roberto Moreira, *Society and Education in Brazil* (Pittsburgh, 1977).

Other valuable studies include Sarah Mansfield Taber, "A History of Schooling and Family Life on Southern Argentine Sheep Ranches," *Journal of Family History* 15, no. 3 (July 1990): 335–56; Ernesto Schielbein and Joseph Farrell, *Eight Years of Their Lives: Through Schooling to the Labour Market in Chile* (Ottawa, 1982); Kathleen B. Fischer, *Political Ideology and Educational Reform in Chile, 1964–1976* (Los Angeles, 1979); and Jeffrey L. Klaiber, "The Battle over Private Education in Peru, 1968–1980," *The Americas* 43, no. 2 (October 1986): 137–58.

On the ideas of Freire, consult: Paulo Freire, *Pedagogy of the Oppressed* (New York, 1968) and *The Politics of Education: Culture, Power, and Liberation* (South Hadley, MA, 1985). See also Myles Horton and Paulo Freire, *We Make the Road by Walking: Conversations on Education and Social Change* (Philadelphia, 1990); Ann E. Berthoff, "Paulo Freire's Liberation Pedagogy," *Language Arts* 6, no. 4 (April 1990): 362–71; and Nancy Squires and Robin Inlander, "A Freirian-Inspired Video Curriculum for At-Risk High-School Students," *English Journal* 79, no. 2 (February 1990): 49–58.

Illich explained his ideas in *Deschooling Society* (New York, 1970), which was soon followed by Alan Gartner, Colin Greer, and Frank Riessman, eds., *After Deschooling, What?* (New York, 1973). See also Illich's "Education Without School: How It Can Be Done," *New York Review of Books*, January 7, 1971, Special Supplement, 25–31.

For a sampling of the evaluations of the interaction among education, television, social change, and popular culture see: Joseph Straubhaar, "Television and Video in the Transition from Military to Civilian Rule in Brazil," *LARR* 24, no. 1 (1989): 140–54, and "Brazilian Television: The Decline of American Influence," *Communications Research* 11 (April 1984): 221–40; Sergio Mattos, "Advertising and Government Influences on Brazilian Television," *Communications Research* 11 (April 1984); 203–20; Conrad P. Kottak, "Television's Impact on Values and Local Life in Brazil," *Journal of Communication* 42, no. 1 (Winter 1991): 70–87; F. Izcaray and J. T. McNelly, "Selective Media Use by Venezuelans: The Passing of the Passive Audience in a Rapidly Developing Society," *Studies in Latin American Popular Culture* 6 (1987): 27–41; Michael Morgan and James Shanahan, "Television and the Cultivation of Political Attitudes in Argentina," *Journal of Communication* 41, no. 1 (Winter 1991): 88–103; and E. J. McAnany, "Cultural Policy and Television: Chile as a Case Study," *Studies in Latin American Popular Culture* 6 (1987): 55–67. Paula Heusinkveld explores the possibilities for intellectual contributions to popular television in "Television: A New Medium for Mexican Intellectuals?" *SECOLAS Annals* 27 (March 1986): 37–45. A valuable set of pioneering studies on the impact of television on politics is presented in Thomas Skidmore, ed., *Television, Politics, and the Transition to Democracy in Latin America* (Washington, DC, 1993).

For a variety of perspectives on the international impact of the mass media see Ariel Dorfman, *The Empire's Old Clothes: What The Lone Ranger, Babar, and Other Innocent Heroes Do to Our Minds* (New York, 1983); Jeremy Tunstall, *The Media Are American: Anglo-American Media in the World* (New York, 1977); Anthony Smith, *The Geopolitics of Information: How Western Culture Dominates the World* (New York, 1980); Robert S. Fortner, *International Communication: History, Conflict, and Control of the Global Metropolis* (Belmont, CA, 1993); Erdener Kaynak, *The Management of International Advertising: A Handbook and Guide for Professionals* (New York, 1989); Armand Mattelart, *Advertising International: The Privatization of Public Space* (New York, 1991); and Joseph S. Nye, Jr., *Bound to Lead: The Changing Nature of American Power* (New York, 1988), especially chapter 6.

On the Latin American image in the U.S. print, film, and electronic media, see Fredrick Pike, *The United States and Latin America: Myths and Stereotypes of Civilization and Nature* (Austin, 1992); George Black, *The Good Neighbor* (New York, 1988); and John J. Johnson, *Latin America in Caricature* (Austin, 1980). For a specialized study see Helen Delpar, *The Enormous Vogue of Things Mexican: Cultural Relations between the United States and Mexico, 1920–1935* (Tuscaloosa, 1992).

In addition to the reference guides cited above, other sources for books and articles in this area include: Susan Poston, *Nonformal Education in Latin America: An Annotated Bibliography* (Los Angeles, 1975); Virginia W. Leonard, "Latin America: Education in a World of Scarcity," *LARR* 23, no. 2 (1988): 234–41; and Rolland G. Paulston, "Ways of Seeing Education and Social Change in Latin America," *LARR* 27, no. 3 (1992): 177–202.

Suggested Films

Several video documentaries deal with the questions surrounding education and social change. Anthropologist John Cohen produced studies of Andean Indians and their relations with changes emanating from the outside world, including "Dancing with the Incas" (Berkeley, University of California Extension Media Center, 1992). The "Inca Cola" segment of the "South American Journey" series (Washington, DC, Public Broadcasting System, 1987) by Australian journalist Jack Pizzey provides an informal survey of the efforts of the descendants of native Americans in Peru to revive and maintain their Inca traditions. Paulo Freire discusses his ideas on education, literacy programs, and their larger ramifications in society in "Education and the Process of Social Transformation" (Los Angeles, UCLA Latin American Studies Center, 1986). The Tlatelolco conflict and the historical trends surrounding it are presented in a video documentary, "Mexico," Part II: "From Boom to Bust, 1940–1982" (WGBH Television, Boston, 1989).

The 1940 film "The Forgotten Village" (available on videotape from Festival Films, Minneapolis), directed by Herbert Kline with screenplay by John Steinbeck, offers a fictional exploration of the impact of the arrival of education and modern medical practices in a rural village in Mexico. This film has a documentary quality because of the presence of native villagers in important roles.

About the Editor

John A. Britton is professor of history at Francis Marion University, where he has taught Latin American and U.S. history since 1972. He earned his undergraduate degree from the University of North Carolina at Chapel Hill (1965) and his doctorate from Tulane University (1971), where he studied under Richard Greenleaf and Lee Woodward. A contributing editor of the *Handbook of Latin American Studies*, he has published books and articles on Mexican history, Latin American-U.S. relations, and the history of communications and popular culture. His publications include *Educación y radicalismo en México, 1931–1940* (1976) and *Carleton Beals: A Radical Journalist in Latin America* (1987). Currently he is working on a study on international history that focuses on the ideological responses of U.S. intellectuals to the Mexican revolution from 1910 through the 1950s.